# THE FRANCHISE

# THE

# FRANCHISE

## A HISTORY OF
## *SPORTS ILLUSTRATED*
## MAGAZINE

Michael MacCambridge

HYPERION

NEW YORK

Library of Congress Cataloging-in-Publication Data

MacCambridge, Michael,
   The franchise : a history of *Sports Illustrated* magazine /
  Michael MacCambridge.—1st ed.

    p.  cm.
  Includes index.
  ISBN 0-7868-6216-5
  1. Sports illustrated—history.    I. Title.
GV561.M185    1997                        97–15864
796'.05—dc21

                                                    CIP

*Book design by C. Linda Dingler*
FIRST EDITION
10 9 8 7 6 5 4 3 2 1

Copyright page continues on page 414.

# CONTENTS

For my mother,

Lois Stob MacCambridge

I have had younger magazine journalists tell me that the *Sports Illustrated* style, which we might describe incompletely as Timestyle infused with personal Texas, was a real influence on American prose. I don't know about that, and I was always wary of lapsing thoroughly into it, but I believe working in its third-person keep-it-hopping context was good for my chops. The job also got me into fancy hotels and people's mamas' houses all over the country and taught me that if you have to write five thousand words in a night, you can.

—Roy Blount, Jr.

# THE FRANCHISE

# A LONG NIGHT

They couldn't see the snow, because there were no windows in the cramped, chilly room. But they could hear it outside, whipping around furiously, just the sort of storm that could ground airplanes and make life miserable for magazine editors trying to move into the modern age.

Inside the makeshift office, the men took off their coats, stamped the snow off their shoes, and prepared for work. André Laguerre sat in the middle of it all, tapping his ever-present white stick on the desk, chewing on his cigar, glancing at the clock as though it might grant them a reprieve.

On this cold night, February 6, 1967, Laguerre was waiting to put the new issue of *Sports Illustrated* to bed. Typically, this would be done over the course of a routinely frantic Sunday night and into the early hours of Monday morning at the Time & Life Building in New York City. But this wasn't a typical week. It was nearly midnight on Monday, and Laguerre, the magazine's managing editor, was huddled with his skeleton crew of lieutenants in a nondescript office in Time Inc.'s main printing facility in downtown Chicago, waiting for the lead news story of the week.

At the same moment, down in Houston's Astrodome, Muhammad Ali had just made his way back to the locker room. The young, pretty, and still undefeated Ali had soundly whipped an overmatched Ernie Terrell for 15 rounds, to defend his heavyweight title by unanimous decision. Under identical circumstances—a major event occurring 24 hours after its regular deadline—any other weekly magazine in the world would have saved its coverage for the following week. But André Laguerre wanted it in this issue, and he wanted it in color.

This was, to say the least, no easy thing. Even in the age of the space race, *Time* and *Newsweek* were finding it logistically impossible to publish color photographs that weren't shot at least 24 to 36 hours prior to their regular weekly deadlines; *Life*'s cutting-edge photojournalism was done in black and white and almost never on this sort of schedule. But Laguerre was driven by a fierce desire to capture the immediacy of sports. This was his vision: less than 72 hours after a Monday night title fight, *SI*'s subscribers would receive a new issue with color photography of the big event, and a masterfully written article that would transcend the platitudes of the newspaper stories and broadcast reports they'd already seen.

And so the forces for the "late close" were deployed, with over 25 staffers working between Houston and Chicago to get the story into the magazine. Immediately after the fight, art director Dick Gangel collected film from four photographers and rushed out of an Astrodome service entrance. He jumped into a waiting limo that sped to the Houston Air Center, where a chartered Learjet took off for tiny Meigs Field in downtown Chicago. Meanwhile, Laguerre and his staff, having just returned from a closed-circuit telecast of the fight shown at the Opera House on Wacker Drive, were doing what they could in the interim. Senior editor Andy Crichton was reviewing the copy that writer Tex Maule had submitted prior to the fight, to see what could be preserved and combined with the main part of the story, which Maule was scheduled to send by telex from Houston at 2:30 a.m. Assistant art director Marty Nathan had set up a drafting table near Laguerre, where dummy pages with proposed copy blocks and gray rectangles (to indicate picture placement) were already laid out.

But the fight had started late, and gone the distance. In the cab over from the Opera House, Laguerre looked glumly out the window at the driving snow and grew more dubious about the jet's chances of getting to Chicago that night. Weather was expected to remain awful through the morning, well past the magazine's 4:30 a.m. "lockout" time, when the last four pages had to go to press.

Usually, *SI* would have a back-up story ready to go, in case something went wrong, but now it was too late even for that. Over a million copies of the cover—featuring basketball star Rick Barry, and including a small teaser line billing the "Clay-Terrell Fight Story"—had already been printed. The table of contents page, listing the four-page piece on the fight as the lead story of the week, had gone to press as well.

At 1:30, the call came: bad weather had diverted the Learjet to Indianapolis; there would be no pictures coming anytime soon. Low, agonized groans went around the table, with Nathan staring longingly at his page proofs. After the grumbling stopped, all eyes turned toward Laguerre. His staff had learned to trust his judgment, his unassuming sophistication, and his unflappable nature. He rarely had tantrums and—like the great athletes that the magazine covered—seemed to be at his calmest when the situation seemed most dire.

Laguerre rose from his chair and walked into the next room, where the portrait artist Robert Handville had been quietly working, undisturbed and largely unnoticed. "Well, old man, it looks like you're on," Laguerre said. With that, Handville quickened his pace.

The entire Time Inc. publishing philosophy was built on certitude by redundancy. Editors made plans with back-ups. They backed up those back-ups with second back-ups. André Laguerre had absorbed these lessons and brought something else to the job. He was blessed with a sixth sense, an acute vision that others lacked, an instinct for when things weren't going to work out and how they might reasonably be fixed.

Resigned to the belief that everything that could go wrong probably would, Laguerre had arranged for Handville to fly out from New York City, attend the closed-circuit broadcast of the fight, and return to the printing plant, where he'd furiously start sketching illustrations from fight action. Just in case, André had explained.

By three a.m., with Maule's rougher-than-usual copy arriving by teletype and the fate of the photographs sealed (the Learjet was grounded until morning), the sketches were finished. *Sports Illustrated* would publish that week, not with color pictures but with Handville's illustrations from Monday night's fight. Ali's victory had finished too late to make many of the morning papers, so most fans wouldn't read the Associated Press account until Wednesday. A day later, amazingly, *SI* readers would get their story in the mail, with what they had come to expect from the magazine: The Last Word.

Laguerre and his cohorts walked out of the building at six that morning—having okayed the last proof pages and watched the presses begin to roll. The irony was lost on no one that after spending a quarter of a million dollars to arrange for a late close that would push the very limits of mass-magazine technology, *SI* had been forced to illustrate that story in the most rudimentary way imaginable, using hastily drawn sketches from a telecast viewer. But the men also knew that the noble failure of the previous hours foreshadowed future successes. The magazine's quick turnaround would spur newsstand sales, recoup the losses, and dazzle the rest of the magazine industry in New York City, which was slowly starting to take notice of just how potent a journalistic force *SI* could be.

At that point, no other publication in the world had the technical capability, the organizational latitude, or the raw nerve to operate on the very precipice of disaster the way that *Sports Illustrated* regularly did. Laguerre was able to do so because he had gained the trust of the most powerful man in American journalism, his boss Henry Luce. Just as important, he commanded immense dedication from a staff that viewed him with a kind of affectionate awe.

Outside the building, Laguerre proposed a quick breakfast before catching the Pan Am flight back to New York City. As the group marched down the snowy sidewalk, bundling up against the harsh cold, straining to see in the near-dawn light, Nathan and Crichton looked at the rotund silhouette of their managing editor, walking a few paces in front of them, and exchanged a knowing look. He'd done it again.

• • •

Time Inc. founder Henry Luce wasn't much of a sports fan, but he always held a special place in his heart for *Sports Illustrated*. He'd launched it in 1954 against the advice of his most trusted aides, who viewed the very idea of starting a weekly magazine devoted solely to sports as an expensive, misguided, and inherently trivial folly. He'd supported it in its bumbling early years, seeing *SI*'s potential even when skeptics within the company were urging him to cut his losses (which would eventually top $30 million) and shut the magazine down.

*SI* was born in an era when spectator sports were commonly viewed—despite all the suits and ties in the stands—as a blue-collar proposition (an early Time Inc. study of the market described sports fans as "juveniles and ne'er-do-wells"). The distinction between watching sports and participating in them was only sporadically made; in a country still enjoying newfound free time and prosperity, both activities counted as leisure.

There was real doubt whether there would be enough activity in the world of sports to justify a weekly. Within the society as a whole sports were more compartmentalized, regionalized, marginalized. In 1954, the football season ended on January 1, and there were more hours of game shows on television than actual games. Baseball attendance had dropped markedly since World War II, and Major League Baseball's westernmost team was the St. Louis Cardinals. There were six hockey teams in the National Hockey League, and the National Basketball Association still had a franchise in Fort Wayne, Indiana.

But a confluence of events that same year helped create an environment in which spectator sports—and a magazine about sports—could eventually thrive. RCA introduced the first color television sets, though a 19-inch black-and-white model ($187) was still the standard. The Boeing

707, the first modern jet, took to the skies, presaging a time when sports teams could travel from coast to coast in truly national leagues. Frozen TV dinners were introduced by Swanson & Sons, yet another hint that the nuclear family was splitting apart. Rock 'n' roll was emerging, along with a new consciousness of teenagers as viable consumers.

*Sports Illustrated* was originally conceived as a high-toned "class" title, partly as a way to offset Madison Avenue's perception of spectator sports as catering to an undesirable, blue-collar audience, and partly due to the company's own Ivy League–influenced provincialism. But as the masses grew and flocked to the suburbs, the money in sports grew as well. There were games to watch on television, and major league ballparks sprouting up in such "minor league" towns as Atlanta, Minneapolis, Kansas City, and Oakland.

After its troubled beginning, *Sports Illustrated* would eventually refocus itself, developing a distinctive tone that resulted from an unforeseen and unlikely creative amalgam. In the late '50s and '60s, the magazine's prose was altered and enlivened by an infusion of Texas sportswriters, whose prose was lucid, irreverent, and unapologetic about the central role of sports in modern society. These pieces would, in turn, become a major element of a complex, nuanced story mix concocted by Laguerre, whose European sophistication gave *SI* a breadth of vision that no sports magazine had ever possessed. From that crucible would emerge the blueprint for modern American sports journalism, and the quintessential American middle-class magazine of the postwar era.

"I think, over the years, it did something that Luce had in mind right from the beginning," said Ray Cave, one of Laguerre's protégés, who would go on to be the managing editor at *Time*. "It legitimized sports. We've seen sport, the role of sport in society, change tremendously through the years. And the existence of *SI* played a significant role in that change. All of a sudden, you could read a sports magazine, and still be considered *able to read*, for starters."

But *SI*'s subscribers did more than just read the magazine—they seemed to absorb it, to need it, to rely on its weekly presence in their lives. "*Sports Illustrated* has become an addiction with me," wrote a New England journalist named John Hubbard, in 1976. "I grab a quick glance when it appears on the newsstand each Thursday here and sulk if my own copy isn't with Friday's mail. There have been hellish weekends when not even Saturday's delivery bore fruit and I was forced to suffer or buy the magazine and endure endless wifely lectures on economics and immaturity."

*Sports Illustrated* mattered to Hubbard and millions of readers like him not only for what it did, but how. Investing the magazine with an assured sophistication and a brilliant journalistic rationale, Laguerre's *SI* gave the American sports fan a sense of himself and his community, of how pervasive the pull of sports had become. It reimagined an adult world in which sports wasn't just a pastime, but a central component. In doing so, it found an audience that hadn't been thought to exist prior to its conception.

In time, its impact within the world of sports was equally profound. "*Sports Illustrated* is like Rolex—the Rolex of magazines," said Chris Evert, two decades after being named *SI*'s 1976 Sportswoman of the Year. "After all these years, it still maintains such a high level. And nobody's topped it. I think it was always a thrill to be on the cover, or be featured in there. I can still remember the headline of the first story they ever ran about me—'More Joan of Arc than Shirley Temple'—and I was like 15 years old at the time. It was a big deal, and it still is."

While athletes took notice, a generation of aspiring sportswriters took their cues from the magazine. "There probably isn't a sportswriter in America between the ages of 35 and 45 who didn't want to be a sportswriter because he was reading André Laguerre's *SI*," said *Esquire* columnist Charles Pierce. Its impact transcended sport; writing in the *Chicago Tribune* in 1984, Stephen Chapman argued that "*SI* is not about athletics but about the human spirit. A century from now, when scholars want to learn how Americans lived in our time, they'll turn to *Sports Illustrated*. Anyone who wants to know now should do likewise."

When historians examine the explosion of spectator sports that reshaped America's leisure time in the last half of the 20th century, they invariably point to two contributing factors: economic prosperity and the advent of television. *Sports Illustrated* was an important third element; it served as a counterbalance to the persistent hype of television, offering a way for new and educated fans to put the endless rounds of games and matches into a meaningful context. It made an art out of in-depth reporting on those games, and thereby made the games themselves more important to more Americans. By setting the agenda of just what sports were important, *SI* pointed the way for much of the television revolution that would follow.

"We helped those sports," said longtime *SI* writer Bill Leggett. "You listen to enough television; it doesn't say a goddamn thing. All television did was broaden the stage for *Sports Illustrated*. People would see the game and want to read about it. Remember, a lot of those games people saw because *Sports Illustrated* told them it was important: 'Oklahoma plays Nebraska this week—it means something.' There was no national scope to college football until the '60s, until *SI* came along. It was just a bunch of guys with animals on their chests running into each other. The national games became important because of *SI*."

Presiding over the magazine's transformation in the '60s was Laguerre: Frenchman, horse player, Gaullist, gambler, gentleman, barfly. His entire personality embodied the paradox—a man of elegant manner but rather disheveled appearance, a gruff leader who laughed easily. His thick, black-framed glasses set off a strong nose; his tie was almost always loosened over his white dress shirt; his tailor-made charcoal suits were invariably rumpled, dotted with cigar ashes. In appearance and demeanor, he resembled no one so much as that incongruous hero of espionage fiction, John Le Carré's plump, stoic spymaster George Smiley.

"What you must know by now is that a great deal of the Laguerre legend depended on this incredible, massive, magical personality he had," said Roy Terrell, his successor as *SI*'s managing editor. "He wasn't any hail-fellow-well-met or anything. He was just this big, stolid, rather distinguished serious guy, who was human, too. And all these people loved him. He was like your father or like a big brother. He'd pat you on the shoulder—that was one of his gestures, but only to people he really liked—and you just kind of melted. We were all affected by that."

"Oh, I thought he should've been president," said Dan Jenkins, perhaps the most influential writer in the magazine's history. George Plimpton, whose *Paper Lion* first appeared in *SI*, described himself as "quite terrified of Laguerre. You worked somewhat harder when you knew he was going to read your story, which is a mark of a great editor, I think."

Laguerre spoke softly and—literally—carried a big stick, an off-white pointer about the size of a golf club's shaft. His presence was so forbidding that many younger staffers were afraid to walk down the same hall with him, afraid to get on an elevator that he alone might be riding. But for those who knew him well, he was the ideal leader. And for years, in a series of small, untrendy bars in midtown Manhattan, Laguerre held forth with an eclectic band of writers, editors, and friends. From these extended drinking sessions came many of the ideas for *Sports Illustrated*'s best stories. If it wasn't Jenkins infuriating Notre Dame fans with his caustically funny analysis, it was Frank Deford delivering clarifying images of some of the era's most celebrated figures, Jack Olsen writing his seminal series on "The Black Athlete," John Underwood examining the most dehumanizing aspects of collegiate sports for profit, or Plimpton engaging in one of his participatory forays into the world of professional sports.

Laguerre believed in the idea of an elite, and in sports journalism, *SI* was it—the publication that would set the agenda in sports. "The magazine was edited in those days from the standpoint of 'What we think is important is what you should think is important,'" said Jenkins. "'And if you don't agree with it, that's your problem.' It was totally arrogant, but I think it was right. And Laguerre stood by his writers. We were the authority. Tex Maule, right or wrong, was the pro football writer, and I was the college football writer. And André's stance was, 'This is what my guy thinks, and therefore he's right, and you're an idiot if you don't agree with him.'"

When Laguerre left *Sports Illustrated*, its reputation for literary excellence was secure. James Michener, in his 1976 book *Sports in America*, observed that "only *The New Yorker*, among contemporary magazines, has been as effective in sponsoring good writing with a certain wry touch." But in journalism, as in war, the winners write history. And so Laguerre's seminal, record-setting tenure as *Sports Illustrated*'s managing editor, which lasted from 1960 to its sad, fractious conclusion in 1974, has been forgotten by many and obscured by a few. When he died, in January 1979, the *New York Times* ran a scant obituary of six column inches.

• • •

By 1997, *Sports Illustrated* stood as perhaps the last magazine in the Time Inc. empire in which Henry Luce might plausibly take pride. The venerable mass weekly *Life* had died in 1972, five years after Luce himself, and was later revived as an unremarkable and largely inconsequential monthly. *Time* was reduced to embarrassing libel lawsuits and numerous editorial retrenchments, leaving it a step behind the resurgent *Newsweek*. Only *People* could match *SI* in terms of bottom-line success, and whatever its strengths, or that of its sister *Entertainment Weekly,* personality-driven journalism was hardly the legacy that the serious statesman Luce had in mind.

But *Sports Illustrated* had become a national institution, the only large-circulation title ever to win consecutive National Magazine Awards for general excellence. The magazine boasted more than 3 million subscribers, and a readership of 24 million adults each week. It also was one of the great financial successes in the world of publishing, the second most profitable consumer magazine in the world (behind *People*), earning more than a billion dollars in profits since 1984. *SI*'s covers were icons of popular culture, and its annual swimsuit issue was perhaps the most recognized special issue in American publishing.

And yet *Sports Illustrated*, for all its recent financial and journalistic success, was still a magazine haunted by the memory of André Laguerre. It was still organized from his blueprint, and still retained an air of his literary sensibilities. And for many readers, it was still judged in the '90s against what he did then.

This last part was perhaps unfair, since the changes in the company over the past generation had been of kind, not just of degree. A different set of pressures had come to bear on Time Inc.'s all-powerful managing editors in the '90s.

The operating conundrum of Time Inc., articulated by Luce in the '60s, by now seemed quaint: "Time Inc. has everything General Motors has—plus our main job, the practice of journalism," he said. "Furthermore, and this is our proudest boast—journalism has the top priority. . . . So, then, the most interesting thing about our company is how we set up a management which is required to produce a profit and yet has no control over our essential product, the editorial content of our magazines."

Luce's principled separation between editorial "church" and business "state" was still observed in theory at Time Inc., but in practice it was violated with regularity. The entire concept was viewed as antiquated in the harsh economic realities of the '90s, when *Sports Illustrated* was a key element in a division that now routinely referred to its magazines as "brands." Time Inc., bragged the Time Warner 1996 annual report, was "the world's premier creator of category-defining editorial franchises."

In line with the new company philosophy, *Sports Illustrated* in the '90s was much more than a magazine. It had become a diverse, far-reaching multimedia enterprise that had successfully launched a spinoff magazine for children (*Sports Illustrated for Kids*), was embarking on another title aimed at female readers (*Sports Illustrated Women/Sport*), and had even established a presence on cable television, with the all-sports news channel CNN/SI.

In the short term, these and other ventures reaped financial successes. But in the midst of all the expansion and "brand extensions," no one was quoting Michener anymore. Few people argued that *Sports Illustrated* was the best-written magazine in America. "You couldn't even argue that drunk," said *SI* alum Mark Kram, the sort of brilliant, prickly, and difficult writer for whom there seemed no place in the modern *SI*. As *Sports Illustrated* had grown more profitable, it had also grown more predictable; there was a greater degree of efficiency than ever before, but also fewer of the editorial surprises that made the magazine special.

And so the challenge facing *Sports Illustrated* in its fifth decade wasn't merely to retain the spectacular profits guaranteed by those 24 million readers. It was to make them care about the magazine as passionately as they had in the past.

# CHAPTER 1

# MID-AMERICAN CENTURY

## The *Columbus Dispatch* said

that the Buckeyes had a good chance against Wisconsin this weekend, and maybe Wes Fesler would get to keep his job, and that if the Cleveland Browns kept winning, they could very well take the title in their first season in the National Football League. But what Robert Cowin was preoccupied with, as he passed by the newsstand of the Deschler-Wallach Hotel in downtown Columbus, was how seriously people took their sports in this part of Ohio.

And it reminded him of the wives. For the past three days, nearly every woman he'd talked to had been complaining about her husband's reading habits. Sure, one would say, I'd love it if he'd read *Time* or the *Saturday Evening Post* or a quality magazine, but instead he's got his head in *Baseball* or *Sport* or *True*. Another said that her husband would probably read *Time* more often if it had more news about baseball and football. And when he'd ask what newspaper their house received—the *Dispatch* or the *Cleveland Plain Dealer* or the *Akron Beacon Journal*—the answer was always the same: We get this one, because my husband says it has the best sports section.

Trying to make sense of comments like this was what Cowin did for a living. Tall, genial, and gray-flannel handsome, he was assistant manager for corporate circulation at *Time* magazine. He'd come to Columbus this early November week in 1950 for reader surveys. It was Columbus and not Poughkeepsie or Topeka or Detroit because Time Inc.'s massive research department had discovered, shortly after World War II, that Columbus was a perfect microcosm of middle-class America. Hard-working, upwardly mobile, overwhelmingly white, and increasingly suburban, it could be counted on to closely reflect the biases and habits of the country at large.

This trip was part of a cutting-edge experiment, in tandem with

O.E. McIntyre, a pioneer in the magazine list business. McIntyre had been to Columbus weeks earlier, talking to bankers and realtors in order to map out the economic strata of the Columbus area. With that map and a reverse telephone directory, he had pinpointed the most desirable customers in the market. Then Cowin and his boss Bernie Auer, a Time Inc. circulation manager, went to Columbus to hit the pavement, make some cold calls, and find out what America thought of their magazine.

"Hello, ma'am," Cowin would say. "I'm Robert Cowin of *Time* magazine. We're not here to sell anything; we're just doing a survey." And then came the clincher, proof of the gravity of their mission: "We're here from New York."

Time Inc. *meant* something in those days. Henry Luce stood astride his self-proclaimed "American Century" secure in the knowledge that his company had emerged from the war as the most powerful and influential journalistic entity in America. The tenets of group journalism—Luce's blueprint for reporting laced with a clear, coherent perspective ("fair, but not objective")—had been codified in the magazines, which dominated middle-class American discourse.

*Time* magazine was still the company's flagship, the most important print publication in the land, delivered to the White House every Sunday night. *Life* was, commercially, even more successful, having survived its spectacular growing pains to become the magazine of the masses, full of the photographs that people craved, glimpses of leggy movie stars and foreign lands, giants of arts and sports and entertainment. And *Fortune*, oversized, overstylized, and self-important, was a weighty, artful success, a journal of American business that was required reading for executives trying to understand the rapidly changing character of a country still reveling in both the psychic and economic spoils of war.

Luce saw that the boom was affecting Time Inc. as well. A decade earlier, the company had been, in his words, "a small big business." But between 1939 and 1945, revenues had doubled, and the company was forced to reshape itself for an inevitable expansion. In 1941, Time Inc. employed 2,500 people; within 20 years, it would employ 5,500. Luce was convinced that the company needed to grow, the same way that everything in America—housing, shopping centers, communications networks, highways—was growing in the first boom of postwar prosperity.

A few days after returning from Columbus, Cowin received a memo sent to all Time Inc. editorial employees by Daniel Longwell, the senior advisor to Luce and editorial director John Shaw Billings. The company was looking to start a new magazine, Longwell's memo explained, and was soliciting the staff for any fresh ideas.

This was just the sort of invitation that would catch Cowin's attention. In his own little corner of the growing company, he was quickly establishing himself as an innovative thinker. In his three years at Time Inc., the Duke University graduate and native Pennsylvanian had cheerfully sent unsolicited memos to several of his superiors, suggesting ways to increase efficiency or improve newsstand sales or bump up circulation. His ambition had been noted, and even when discarding his suggestions, his superiors encouraged him. So as he sat in his living room on Thanksgiving Day, 1950, Cowin was thinking of ideas for Longwell, thinking of ways to make an impression and, after a while, thinking back to Columbus, Ohio, and the wives.

The next day, he came into the Time Inc. offices and typed up a memo to Longwell:

> There are very few subjects which are not pretty well covered by the magazines with large national circulations: *Time* and *Newsweek* in the news field; *Life* and *Look* cover the picture field; *House and Garden* and *Better Homes & Gardens* take care of "home improvement"; *Ladies' Home Journal*, *McCall's* and *Woman's Home Companion* keep the ladies happy; and so on down the line. However, there is one very broad field which is not adequately covered by any publication with a large national following—sports!

> Aside from a number of pulp magazines—and near pulps—and a few "one shots" put out by such publishers as Dell, there seems to be only a handful of sport magazines which have good, well known reputations in this area and nationally. None of them have a circulation over 1,000,000....

> I'm sure that Time Inc. with its facilities and appealing editorial "know-how" could put out a sports publication so far above and ahead of anything being published today that the demand would be overwhelming. It would be a magazine that is at home on every cocktail table of the millions of wide awake people who crowd the public and private golf courses at 6:00 A.M., the high school tennis courts, as well as Churchill Downs.

> With the trend toward a shorter work week and more holidays, the number of people—and the time they spend—engaged in their favorite sporting activity is growing at an enormous rate. Why not cater to this obvious interest?

In the rush of the holidays, Cowin didn't hear from Longwell, and besides a few words of thanks in the hall, he never did receive a direct response. Instead he went about his business and waited for the nearly three years that would elapse before the company would take him up on his proposition.

• • •

The genesis for Longwell's memo was an October 30, 1950, meeting called by Time Inc. president Roy Larsen, the cautious entrepreneur who had been Luce's business-side counterpart since the death of company co-founder Briton Hadden. He was joined by Billings, Longwell, Time Inc. advertising director Howard Black, and vice-president and treasurer Charles Stillman. Larsen announced that he and Luce were looking for a "Big Idea" for the company's next publishing venture. They weren't interested in merely improving the existing magazines; instead, they wanted a concept for a new magazine, one that would not compete with the existing titles for advertising revenue.

By 1951, plans for new ventures became more explicit. In a letter to his associates, Luce noted that the company had more than $10 million "sitting idle . . . not needed as protection against 'hard times' because we have plenty of protection in our breakeven point plus capital and surplus against the ordinary hazards of the business cycle." Time Inc. couldn't hold on to the money forever—the government's 80 percent marginal tax rate would see to that—so the company had to either invest it or watch it disappear.

Ideas for a new magazine, of one kind or another, had been percolating at the company since the end of the war. In May 1947, Luce detached *Time* editor Thomas S. Matthews to work on an experimental project called *Measure,* meant to be a monthly magazine of cultural and intellectual discourse similar to the *Atlantic Monthly* or *Harper's.* Luce also had been intrigued with an idea for a periodical called *Murder,* a true crime magazine that would explore the most spectacular cases of the day in exhaustive and intricate detail. The company tinkered with all these ideas, as well as a compendium of new short fiction, without reaching consensus. None of the ideas seemed like quite the *right* one; none seemed big enough to seize the imagination of a company that was respected in Washington D.C., trusted across America, and known throughout the world.

The new magazine committee languished until a lunch hour in March 1953, when a casual bit of praise pricked Luce's pride. Editorial director John Shaw Billings, Luce's trusted adviser and the second ranking executive on the editorial side of the company, mentioned how impressed he was with the work of treasurer Charles Stillman, whose investments were increasing Time Inc.'s holdings. The idle praise rankled Luce. "Well, anybody can make money *with* money," he said. "We're supposed to be publishers. A real test would be, Can we bring out a new magazine?"

The answer was forthcoming. Later that month, Harry and Clare Boothe Luce left for Naples on the Italian ocean liner *Andrea Doria*, where Mrs. Luce would take her appointment as U.S. Ambassador to Italy. On his last day in the office, Luce left Black and Stillman with orders to pursue the idea of a new magazine; he wanted to decide, within the coming months, on a single idea that could be examined for its possible viability. By this time, Cowin's idea—altered, diluted, tricked up, and with someone else likely taking credit for it—was among the finalists.

Luce had heard the sports idea as well, though he had not been immediately captivated. From his early childhood days in China as the son of a Presbyterian missionary, he'd lacked the correct disposition for games. He indulged casually in sports during his college years at Yale and Oxford, but as an adult, he seemed unable to enjoy recreation. He sped through his infrequent outings of golf, playing nine holes at a time and always using an electric cart, lest he tarry too long. On the tennis court, Luce was an aggressive, artless player, rushing the net for reckless volleys, as though the mere thought of long baseline rallies was a waste of time.

But that spring in Europe, Luce couldn't help noticing how many dinner-party conversations seemed to wind up on the subject of sports, exposing large gaps in his otherwise encyclopedic knowledge. Upon leaving one party, he asked *Life* articles editor Emmet Hughes, who had joined him for the evening, "Why does every conversation end up being about sports?" Walsh knew of Luce's utter ignorance of the particulars of the subject, so he framed his answer carefully. "Well, Harry," he said, "because sports, like music, is a universal language. Everyone speaks it."

Neither Larsen nor Billings were enthusiastic about a new venture. But the company's advertising director, Howard Black, was. A hard-drinking, chain-smoking, street-smart Irish carouser, Black had always been a breed apart at the company. He was prone to fits of self-absorbed rambling, pacing the den of his Brooklyn home, muttering aloud to himself about "that goddamn Luce" or "that goddamn Larsen." Billings was keenly aware of Black's fervor to start a new magazine, but gave it little credence. "Black is crazy to publish," he wrote in his journal, "but as an illiterate, he doesn't know what."

While Black rarely corresponded in print, he did send Luce a 6½-page memo later in May, reviewing the different possibilities for magazines, among them a newsletter about international politics and, finally, "a Sports Weekly—everything in sports—hunting, fishing, boating—a picture magazine—10 cents a copy. I'm not sure of the price for I feel that we should not have more than 1,500,000 circulation." Luce cabled back and, summing up his thoughts, remarked that the "compass needle always came back to sport." At the very least, he felt it was time for the company to finally explore the idea further.

In June, Luce returned to New York and called a meeting of Larsen, Black, Stillman, and a few other executives. Billings recognized quickly that Luce was in "an empire-building mood." He began the meeting by tossing the printed agenda aside and suggesting that they discuss the idea of a sports magazine. "Within 60 seconds everyone present agreed," Luce would remember later. "During the meeting, which lasted two hours, there was no discussion about *whether* there should be a Time Inc. sports magazine, but *how* it should be." Others would recall the meeting differently. Charles Stillman produced a report stating that the advertising universe for sports magazines wasn't large enough to sustain a weekly, but his findings were ignored. Both Billings and vice-president Allen Grover pointed out that Time Inc. wasn't really "a sporting outfit," and that much of the staff would have to come from outside the building.

That point was ignored, but they were right. Although Time Inc. spoke to the American middle class, its staff did not closely reflect its readers' middle-class pastimes. Knowledge of sports within the company, from Luce on down, was shockingly low, owing less to the company's supposed Ivy League predominance than an overarching, serious-minded gentility. Time Inc. people didn't sweat; their sports were rich men's pursuits—yachting, golf, croquet. But by now Luce was intrigued, and when the group met again a week later, he formally put forth a proposal for a mass magazine, a sports weekly with a cover price of 15 cents and a circulation of 1,500,000. Luce suggested that Sid James, an assistant managing editor at *Life*, could edit the magazine, and that Bernie Auer might make a good publisher.

To explore the viability of the idea, Billings tapped one of his star writers, *Life*'s Ernest Havemann, to make a confidential survey of the sportswriting universe. The cool, slightly detached Havemann had been pursuing a Ph.D. in psychology at Washington University in St. Louis when he abandoned it to work for the *St. Louis Post-Dispatch*, where he was briefly a sportswriter. About sports, as other matters, Havemann was really more of a student than a fan.

On Thursday, July 2, Billings and Havemann went to Luce's office to discuss the new magazine. "They're on the same track, going in the same direction," wrote Billings in his journal. "But I'm not yet on fire about

Sports as a subject for journalism." While Larsen was the general care-taker of the overall project, Billings would, during Luce's time in Italy, be the main editorial-side executive over the project . Billings had been the obsessively punctilious managing editor of *Time* from 1933 to 1936 and *Life* from its first issue in 1936 to 1944, when at Luce's request he rose to the newly created position of editorial director, where he often acted as a buffer between Luce and his managing editors.

For a representative on the publishing side, Larsen had summoned Richard Neale, then the director of promotions at *Life* magazine. He'd been a dynamo at the *Life* promotion department, playing an important role in a spectacularly successful promotion called National Golf Day, in which America was invited to play a round "against" Ben Hogan. On May 31, 1952, more than 87,000 contestants played a round of golf on their home courses. With the help of their USGA handicaps, nearly 15,000 beat Hogan's medal round of 71, shot the same day at the Dallas Northwood Club, site of the '52 U.S. Open. The event had been Howard Black's idea, and its success seemed proof to him both of the emerging leisure class in America and Time Inc.'s ability to tap into it.

On July 7, just before returning to Italy, Luce hosted a luncheon meet-ing with all the sports magazine participants, who would begin work just two days later. There was a hint at the lunch that Luce and Havemann had different magazines in mind. "Havemann led off with his ideas," Billings reported in his journal. "He proposed a staff-written magazine. Luce dis-agreed completely, wanted the editors to find and encourage outside writ-ers." Billings also noted that there was much talk of a "search for a 'com-mon denominator' with which to unify the magazine philosophy."

• • •

A search for a common denominator had been a historical problem for American sports magazines. Havemann was not the first person, or even the first Time Inc.-er, to consider the idea. In one of company co-founder Briton Hadden's notebooks from the late '20s, there was a nota-tion about exploring the idea of a "spt. mag." Hadden also dreamed of owning a major league baseball team.

But a general magazine about sports had never flourished. The first real effort to appeal to such a general spectator sports fan came in the mid-'30s, with the underfunded, independent effort by a pair of former Time Inc. employees, *Fortune* production man John Escher and *Time* assistant circulation manager Samuel H. McAloney. McAloney had left *Time* early in 1935, to work with *Story* magazine, a middlebrow literary title owned by a Jewish émigré named Kurt Simon. Escher and McAloney sold Simon on the idea of a general interest sports magazine, which they began publishing under the title of *Sports Illustrated* in January 1936.

The first issue of *Sports Illustrated*, on newsstands in December 1935, carried a steep cover price of 25 cents. Running 50 pages, it featured a piece by Paul Gallico about watching sports events from a plane, a six-page lead feature previewing the Rose Bowl, and a front-of-the-book section clearly modeled on *The New Yorker*'s Talk of the Town. The problem, inevitably, was advertising. The distillers of Mount Vernon Christmas Punch bought a four-color ad on the back cover, but the only full-page ad inside was taken out by McAloney's former colleagues at *Time*.

Among the worried investors in the new magazine was Stuart Scheftel, the restless heir to the Strauss family that owned the Macy's department store chain (his grandparents died on the *Titanic*). Scheftel was already publishing a magazine called *Young America*, with a circulation approaching 100,000. Within a few months, when *Sports Illustrated* needed money, he bought out Simon, Escher, and McAloney for an 80 percent interest in the new magazine. Under Scheftel's watch, *Sports Illustrated*'s profile increased instantly, as he poured more money into it and converted it to a stylish oversize format resembling *Esquire* and *Fortune*. But in late 1937, Scheftel lost most of his fortune in the stock market. While *Sports Illustrated* had by then attained a circulation of 65,000, he felt that *Young America* had the more promising future. In March 1938, convinced that one but not both of the magazines could succeed, Scheftel shut down *Sports Illustrated* and sold his subscribers' list, but retained the rights to the title.

Eight years later, in August 1946, MacFadden Publications president O.J. Elder launched a personality-driven magazine called *Sport*. Loaded with breezy profile pieces and quizzes, photos and season previews, it quickly attained a circulation of 300,000 and grew marginally in the coming years, becoming a favorite of teenage boys. By 1948, Dell Publications wanted to get into the sports publishing game as well. It launched a magazine broadly imitative of *Sport*, called *Sports Album*, only to find MacFadden threatening to sue, arguing that *Sports Album* was a deliberate imitation. Dell ceased publication of *Sports Album*, but didn't give up. Stanley Woodward, one of the premier sports editors of his era, had just finished a cantankerous first term at the *New York Herald Tribune* when he approached Dell with the idea of doing a serious sports monthly. The first issue hit newsstands in February of 1949. It, too, carried the title *Sports Illustrated*, which Scheftel had leased to Dell late in 1948.

From the first few pages of Vol. I, No. 1, it was clear that the Dell publication would focus much more on spectator sports than the earlier incarnation of *Sports Illustrated*. Oversize (like *Life*), printed on flimsy, coated paper (like *Life*), and suffused with black-and-white photos (like *Life*), it was a publication for the masses, albeit one committed to a harder journalistic edge than sports pulp magazines of the era.

Under Woodward's editorship, the first issues would include articles by John Lardner, Jimmy Cannon, Clair Bee, and Red Smith. The April issue featured a sparkling photo essay about the birth of a thoroughbred, showing the first few minutes in the life of a horse that would, in three years, be one of thousands eligible for the Kentucky Derby. There were stories on the new baseball season, a lengthy analysis on the future of television in sport, and plenty of good writing.

For its time, the magazine was visually impressive, topical, and authoritative. It was written with verve and style and a real editorial viewpoint. It assumed a universe of intelligent spectator sports fans that wanted more than just superficial personality pieces on the biggest stars, and it delivered a magazine just for them.

And it went out of business within five months. Plagued by low circulation and a high overhead, Dell pulled the plug in the middle of the summer, and the rights to the title *Sports Illustrated* reverted again to Stuart Scheftel. America wasn't ready yet.

• • •

The seven people who reported to work on Time Inc.'s top-secret "experimental sports magazine project" on July 9, 1953, were only dimly aware of this history. Project X, as it came to be known to some within the building, was based on the 17th floor of the Time & Life Building at 9 Rockefeller Plaza.

Havemann was joined by *Life* reporter Clay Felker, the son of an editor for the St. Louis baseball newspaper *The Sporting News*, and *Life* writer Don Schanche. Felker was a magazine lover of almost boundless ambition who seemed cursed by being typecast as a sports reporter at Time Inc., though his first love was politics. Another product of Time Inc.'s rich *St. Louis Post-Dispatch* pipeline that had produced Havemann, *Time* editor Roy Alexander, and *Life* assistant managing editor Sid James, Felker had more of a sports background than almost anyone else in the company. He'd worked with the New York Giants' radio broadcast team, and double-dated with Bobby Thomson back on Coogan's Bluff. Schanche had been a foreign correspondent for the company, and freely admitted to knowing far more about Laotian politics than American football. But he was talented, and good friends with Havemann, who coaxed him down. Efforts to recruit writers or editors from *Time* had failed. As Billings reported to Luce, "nobody on that magazine would volunteer for the experiment. They claimed they had more important jobs to do, and besides, they weren't really interested in sports—an ominous note." Rounding out the experimental editorial staff was designer Francis "Hank" Brennan, working then in the amorphous position of art adviser to Luce. Brennan had been art director of *Fortune* and *Life*, but the prevailing opinion among designers in the building was that he was still stuck in the classical prewar era.

The initial editorial planning sessions proceeded haltingly. Havemann would sit with Felker, Schanche, and Brennan in the conference room and discuss the theory of what a Time Inc. sports magazine might look like. But he realized quickly that he needed someone who was a legitimate sports expert. Felker had suggested *Life*'s fast-rising Hollywood correspondent, Jim Murray, who had established himself as a perceptive student of the high life, able to mix smoothly with the glitterati and still turn a sharp phrase. He was living in Pacific Palisades and filing regular dispatches on the movies and popular arts, and was well-known among the staff as a passionate, knowledgeable sports fan. Havemann called him up and explained the concept. "My backbone kind of shrank at the thought of going to New York in July," said Murray, "because air-conditioning was not widespread then. Only a few hotels had it [the Time & Life Building did not]. But I said, okay, if I could come back on the train so I could noodle some ideas." When Murray got to New York in mid-July, he found the department in a curious state of animated disarray. Havemann greeted him warmly, but then spent most of his days in his small adjoining office, with the door closed. So it was left to Murray to handle many of the administrative duties, like giving out the writing assignments in an effort to get a sense of the field: Don Schanche to the College All-Star Game in Chicago, Clay Felker to the Hambletonian, Murray himself to a fight card at the Garden.

On Tuesday, July 21, Billings and Larsen joined Havemann and Brennan to discuss the project's progress. It was an awkward meeting, leaving Billings with the sense that Havemann was still stuck on many of the same theoretical questions that he'd worried over at the meeting two weeks earlier. While Billings was waiting for some tangible specifics, Havemann was asking for guidance on the ratio of pictures to text, an "off-the-cuff reaction" on whether humor should play a great part in the new magazine, and whether the executives thought fiction should be a major component. *These are the things we need* him *to figure out,* mused Billings at the time.

He couldn't. Privately, Havemann was chilling to the whole idea. He was coming around to the prevailing opinion within much of the building, which was that a magazine about sports was a poor project for an important company that was influencing world events. Luce's belief in the start-up did little to heighten the enthusiasm of his lieutenants, who viewed him in much the same way that journalists have viewed great press moguls for generations—with a curious mixture of respect and condescension. During furtive conversations in the executive washroom, top-level editors and writers were referring to the new magazine as *Muscles*.

It was also true, as Murray had sensed, that Havemann's mind was otherwise occupied. He was spending most of his days in his small office with the door closed, poring over a bulky manuscript: the advance galley proofs of Alfred C. Kinsey's *Sexual Behavior in the Human Female*, the much anticipated follow-up to Kinsey's earlier study of male sexuality. Havemann would wind up writing a long analysis of the book for the August 24, 1953, issue of *Life*.

The sports magazine idea was no competition for Dr. Kinsey. In between chapters, Havemann paused to take stock of what his tiny staff was producing, and traded memos with Billings. Finally, writing Billings from his home on Sunday, July 26, Havemann begged off the project. His intensely personal cover letter assumed an air of weary fatalism: "Everything I have studied since I started this project, everybody I have talked to, all my own thoughts, have seemed to me to lead inescapably to this conclusion: Our idea for a sports magazine just won't work. . . . I naturally feel that we should abandon the project, that any time or money we spend on it will be wasted and that if we should ever actually publish the magazine it would be a costly failure."

He promised that his accompanying "Report on Sports" would dispassionately weigh the pros and cons of such an effort, should anyone else decide to take it up, and that he wouldn't say anything to his staff, since such a disclosure could only hurt morale. Billings received the memo and the report Monday morning, July 27. Havemann's 11-page single-spaced summary, "A Report on Sports," opened with the assertion that during the winter months, "a weekly sports magazine cannot depend on news." Havemann also argued that most sports fans were simply too wrapped up in their own specific passions to care about others:

> The point I'm trying to make here is two-fold: (1) the word sports covers a multitude of subjects, and (2) there is less interest and good copy in any of them than one would at first suppose. Indeed I have come to believe strongly that we are dealing here with a great number of little splinter groups, one might call them. There are scores of sports

magazines on the market, ranging from a little newsletter sort of thing on West Coast bowling to the rather handsome and elaborate *Yachting*. They all serve a purpose and all have their fans, ranging from a few thousand to 800,000. They are strictly for devotees; nothing in them would interest an outsider.

And here I think is the heart of the dilemma. In practically all participant sports there is a definite and very low limit on the number of stories you can dream up or words you can write without getting detailed and technical. Yet as soon as you get at all technical you find yourself writing to a mere handful of people.

You are bound to wind up, in seeking enough stories to fill a weekly magazine, with a hodge-podge that pleases nobody.

But Havemann granted that there *was* one area that had to be examined seriously, that being the burgeoning world of spectator sports. Baseball had for decades been a hallowed institution in America, and both boxing and football were enjoying huge audiences. But here Havemann reached the same conclusion that then prevailed on Madison Avenue, a view that would influence virtually every subsequent decision made by the Project X committee. "Our business department is working up a report on the finances of sports magazines," he wrote. "It will show, I am sure, that only males read sports magazines; that most of the males are either juveniles or ne'er-do-wells and the advertising agencies know it, and that even having the word Sport in a magazine title may be financial folly."

And if the audience was bad, suggested Havemann, the quality of sports reporting was even worse. While he granted that *Time* could produce a magazine that "would make all previous coverage of spectator sports look silly," he warned that it would be a much bigger job than expected, because the company "would have to give the current practitioners a lot of editorial guidance and rewriting." He further warned that the staffing requirements for the new magazine would be monumental. *Life* already had an editor, an assistant editor, and two to three reporters working full-time to produce one sports story a week, along with one or two photographers to supply the pictures. Multiplying that to come up with 40 pages of editorial matter a week seemed a daunting, futile proposition to Havemann. "I wonder how I could ever have been enthusiastic about the idea," he wrote in closing. "I can't answer that."

Billings privately agreed with many of Havemann's conclusions, but was alarmed by the suddenness of his surrender, and dismayed by the timing. Luce's next scheduled New York visit was just six weeks away, and the experimental department was expected to have an internal specimen magazine to show him. That afternoon, he took Havemann to lunch at Louis XIV, the favorite dining spot for Time Inc. executives, and convinced him to stay on another week, until Roy Larsen returned from his vacation. Both men agreed that Havemann shouldn't share his skepticism with the staff.

But in Billings's mind, Havemann's argument against the idea was both persuasive and decisive. "[Havemann's] memo has effectively killed off all idea of a 100 percent sports weekly—the original Luce idea," he concluded in his journal entry of August 5.

• • •

Many of Havemann's concerns about spectator sports and the sort of audience they attracted must have seemed well-founded to his colleagues. In 1953, there were few encouraging trends to argue for the longtime health of any of the major sports.

Major league baseball attendance had fallen steadily since its record high of 20.9 million in 1948, drawing just 14.3 million in 1953. The decline would have been even sharper if the Boston Braves, who drew less than 300,000 fans in 1952, hadn't moved to Milwaukee, where they drew 1.8 million in their first season. At the same time, the vast network of minor leagues was contracting painfully, threatened by the advent of television.

Pro basketball was described by one observer as "a small-time, penny ante sport, because it attracted so many small-time, penny ante operators." The NBA had lagged behind even major league baseball in permitting blacks in the league, with Chuck Cooper and Harlem Globetrotter Nat "Sweetwater" Clifton first playing in 1950. College basketball attendance dropped by half in the first four years of the decade, rocked by point-shaving and grade-fixing scandals at City College of New York (which had won both the 1950 NCAA and NIT championships) and Kentucky (which dropped the sport in 1952 and 1953). Even at its best, it remained essentially a regional sport; the two top-ranked teams in the 1953 wire-service polls, Indiana and Seton Hall, went to different postseason tournaments.

It would be 1958 before pro football would average 30,000 fans a game, though it was picking up a following on television. In 1951, the Dumont Network had presented the first national telecast of an NFL title game. But broad sections of the country still preferred the college game. In 1952, the supposed football hotbed of Dallas greeted an NFL franchise with complete indifference. The Dallas Texans, the remnants of the defunct New York Yanks franchise, drew just 13,000 fans a game at the Cotton Bowl, and its owners turned the franchise back to the league midway through the season. While college football enjoyed popularity, interest waxed and waned across the country, and there was no sense that the game being played so passionately in the Big Ten carried much intrinsic interest to fans in the Ivy League, or vice versa.

In tennis, Jack Kramer's grinding pro tennis circuit labored on, helping to create stars like Pancho Gonzalez, though so-called amateurs were likely making more money. Golf had enjoyed a postwar renaissance, but there was little to suggest that its popularity would go beyond the major championships.

And there was a taint of impropriety surrounding both of the certifiably healthy spectator sports, boxing and horse racing. The former was dominated by Rocky Marciano and Sugar Ray Robinson, but television overexposure was hurting the sport—there hadn't been a $1 million gate since the Joe Louis–Billy Conn rematch in 1946—and the public had become justifiably suspicious of many results. And horse racing was, in the mind of some, not a sport at all, but merely a convoluted justification for gambling.

Finally, the perception persisted among Time Inc.'s management that, whatever the strengths and weaknesses of the individual sports, there was nothing in the culture that bound them together, no natural impetus for the college football fan to follow ice hockey, or for the baseball fan to care about tennis.

And everywhere, there was the fear that television was destroying all the games. There had been 7,000 sets in the United States in 1946; by the end of the '50s, there would be 50 million. Even the most cautious analyst could tell that the TV explosion meant *something*, but few observers saw it as a boon to spectator sports.

If anything, the most impressive gains from the postwar boom were being seen in participant sports. Studies showed that table tennis, softball, and bowling had about 20 million participants each, and another 17 million were skating at the country's 4,000 roller rinks. The new suburban dwellers seemed to be drawn to pursuits that were once the exclusive province of the rich. Five million had taken to the increasingly democratized public golf courses. Or they were going boating, where between 1936 and 1952 the volume of boat-trailer sales increased fortyfold.

Of course, because there were no real sports fans among Time Inc.'s upper echelon, no real studies done of potential readers, no surveys of sports fans, these were all guesses, and mostly uneducated ones. But they would inform and guide the company's thinking about the entire field of sports for years to come.

• • •

At lunch on August 13, Ernest Havemann formally resigned his post and Roy Larsen accepted his resignation. The next day, Billings and Larsen spent the afternoon poring over all the documents that Havemann's department had gathered. Two crucial decisions would come out of the meeting. The first one was conceptual, and explained by Billings in an August 26 letter that gave Harry Luce in Rome his first glimpse of the crisis:

> Speculating that the publishing formula of 1,500,000 circulation may have stymied editorial development, Larsen came up with another general concept for the magazine: a *class* sports weekly of 350,000 instead of a *mass* magazine of 1,500,000. Its writing and attitude could be sophisticated, intelligent, even critical, with no pandering to fans. It would be "rich" in content and format—25¢ per copy—and would appeal to the *Sportsman* which might be its name. In advertising it would go after a class market now being neglected by all save the *New Yorker*.

They also concluded that it was time to bring all the elements together, to bring on an editor who could be relied upon, as Billings would put it, to construct "something tangible in the dummy form on which a reasonable judgment could be made. And to hell with theory for the time being!"

But none of the task force members had enough experience to direct such an operation. And while there were other writers in the building who'd touched on sports, it now seemed clear that an experienced editor was needed. Billings and Larsen eventually arrived at Sid James, the assistant managing editor at *Life*, longtime Time Inc.-er, a man of unvarnished enthusiasm. James had been a successful bureau chief in Los Angeles, but since moving to New York as an assistant managing editor, he had been eclipsed in the sizable shadow of *Life*'s autocratic managing editor Ed Thompson, who didn't much care for him. Billings knew that Luce would approve, because Luce had mentioned James as a possible editor early in the planning stages. He also knew that the Luces were particularly fond of James because the chipper AME had played a crucial supporting part in

Clare Boothe Luce's worst hour, in 1944. While returning to Stanford University after meeting the Luces in San Francisco for dinner, Ann Brokaw, Clare's daughter from a previous marriage, died in an auto accident. James, then working as Time Inc.'s L.A. bureau chief, happened to be in San Francisco that weekend, and his discreet, assured handling of the grisly identification and transportation arrangements permanently earned the Luces' favor.

Ed Thompson was just returning from a European vacation, but Larsen and Billings moved fast. On the morning of August 18, Larsen called him to his office and made a pitch for James, with Thompson consenting to let James be detached for the project. The same day, Billings took Thompson and James to lunch to outline the situation. James agreed immediately, earning Billings's gratitude ("The good soldier," he wrote. "I liked him a lot.")

While James lacked the presence or intellectual firepower of Ed Thompson or *Time* editor Roy Alexander, he had proven himself over several different assignments in the company. His shortcomings—blind optimism, an inability to critique his own work, a patent disinclination to think skeptically or see the larger picture—had eliminated him from any serious shot to be Thompson's successor at *Life*. But they could be just the qualities, Billings thought, to get the sports magazine idea into motion.

James, born in 1906, had been a journalist virtually all of his adult life. His father Harry had been a humor columnist for various St. Louis papers, mostly the *Post-Dispatch*, where he provided the light verse and wisecracks so common in papers of that era, under the headline "Jests and Jingles." At home, he played the banjo to entertain his five children, whom he raised after the death of his wife in 1911. Sid James began as a cub reporter for the *St. Louis Times* and quickly graduated to the *Post-Dispatch*. He started stringing for *Time* while at the *Dispatch* and, after serving in New York as a national affairs writer for *Time* from 1936 to 1938, he was hired as the head of the Chicago bureau in 1938. In 1941, he was promoted to chief of Western editorial operations, serving in Los Angeles from 1941 to 1946, when *Life* magazine was viewed as a nearly omnipotent force by the Hollywood studios. Possessed of a strong face that always looked more stern in pictures than in real life, James seemed a man positively propelled by his own optimism, with abundant faith in America, technological progress, and the press. He was a cheerfully earnest and well-respected boss, and his tenure had been a grand success in L.A., where he presided over a talented stable of writers and an all-star collection of photographers, including Peter Stackpole and Bob Landry.

James was summoned back to *Life* in 1946, where his career stalled. The blustery, Montana-born Thompson was a force of nature, a man James described as "the best editor I ever worked for," but the respect was not mutual. Thompson bristled at James's breezy, glib style, and blanched at his presumptions to power. By the early '50s, James had been marginalized, put into the position of booking the outside guest for the weekly lunch with Thompson and his assistant managing editors. But he still gave it his best. From one of those bookings came the opportunity, through James's efforts, that allowed *Life* to print Ernest Hemingway's *The Old Man and the Sea* in its entirety.

Amazingly, news of Havemann's resignation had remained secret, hidden from the staff on the 17th floor, where Murray, Felker, and Schanche continued to work on story ideas. But on August 20, James burst through the office door. Jim Murray had known James in L.A., having started work with the company shortly before James was transferred to New York.

"Hey, Sid!" said Murray, pleased but perplexed. "What are you doing here?"

James walked up to Murray, poked a finger in his chest, and asked sternly, "Do you believe in this magazine?"

Murray was more startled than stirred.

"Oh, yeah . . . sure," he said.

James circled the room, posing the same arch question, with the same pointed finger, to Felker and Schanche. After both answered in the affirmative, James disclosed the fate of Havemann. Murray, for one, wasn't surprised.

Then Sid James began taking stock. It had been years since he'd really been in charge of anything. Now, emboldened by the confidence shown in him, he set about turning his enthusiasm into a larger reality. A more circumspect man might have considered submitting to Billings a point-by-point refutation of Havemann's analysis. But James answered that memo in only the broadest of terms. He planned a lunch on August 26 with Larsen, Billings, Neale, and Black, where he would present his findings. That morning, he had delivered to their offices a one-paragraph summary of his vision of the magazine. What it lacked in specifics, it made up for in enthusiasm:

## PROJECT X

It would not be A sports magazine. It would be THE sports magazine, with capital T, H and E. It would bring a reader all THE sports news in THE best way, and THE best advice, THE best in adventure, fiction, etc., etc. The writing would be the best we can get. There would be fine color both photographic, painting, and commissioned drawings. There would be the finest photographic portraits of sports personalities we can get and the photographic portraits of animals will be even better if we can make them so. The paper will be of good enough quality to make the most of all of this.

At the lunch that day, James argued that the current sports pages were inferior, that there was no real competition in the weekly field, and that the combination of increased postwar leisure time and spending, as well as the advent of television, could increase sport's profile enough to support a weekly magazine.

He also left them with a longer memo, endorsing Jim Murray's suggestion, to call the new magazine *Fame* (a title then owned by Quigley Publications, for an annual movie fan magazine). That title, of course, would have the added benefit of giving the company complementary titles for its four major periodicals: *Time* and *Life*, *Fame* and *Fortune*. Nothing was decided then, although the rest of the committee quickly rejected Larsen's idea to call the magazine *19th Hole*, meant to suggest the country club tone that he wanted the magazine to adopt.

James proposed that the magazine open with a section called "Soundtrack," that would be "more like the *New Yorker*'s opening than *Time*'s or *Life*'s." He would follow that with regular departments, on Baseball, Football, Hunting, etc. Ever confident, he closed the memo with the same effusive paragraph that he'd sent to Billings and Larsen that day. They shook his hand, thanked him, and went up to Larsen's office to meet privately. Neither man thought much of the new suggestions, but they also knew that the ultimate decision would rest with Luce. Writing to Luce August 26, Billings promised that "your project is very much alive—and we'll have a baby for you in September—a seven pounder, if not a ten pounder."

Luce arrived in mid-September and looked with fascination at the rough pages that James and Brennan had constructed. A few days later, Billings called James with the good news: "Sid, Harry wants to know if you could take this on. He's all for it." James eagerly accepted and began to assemble a staff.

Then Billings went back to his office and wrote a letter to commiserate with his friend, Time Inc. vice-president C.D. Jackson. Billings's opinion would reflect that of most of the hierarchy at the company. "When Harry came up with this experiment my heart sank with personal dismay," he wrote, "because here was a publishing enterprise for which I had no heart, no knowledge, no enthusiasm."

# CHAPTER 2

# "MUSCLES"

The first game of the 1953 World Series was played on Wednesday afternoon, September 30, at Yankee Stadium, where the Brooklyn Dodgers sent 20-game winner Carl Erskine against the Yankees' Allie Reynolds. With their team aiming for a fifth straight world title, Yankees fans were worried about whether their pitchers could hold up against Brooklyn's imposing batting line-up. Dodgers fans were worried about the curse of Brooklyn, and the specter of losing yet another Fall Classic.

Richard Neale and Sid James were worried that their guest would be bored.

Henry Luce, having approved the idea of exploring the sports magazine concept, was now immersing himself in the world of sports with the same methodical approach that he would use to get up to speed on an obscure foreign culture or an emerging political story. His ignorance of the subtleties of sport was complete, but he brought a voracious mental acquisitiveness to every new pursuit. He spent much of his free time joining reluctant employees at sporting events, where he would pepper them with an unending stream of questions: Why is there tape around the boxer's gloves? Who's that man standing by the base? What are they saying in the huddle?

Having no frame of reference, no sense of the tradition of the Yankees or the perennial rivalry between Brooklyn and the Bronx, Luce might have been watching any baseball game. And that was unfortunate, because by the time he arrived in the second inning, the Yankees had knocked Erskine out and were ahead 4–0, at which point the game fell into a drab, sluggish rhythm. "When you hear the boys selling peanuts instead of the fans riding the pitcher, it's a dull ball game," recalled Neale later. "And it was." By the end of the fifth inning, even the insistent questioning from Luce had subsided, and now the editor-in-chief was growing restless and distracted.

Then the Dodgers' Gil Hodges homered to start the sixth, and after a deep flyout by Carl Furillo, Billy Cox singled. Dodger manager Chuck Dressen sent in utility outfielder George "Shotgun" Shuba to pinch-hit for pitcher Jim Hughes, who'd held the Yankees to a run in four innings of relief for Erskine. Allie Reynolds looked tired, but there was no sign of Casey Stengel emerging from the Yankee dugout.

Shuba sent Reynolds's first pitch into the right-field stands, tying the game and sending the sizable minority of Dodgers fans into a celebratory frenzy.

Moments later, with Stengel summoning Johnny Sain for Reynolds and the stands still crackling with residual excitement, Luce turned to Neale and James and smiled.

"Well," he said, "looks as if it could be a pretty interesting subject for a new magazine."

Luce left in the seventh inning, but he'd glimpsed a bit of the drama that big American sporting events could offer. His curiosity had been satisfied, and he emerged more committed than ever to the idea of a sports magazine. During his brief trip from Rome, Luce surveyed Brennan's specimen layouts and remarked that they opened up a "whole new wonderful world of sport" for him.

The rest of the fall of 1953 was spent in a constant churn of activity, with James hiring dozens of new staffers, while at the same time trying to produce a blueprint for the prospective magazine. Because he was spending such long days with his staff, James handled his voluminous correspondence from Luce while riding on the train to New York in the morning. He belonged to a coterie of Westchester County businessmen who had leased their own private rail car on the New Haven Railroad. James would meet the 8:18 train at Rye, where he was greeted by a porter, who also shined shoes and served ice water on the 40-minute trip into New York City. With his briefcase on his lap, James composed longhand memos to Luce on a legal pad, before having them retyped and cabled to Luce in Rome. For his part, Luce often sent two or three letters a day, responding to developments, suggesting story ideas, analyzing budgets.

By the time of Luce's late September visit, James had outlined his new vision of the magazine. In it he reiterated, yet again, his paragraph about THE magazine. He described the current working format for Luce:

a. Photographic color cover.
b. Front of the Book consisting of contents table, The Record, The Week's Winners, and The Sportsman at Large.

    c. Body of the Book consisting of The Soundtrack, The Spectacle [a four-page color photographic portfolio], an important coming event, a feature, an adventure story, a foreign sports story. (These to be jumped past the center ad well if necessary).

    d. Back of the Book consisting of specialized departments such as Health, The Sporting Look, Cookery, Cash on the Barrelhead, Fun and Games, Column of the Week, Fiction, Post Mortem.

The plan was made for a first dummy issue to be published in January (dated in December, so Time Inc. could write it off on 1953's books). The dummy would give Time Inc. executives a sense of what such a magazine would look like. Only then could they decide whether to go ahead with the launch.

While Luce was encouraging the editorial side, Neale's team was analyzing the magazine's potential for profitability. The central, cherished assumption that the business side made was that it would be a class magazine, aimed at a select audience of country club members and upscale families.

Even as the business side was grasping for justification for a class magazine, another Time Inc. publication was arguing indirectly for the legitimacy of a magazine directed to a more diverse audience of new suburbanites. Beginning in August of 1953, *Fortune* managing editor Hedley Donovan published a sprawling 11-part series on "The Changing American Market," written by Sanford Parker and a variety of collaborators, which argued that the '50s would see an amazing growth in the "moneyed middle-class," with a commensurate demand for leisure-time products and services. The series noted that the country was devoting $18 billion annually to "unmistakable leisure-recreational expenditures on spectator amusements, spectator and participant athletics, hunting and fishing, gardening, domestic recreational travel . . . foreign pleasure travel, boating, games and toys, certain books, magazines and newspapers, etc."

The broader numbers also showed that real per capita income had more than doubled in 50 years, and that the U.S. was quickly becoming a "one-class market of prosperous middle-income people," a large percentage of which was migrating to the suburbs. Starting in August and appearing every month through the summer of 1954, the series was a constant reminder that the American market was becoming more affluent.

On a Thursday night in January 1954, a festive, expectant mood permeated a dinner meeting of the experimental project's main players, held at the posh Lynx Club in Manhattan. After much discussion about the reader universe, cover price, subscription rate, and start dates, Roy Larsen asked

*Time* circulation chief Bernie Auer how long it would take to get a first test mailing sent out. Larsen wanted to send it to *Time* and *Life* subscribers in Minnesota (where *Time* subscribers had received the first test mailing prior to the *Life* launch in '36). Auer estimated that something could be done by the first of March, but when Larsen asked him to have it done by mid-February, Auer assured him it would be ready. The sports magazine idea was on the fast track.

And then the time came for Luce himself to speak.

"When I first arrived in Rome," he said, "the Ambassador took me to many dinners, events and celebrations, some of which both of us undoubtedly could have skipped. One of them was a sports event where the Ambassador threw the ball in to start the basketball game between the Globemasters and some other team."

"Globe*trotters*, Harry," interjected Howard Black.

"Globemasters, Globetrotters—it doesn't make a difference. I am impressed with what you all have done and I'm impressed with the concept of the magazine. But let there be not a word in it about that game basketball."

He was smiling by then. Before he left New York, Luce approved the suggestion of Black and Larsen, installing H.H.S. "Harry" Phillips, Jr., then the advertising director of *Time*, as the magazine's first publisher and William "Bill" Holman, previously the Eastern advertising manager for *Life*, as the advertising director. Richard Neale was named assistant to the publisher. Appropriately, Bob Cowin, whose idea had started it all, would be the magazine's first circulation director.

The first dummy was printed in mid-January, and sent out both to prospective advertisers and sports editors at newspapers around the country, in the belief that it would increase confidence in and word-of-mouth about the new venture.

"The New Sport Magazine" read the cover logotype, dated "Dummy No. 1, December 5, 1953." Selected elements of the production were undeniably impressive: Time Inc. photographer Mark Kauffman had five pages of crisp, dazzling color from the Bobo Olsen–Randy Turpin middleweight title fight; there were two pages of dense, cribbed scouting reports, written by conference opponents of Michigan State and UCLA, part of a comprehensive Rose Bowl preview that included everything from jersey numbers of key players to fight song lyrics.

And yet the overall issue was as shapeless as James's open-ended conception of the magazine. Brennan's art direction was comically uneven (many stories didn't even have headlines) and the front-of-the-book section, Soundtrack, was so broadly imitative of *The New Yorker*'s Talk of the

Town section as to be an embarrassment. Havemann wrote a memo to Billings, stating, "I still think it merely proves—by being no better than it is after all the effort that has gone into it—that you just can't lick the problems. I further think that to compose a critique of the dummy would be like trying to pick the deadest fish on a mackerel boat."

Shortly after that issue, James would dismiss Brennan in perhaps the only preemptive firing during the year of preparations for the new magazine. After Brennan, *Fortune* art director Leo Lionni was brought in for the second dummy, which would be produced under real deadline conditions and go to press the weekend of the Masters golf tournament in early April. Lionni quickly set about redesigning Brennan's efforts, coming up with a new headline typeface and a more unified overall look.

Before returning to Italy, Luce called a February business luncheon for the new ad sales staff, where his rationale for the new magazine drew bemused stares and frozen smiles. "Sport has aspects, too, of creativity. Man is an animal that works, plays and prays. As a boy, I remember reading a book entitled *Four Things Men Live By*. These four things were Love, Work, Play, and Prayer. No important aspect of life should be devalued. And if play does correspond to some important elements in spiritual man, then it is a bad thing for it be devalued. And sport has been devalued. It has become a lowbrow proposition. It does not get serious attention. The new magazine will be a reevaluation of sport—not an overevaluation—to put it in its proper place as one of the great modes of expression."

This kind of overtheoretical analysis was typical of Luce's attitude toward sport. His emotions followed his intellectual engagement, and while he was enthusiastic about the prospect of a new sports magazine, his interest in sports remained purely abstract. While he would continue to have editors take him to sporting events, sporting personalities had no hold on his imagination. When Joe DiMaggio paid a visit to the U.S. Embassy at Palazzo Margherita in the winter of '54, it was Clare and not Harry who greeted him, suggesting they stroll through the Via Veneto and stop at a café for a cup of coffee. Luce attended a few sporting events in Rome, but this was work for him, just more research for another project. In his leisure hours, he spent his time at Rome's zoo.

Whitney Tower was back for his second interview. The stocky, vaguely aristocratic young horse racing writer knew plenty about thoroughbreds; he was part of the Whitney and Vanderbilt lineage. In 1949, he had come to interview for a job with *Time*, but was told to get more experience. By the spring of 1954, Tower had put in four years for the *Cincinnati Enquirer*, and he had returned seeking a job for the new sports magazine. Tower affected a nervous cheerfulness as he showed up for his crucial meeting with Dick Johnston, the *Life* magazine senior editor who had been hired by James as his assistant managing editor. Tower was dressed sharply and was bravely attempting to conceal his slight stammer, which became more pronounced when he grew self-conscious.

Johnston greeted the young writer warmly, sat back in his chair, put his boots up on his desk, and took a quick look through Tower's personnel file. "Ah, Cincinnati," he said brightly. "Are all the good whorehouses still in Kentucky?"

Given the dearth of Johnston's sports knowledge, it seemed as good a question to open with as any. With his sweeping black hair combed high on his head, his slim mustache, and a glint in his eye of playful malevolence, Dick Johnston looked like an erudite gangster—and often acted like one. Legendary *Esquire* editor Harold Hayes once remarked that Johnston's epitaph ought to read: "If you can't drink it, or smoke it, or fuck it—what good is it?" Johnston's public drinking and unabashed carousing were at odds with the more polished Time Inc. style of furtive dalliances, but Johnston was such an excellent word editor that he was valued in spite of his social sins.

Johnston was no antidote for Sid James's casual acquaintance with the proposed magazine's subject. In the words of one colleague, Johnston "didn't know his ass from third base about sports." In actuality, he knew a little more than that, having been a strapping, all-district catcher in high school at Eugene, Oregon. He'd worked at the local newspaper, the *Eugene Register-Guard* right out of high school, before matriculating at the University of Oregon, where he became something of a saloon socialist. Before going to work for Time Inc., he covered the war in the Pacific for the United Press, and worked as a manager and publicist for the wrestler Gorgeous George. Shortly after the war, Johnston was sent to Shanghai to work as a foreign correspondent, but his left-leaning dispatches didn't sit well with Whittaker Chambers, who after disavowing Communism had become *Time*'s national editor.

James knew of Johnston's talents and, though he didn't approve of his habits, he knew he could be an asset. On the day he hired him for the sports magazine project, James had fixed his colleague with a solemn stare and cleared his throat. "Dick, there's one condition," he said. *"Don't fuck the help."* Johnston laughed heartily, shook James's hand, and ignored the admonition, as he usually did when his superiors tried to tell him how to behave.

While Johnston was destined to be a career iconoclast, James's top senior editor hire, John Tibby, fit the clubby Time Inc. style, right down to his rep tie and wing-tips. It was Tibby's misfortune to appear the perfect caricature of the Time Inc. functionary—serious in intent but somewhat vacuous, good-tempered, and literal. He began his career in his hometown of Pittsburgh at the *Post-Gazette*, later moved to the Gallup Poll, and finally joined Time Inc. as a United Nations correspondent in 1946. He went to the *Time* foreign news desk a year later, and became senior editor in charge of the back of the book in 1948. There he languished, much as James had at *Life*. When the prospect of promotion came up for the sports magazine, Tibby jumped at it.

For James, Johnston, and Tibby, the sports magazine meant a last chance at climbing the corporate ladder. All had enjoyed productive years with the company, but none were destined to play a crucial role with any of the existing magazines. And while they were hardly qualified to run a sports magazine, each man had to feel he'd finally been recognized and valued.

One other crucial management hire was the stern, exacting Honor Fitzpatrick, as chief of researchers. She was a logical choice, having been with the company, off and on, since 1936. She had been a meticulous researcher at *Life*, where Johnston—the most active Lothario in a newsroom full of them—took a shine to her bright red hair and jaunty green berets. She finally married, though not especially happily, divorced a few years later, and was stuck on the research track when Johnston nominated her for the chief of researchers.

Well versed in the Time Inc. traditions that she would be expected to pass on to a new generation of company employees, Fitzpatrick also possessed the sort of erect bearing and crisp demeanor that would make an impression on the young reporter-researchers, many coming straight out of college. The entry-level position for the new recruits required hours of painstaking work, doing background interviews and research to supply the main staff writer with additional information for the story, then turning around and checking every word of the text that was finally submitted. Presiding over these young troops, Fitzpatrick seemed—in one reporter's words—"a combination of a mother and General Patton."

James sent the skeleton staff of writers around the country to do what amounted to dry-run writing assignments, where they were frequently exposed as less than expert in the field. When early hire Coles Phinizy went to a Dodgers-Giants game at Ebbets Field, he saw Duke Snider hit a home run.

"How far was that?" he asked aloud in the press box.

"Well, about 390 feet," estimated one scribe.

"Exactly, please."

Often it was a case of the wrong people being sent out for the right job. Writers Ezra Bowen and Don Schanche were sent down to spring training in 1954. After three weeks of research in which they weren't heard from, Bowen wired the office with the message, "Not much happening here."

One of James's first editor hires with a real grounding in sports was Andrew Crichton, the gifted, eccentric product of a literary family. His father Kyle Crichton was a sprightly writer on sports and movies for *Collier's*, whom Groucho Marx called the funniest man he'd ever met. His brother Robert would go on to write a series of best-selling novels. (Michael Crichton, of such modern mega-hits as *Jurassic Park*, is a distant relative.) Andy had been constructing his own newspapers by age six and attended Harvard at the end of World War II. The comically near-sighted Crichton was a garrulous, precise man, frequently sporting a smile, a squint, and a cigar. His laugh at the upper registers transmogrified into a manic giggle. He was an intuitive editor and writers admired him for the same reason that some of his bosses didn't, because he had an exceedingly light touch with copy.

Crichton was hired as a senior editor, as assistant to Johnston in acquiring outside pieces. "Part of the idea was that most of the magazine could be done by outsiders," Crichton said. "Of course, Time Inc. couldn't stand freelancers. But in the meantime, somebody had to buy the articles and we had to get a lot of articles quickly. We bought some bad stuff, and there was mostly bad stuff being done." The experience also exposed a central flaw in the magazine's conception. The idea that it could survive primarily on outside submissions, with a small staff, and still publish a Time Inc.–quality publication was sheer folly.

Johnston and Crichton would leave the office each Friday, briefcases bulging with solicited material. They'd frequently return Monday morning to halfheartedly place one or two stories on the other's desk, the extent of publishable material each had read. Havemann had been right about one thing: the present level of sportswriting was rife with cliché, devoid of perspective (some writers were still on the dole with the teams they covered), and with but a few exceptions, lacking in rising young talent, at least in the large East Coast cities and metropolitan areas like Chicago and Los Angeles, where Time Inc. operated bureaus.

Hired around the same time as Crichton was an oft-fired advertising salesman named Robert W. Creamer. After graduating from Syracuse shortly after the war, he had bounced around several agencies in New York City until Bill Bernbach, of Doyle, Dane Bernbach told him he was in the wrong business. Creamer found a steady job at *Collier's Encyclopedia* in 1950, where his extensive sports knowledge and attention to journalistic detail made him a valuable asset. Broad-faced and sandy-haired, Creamer was a small-town boy who retained his wonder for the city, along with his villager's charm. He grew up in the bucolic hamlet of Tuckahoe, about a 30-minute train ride from the city, and moved with his wife Margaret into the very house where she grew up.

Creamer had known Crichton from a somewhat distant remove, having spent much of his high school career chasing the Bronxville High middle-distance runner around the track. Their personalities complemented each other well. While Crichton had the aspect of a brainy, slightly absent-minded class clown, Creamer was a down-to-earth Irishman, a constant kibbitzer who was universally well liked. What both brought to the offices of the new magazine was a thorough knowledge of sports.

They were hired right before the second dummy was due. The frenzy suited James, a man of boundless energy. "He was very friendly and you liked him instantly," said Creamer. "Always had a grin, always cheerful, all this energy, go-go, great, everything's terrific—very upbeat all the time. But he used to drive you crazy because you didn't know what was going on."

This was reflected in the frantic and often misdirected energy on the 17th floor. Whitney Tower thought he'd aced his interviews with both Johnston and James, so he returned to Cincinnati and waited to hear whether he'd gotten the job. After six weeks with no word, Tower finally called James's office. "Oh, my goodness, didn't I tell you?" said James when he got on the line. "You're hired. I just forgot to call."

In March 1954, James changed the business plan to account for more staff writers, and renewed his search within the company for candidates. His first hiring coup was coaxing *Time*'s Paul O'Neil, then among the top writers at the magazine, to come over to the project. With a background as a distance runner from Seattle, O'Neil knew the lure of sports, and though he'd been writing about politics well enough to earn 30 cover stories in *Time*, he jumped at the new challenge. "Paul was the best," remembered James. "He could take a subject and just kind of surround it in a very short time, and was a fast writer. And he had a great, almost fiendish, sense of humor." An oft-told, perhaps apocryphal, story had O'Neil informing *Time* managing editor Roy Alexander that he was going over to the new sports magazine. Alexander is reputed to have said, "Why would a writer, on a magazine for people who think, want to go work on a magazine for people who sweat?"

For all his skepticism about the state of contemporary sportswriting, James was convinced that the only way to differentiate the new magazine from previous sports periodicals was to hire big names. Red Smith had tentatively agreed to be the magazine's baseball columnist, supplementing his heavy weekly schedule for the *New York Herald Tribune* with a signed weekly piece. Herbert Warren Wind had been recruited from *The New Yorker* to write golf, and Budd Schulberg—whose screenplay for *On the Waterfront* was well into postproduction—had signed on as the first boxing editor.

The second dummy promised to be an ordeal. Herbert Warren Wind, a notoriously poor deadline writer, was sent to Augusta to cover the Masters for the lead story. Much of the rest of the issue would close early (as it would during the course of a normal publishing week), but Wind's account of the Masters would be held out until Sunday night. When the Masters went to a playoff, Sam Snead edging Ben Hogan on Monday, the magazine had to scramble. Wind filed two paragraphs to top the story that he turned in on Sunday, allowing the magazine to close three of the four late pages on time.

The title on the cover of the second dummy was *Dummy*. (The company, hoping to acquire from MacFadden the title *Sport*, had spent months producing internal test sections under the nonsense title *Mnorx*, which approximated the spacing and lettering of the desired title.) *Dummy*'s cover photograph was a golf scene from Pebble Beach, not Augusta. Inside, the overall look was more assured. Lionni had incorporated a slim, capsule-shaped horizontal oval, usually in red, to signify the departments and also serve as a keynote to run throughout the magazine. It was called the "sausage" by the rest of the art department, and would become a cornerstone in design planning thereafter.

Response to the second dummy was generally more positive, though advertising agencies were still cautious. The advertising journal *Tide* surveyed its leadership panel (a group of ad execs) and found that less than 50 percent said they would advertise in it. The panel's consensus was that the magazine would be a "hard book to sell space for, with an audience all over the lot." This would become a resounding complaint from Madison Avenue. Buyers there felt the magazine didn't speak to an identifiable audience. "It covers too much ground," said one panelist. "It's a hybrid. Do baseball and boxing fans mingle with fox hunters in pink coats?"

There was better news from the circulation side. By late March, results of the first test mailing had started to come in. Larsen oversaw the project—or "copy test," as it was referred to within the building—beginning with essentially the same salutation as the first letter sent out to announce the launch of *Life*. The response was staggering: in an industry in which a 4 percent draw from a list was considered wildly successful, Time Inc. received a 5½ percent response rate (that is, orders for a charter one-year subscription, priced at $6) from *Life* subscribers and nearly 8 percent from *Time* subscribers.

That would give the ad staff ammunition to demonstrate that there was significant reader interest. But it was still left for James to come up with a coherent internal prospectus, which would announce his intentions and give the advertising and circulation staffs something to work from. James finally sent a 54-page prospectus to Luce on April 16. It provided the clearest view to date of what sort of magazine James and the company now envisioned—as well as the continued influence of *The New Yorker* on James's thinking and aspirations.

The new magazine would open with three departments—The Week's Winners, Coming Events, and The Footloose Sportsman (a travel guide to American cities). Next came The Lead Story, which would focus on a big event, a major revelation, or "personal stories which are of high news value because of their tellers and because of their telling as well— Churchill on 'My Thirty Seasons of Polo' . . ." This would be followed by an unwieldy section titled News Comment, News Pictures, that included the Spectacle section, a four- to six-page color photographic portfolio. James suggested following that up with an editorial page, then leading into the expanded preview section, which most agreed was the one editorial highlight of the two dummies. That was followed by features and perhaps fiction and then a glut of departments. They would be referred to internally as columns, perhaps because many were charged to a single celebrated writer: Red Smith on baseball, former coach Herman Hickman on football, Budd Schulberg on boxing, Bill Talbert on tennis. Sprinkled throughout the departments would be "oddments," Luce's term for the single-paragraph bits of information, arcana, or drollery that *Reader's Digest* employed to fill its columns. The back section would also include a Column of the Week (a reprint of an outstanding sports column, culled from newspapers around the country). Cash on the Barrelhead (about the business of sports), Sport in Art, and Weekend (suggested vacation outings) would be occasional columns.

Even more departments would follow, including Pat on the Back (highlighting as yet obscure sports standouts), The Hot Box (in which New York photographer Jimmy Jemail would ask a group of people an

identical question and run their capsulized answers next to their pictures),
Health, and Sporting Look—the fashion column that Neale had been
pushing for, to attract female readers. Then came James's own invention,
the Matchwit Puzzle. It was two crossword puzzles, reading in opposite
directions on facing pages, with a few clues intersecting. He conceived it
as a contest for a couple, to see who could finish first. The magazine
would end with its letters section, called The 19th Hole.

• • •

All signals were pointing toward a late summer launch. With that in
mind, ad director Bill Holman felt that a spring ad conference could be a
show of strength, a high-profile signal to the industry that Time Inc. was
squarely behind the new enterprise, and would spare no expense in ensur-
ing its success. So on April 22, nearly 60 Time Inc. ad salesmen gathered
in Myrtle Beach, South Carolina, for pep talks, strategy sessions, and a
weekend of relaxation before they went out to sell the new magazine.

That Friday evening, Harry Phillips made the announcement that the
magazine would start publishing in August. There were cheers all around,
and an open bar. Then a hotel staffer discreetly pulled Sid James out of the
crowd. It seemed he had a call from a Mr. Luce. When James—who began
the night with a rousing speech to the advertising side troops—got on the
phone, he received stern orders from Luce to return to New York immediately, and to bring business manager Ray Ammarell with him. Luce had
just gotten a copy of James's latest estimates for the first year of editorial
operations, which at $2.8 million were about twice what Luce had in
mind. "This may be the end of the magazine," he crossly told James. Time
Inc. historian Robert Elson wrote that Luce "never reconciled himself to
the ever-increasing editorial budgets of his successful magazines. He had
told James that he hoped the new magazine would operate on a lean budget and thus serve as an example to the other managing editors."

As furtively as possible, James and Ammarell caught the next connection back to the city. Ammarell headed for the Time & Life Building to
pick up his complete set of figures, then met James back at his house in
Rye. With Sid's wife, Agnes James, keeping them well stocked with coffee,
the two men spent all day Sunday in the Jameses' dining room, making
cuts in every area they could think of.

Monday morning at 10 a.m., they showed up at Luce's office and cut
some more, removing nearly $1 million from the editorial budget. By mid-
day, Luce closed a file folder, pushed it back across his desk, and
announced solemnly, "Okay, you've got a magazine."

James was flustered, still reeling from the adrenaline rush of fear, frustration, and anger.

"Goddammit, Harry," he said, trying to sound collegial and casual. "Do you mean to tell me that if we hadn't been able to fix these numbers, you would have killed this magazine right here?"

"No better time than the present," said Luce, already concentrating on his next task.

The weekend's work resulted in cutting 20 positions from the proposed staff, and plenty of number-juggling in the business plan. A crucial savings came when Luce agreed to allow the new magazine free use of the Time Inc. news bureaus, picture collection, and photo lab, an expense previously shared equally by all the magazines. The free ride would engender considerable animosity among staffers of other magazines, who resented the preferential treatment given to an enterprise that many found trivial in the first place. But with the Luce meeting at the end of April, the last real hurdle had been cleared. Time Inc. was going to have a new magazine on sports.

On May 12, 1954, Time Inc.'s publicity department issued a release to other media outlets, announcing that an as yet unnamed national sports weekly, "designed 'to heighten your enjoyment of the wonderful world we play in . . . ,' will be announced to the public in June." The May 14 edition of the Time Inc. house organ, *FYI*, announced the launch, and a public release came on June 1.

Young & Rubicam, the high-powered ad agency that handled all of Time Inc.'s promotional campaigns, was flustered early, because some of the company's biggest clients said they already had their magazine budgets tied up in *Time, Life,* and *Fortune.* Between Y&R and the two promotional departments within the magazine—one for advertising, one for circulation—the magazine launched a full-scale promotional offensive at the beginning of the summer. Two-page ads in *Time* and *Life*'s June 7 issues were scheduled to announce the launch. But no one could articulate the vision of the new magazine. Several writers at the agency, as well as on the business side, took a swipe at it. None succeeded and, finally, Harry Luce wrote the announcement himself, at once hinting at the promise of the new project as well as its convoluted past:

> There has never been a National Sports Weekly. Furthermore, it has been brilliantly proved that there never can be. People's interests are too varied. The fisherman cares nothing for baseball. The skier couldn't care less about the Kentucky Derby.
>
> Maybe. Maybe that's the way it was. Maybe that's still the way it

partly is. But one thing is sure: the world of Sport is a wonderful world and everyone enters it with Joy. . . .

You don't have to read it—not any of it. Sport is Liberty Hall. It compels nobody. You don't have to read about it in order to be a better executive or a better housewife or to do your duty as a citizen in the Hydrogen Age.

But you'll surely want to have a look at this new magazine of Sport. Not just one issue, please. Take a year's subscription and see how you get on together. You may find that it makes more enjoyable what you already enjoy. And *that* could have consequences.

One consequence would be that, at last, America will have a great National Sports Weekly.

George Gribbin, the Young & Rubicam creative director, read the ad without knowing who had written it and exclaimed, "Whoever wrote this—we ought to hire him."

But the magazine was still without a title. Luce had held out as long as possible because he badly wanted to secure the title *Sport* from Mac-Fadden. Harry Phillips offered MacFadden $200,000 for the rights, but the company wanted $250,000, and neither side would budge. One afternoon early in June, at the Plaza Hotel, Phillips ran into an old friend, Stuart Scheftel.

"Harry," said Scheftel, "I think the real reason your title is a secret is because you don't have one yet. Well, I've got one for you: *Sports Illustrated.*" Scheftel explained his experience with the title, then went on his way. When he returned from a weekend in the country, he had three phone messages from Phillips. Time Inc. was interested in the title, and wanted to know how much he wanted. Scheftel asked for $10,000. Later that day, Phillips called back, having secured approval from Luce in Rome.

"There's just one more thing," said Scheftel.

"Now, Stuart, I've always known you as a man of your word," said Phillips. "I don't want to go back to Luce with any more demands."

Scheftel laughed. "All I want is a subscription," he said, and it was agreed.

And so, more than three years after Cowin's first memo, nearly a year after the task force had started work on the project, and just six weeks before its first issue would go to press, Henry Luce's new magazine had a name: *Sports Illustrated.*

● ● ●

That summer, *SI* moved into its new offices on the fourth floor of the Time & Life Building, replacing the National Association of Manufacturers.

Late in June, Luce had returned to oversee the push toward the first issue. For years, he had been seen as a distant figure by most of the staffers. But now, in the summer of 1954, he was involving himself in the minutiae of magazine-making once again. C.D. Jackson, in a note to Billings, observed that Luce seemed nervous, due partly to the fact that "while he is not flying blind, this is really quite different from any previous endeavor of his. What I mean is that there was a fairly solid line tying *Time, Fortune,* and *Life* together . . . the line to *Sports Illustrated,* is, at best, dotted, and when Harry solemnly considers cartoons and finds it difficult to smile as he leafs through several dozen, or when he tilts back in his chair, puts the tips of his fingers together and goes into a deadpan dissertation on 'jokes,' those dots get spaced quite far apart."

James had an intuitive understanding of how to stay on his boss's good side. When Luce made his remark about "the wonderful world of sport," while looking at Brennan's preliminary dummies, James seized on it as the cornerstone of the magazine's editorial pitch. By the summer of 1954 it was becoming a mantra. A *Business Week* story noted that the new magazine's staffers "have this phrase so much on their tongues that one man, in speaking of *Time* magazine, recently said that the latter's sphere was 'the whole wonderful panorama of everything.'"

While James spent much of June and July wrangling with budgets and titles, his lieutenants were trying to fill out the staff and get used to the rhythms of weekly magazine-making. The hiring process remained disorganized and meandering. A talented young writer named Gilbert Rogin started out on the clip desk, because a spot was open there. Creamer began as an editor and moved over to the writers' pool, only because of a mix-up in assignments. Johnston, the word specialist, was at first fielding a wide range of administrative duties. And Tibby, the ponderous Time Inc. veteran, was working on Soundtrack, which would require (and for years be denied) a light writing and editing touch. He was also charged with overseeing the reporters who would contribute to the news photo section Wonderful World of Sports, where the staff was putting together internal specimens under deadline conditions.

"Welcome aboard," said Tibby brightly, after meeting a new reporter hire, a disheveled young writer named Kurt Vonnegut.

In the bustle of activity on the fourth floor, Vonnegut was put to work at a desk that didn't have a chair. On his first day, Tibby came over with an assignment.

"What do you know about flat racing?" he asked.

Vonnegut looked at him evenly and said, "I figure it can't possibly involve hurdles."

Despite the irreverence, Tibby took him under his wing, assigning him several pieces, one about the Chicago White Sox and their use of wheat-germ oil, another about a group of sportsmen who protected flyways for ducks flying south. Every time Vonnegut was set to go across the street or across town to report on a story, Tibby ordered him to stay in the office and make some phone calls—it was the Time Inc. way.

Vonnegut wasn't destined to last very long at the new magazine. His demise came when he was assigned to write a caption for a picture in The Wonderful World of Sports about a horse that had veered off a track, jumped the infield fence at Aqueduct, and trotted across the infield.

"I was working on this goddamn story with nothing else to do," he remembered, "working eight-hour days and sitting around. And it ceased to be amusing to me that this horse just took a shortcut across the infield. I was going to go out to Aqueduct to investigate, but they told me it wasn't necessary. So I could only get so much amusement out of the story, and I figured I was in the wrong job. So I left that in my typewriter and departed."

What Vonnegut left in his typewriter was a single sheet of paper, with a one-line caption: "The horse jumped over the fucking fence."

While Tibby's ability to foster brash young writing talent was poor, the rest of the staff was shaping up. Among the staff writers, Paul O'Neil was joined by the multitalented Gerald Holland, yet another Time Inc. employee with *St. Louis Post-Dispatch* roots, who was assigned to write the keynote piece of the first issue, in which he would argue that the '50s—not the '20s—were the true golden age of sports.

The circulation push had yielded 350,000 charter subscribers, making *SI* the largest circulation launch in magazine history (even *Life*, the fastest magazine success ever, had started with less than 200,000 subscribers). The company had also made the relevant production decisions. Some at the new magazine pushed for a Sunday night or Monday morning close, but the new magazine got this more from happenstance than design. "*Time* magazine had its own battery of press equipment in various print-ing plants," said Jim McCluskey, who rose out of the Time Inc. production department to become vice-president of manufacturing and distribution in the '60s. "When *SI* was started, in order to do it as economically as possible, it was fitted in behind *Time* magazine, so that it could use the same press equipment. You have to remember that there weren't a lot of presses around at that time that could handle the volume that was being asked." With Thursday being the target day for newsstand distribution, and most subscribers expecting to get their copies by Friday, *SI* had to print fast and ship quickly. Possible locations in Dayton and Louisville were dismissed because of the time it would take to move the printed copies to the midwestern rail distribution point of Chicago. R.R. Donnelley's Lakeside press in Chicago wound up being the main point, but it took too long to get the copies to the West Coast, so a second run would print in Los Angeles, at Pacific Press, Inc.

The *Business Week* story, which ran a week before the start-up, gave the magazine a chance based on its marketing strategy. "*Sports Illustrated*, or *SI* as its staff calls it alternatively, will probably never top a million. Its business managers insist that they are trying to keep a brake on circulation. They want to direct the magazine's appeal to the country club set, the upper-income people who are—or would like to be—familiar with sports cars, skiing at Davos, the National Open. . . . No one was interested in a straight sports magazine of the familiar kind, largely masculine in tone."

• • •

The first issue went to press on Sunday night, August 8, and the timing turned out to be fortuitous. On August 7, the main event in Vancouver's Commonwealth Games was the nationally televised mile that would match world-record holder John Landy and Britain's Roger Bannister in the first-ever meeting of sub-four-minute milers. James sent his first team—writer Paul O'Neil (whose track background would serve him well) and photographer Mark Kauffman. The office was crowded that Saturday afternoon, as much of the staff paused to watch the telecast of the scintillating race, in which Bannister held off Landy down the home stretch.

Then they waited. Late that Saturday night, O'Neil's piece started coming in, from the Western Union teletype machine. After reading O'Neil's story, Crichton looked up excitedly at Johnston and said, "I think we're going to be a success. He's done exactly what we want—not what those publicity people are telling everybody." The eternal optimist James had expected a marvelous piece from O'Neil, and wasn't disappointed. What O'Neil had done for his lead story was write about the track meet with the same clinically detached and yet illuminating style—edifying without being pedantic—that marked the best of *Time*'s prose. "Duel of the Four Minute Men" blared the headline. The lead, with a Vancouver, B.C., dateline, read:

> The art of running the mile consists, in essence, of reaching the threshold of unconsciousness at the instant of breasting the tape. It is not an easy process, even in a setpiece race against time, for the body rebels against such agonizing usage and must be disciplined by the spirit and the mind. It is infinitely more difficult in the amphitheater of competition, for then the runner must remain alert and cunning despite the fogs of fatigue and pain; his instinctive calculation of pace must encompass maneuver for position, and he must harbor strength to answer the moves of other men before expending his last reserves in the war of the home stretch.
>
> Few events in sport offer so ultimate a test of human courage and human will and human ability to dare and endure for the simple sake of struggle—classically run, it is a heart-stirring, throat-tightening spectacle. But the world of track has never seen anything quite to equal the "Mile of the Century" which England's Dr. Roger Gilbert Bannister—the tall, pale-skinned explorer of human exhaustion who first crashed the four-minute barrier—won here last Saturday from Australia's world record holder, John Michael Landy. It will probably not see the like again for a long, long time.

O'Neil's prose was accompanied by an opening shot, running across two-thirds of the opening spread, of Bannister passing Landy on the final turn. By Sunday night at midnight, the rest of the magazine closed, although not without some glitches. For that weekend closing, while his father was dying in Pittsburgh, Tibby took over several departments, and did a careful editing job on O'Neil's story, which had come in long. Rather than cutting it, Tibby arranged to have the typeface shrunk on the second spread, a difficult task in the 48 hours before the close. "Jack was really valuable," said Creamer. "He peaked in that first issue and was never as good again."

The cover  was a Mark Kauffman photograph showing Milwaukee Braves slugger Eddie Mathews at bat in a night game at Milwaukee County Stadium. Inside was an impressive but uneven finished product, a compendium of stories, pictures, and departments that was already trying to be all things to all people. After opening to a quick quiz on sport, Jimmy Jemail's Hot Box (eliciting single-paragraph answers to a single question from a variety of celebrities), and the brief profile feature Pat on the Back, readers found a Memo from the Publisher, signed by H.H.S. Phillips, Jr.

Soundtrack, still derivative of *The New Yorker*'s Talk of the Town, followed O'Neil's lead story, and fed into Spectacle, a four-page color section (with Kauffman photos on the Ezzard Charles–Rocky Marciano fight). Next up was The Wonderful World of Sport, a five-page photo gallery of recent sporting pictures. That was followed by a single-paragraph story, accompanying a spread on Philip, the Duke of Edinburgh, and, then a pair of single-page stories on baseball-card collecting, sandwiching a six-page color foldout of reproductions of Topps trading cards.

The longest story in the issue was Gerald Holland's lengthy account of the '50s as a boom time for sport. "The Golden Age is Now" argued that America was in the middle of "the greatest sports era in human history." Holland's essay, alternately measured and hyperbolic, codified James's view of The Wonderful World of Sport. "There is nothing bad about sports," he wrote in conclusion, and throughout the first issue, the numerous advertising images of smiling faces—upwardly mobile Americans enjoying "the champagne of beers" or moving into the passing lane on the power of high-octane ethyl gasoline—reinforced the vivid editorial documenting the heart of what Luce had already described as the "American Century."

The Great Outdoors followed Holland's piece, with two stories for hunters and fishermen, then several departments—Under 21, Health, Red Smith's baseball column, and a football column written by Grantland Rice (who'd died just weeks earlier), originally commissioned for the promotions department earlier in the summer, by assistant publisher Richard Neale and promotions man Bill Scherman. Three cartoonists shared the back-page Last Laugh.

It was done. The first issue of *Sports Illustrated* was 144 pages long and it would be an instant hit on the newsstands. And in the dim hours of that hazy August morning, as Creamer and Crichton took the elevator down to the lobby of the Time & Life Building and headed out to the luxury of a cab ride home (it was a special dispensation for Time Inc.-ers who worked late on closings), they were full of the heady pleasure that came with hard-won accomplishment. For Crichton, though, the weary satisfaction was accompanied by a vague panic.

"I was wondering, 'My God, now what are we going to do about the next one?'"

# CHAPTER 3

# MEANWHILE, BACK IN TEXAS

It was a Friday afternoon in the dead of summer in Texas in the early 1950s, and on the cramped, sweltering second floor of the *Fort Worth Press*, Blackie Sherrod was getting ready to go home. Sherrod, who'd just completed his sixth column of the week, was the tanned, brawny sports editor of the the *Press*. The tabloid operated out of a boxy, soulless two-story building, within earshot of the railyards and just downwind from the farmers' market. Writers climbed the dark stairway to the second floor, where the grimy newsroom sat right next to the pressroom, and was cooled in the summer and heated in the winter by the same ash-spewing ventilator duct in the corner of the sports department. For copy paper, reporters often resorted to triangular-shaped sheets of excess newsprint scrap, or the back side of press releases. When a staffer had used up his pencil, he returned the nub to the cashier and received a replacement. Understaffed, underpaid, inexperienced, and overworked, Sherrod's sports department still managed to regularly beat the stodgy, respectable *Fort Worth Star-Telegram* on stories.

The *Press* was an afternoon paper, which meant that Sherrod and his staff had to stay up late covering games and get up unconscionably early, showing up at 6 a.m. for the paper's 8:30 deadline. It was never easy, but after flying reconnaissance missions in World War II, Sherrod didn't mind writing ten stories a week, covering half as many events, spending many of his afternoons at practices or on the phone, handling all the administrative duties in his six-man department, and, in his spare time, trying to teach sportswriting to the rambunctious band of college students that made up the large part of his staff.

Before he could leave for his short summer weekend, the phone rang. The operator sounded far away. "Yes, sir, I have a long-distance collect call from a Dan Jenkins. Will you accept the charges?"

Sherrod smiled and said yes. Jenkins was his frighteningly talented prodigy, still in school at Texas Christian University, where by all accounts he seemed to be majoring in golf and minoring in bridge. Jenkins had left that morning for his first trip to Las Vegas, promising to come back a rich and more worldly man.

"How's it going Dan?" asked Sherrod.

"Not so good," said Jenkins in a deep voice, once described as sounding slicker than Tupelo honey on oilcloth. "Could you wire me some money?"

"You broke *already*?"

"Yep. Lost it all."

"Okay," said Sherrod. "What room are you in?"

There was a beat of silence.

"Uh, I don't know. Blackie, I haven't even checked in yet."

Sherrod laughed and wondered when Jenkins was ever going to grow up, and what might happen if he did. And he marveled at the young man's preternatural confidence. Dan Jenkins was going places.

Throughout the Time & Life Building in 1954, executives were engaged in long, weighty discussions to decide how large a place sports might take in postwar society. They worried over it, argued over it, and launched *Sports Illustrated* even though many of the questions had never been resolved to their satisfaction.

But in Texas it was different. Knowledgeable, passionate fans—the true believers who were the bedrock of spectator sports—existed everywhere. The difference was that back East or out West, sports didn't insinuate themselves so completely into mainstream society, the way they did in Texas or other parts of the Midwest. Boys grew up in Texas with a knowledge of sports heroes common to boys everywhere, and something more: an ineffable sense that sport belonged in the center of things, less a pastime than a constant companion. There are two sports seasons in Texas, went the old saying, football and spring football. There was no analogous boast about baseball in New York, or any sport anywhere else.

Blackie Sherrod would have agreed with Ernest Havemann's analysis of the level of sportswriting talent in 1954, but he was on a personal crusade to elevate it. The *Press* never had a circulation of much above 60,000, and never had the financial wherewithal to challenge the *Star-Telegram* on a conventional basis. But under Sherrod, the sports department exhibited a relentlessly impertinent style, a mixture of sensationalism, analysis, irreverence, and showmanship that embraced broad elements of what would later be called New Journalism. At a time when virtually every sports department in the country was sticking to basics, trying to find out Who, What, Where, and When, Sherrod's charges asked Why, and did so with an attitude .

• • •

Dan Jenkins had inherited his restlessness from his father. In the '20s, Elzie "Bud" Jenkins was a notorious figure around the nightclubs of Fort Worth. Tall, confident, and rakishly handsome, he had a greater talent for enjoying himself than for any particular vocation, although he made enough in the furniture and carpet business to keep him in new suits and golf clubs. He'd once won a talent show with a young looker named Ginger Rogers, at about the time she was getting her start with Eddie Foy's vaudeville troupe in Fort Worth. There had been several marriages, one of the shortest to the high-strung but elegant beauty Catherine O'Hern, a globe-hopping, antique-dealing, chain-smoking daughter of a Fort Worth socialite. When Catherine got pregnant, she and Bud got married, and she gave birth to Dan Jenkins on December 2, 1929. Bud and Catherine would be divorced before Dan's first birthday.

Young Dan Jenkins would be just fine. He went to live with his paternal grandparents, Elzie and Sally Jenkins, in a house on Travis Avenue in an unprepossessing section of south Fort Worth. The large house formed the spiritual center of the Jenkins family compound—Dan's aunt Inez and uncle Sid lived across the street; his cousin was next door. His grandfather had been a barber, before signing on as a U.S. deputy marshal. Sometimes he'd let young Dan sit in the front seat with him while he transported a convict down to the prison at Huntsville. But Dan's strongest parental influence was his gregarious grandmother Sally, one of 14 siblings, who had been born in a covered wagon in Choctaw Indian country in Oklahoma.

"I never had any *angst*," was how he would put it later. Growing up in Fort Worth in the '30s, in an extended family of sports fans, a boy could think he was living in the capital of the sports universe. Just three days before his seventh birthday, he went with his dad to see one of the biggest football games ever: the hometown team, 10–0 Texas Christian with Slingin' Sammy Baugh, played host to the 10–0 Southern Methodist Mustangs, from 30 miles away in Dallas. On that day, Bobby Wilson and SMU prevailed, but three years later, TCU would win the national championship and go to the Sugar Bowl, behind the wondrous Davey O'Brien. Fort Worth was also home to the two best golfers in the world, Ben Hogan and Byron Nelson. In 1937, Dan's aunt Inez had taken him for his first round of golf to Katy Lake, the same nine-hole course with sand greens where Hogan had learned the game. Later, his uncle Mack introduced him to Worth Hills, a raggedy public course adjacent to the TCU campus that everyone called Goat Hills. He said Dan had a natural swing. At the Colonial Club in Fort Worth, Dan watched Craig Wood win the 1941 National Open. By that time, he felt sorry for anyone who *didn't* live in Fort Worth.

When he got back from classes at Daggett Elementary, Dan would run down the street to visit his aunt and uncle at their business, Whitley's drugstore, where he could sit at the soda fountain and page through the new titles in the magazine rack. From an early age, he'd been known to play sick so he could stay home from school, listen to radio shows, and order a care package from Whitley's: a vanilla shake, the new *Captain Marvel* comic, a set of drawing paper, and a box of Crayolas so he could fashion some more portraits of football players and golfers. Magazines exerted a strong pull on his imagination, documenting a world far beyond Fort Worth. One ad, from *Esquire* in the fall of 1940, particularly stood out. It was a color shot of that year's U.S. Open winner Lawson Little, taking a smooth swing at a posh country club, with a lagoon in the background. "It looked like the most exotic thing in the world," he recalled later. "Because at that time I had never seen Colonial, the U.S. Open hadn't come yet. *Wow, wouldn't it be something to play on a golf course like that someday.* I just remember it being extremely exotic—damn near *erotic.*"

He was the first one out the door to get the newspaper in the morning, and he loved sitting in the kitchen with the adults, listening to his aunts and uncles argue about sports or politics or the movies while his grandmother made breakfast. He'd keep scrapbooks of the exploits of Fort Worth's sports heroes, and on Saturdays when he wasn't at games, sit in his grandma's parlor and listen to broadcaster Kern Tips, calling the Southwest Conference Game of the Week. In the fifth grade, his grandmother brought an old typewriter down from the attic, and Dan began copying stories out of the paper. It wasn't long before he started adding to those stories, and then writing his own. He loved movies as well, and after seeing *The Front Page* and *His Girl Friday*, he decided he wanted to be a newspaper writer.

By the time he got to Paschal High, Jenkins was a rangy, long-nosed kid with black hair and a smallish, almost delicate, mouth. He wasn't conventionally handsome, but he had a presence, the same confidence that Sherrod would see years later. The same school building, under various names, had sent forth Ben Hogan, Ginger Rogers, 1936 Olympic pole vault gold medalist Earle Meadows, gossip columnist Liz Smith, and, just a few years after Dan, astronaut Alan Bean. At Paschal, Jenkins was a charismatic figure, the first kid in his class to get a car, the first to get a deep voice. He was taking his sweetheart Pattie O'Dell on car dates well before his 16th birthday, and because Elzie Jenkins was a U.S. marshal, the family had an E ration ticket, meaning they could get all the gas they needed. They often wound up at a drive-in called The Pig Stand, where they'd sit in the car listening to music, smoking cigarettes, sneaking a beer and a few kisses. And they often double-dated with Pattie's best friend, the gorgeous and funny June Burrage, who was struck by Jenkins as well. "He was tall, very thin, very cynical," she remembered. "Everybody was terrified of him. He wasn't classically handsome at all, but he was enormously talented and he never lacked for dates."

His best friend, sharing the same nickname as his father, was Edwin "Bud" Shrake, tall and classically handsome in all the ways that Jenkins was not, but sharing a similar sense of humor and precociously jaundiced worldview. During the day, they were practically inseparable, except for basketball. Dan was so devoted to the authoritarian coach Charlie Turner that he took advantage of the Texas high school "redshirt" rule, which allowed him to stay in school and play another year of varsity basketball. Bud, two years younger, chose not to go out for basketball simply because he thought the authoritarian Turner was "a sadistic Nazi." After school and in the summers, they'd head out to Herb Massey's Cafe, to drink soda, eat chicken-fried steak, and play games on the puck-bowling machines. When just facing the table and doing their best grew tedious, they invented variations. The most competitive had the contestant standing in a hedge *outside* the restaurant, reaching in through the window, and taking a blind shot. It was at Massey's one afternoon that Dan and Bud had devised their rating system for females. Even this was touched by the influence of sports; rather than ascending from 1 to 10, it went from 10 to 1, just like the Associated Press college football poll.

In the spring of 1948, just months before his high school graduation, Jenkins wrote a parody of the *Fort Worth Star-Telegram* sports columnist Amos Melton in the *Paschal Pantherette*. A *Fort Worth Press* stringer named Julian Reed saw the column and showed it to Sherrod, adding that Blackie really ought to check out this smart-aleck kid over at Paschal. That was how, in the summer of 1948, just out of high school, Dan Jenkins had a byline, working for the *Fort Worth Press* at $25 a week.

His first journalism lesson came quickly. Assigned by Sherrod to write a piece on a local golf tournament, Jenkins composed a straight lead and turned it in. A few minutes later, Sherrod gave it back to him. "Send me paragraphs you can write without putting the score in," he said. And that was all he had to say. "I understood right then," Jenkins would recall later. "Yeah—we're an afternoon paper. Of course. Feature. It was a very fast journalism lecture, but I was smart enough to understand it."

Jenkins started at TCU in the fall of 1948, but even before then, he had begun to acquire a certain worldliness—his buddy Don Matheson called him a "sentimental cynic." Who but the sentimental Dan could marry the same girl, Pattie O'Dell, not once but twice? They'd first eloped when they thought Pattie was pregnant, had the marriage annulled when they found out she wasn't, then decided to do it the right way, in a church wedding with Pattie's friend June standing up as a bridesmaid. That marriage ended within a year, on the very night that Pattie threatened, "If you go to Massey's one more time, I'm gonna get a divorce." And who could be anything but a cynic after three marriages—the third to a beautiful TCU literature professor named Joan Holloway—and three divorces, all before the age of 25?

Despite the romantic trials, the college years were an exquisite five-year romp. Jenkins was a bigshot at the newspaper and the captain of the TCU golf team. Through the early '50s, he and Shrake and their friends would frequently find themselves at Jack's, a cramped roadhouse out on the Mansfield highway, parking out back and walking in under the sign of the kicking mule. There were padded booths around the walls, and a spacious dance floor where they'd dance the Poly Drag—a variation on the box step that Shrake once likened to a Fort Worth Tango—to songs like "Sixty-Minute Man" by Billy Ward and the Dominoes. Shrake remembered the Fort Worth nights well: "We'd be in some joint staring at some really good-looking girl, and Dan'd always say, 'Remember—somebody somewhere is tired of her.'"

And after they took their dates home, Dan would head with his friends out to the Griddle, where they'd bet on how quickly a football player named Hal Lambert could inhale a bowl of chili (the record was under two minutes). Then they might go down to the Texas Hotel for chili and eggs. By 3 a.m. or so, Jenkins would head home, prompting Shrake to remark that for years his friend "averaged three hours' sleep a night and drank more coffee than any other writer except Balzac." The hours were brutal, but it was fun. Jenkins would get up at 5:30 a.m., struggle into the *Press* just after six—Shrake would usually be there by then—and work until deadline at 8:30. Then they'd jump in their cars and race to the campus, heading out on West Freeway, Jenkins in his black-and-yellow Chevy Bel-Air, Shrake his '47 Dodge sedan, weaving in and out of traffic, and finally accelerating down University Drive at an insane speed toward the "finish line," the front door of TCU Drugs. But then they'd stop in the drugstore for the inevitable cup of coffee, as often as not missing their first class. By two p.m. Jenkins would be heading out to Goat Hills for golf or to the football field or basketball court to cover a TCU practice. And then it would be another night out.

And at TCU, it all ran together—sports and literature, music and politics, work and play—into one vital, continuous whole. Ernest Hemingway and Bob Wills. Slingin' Sammy and Fyodor Pavlovich. They all enriched Dan Jenkins's life, working their way into a quilt of voracious reading, fevered writing, intense competition, elusive romance, and serious spectating. Literature wasn't something to be enjoyed at a distant remove, under a reading lamp in an overstuffed chair. It became a part of their days, another element in the seamless mix of serious fun and enjoyable work that made up their lives. At Goat Hills, when Jenkins was waiting for a tee time or for the group ahead of him to putt out, he might have his nose buried in *The Brothers Karamazov*. When Life announced it was going to publish Hemingway's *The Old Man and the Sea*, the young *Press* writers started a pool to pick the first word. Shrake won with the darkhorse "He," certain all along that Jenkins's choice of "It"—the early line favorite—was going to be the winner.

Shrake spent a year at the University of Texas in the prelaw program before returning to Fort Worth to attend TCU and, eventually, got a job at the *Press* as well. Both men knew they wanted to work in New York City one day, but they often referred to their college years as Chicago Days, since they dressed like the reporters in *The Front Page*, in dark suits with snap-brim hats and an air of self-importance. (When he moved to the police beat at the *Press*, Shrake found that if a reporter looked like a detective, he could walk right into a crime scene and get vital information before the real police rousted him out.) Dan's wife Joan knew they wouldn't be around long. Sitting up one night, listening to Bud and Dan talk about their planned conquest of New York City, she broke down. "Listen, you assholes," she said. "There's 14 roads leading out of this town. Why don't y'all just *get on* one of 'em?"

While they planned their escape from Fort Worth, they toiled for years at the *Press*.

"Oh, the *Press* was great; it was like a zoo," remembered Shrake. "It was hot and dirty and crowded, and everybody there was some kind of half-insane character. We all belonged together. The first day I walked into the *Press*, I could hear the clacking of the teletype machines, and all these people were running around with their sleeves rolled up, and their hair was blowing in the so-called air conditioner. Everybody had this sense of urgency and excitement, and right then I thought, 'This is what I want.'"

While at the *Press*, they ran with another Paschal grad, Dick Growald (who would go on to become an international correspondent for UPI) and a squat, slyly clever writer named Gary Cartwright, who would be a willing participant in much of their low-grade rebellion.

While TCU was teaching them about literature, Sherrod was teaching them about journalism, exposing his young charges to John Lardner, S.J. Perelman, Damon Runyon, and Westbrook Pegler. "You want to learn how to write sports?" Sherrod told Jenkins one day. "Go read Henry McLemore." McLemore wrote sports for the United Press. When Grantland Rice was the best-known sportswriter in the country, McLemore was working in a less mythic, more sardonic style. Jenkins went to the stacks and opened one set to the 1936 Olympics, to a McLemore story that led: "Berlin—The Olympic marathon was run on Tuesday. It is now Thursday and I'm still waiting for the Americans to finish."

The worst, most egregious examples of bad sportswriting got posted on Sherrod's dreaded bulletin board, without comment. If one of his writers referred to a game as a "melee" or a "tilt" or a "stemwinder," Sherrod would put the sentence on the board. And if anyone was overcome with a desire to mimic the revered Hemingway or Fitzgerald—still the biggest influences on the staff—Sherrod would put that on the board ("So we beat on, boats against the current, borne back ceaselessly into the Southwest Conference track meet . . .").

And because Sherrod was their mentor, and perhaps because they were quite sure no one was reading them, they learned to leaven their stories with humor. Sherrod was a terrific columnist, at once knowing and wry, able to deflate the pompous, always with a quick wit and a quick opinion. Cartwright was a loose cannon, capable—given the right circumstances and right amount of alcoholic inspiration—of almost any act. And Shrake was a crack reporter, an intuitive sleuth with a thrill for the chase and a contrarian's heart. And no one was as effortlessly irreverent as Dan Jenkins.

Six days a week, Sherrod and his charges put on a show, mostly for themselves. "We survived on the assumption that no one read our paper anyhow," Cartwright explained later. "It is the same feeling you get on a college newspaper or on mind-expanding drugs." At its best, it could provide both an intellectual and visceral jolt. At its worst, it was embarrassingly self-indulgent, but it was daring throughout. After making an argument for a golfer's inclusion in an upcoming tournament, Jenkins deprecated his own influence in one of his columns by adding, "The reader must remember that it was our cunning which earned Vladimir Zilch a birth in the international face-slapping matches at Kiev in '34."

Jenkins loved the rude, rhythmic language of sport and found a sort of eloquence in the ramblings of TCU football coach Abe Martin, a man who never met a shopworn southern football cliché he didn't like. "You gimme a gunny-sack full of little old pine knots who'll hit-chee and we'll have us a spellin' bee come Saturday" was how Martin might describe his chances with his undersized, overachieving cast of players. Rather than cleaning up Martin's scattershot quotes, Jenkins learned to distill the most colorful elements and bring that language into print, such as when Martin would refer to a game as "a choir practice," "a formal dance," "an ear roastin'" or "a story tellin'." Martin was notoriously suspicious of the new-fangled terminology coming from the pro game. "They talkin' about *pursuit* in football," he told Jenkins once. "Well, that ain't nothin' but chase 'em and catch 'em."

David Halberstam has suggested that the roots of New Journalism occurred in sportswriting in the '40s and '50s, and Blackie Sherrod saw evidence of it. "Dan was doing something when he worked for the *Press* that later became very popular with Tom Wolfe and Gay Talese and Hunter Thompson—the New Journalism," said Sherrod. "Dan Jenkins was doing that when he was 19 years old, and he didn't know it. It was new and different. It's a trait of transposing himself into the person he's writing about. He doesn't have to say, 'He thought . . .' He becomes that person."

Before he was out of TCU, Jenkins had invented a character named Billy Clyde Puckett, who made a few appearances in Jenkins's column in the *Press*, expressing his philosophy through the limited but colorful vernacular of the gridiron. He was also injecting humor, crisp analysis, and a columnist's point of view into his news stories. While he wouldn't perfect that style until well into the '60s, the roots were established at the *Press*. "Exaggerated outrage grounded in truth" was how he would describe it later.

In the midst of it all, Jenkins was developing a long, potent golf game. He'd learned about pressure and gambling and life at Goat Hills. Hard by the TCU campus, the barren, treeless public course was the site of several golf games with which Herbert Warren Wind would not have been familiar. Sixsomes. Eightsomes. Gangsomes. It was a course that inspired daring, to ward off the ennui. "There's more grass in my office than there was on that golf course," said Jenkins's friend Donald Matheson, four decades later. Green fees were 75 cents, but the gambling made things interesting. The Goat Hills gang knew all about the legendary Titanic Thompson, who had been immortalized in an essay by John Lardner. They'd try shots made famous by Thompson and local trick-shot artist Joe Kirkwood, and Matheson was the inventor of the drop-kick tee shot on the first tee, with which he fazed more than a few of Paschal High's match-play opponents in the '50s.

Like Ben Hogan and Byron Nelson before him, Jenkins finished second in the Fort Worth city championships. When Hogan would spot the young writer at the Colonial, he'd say, "Hi, fella," which was more than Hogan said to any other writer in town. One day they golfed together at Colonial, and Hogan shot a 67 while Jenkins, outdriving him consistently, wound up in the low 70s. Sitting on the clubhouse veranda after their round, Hogan paid the younger golfer a great compliment, along with issuing a subtle invitation. "You know, you're a fine golfer, and you could win the U.S. Amateur," said Hogan. "But you'd have to work. You'd have to do everything I say for the next year."

Jenkins said, "Why would I want to do that?"

He had learned enough about pressure in golf to suit him a lifetime, and he realized that his writing came a lot easier and more naturally to him than his fairway-iron fades.

Jenkins and Shrake kept their eyes on New York. Shrake wanted to be a foreign correspondent for the *New York Herald Tribune*, and he wanted to publish his first novel by the age of 23, like Fitzgerald, or failing that, by 28, like Hemingway. Jenkins was intrigued with all these things, but for him sportswriting was enough. He didn't know exactly where he wanted to go, until one August day in 1954 when, standing around Sherrod's desk, he saw a copy of a slick new magazine with the Braves' Eddie Mathews on the cover.

"What's this?" he asked.

"That's the new weekly sports magazine from Time Inc.," said Sherrod.

Jenkins looked through it. And thought, *Jesus Christ, what a great idea—it's got to be a hit*.

And that was it. *Sports Illustrated* didn't pick Dan Jenkins. He picked *Sports Illustrated*.

"It seemed important at the time," he said. "Only later, when I was smarter, did I realize how awful it was. Or how naive it was, really. It wasn't awful because they had wonderful writers like Paul O'Neil. And at the time, all we had was *Sport* magazine. And here, all of a sudden, was a weekly, and Time-Life was behind it, so how could it fail? It looked like it was the New York Yankees."

• • •

When Hamilton Prieleaux Bee "Tex" Maule was growing up in Florida, undereducated and uncultured, his mother gave him a dictionary. She instructed him, whenever he came across a word he didn't know, to look it up. By the time he was out of high school, and heading to St. Mary's University in San Antonio to play football, he'd grown into a tall, rawboned man exuding an obvious self-regard. He maintained the habit of studying over the dictionary, so as to know words that his more pampered and affluent peers wouldn't know. Their double takes were a source of pleasure; Maule enjoyed being the expert.

Before he could finish at St. Mary's, he was called off to fight in World War II, then came back and graduated with a degree in journalism from the University of Texas. After college, he bounced around, finding work as an insurance investigator, a merchant seaman, a gymnastics teacher, and a flying trapeze artist with the Cordonas, a low-grade circus act of the '40s. He also spent some time on the sports desk of the *Austin American-Statesman*, where he befriended a bright, focused writer named Tex Schramm. The two used to talk sports at all hours over beers at Scholz's Beer Garden, the oldest saloon in Texas. At the *Statesman*, the pair were known as "the co-Tex."

Maule developed a fondness for a wide range of sports, from track and field to boxing to baseball. But what Tex Maule loved more than anything was pro football. It seemed purer to him than the unruly combination of loyalty, sex, pageantry, and pressure that made up the college game. Instead, it was controlled, almost antiseptically uniform, with a patina of officially recognized legitimacy. In this limited universe, Maule could excel; he could be an expert. Schramm left the newspaper in 1947 to become the publicity director of the Los Angeles Rams; after a promotion to assistant general manager in 1949, he hired Maule to be the team's new publicity director. For three years, Maule and Schramm would literally help the Los Angeles newspapers cover pro football. As often as not, if the team wanted a story in one of L.A.'s five daily newspapers, Schramm and Maule would have to write it themselves.

The National Football League in the '50s was not quite the media savvy institution that it would later become. Prior to the 1951 NFL championship game in L.A.—where the magnificent Rams team, with Bob Waterfield throwing to Tom Fears and Elroy Hirsch, would beat the Cleveland Browns, 24–17—the league imposed a rule that said no tickets could be given out free of charge, hoping to further establish its own legitimacy as a major league organization. But when the Rams informed the L.A. media that there would be no free passes, the scribes in the area had a meeting and decided the event really wouldn't be worth covering. It was Schramm and Maule who convinced the Rams management that the only choice was to buy a few hundred tickets from the league at full price and distribute them to the media. The paid attendance was 57,522 at the Los Angeles Memorial Coliseum, but it was the 300 tickets paid for by the club that helped establish the sport on the West Coast. The next day, the game got great coverage in all of the city's newspapers; the Rams were world champions.

A few weeks later, the New York Yanks' struggling NFL franchise was taken over by the league office, which in turn sold it to a group in Dallas, where it became an "expansion" franchise named the Dallas Texans. Maule had the chance to go back to Dallas and be the head of publicity for the new franchise, with the possibility of moving up to a personnel job in the future. So he left L.A., turning the publicist's job over to a polished 25-year-old press agent named Pete Rozelle.

But Texas wasn't ready for pro football. The Dallas media was less enamored of the NFL than they were of the college game. Even the sportswriters treated it as a joke. Maule never forgave the *Press* writers for what they'd done during an early-season Texans game. Shrake was covering a game for the *Press* one week and had trouble getting into the media parking lot. After sending a letter of complaint to the Texans' office, he received a Maule apology along with about 50 parking passes and as many press-box passes. The next Sunday, Shrake and Jenkins parked at the Fairgrounds before the game, then decided to have a few beers at a nearby bar. Afterward, no one could quite remember whose idea it was to use press passes as chits for their drinks, but the result was that Jenkins and Shrake got drunk and never did make it over to the Cotton Bowl. Maule's pressbox was besieged with all manner of waitresses, cooks, cheerleaders, and housewives. He didn't think it was very funny.

The Texans drew poorly and by the middle of the season, the franchise was sold back to the National Football League. A year later, its meager holdings would be awarded to a Baltimore ownership group headed by Carroll Rosenbloom, and rechristened the Colts, where they began the 1953 season.

So Maule decided to go into sportswriting, getting a job with Bill Rives at the *Dallas Morning News*, where he started out working the slot on the night sports desk. Eventually, he'd get his own column. He would never let Dallas forget that it had rejected professional football, and he never stopped lobbying for the sport's return. (It finally did return, in 1960, when the Dallas Cowboys joined the NFL with Maule's old friend Tex Schramm as the new club's general manager.) But even in the early '50s, Maule sensed that pro football, on the verge of exploding in popularity, would be his ticket to the big time. When he heard that *Sports Illustrated* was starting to publish, he told his friend Bill Rives that he wanted to work there someday.

Maule and Rives would occasionally grouse about Sherrod and his disrespectful followers. Maule thought they were annoying, but he at least understood they were talented. Rives found them purely evil. They'd once nearly cost Rives a coveted award, as Texas Sportswriter of the Year. When the National Sportscasters and Sportswriters Association was started in 1957, it sent out a query to every sports department in the country, asking how many staff members it had. The *Press* had six, but when Gary Cartwright returned the query letter, he listed 24 staffers, and that's how many ballots the Association sent to the *Press* in the voting for Texas Sportswriter of the Year. If Rives hadn't gotten wise and interceded on his own behalf, the Association would have given the first Texas Sportswriter of the Year award to the legendary *Fort Worth Press* writer Crew Slammer. Who, among his other shortcomings as a writer, didn't exist.

• • •

Far away from the contentious mix of Dallas and Fort Worth sportswriters, one of the best young writers in the state was working in relative anonymity. In 1951, Roy Terrell had started his new job as the sports editor of the *Corpus Christi Caller*, where his main innovation had been to fill up Monday's sections with pro football results, giving it the same sort of coverage that college football received in the exhaustive Sunday sections around the state: full stories on each game, statistical summaries, photos with dotted lines showing the arc of a pass, small labels identifying each player.

Terrell had grown up in Kingsville, hard by the King Ranch, with a father who worked on the Union Pacific railroad. Kingsville's population was just 8,000 and that, by all rights, should have made it as backward as the rest of southeast Texas. But it had Texas A&I college, the UP railroad, and old-money families like the Kings and the Clayburghs, so it was less provincial than many larger Texas towns. Young Roy Terrell and his sister knew a ranch hand at the King Ranch, and he would help them sneak on the land occasionally, to hunt in the pastures, or ride horses, literally, out on the open range.

Terrell was only about six years older than Dan Jenkins, but it was a crucial six years. They shared a state of origin and a love of sports, but their outlook was drastically different. During the depression, Terrell's father was laid off from the railroad, and the family moved to Indiana for a while, to stay with his mother's parents. His mother supported the family with her superior secretarial skills, and his dad took odd jobs. Roy grew up tough and agile, with a firm jaw and a ready smile. But even as an adolescent, he was more serious-minded than most of his peers.

After the family returned to Texas in the mid-'30s, Terrell graduated high school a month after his sixteenth birthday and enrolled at Texas A&I, where he played college basketball as a freshman. The next year he transferred to the University of Texas, where in the fall of 1940, he was in the crowd, along with a UT upperclassman named Tex Maule, for the Longhorns' historic 7–0 upset of Texas A&M. Texas scored on the first drive, and staged one heroic defensive stand after another, each seemingly deeper into its own territory, to snap A&M's two-year win streak, preventing them from a repeat national championship and costing them a trip to the Rose Bowl.

A year later, Terrell went back to Kingsville, this time to join the Civil Aviation Administration's civilian pilot training school. He was in the air over Kingsville on December 7, 1941, when news of the Pearl Harbor invasion broke. That clinched it; Terrell went into the navy's flight training program, intent on becoming a marine. In World War II, he would fly two tours of duty, first as a dive bomber over the Marshall Islands, then as a fighter pilot in the capture of Peleliu, in the Palau Islands in the Pacific.

By the time he returned from the war, he had decided to be a sportswriter and not a doctor. He went back to A&I and got his bachelor's degree, and married his sweetheart Charlyne Skipper, whose father had been Terrell's Boy Scout troop scoutmaster in the '30s. They moved from Kingsville to Corpus Christi when a job opened up on the sports department at the *Caller*, and by 1951, Roy Terrell, only 28 years old, was the sports editor and columnist. He'd grown fond of writers like Paul Gallico and Red Smith, who could write about sports in lucid, civilized tones. In his mind, the games deserved serious treatment. In the spring of 1954 when Terrell saw the two dummies for the new sports magazine from Time Inc., his first reaction was almost identical to Jenkins's: *Oh, man, this is the greatest thing that ever happened.*

But in this case, the magazine would come to him. Terrell had developed a following in Corpus Christi. One of his faithful readers was a Texas stringer for Time Inc. named Jim Roe, who had done some exemplary reporting for the magazine about Lyndon Johnson's rigged congressional election victory over Coke Stevenson in 1948. And in the summer of 1954, when a note went out to bureaus and stringers, Roe saw that *SI* would be running a column of the week, and he started collecting some of Terrell's clips and sending them to New York.

On Saturday, August 21, Terrell was in Dallas with the National Reserve air squadron there, when one of his fellow officers told him his picture and column were in *Sports Illustrated*. The prestige meant something, as did the $250 (Terrell was making $90 a week at the *Caller*), though it would have been nice if they hadn't listed his name as "Ray Terrell."

Terrell winced as he read the rest of the second issue. "I read those two issues, and then I probably read three or four more, then I just quit reading," he said. "It was so bad, I quit reading. And when they called me, early March or April [of 1955], and asked me to come up, I went down to the library and got a stack of them, and I'd read and read and read." His opinion didn't change much, though when he got to New York and started talking to Sid James, he tried to be diplomatic about it.

The news of Terrell's hire, in May 1955, was greeted with befuddlement and a certain amount of envy elsewhere in Texas.

"When Roy Terrell was hired, we were shocked," said Dan Jenkins. "Corpus Christi?! Even people in Texas didn't know him. I mean, if you sat around and asked, 'Who are the best sportswriters in Texas?', they were Blackie Sherrod, Clark Neelan at the *Houston Post*, Bill Rives at the *Dallas News*. And suddenly, *Sports Illustrated*, the only national weekly sports magazine, hires a fucking guy named Roy Terrell? From Corpus Christi? We thought, 'Well, they must not be as important as they think they are. They're stupid—why didn't they ask?'"

In time, Jenkins would grow to appreciate Terrell's talent. And Terrell, when he got to New York, instantly recognized an elemental distinction in the regional attitudes toward sports. "In Texas," he recalled, "sports was part of the daily fabric, while in the more sophisticated East it was an amusing sidebar. Without apologies for our cultural level circa 1954— what else are you going to do in a small Texas town on Friday night except get ballistic over high school football?—there was a major difference between the way easterners and Texans viewed sports."

Terrell, and the Texans who followed him, would bridge that difference.

# CHAPTER 4

# ADRIFT ON "HARRY'S YACHT"

*Sports Illustrated*'s premiere was both a public and commercial success. The 144-page issue, dated August 16, 1954, carried 74 pages of advertisements, bringing in over $1.3 million. Among the ads was a lavish four-color spot running across the center spread that formally launched the marketing of Ford's new model, the Thunderbird. Across the country, nearly 90 percent of the issues were snapped off the newsstands during their first day of sale, Thursday morning, August 12. On the strength of the advance build-up and a morning mention by Dave Garroway on NBC's *Today Show*, the magazine sold out in New York City by noon that day. In Chicago, dealers were offering cash for more copies of the magazine, a departure in a business where everything was handled on consignment.

Luce sent a copy to President Eisenhower, who wrote back saying he knew he would "find much of interest in it, perhaps too much for my own peace of mind." In the press, response was also favorable. *Kansas City Star* sports editor Ernie Mehl called the new publication a "really extraordinary addition to the field of athletics." And the publisher of *Look*, Gardner Cowles, praised the first issue as a "superior job."

But there was a strident minority that disagreed. In a confidential memo to the *SI* management team, Luce recognized a complaint from many readers that would hound the magazine for years: "*Sports Illustrated* was for the 'martini set' rather than for the 'beer and pretzel gang.'" Another complaint was that, in Luce's words, "the magazine as a whole did not appear to be a sufficiently topical review of the week's events in Sports. And this was related to a feeling that *Sports Illustrated* is not sufficiently a 'real' sports magazine."

While taking the general criticism in stride, Luce would go on to make two recommendations. First, he urged the editors to "review our format to see whether we can work out a better and a better organized 'news cover-age.'" His less astute suggestion, to the advertising department, was that it aggressively go after "those 2-inch and 3-inch advertisements" so common in sports magazines. This seemed an extension of Luce's unconsciously patronizing view of the magazine as a humble journal, full of "oddments and information," like *Reader's Digest*. The advice to strive for smaller ads, besides making page flow and layout more difficult, would send *SI* ad reps chasing after hundreds of small accounts that, even if landed, would yield only small financial benefits and contribute further to the widely held opin-ion in the advertising industry that *SI* was good for selling little more than, as James would paraphrase it, "piles cures and jockstraps." Advertising vol-ume began free-falling with the second issue. The 74 pages of advertising in Vol. I, No. 1 would account for nearly one-quarter of the year's total ad pages, which would come in at a disappointing 318 pages, far short of the conservative target of 500.

In January 1955, James put the entire editorial staff (save the letters department) on a Thursday–Monday schedule. The overdue change would have some unforeseen effects. It further isolated *SI*'s staff from the other Time Inc. staffs, by making it the only magazine to work both weekend days. And the odd Tuesday–Wednesday weekend guaranteed that the staff would become even more insular. Who else would go out on a Tuesday night? "Our only friends were us," said Andy Crichton of the early days. "We sort of lost a lot of our friends. You couldn't really see them very often, although we tried. I remember the times going to parties, then arriving the next day at eight in the morning with a hellish hangover, and having four articles come in and every one of them needing to be rewrit-ten. Oh, my God! I'd do a lousy job."

Within the Time & Life Building, the general attitude toward *SI* was one of arrogant, barely concealed ridicule. The weekend of the first issue, one executive had raised a toast to "Harry's Yacht," betraying a measure of the condescension with which the other staffs viewed the upstart. The knowl-edge that *SI*'s losses would reduce profit-sharing returns for the immediate future put many in a hostile mood. And then there was the change, one weekend in the fall of 1954, in the lobby of the Time & Life Building. Just above the reception office, for years, the names of *Time, Life,* and *Fortune* had appeared in huge block capital letters. But there wasn't enough room to put the title of the new magazine below the others. Staffers returning to work one Monday walked in and saw:

SPORTS ILLUSTRATED

TIME LIFE FORTUNE

*SI's* positioning only exacerbated the already palpable resentment. Occasionally, other Time Inc.-ers expressed their derision verbally, half-kiddingly upbraiding *SI* staffers in the office elevators. At the Time Inc. cafeteria, *Life* sports editor Marshall Smith made it a point to avoid anyone from the magazine. Crichton and *Life's* Scot Leavitt had angry words in the lobby one morning, after Leavitt dismissed the magazine's quality. "I tried to talk to him later and he just ignored me," said Crichton. "There was a real feeling that we were taking money out of their pockets or food out of their mouths, or drink out of their flasks."

On the fourth floor, where the edit and ad departments were sharing space, James allowed none of the negativity to affect morale. Marching through the halls and encouraging the troops, heaping praise on his favored employees, James seemed convinced from the beginning that *SI* was changing the world. "Sid would come along," said Whitney Tower, "and he'd pat you on the back and say—whether it was true or not, it usually was not—'God, this was a great issue. This is the best issue yet.'"

*SI's* staff was significantly smaller than *Time's* or *Life's*, and yet, because of its trouble generating ad pages, the magazine was often forced to produce up to 20 extra pages of editorial material every week. Rather than grumble, James celebrated this as a way to get the entire staff involved. If more people took part, there was also more confusion, exacerbated by the consistent lack of hard-sports knowledge on the part of most of the editors. Tower remembered that associate editor Eleanor Welch "wouldn't know a Ping-Pong ball from a football." Numerous writers had vexing planning sessions with Jack Tibby, who once asked Roger Kahn, preparing to leave to cover a college football game, what his lead was going to be. "I don't know, Jack," said a rankled Kahn. "They haven't played the game yet."

Kahn bridled under the relentless pencil edits and left at the end of the year. "I wrote 'slider' in a story," he remembered. "They put the word 'pitch' after slider. And I said, 'Well, you don't really call it a curveball *pitch*.' They explained that slider was obscure."

Yet the magazine's lack of expertise was incidental to its main editorial dilemma. It was selling two things—timely sports reporting (as many as 32 editorial pages could close on Monday morning) and dazzling color, in unprecedented quantity. But because of the six-week lead time required to process color, these two elements couldn't be mixed.

Still thinking along the same pedantic lines that prevailed at *Life*, James saw the weekly color section Spectacle as an opportunity to open new worlds to his readers. One week, portraits of the nation's best basketball players, the next week, midget race cars. Or flamingoes in the West Indies. Or the charge of a rhinoceros. Or harpoon fishing for sharks in Mexico. Any of these elements might have worked. But often they appeared without any supporting or corresponding written material, or were placed behind the lead news story and before the stilted Soundtrack (which more logically should have been in the front of the book). The magazine lacked any identifiable internal rhythm.

For all that, the color that did run was impressive. Prior to *SI*'s launch, color sports photography had been a nearly barren field, save for portrait artists like Ozzie Sweet (much of whose work appeared in the pages of *Sport*). But *SI* had recruited two pioneers before the launch—the elegant traditionalist Mark Kauffman and the irrepressible action photographer Hy Peskin—and another one shortly thereafter. Late in 1954, Kauffman convinced *SI* to give a contract to his friend John G. Zimmerman, a product of the Frémont high school in Whittier, California, whose program would produce eight Time Inc. photographers. While Kauffman was a visual classicist, Zimmerman was an innovator, a photographer whose restless inquisitiveness was always producing new angles, different shots, unprecedented images. He would prove to be perhaps the most technically original photographer in the magazine's history.

The technology at the time was rudimentary. It was impossible to get the sort of clarity with color film that was routine in black-and-white shots. And the heavy, groaning, painfully slow letterpress engraving process tended to mute the sharpest elements in either kind of picture. The first breakthrough occurred with cameras. In 1954, the dominant equipment for news photographers was the Graflex, a blocky 4-foot-by-5-foot camera that allowed long lenses but provided little mobility ("You could get run over at a football game," said Zimmerman, "because you're looking down in this big hood"). But within a year, Kauffman and others became enamored of Bell & Howell's Photon, an ideally designed camera for sports photography because it had a motor drive and zoom lens capacity. The problem was that the cameras were notoriously unreliable and had been a commercial dud. "I ran around buying all of the Photons I could find," said Gerald Astor, who became photo editor in 1956. "Anytime one was available, I would get them to buy it, because you had nothing else. And you could put a long lens on them and get the photograph—a string of them, so in a football game you would get the sequence of three or four pictures, and in there would be the good photograph."

While Peskin excelled in color as well, it was his black-and-white photography that would set the standard for the era. The theatrical images— heavily backlit action, fighters limned against a dark background, with a simple, heavenly overhead light bearing down on them—could be seen a generation later, in the cinematography of Martin Scorsese's *Raging Bull*. But the innovations came at a price, as Peskin alienated many of his colleagues in the loose fraternity of shooters. Sports photography in the '50s was an art of sharp elbows and pushy persistence, but even in this competitive crowd, Peskin was in a class by himself. Once, following the progress of a batter trying to stretch a line drive to right field at Ebbets Field into a triple, Peskin ran from the photographer's box behind first base across the diamond to get a closer shot at the play at third base.

But even in the uneven first year, the magazine wasn't without cogent analysis. Under the headline, "A Fan Fights Back," in the October 11 issue, there was this observation:

> One of the problems of television is that it is so much with us. It is not only a hungry giant but a Gargantua with an oversized tapeworm of an appetite. It devours comic and dramatic plots until supply has got to run thin. And this same insatiability can result in fights which are hastily arranged between two men who have no business (except the beer business) being in the same ring together.

The writer was Budd Schulberg, already something of a celebrity when he agreed to be *SI*'s first boxing editor. Born in New York, Schulberg inherited a love of boxing from his father, Hollywood film producer B.P. Schulberg. After growing up in Los Angeles, he attended Dartmouth, served in the navy in World War II, then was in charge of photographic evidence for the Nuremberg Trials. Following the war, he began a writing career, solidified in the early '50s with the sale of the screenplay for *On the Waterfront*, for which he'd win a 1954 Academy Award.

Schulberg was the leading force in *SI*'s first newsworthy investigative coup, a series exposing the dubious tactics of Chicago promoter James Norris in particular and "boxing's dirty business" in general. Steady, solid reporting by Schulberg and other staffers such as investigative writer Martin Kane and the Brooklyn-raised, Yale-educated Robert H. Boyle, paid off with exclusives like a December 13, 1954, story in which former heavy-weight Harry Thomas charged that Norris had paid him to throw fights. The piece included a photo of Thomas taking a lie-detector test and an accompanying editorial, by James, that closed with the rhetorical question: "Is Boxing Going to Be a Legitimate Sport or a Dirty Business?" He put the two alternatives in red ink.

Months later, Norris was finally ousted, stripped by a New York circuit court judge of his official oversight powers in boxing. For his exposés, Schulberg won the Bengal Bouts award from Notre Dame, given annually to "the man who has done the most for boxing in the last year." It was the first instance in which *SI* could claim to have affected the condition of sports.

Within the first few months of publication, the magazine's strengths and weaknesses were becoming clear. *SI* had more color than any sports magazine before it, and whatever its technical drawbacks, the color was a hit. The scouting reports, from the World Series preview to a New Year's Day bowl roundup (including two pages of rosters, write-ups, diagrams, season's results, and analysis for each of the four major bowl games), were a true innovation, allowing television viewers to be more informed prior to a big event than ever before. *SI* got plenty of publicity in December 1954, when James named Roger Bannister the magazine's first Sportsman of the Year, *SI*'s equivalent to *Time*'s Man of the Year.

But while *SI* was consistently previewing the big events, there existed no logical approach to weekly news coverage, and a lack of a coherent perspective on any sport. The lead football piece in the October 11 issue was an as-told-to story bearing Cleveland quarterback Otto Graham's by-line, on the increased violence in football. It ran opposite the beginning of a four-page color portfolio by Mark Kauffman on night football, whose closing caption carried the same dry air of pedanticism as so many other cutlines in *SI*: "Preseason games help pro teams financially, also help condition players." Facing the final page of color was the first page of Sound-track, composed of items gleaned from the World Series.

Because of the focus on high-income pastimes, the magazine's editorial mix was at once curious and haughty. "There were so many goddamn people covering yachting," said Robert Creamer of the early months. "And those of us who did hard sports resented it." One staffer, Ezra Bowen, wrote 36 stories on yachting within the space of a single year.

Meanwhile, the design was a melange of ungainly, unrelated elements. Soundtrack even took to running full-page cartoons, and sidebars of cloying light verse, such as: "When playing squash rackets / He's lousy. But gosh, / No wonder—his racquet, / You see, is a squash!" (While the title of the section would be changed to Events and Discoveries in March 1955, the style remained unchanged.) Art director Jerry Snyder peppered the pages with his own self-consciously whimsical line drawings. On longer captions, Snyder used typefaces identical to the magazine's body copy, creating visual logjams in which it was hard to tell where one column of type ended and another began.

"In the case of *SI*," said Andrew Heiskell, watching closely from his *Life* publisher's chair, "we really weren't creating what the dogs wanted. Reader dogs or advertiser dogs. I don't think anybody could have sold that. The magazine didn't seem to come together. It seemed to be bits and pieces. It had no form. The most important thing for a magazine is to have a form in which you create variations from week to week."

Behind the scenes, the start-up was losing money far beyond what the financial experts at Time Inc. had forecast. After spending $3.2 million during the 13 months of planning, the magazine lost $6 million more during the last five months of 1954, nearly doubling even the most pessimistic expectations. "The big problem was that advertisers couldn't believe that an audience interested in sport would be upwardly mobile," said Bill Scherman, promotions director for *SI*. "I guess they were thinking of people in the bleacher seats, fight fans, bowlers, public course golfers. Agencies were reluctant to accept us as well. Time Inc.'s own agency, Young & Rubicam, complained that their biggest clients, many of them naturals for *SI*—Arrow shirts for example—already had big budgets committed in *Time, Life*, and *Fortune*."

But Larsen, for one, was sure that the key to *SI*'s salvation was to go upscale. He'd come into James's office every week, to tell him what he did and didn't like about the previous issue. What he seemed to want most, according to circulation director Bob Cowin, were articles about "cooking lobster on the fantail of a 40-foot yacht in Nantucket." John G. Booth, one of the magazine's early ad salesmen, put the problem succinctly: "In the early days they seemed to be writing for a sports-worldly upscale audience while the promotion department gave too much emphasis to women, and we were out soliciting business from family-oriented advertisers." The haphazard approach prompted one *Time* ad exec to joke that *SI* was "the magazine for teenage millionaires."

The result was a hydra-headed enterprise at serious cross-purposes. Meanwhile, *SI*'s most likely readers—suburban-bound, middle-class Americans who were searching for outlets for their growing spectator sports fanaticism—were disappointed with early covers devoted to an antique car rally, a Swiss ski resort, and a horse show, all in the heart of football season.

The ad picture darkened at the beginning of 1955. There was a six-week stretch in which *SI* failed to sell the prime space of the inside back cover (house ads for *SI* ran instead), and was similarly unable to communicate a sense of sophistication with the ads they did sell. "When your magazine was trying to appeal to adults," said executive Tom Griffith, "it was very embarrassing to have ads on the back cover for Pedwin shoes for stuffy eight-year-olds."

• • •

The January 31, 1955, issue carried the first cover photo of a prominent female athlete, and inaugurated the superstitious fear of an "*SI* cover jinx." Hy Peskin's cover shot showed skier Jill Kinmont, a hint of a smile on her face, standing against the backdrop of the Sun Valley, Idaho, resort, where top amateurs were practicing for the Olympic trials. Three days after the magazine hit the newsstands, Kinmont fell during an icy late-afternoon run at a meet in Alta, Utah, damaging her spinal cord in a spill that left her paralyzed below the neck.

But the most discussed cover of the spring was on the April 11, 1955, issue celebrating the beginning of the new baseball season. It showed Willie Mays and his manager Leo Durocher flanking Durocher's wife, starlet Laraine Day. It prompted 25 cancellations and hundreds of negative letters. "They consider it bad taste to show a Negro [Willie Mays] with his arm around a white woman," noted letters editor Henry Romney, in his memo to James.

Inside the magazine, James's repeated use of celebrity bylines drew attention. The October 4, 1954 issue featured a short essay by John Steinbeck on fishing, novelist James T. Farrell on his first World Series, actress and essayist Cornelia Otis Skinner on her life as a "sports widow," and a two-page photo collage on Ernest Hemingway, sportsman. In the spring of '55, a four-part series written by Tenzing Norgay, the Sherpa who led Sir Edmund Hillary up the face of Everest, proved to be both a spectacular read and a revisionist take on Hillary's triumph.

William Faulkner wrote two pieces for *SI* that year, one on his first hockey game ("An Innocent at Rinkside") and another a journal of his experiences during the week leading up to the Kentucky Derby ("Kentucky May Saturday"). The Derby assignment required special care and handling. Whitney Tower was assigned to chaperone Faulkner in Louisville, to encourage him to file 300 words a night as a hedge against writer's block at deadline, and "to see that our guest did not become so preoccupied with the available whiskey that he neglected his assignment."

Faulkner arrived Tuesday, May 3, the day it was announced that he'd won the Pulitzer Prize for fiction for *A Fable*. Tower spent the next four days taking Faulkner around the track and to the horse farms in Lexington, as well as rescuing him from the vacuous cocktail party chatter that he abhorred. For his part, Faulkner fulfilled his end of the agreement by supplying 300 words a night. Tower was alarmed the first night, when he picked up Faulkner's copy to take it to the Western Union wire office. "There it was, 300 words of prose with not a single punctuation mark of any sort, no capital letters and no periods," recalled Tower. "Just 300 words strung out all together, starting with: 'this saw boone the bluegrass the virgin land rolling westward wave by dense wave from the allegheny gaps . . .'" In New York, Dick Johnston remarked that at last he'd found a scribe who could write to fit.

The most popular of the early star turns came from the satirist John P. Marquand, who wrote a series of gently mocking satirical essays on country club culture. His collection of letters from Roger Horlick, member of the Board of Governors of the fictitious Happy Knoll Country Club, crisply captured the martini-dry humor of the upper middle class (to say nothing of the Ivy League sensibilities of most Time Inc.-ers). The Marquand series would continue over the course of the next two years, with *SI* printing up Happy Knoll Country Club "membership cards" for readers. Its popularity delighted James and the ad staffers, not only because they thought it genuinely funny, but because it seemed to them that it would appeal to *SI*'s ideal reader.

Not all the celebrity items worked. Red Smith stopped writing his weekly baseball column after the '54 season because he disliked the editing. But even *SI*'s most ardent baseball fans could tell that Smith (already writing six stories a week for the *Herald Tribune*) wasn't doing his best work for the magazine. And other celebrities simply couldn't write; when coaching legend Bob Neyland was asked to write about the 1955 Orange Bowl, in which Duke pounded Nebraska, 34–7, his lead was: "From the personal point of view of an old-time coach, I was surprised at the weakness in punting shown by Duke in this game, at the climax of a successful season."

*SI*'s larger problem was that it lacked the sharpness of first-class deadline journalism. Too many stories, like Al Wright's piece on the 1955 Indianapolis 500, amounted to little more than a chronological retelling of the event, the same kind of "running" account that newspapers were producing on tight deadlines, as dry as a "first lede" story from the Associated Press. The editors who wrote captions, often ignorant of the particulars of sport, tended to generalize, emphasizing the grandeur and pageantry at every turn. A Masters color portfolio opened with: "A major golf tournament is one of the ranking spectacles in the vast vivarium of sport."

Then there were the odd priorities that the magazine displayed. The March 28, 1955, issue led with a four-page piece on the "The Maharaja of Mysore Takes *SI* on a Tiger Hunt," about the monarch's bagging of a Bengal tiger, with a diagram of the more than 25 men who helped flush the animal for the hunt. Seven pages later, at the beginning of The Wonderful World of Sport, was a short story on Bill Russell and the University of San Francisco winning the NCAA basketball title. Certainly, college basketball hadn't exploded yet, but the tournament had become big enough for newspapers (even as tiny as the *Fort Worth Press*) to send their writers out of state to cover the hometown team's progress; the magazine hadn't responded to the growing popularity of the sport. When *SI* ran Herbert Warren Wind's account of Cary Middlecoff's Masters win in '55, it appeared behind pieces on country club bowlers and "The Wonderful Woo of the Sage Grouse."

In the summer of '55, the magazine made its biggest splash in the sports community. After Swaps upset Nashua in the '55 Derby, the air was taken out of the Triple Crown; Swaps owner Rex Ellsworth hadn't paid the $100 entry fees to make his colt eligible for the Preakness or the Belmont. In an unsigned Events & Discoveries piece, Tower wrote about the technicality preventing a return engagement, and suggested a possible date and location for a match race. In the June 13 issue, *SI* broke the story that both sides had accepted the challenge. The 1¼-mile race, for a winner-take-all purse of $100,000, was run Wednesday, August 31, at Chicago's Washington Park. In a country that was still acutely conscious of region and class differences, the match-up was a natural: Ellsworth was a California rancher more comfortable in jeans than a suit; Bill Woodward, the heir to a fortune and the owner of a full-powered racing stable, was his aristocratic opposite. Nashua won the rematch, and in reporting on the race, *SI* patted its own back, quoting Swaps-Nashua race promoter Ben Lindheimer, who said, "At the contemplation stage of the race, *Sports Illustrated* showed a compelling desire to bring about a contest everyone knew would be a credit to both sport and racing. Your magazine was, in fact, the spearhead."

There was a bizarre postscript to the Swaps-Nashua duel. One Sunday morning in November, Whitney Tower was driving to midtown Manhattan (he'd been in the country over the weekend), pondering how to approach his profile on Bill Woodward, whom James had decided would be *SI*'s

Sportsman of the Year for 1955. That very morning, the editors were planning to approve and close the cover for the year-end issue, with a photo of Woodward, his wife Ann, jockey Eddie Arcaro, and Nashua. Tower was just turning downtown when he heard the radio report: Ann Woodward had shot and killed her husband the night before (the police ruled the shooting an accident). At a frantic office that morning, James made a snap decision, throwing out the cover art and instantly deciding that Brooklyn Dodgers pitcher Johnny Podres, who had won Game 7 of the World Series that year, would be named Sportsman of the Year. The editors quickly located a bland head shot, the only color close-up they had of Podres, and sent it through to engraving.

• • •

But while *SI*'s emphasis was often elsewhere, there were some signs of first-class mainstream sportswriting: Creamer was showing a graceful writing touch and the workmanlike Tower was able to convey the drama of an event. But the two early hallmarks were Jim Murray, who had returned to the West Coast, where he served as a de facto Los Angeles correspondent, and Roy Terrell, who was hired in April 1955.

Murray would play a valuable role for a magazine that was slowly warming to football. *SI* devoted four pages to the 1955 NFL preview, compared to football columnist Herman Hickman's college forecast, which spanned six issues (meaning that by the time some teams were previewed, their seasons would be half over). But James still hadn't seen pro football as a major sport; Murray's short pro football department piece was the only coverage of the December 1955 NFL title game, a 38-14 Browns win over the Rams.

A week later, Murray's writing on the January 1956 Rose Bowl didn't just sum up the game, but the buildup before it as well. It was one of the first instances of *SI* surveying the scene *around* the game rather than simply at it. Murray opened with an anecdote about an exchange between the opposing coaches, Michigan State's Duffy Daugherty and UCLA's Henry "Red" Sanders, at an early December football awards dinner, then moved to Daugherty's cocky, curious behavior during pregame preparations in Pasadena: "Accustomed to dour, cloak-and-dagger characters who behaved in Pasadena as though they were abroad in a jungle full of Mau-Maus, West Coasters did not know at first what to make of Daugherty. He not only permitted hostile (i.e., California) newspapermen in his practice sessions—an unheard-of breach of security to the likes of Fritz Crisler at Michigan or Woody Hayes at Ohio State—but he even waved the public in and not only ran off his whole repertory of plays but even took the micro-phones in hand personally to explain them to the crowd." Murray contin-ued writing pieces from the West Coast for the balance of the decade, before being lured away to the *Los Angeles Times* in 1961, where he would eventually win a Pulitzer Prize and be regarded by his peers as the best sports columnist ever.

The hiring of Roy Terrell turned out to be a pivotal moment in the magazine's history. When *SI* flew Terrell to New York in April 1955, he dined with Tibby and Johnston, a precedent in itself, since the two loathed each other. After the lunch, Johnston was talking about Terrell in bemused tones. "I can't figure this Terrell guy out," he said. "He's a Texan and a Marine and he's a *nice* guy." Later that night, Johnston took Terrell out for drinks, and offered him much unsolicited advice on where to find women in New York City. A month later, the Texas invasion began. Roy Terrell, in two-tone bucks, showed up on Memorial Day weekend, to an empty office. He had to borrow $20 from Johnston's secretary Kay McCarthy, so he could eat until he received his first paycheck.

While many of *SI*'s early staff writers were limited to one or two sports, Terrell quickly proved himself a generalist with a comprehensive knowledge of the major spectator sports. He covered 1955's National League pennant race with insight, helping to establish an emerging lead-story style based on the assumption that the reader knew an event's out-come and was looking for analysis behind the result. Terrell was both a graceful writer and an adept student of sports, able to write not just about a game, but its resulting implications. In the spring of 1956, on the college basketball beat, he reported on the University of San Francisco's second straight national title. *SI* ran the story as a basketball department in the back of the magazine, with a tiny one-column photo of Bill Russell stuff-ing a shot in the title game against Iowa, held in Evanston, Illinois. "Meanwhile, over in the Edgewater Beach Hotel on Chicago's Lake Shore Drive," concluded Terrell, "the rules committee of the National Basketball Coaches Association was paying Bill Russell perhaps his biggest tribute: in executive session they were seriously considering a new set of rules to pre-vent the inordinately tall and agile player from vaulting in the air and slap-ping the ball *down* into the basket."

Terrell's opinion of the magazine and its central problems hadn't changed much. "It became obvious to all of us, a lot of us, that it was really a bad magazine," he said. "And there was such a simple reason why: none of the three people—Sid, Johnston, or Tibby—knew anything about sports. Nor did they care that much about sports. They didn't really think they were important."

• • •

The magazine covered its first Olympic Games in 1956, beginning with the Winter Games in Cortina d'Ampezzo, Italy. In previewing the Games, Creamer wrote a penetrating profile of legendary International Olympic Committee chieftain Avery Brundage. The results from Cortina were filed by Time Inc. senior European correspondent André Laguerre, whose trenchant, detailed pieces from Cortina were the first authoritative writing in the Western press about the growing Soviet athletic arsenal.

Only Luce and a handful of other New York staffers knew of Laguerre's love of sports. In any case, his preeminence as a political reporter made it surprising that he would take on the Cortina assignment. The bigger surprise came several weeks later, when it was announced that Laguerre would be leaving his bureau chief post in London to become assistant managing editor for *SI*. Luce's memo, dated March 19, 1956, also announced that Jack Tibby was being promoted to assistant managing editor as well. But the buzz throughout the magazine—and, in fact, the whole Time & Life Building—was why one of Luce's favored employees and the company's most respected European political correspondent was coming to the States to work on "Harry's Yacht."

For the staffers who were pushing to move *SI* toward a harder-edged focus on spectator sports, the move did not bode well. What could a Frenchman possibly know of American sports? But at the same time, those who had met Laguerre spoke of him with a strange respect. The scuttlebutt eventually reached Jim Murray out on the coast. One call was openly derisive.

"Can you believe they're bringing this Frenchman over to *SI*?"

"Let me tell you something," Murray said quickly, "this guy *knows* sports—believe it or not."

Then Murray recounted an experience from the summer of 1951, a strange, almost mystical moment that had remained lodged in his memory. It happened on a train ride up to Lake Placid, where a broad cross section of Time Inc.-ers were gathering for a meeting. Sitting around the lounge car on the trip, Murray was joined in a long, boisterous conversation about sports with *Time* congressional reporter Frank McNaughton, Washington bureau chief James Shepley, and a few others. The conversation flowed toward a reminiscence of the Gashouse Gang of the St. Louis Cardinals, as well as the players that took their place in St. Louis immediately thereafter. Round and round it went, talking about Musial and Slaughter and Ol' Diz. But try as they might, none of the assembled sports experts could come up with the name of one of the Cardinal second basemen who followed Frankie Frisch.

"And we're all sitting there," said Murray, "just talking about this, and we couldn't remember the name of this guy. And suddenly, we're aware of this presence on the train, standing by the door. And this voice says, 'Emil Verban.' And he was *right*—it *was* Emil Verban. It was the answer to the Double Jeopardy question."

They turned back toward the door and saw a stocky, bespectacled man, with the hint of a smile on his face. It was André Laguerre.

# CHAPTER 5

# LAGUERRE

*Prestige cannot exist without mystery, for people revere little what they know too well.*

—CHARLES DE GAULLE

## The plane out of Paris was

having trouble long before it neared London. Now, as it made its final approach toward Heathrow, wings listing precariously on descent, the passengers were told to prepare for a difficult landing. Moments later, the jet's wheels smacked loudly on the macadam and screeched toward a skewed, ungainly stop. But the worst had been averted; a few passengers suffered minor scrapes, but most were simply suffering from nerves.

As the late afternoon fog enveloped London, a stout figure could be seen among the first deplaning. Dressed in a well-made but ill-fitting charcoal pinstriped suit, with white shirt and blue necktie, he stepped hesitantly down the metal ladder stairway, with his bulky black briefcase in one hand and an unlit cigar in the other. He walked away from the approaching ambulances and police cars, and moved toward a fence bordering the airport grounds. Stepping gingerly over the fence, he scaled an embankment to a nearby road, and hailed a taxi.

As the cabbie drove toward Orange Street in the West End, the man took out his handkerchief and dabbed the cold sweat from his pouchy face and neck. Within minutes the taxi pulled up in front of a squat building whose unprepossessing basement tavern was advertised by a plain, humble sign that said "Jack's Club." After descending the stairs, the man walked in and moved toward the bar. There, placing his briefcase down on a stool, he remained standing and waited for his usual scotch and water. They knew him here. He didn't have to ask, and he didn't have to wait long.

"Start working on another, if you will, old man," he quietly told the bartender, in his stately Continental cadence, still with the dollop of British accent he had acquired during his boyhood. And there, self-possession returning, thoughts clearing, the man drank in silence.

But it wasn't until days later, when a coworker at the Time bureau mentioned the scary landing out at Heathrow, that André Laguerre mentioned his experience. "Yes, I know," said Laguerre. "I was on it."

"My God!" exclaimed the man. "What did you do?"

"I caught a cab."

That flinty Gallic stoicism had served André Laguerre well. It sustained him through the most harrowing of circumstances, when he was making night drops behind enemy lines in occupied France or swimming for his life off the shores of Dunkirk; and it would temper him through the greatest of his triumphs, moments of signal achievement when he gained the everlasting respect of the two men he most admired, Charles de Gaulle and Henry Luce.

The executives of Time Inc. launched *Sports Illustrated* as much on faith as wisdom. They envisioned a smaller, more prosperous world, a world connected by news media and air travel, bound together in sophistication and leisure. But while they could only vaguely discern, as if in the distance, the broad contours of this world, André Laguerre had *lived* it. Born in England, raised in San Francisco, ever loyal to France, Laguerre's cosmopolitan upbringing was a fact, like his love for horse racing, cigars, and scotch. As bizarre and unlikely as his 1956 summons to New York seemed at the time, it all made a kind of poetic sense later.

• • •

Perhaps editing was in André Laguerre's blood. His grandfather Maxime Laguerre hailed from the eastern part of France, and served for eight years as a deputy in the AIN, the French congress; it was a source of pride that he made only one public speech during that time. Maxime's cousin Georges Laguerre was equally prominent, a flamboyant French lawyer, longtime ally of Boulanger and Clemenceau, and a friend of Emile Zola. In January 1898, when Zola was preparing to publish his long letter to President Faure on the Dreyfus affair, it was Georges Laguerre who read it, considered the overly verbose title, and suggested it was too long. Zola listened and shortened the title to *J'Accuse.*

André Laguerre was born February 21, 1915, in the parish of Ottery St. Mary in Devon, England, the first child of a lifelong French diplomat and an aristocratic Englishwoman. His father James Laguerre was a handsome, vain man, capable of great charm but also diminished by a limiting literalism. His wife Dorothy, daughter of Lord Grey, was a beautiful woman once described by a family friend as "the stupidest woman I've ever met—just a little piece of fluff."

The oldest of three children, the shy, purposeful André was fiercely protective of his younger siblings, Leon and Odette. He weathered his father's failures and his mother's foolishness with a stolid equanimity, even as the family moved from England to France to Syria and back to England, all before his tenth birthday. Possessed of a taciturn nature and a burning intelligence, he grew up studious and remarkably observant, reminding many family members of his grandfather Maxime.

In the summer of 1927, James Laguerre received another diplomatic posting, this time as a commercial attaché for the French government in San Francisco. The family made its move to the States and André, at age 12, was placed in the eighth grade at the Santa Monica School. Living in the fashionable Seacliff section of San Francisco, he would become acquainted with some quintessentially American pleasures, often traveling to Recreation Park to watch the San Francisco Seals minor league baseball team or out to the horse races at Tanforan, where he'd stake his allowance on a *Daily Racing Form* and some longshots. Because the St. Louis Cardinals were the westernmost major league team at that time, André became a Cardinals fan. And in 1928, after moving to St. Ignatius College preparatory school, he found work as a copyboy at the *San Francisco Chronicle*, where he learned to look for the Cardinals scores on the clattering Associated Press wires.

These pastimes distressed his parents; James Laguerre wanted his son to be a diplomat, Dorothy wanted him to be a priest. But neither his mother's babying or his father's shouting had an effect beyond making him more stubborn. André Laguerre had long ago decided he would be a journalist.

In 1929, he returned to England to attend the St. Martin School in Devon, and in 1931 he obtained an Oxford School Certificate with highest possible honors. He could have attended Oxford University, but instead took a correspondence course and began writing freelance stories. To make the rent, he found work in London at Smith's Bookstore, piling parcels and delivering papers. By the mid-'30s, he was among the youngest successful journalists on Fleet Street, securing writing assignments for several newspapers, in England and abroad. When Neville Chamberlain went to Munich, André Laguerre went there as well, covering the 1938 Munich agreement as a foreign correspondent for *Paris-Soir* at the age of 23.

When France declared war on Germany a year later, Laguerre joined the French forces as a corporal. He spent some time on the Maginot Line, then was posted to British General Headquarters at Arras as a government liaison. But it was in May 1940, while he was with the French forces at Dunkirk, that Laguerre's life changed. In the confusion that prevailed prior to the evacuation, while the French troops waited for the British fleet to rescue them, he spent a week on the beaches, searching for an escape. On the morning of June 1, he climbed aboard a French destroyer that moved unsteadily out to sea. With the coast still visible, the ship hit a mine. Laguerre was among the first to jump overboard, swimming away from the wreckage. As he frantically trod water, he turned to see hundreds of French soldiers clinging desperately to the rail, trying to climb up on the keel of a ship that was slowly sinking into the North Sea. He was a half mile away when the whole ship went up in flames.

Swimming around, trying to elude German machine-gun fire and stanch the bleeding from a fragment in his neck, Laguerre was near the point of exhaustion when he was finally rescued by a British destroyer. On the way to Britain, he saw many of his countrymen trying to climb aboard as well, only to have British soldiers, realizing the ship was already overloaded, push them back into the sea. Laguerre was still convalescing on June 18, 1941, when he heard the broadcast of de Gaulle's message of resistance. After being discharged from the hospital and cleared by the British military authorities, he was given a choice between repatriation in England or joining the Free French troops. He chose the latter, and throughout the months of the Blitz, stood sentry outside de Gaulle's headquarters at Carlton Gardens. It was an odd posting. André was clumsy with the bulky French infantryman's rifle and longed to be more than just a grunt with a weapon.

One night, over drinks, he had a long discussion with an American journalist, who argued passionately that de Gaulle was hurting his cause by the imperious manner in which he dealt with the American press. Only days later, de Gaulle happened to send a directive to all ranks within the Free French for ideas to improve the morale and standing of the Free French. Laguerre typed up a communiqué—in his blunt, authoritative fashion—that so impressed de Gaulle that he summoned the corporal for a meeting. De Gaulle quickly appointed him assistant to the chief press attaché, whom Laguerre replaced in a matter of months. Within a year of his near-death off the shores of Dunkirk, André Laguerre, just 26 years old, was the journalistic point man for Charles de Gaulle.

De Gaulle grew to trust his youthful press officer and, in the fall of 1943, took Laguerre with him to North Africa and, in 1944, to Wash-

ington for his meeting with Roosevelt. In 1945, as the postwar government established itself, André spent much of his time briefing the international press from De Gaulle's headquarters at the Scribe Hotel in
Paris. The Scribe was just minutes away from *Time*'s Paris bureau, an
aristocratic French building on the rue Royal and Concord, where *Time*
bureau chief Charles Wertenbaker was flooding New York with voluminous updates on the reconstituted French republic. His reporter
Nathalie Katchoubey grew to dread the trips over to Laguerre's office at
the Scribe. This regal, handsome daughter of a Russian princess and the
direct descendant of Napoleon's first wife, Joséphine de Beauharnais,
was raised in a cultured atmosphere, studying to be a ballerina, spending her free time in her bedroom, listening to Maurice Chevalier records
and dreaming that she was dancing with Fred Astaire. But her patrician
politesse seemed lost on the de Gaulle spokesman. "I would wake up
every morning," she recalled, "and say, 'Oh, God, I hope Charlie
Wertenbaker doesn't send me over to see that awful man André
Laguerre,' who was always so difficult. I'd be given questions to ask
him, like 'What is the government going to do about this?' and he was
very gruff. He'd say, 'You're not precise—please be more clear. I don't
understand what you're saying.' Everyone was scared. It was torture
every time."

Within a matter of months, the unlikely pair would be working side
by side. De Gaulle knew that André Laguerre didn't want to be a mere
political functionary, and sent him on a mission to America to "investigate
the press situation." The trip was actually a job-hunting tour for Laguerre.
After an interview with Henry Luce in the spring of 1946, he returned
with a job as *Time*'s Paris political correspondent.

Laguerre would grow steadily less gruff with Katchoubey, though she
still found him imposing. They shared a small office, and days would go
by without him ever recognizing her presence. Then one day, she'd show
up for work and he'd remark, "Well, hmm . . . that is a very handsome
dress you're wearing." And then for days at a time again, nothing.

They began courting, in Laguerre's casual fashion, though he was
much more concerned with living a bachelor's life. He had grown friendly
with André Malraux during the war, and although they disagreed about
much politically, they were tight drinking companions. Laguerre was a frequent dinner guest of Albert Camus, who loved nothing more than to
stand in his living room with Laguerre, both men with a drink, kicking a
soccer ball back and forth. It passed for exercise.

Laguerre retained the love of sports he'd gained in the States. In the
fall of 1946, he scolded Jim Knight, the Paris bureau chief of the *Interna-*

*tional Herald Tribune*, for his shoddy handling of the paper's reporting on the World Series (Laguerre was disappointed that the *Tribune* hadn't emphasized the daring nature of Enos "Country" Slaughter's Series-winning sprint from first on Harry Walker's double). That same year, he began writing a Paris sports column for the *Herald Tribune*, under his sports nom de plume Eddie Snow. "What was remarkable about the columns, whether they were written about tennis from Roland Garros or the horses at Longchamp, was that they were perfectly pitched in the American vernacular," said Jim Knight. "You would have thought they were by some smart, cynical American." In 1947, Laguerre organized—and then starred in—a softball game between Time Inc. and the *Herald Tribune*, held in front of a largely mystified crowd on the the lawns of the Bois de Boulogne, the stately park in Paris.

A Letter from the Publisher in *Time* in 1947 quoted Laguerre's analysis of a U.S.–U.S.S.R. diplomatic tiff earlier that spring, and gave a hint of his grounding in American sports: "It is undeniable, of course, that Soviet trickery got the U.S. into a jam. Somehow, I can't get indignant about this trickery, anymore than I can about the first baseman who hides the ball in his glove and waits for the runner to take a lead off the bag. In the major leagues, you just don't fall for tricks like that."

During those years in Paris, Laguerre often drank at a bar in the Hotel Californie or the dilapidated Michel's, run by a retired British naval officer. Harold King of Reuter's often join him, as well as Frederick Klein from the *Time* bureau. Everyone, it seemed, drank with Laguerre. Red Smith stopped by when he was in town; the author Georges Simenon often paid him a visit; even the fabled photographer Robert Capa joined Laguerre and his group for an occasional game of poker. On one occasion, Capa's girlfriend at the time, Ingrid Bergman, sat in the corner until 2 a.m. while the men went about their business.

In January 1948, Laguerre was named head of the Paris bureau, though his lifestyle didn't noticeably change. "When André was running the bureau, he only cared about three things," said Time Inc.-er Frank White. "Firstly, journalism, his job. Second, he was a sports fan, mainly horse racing. And the third one was bars."

Decades later, Frederick Klein and Frank White used to reminisce about the night they joined Laguerre in a small, touristy bar near the shadow of the Arc de Triomphe. As they walked into the establishment, called the Scotch Bar, Klein and Laguerre were speaking English, mainly for White's benefit, his French being subpar at the time. The bartender had no reason to think anything other than that the three men were American tourists. After the first round of drinks were served and emptied,

Laguerre fixed the bartender with a grave stare, and spoke French for the first time since entering the tavern.

"Jeune homme," he said sharply. "Pourquoi vous nous servez maintenant du vrai whiskey?" *Young man—why don't you now serve us some real scotch?*

The bartender was just beginning to feign offense when Laguerre cut him off.

"Look, this is not only not scotch, but I can tell you the exact brand of *mar* that you used to cut it with."

The bartender's eyes twinkled. He opened the trap door behind the bar to the cellar and disappeared, returning a moment later with an unopened bottle of Glenlivet, the fine single malt. "Gentlemen," he said sheepishly, "this is on us."

Even then, a myth was growing up around Laguerre and his astonishing capacity at not only holding but discerning alcohol. He boasted to reporter Dita Camacho, in the Paris bureau, that he could identify scotches in a blind taste test. He nailed every one until he reached a glass that she'd surreptitiously mixed with three different brands. "This one was planted," Laguerre said instantly, then looked toward Camacho with mock sternness. "It's a mixture, and I won't even try to tell you who did it."

Through it all, he provided *Time* with a series of scoops on the Paris beat, many of which so enraged French government officials that they threatened to deport him, before realizing that he had dual citizenship. By 1950, Luce was so impressed with Laguerre that he appointed him to his staff in New York for a year's tour of duty. In the house organ *FYI*, Billings said that "Laguerre's assignment will be editorial work on political analysis on which he will report to top editors through me."

Laguerre began his duties in New York on December 1. He was ill suited to the political advisory role for which Luce had drafted him, disliking the long hours of solitude, missing the bars and the friends and the revelry of the Paris days. But he still made an impression on Luce and the company.

The defining moment of Laguerre's stay in the States occurred at a luncheon at the Commodore Hotel, before the train trip to Lake Placid in which Murray would meet Laguerre. Luce held the floor and was waxing ebullient over his conclusions, surveying the condition of Europe and the score in the Cold War, while his lieutenants sat in rapt silence. Concluding his remarks, Luce looked down the dais to Laguerre, who had been sitting in his chair with his arms folded, and asked solicitously, "Wouldn't you say so, André?"

Laguerre hadn't budged since the soliloquy started. But now he sat up in his chair, looked back at his boss, and said evenly, "Not quite, Harry."

"There was utter consternation going on around the table," recalled one veteran Time Inc. staffer. "Nobody talked to Luce that way. And André wasn't trying to make any points, and he wasn't being a wise-ass. It was just the way he was."

Laguerre earned Luce's respect nonetheless, and went back to Paris in November 1951 having solidified his position as one of Luce's most prized and trusted employees. In 1954, he was promoted to chief of the London bureau. A year later, when Paris bureau chief Eric Gibbs died, Luce requested Laguerre serve as chief of both the London and Paris bureaus.

It was during a trip back to Paris, in the fall of 1954, that Laguerre first received a call from Luce, inquiring about whether Laguerre would consider moving to New York to work on *Sports Illustrated*. "André was dismayed," remembered Frank White, who was in Laguerre's office with him when he took the call. "He wanted to be the managing editor of *Time*, not *Sports Illustrated*. He was, if not dejected, definitely disappointed. He loved sports and all that, he was an avid fan. But his real drive, his real bag, was political and international news. And that's what he thought he was good at, and that's what he trained for and that's what he hoped he'd get."

It privately rankled Laguerre that Luce was so preoccupied with his thorough knowledge of sports. Luce was amazed that his Paris bureau chief was conversant in such pastimes and always relied on him to take him to one sports event or another. In 1949, Luce joined Laguerre and White for a French league soccer game, which quickly left the editor-in-chief bored. He tried to follow the action for a while, but his mind began to wander. Midway through the first half, after spending the previous few minutes scanning the stands at the Parc des Princes, Luce nudged Laguerre in the ribs. "André, André," he implored, looking around. "How many of the people here are Communists?"

Whatever Luce thought, it had become clear to him that Laguerre had sufficient leadership skills to be trusted with running the company's two most important European bureaus. Laguerre was becoming a Luce favorite, as well as a respected figure in political circles. When asked in 1955 who was the best political reporter in England, Winston Churchill responded, "Why, André Laguerre, of course." The two often shared lunch together at 10 Downing Street, or talked about the latest books and plays, as well as their shared fascination with America and its culture. On a lark, Laguerre even spent a night as a chorus member of his favorite musical, *Guys and Dolls*.

André Laguerre might have stayed a bachelor for the rest of his life—by all accounts he loved the freedom—but Nathalie Katchoubey wasn't going to just continue dating him until one of them died. "Look," she explained in 1955, after they'd been seeing each other for ten years. "The time has come for you to make up your mind."

"But I don't want to get married," he said.

"Well, then you don't want to get married. Very fine. That's the end of our relationship. This is not going to go on, because I'm getting older."

"You can't do that!" he protested.

"Yes I can. You make up your mind one way or another. You say yes, okay, we'll get married in six months' time."

André was stunned; he called Freddie Klein to commiserate. But there was little sympathy from Klein. "André, *good God*, this has gone on for so long—why are you surprised?"

So André Laguerre drank. For three days and three nights, he went on one long, scotch-driven bender. And on the fourth day, two dozen red roses appeared at Nathalie's apartment, along with a note, which read, "Let's have a peace conference."

If there was going to be a peace conference, Nathalie felt she needed an interpreter, so she brought Klein along. During the protracted negotiations that followed, Laguerre argued every angle he could. He offered to support Nathalie, put her up, buy her anything she wanted. And she resisted every entreaty, explaining that she didn't want to be a kept woman.

Finally, Freddie Klein broke in. "You know, make up your mind old boy, or that's it."

André looked at his drink. It seemed to be empty.

"Well," he said balefully. "I guess I have to."

Nathalie bristled. "You don't have to suffer that much."

So they married, on June 7, 1955, in almost complete secrecy. On their wedding day, they went to a small track out in the British countryside. There, in the late afternoon sun, Nathalie bet on a colt named Heavenly Bliss that came in at 30–1. Her other longshot had come in that day, as well.

The Laguerres moved in together in an elegant apartment in London. André liked the city, although there were occasional reminders of his troubled past. Talk of the war could make the British particularly effusive. André almost never spoke of it. And in London one night, when a British ex-officer began hailing the glory that was Dunkirk, Laguerre fixed him with a poker face and remarked dryly, "Yes, you were very, very good. All the Frenchmen who tried to climb into the ships, you pushed their heads down under the water and drowned them." And yet at other times, among Frenchmen, he would wonder about the flaws of their national character. *If it had been us, we'd have brought them on board. And the boat would have sunk.*

January brought Cortina and the 1956 Olympics, which Laguerre covered on special assignment for *SI*. A month later, Luce visited the Laguerres in London. Nathalie, newly pregnant, fixed dinner for the three of them and, during the meal, Harry asked expansively, "Are you happy here?"

"Yes, quite," said André.

"Fine, then. Well, stay on."

After he left, Nathalie went out and restocked the liquor cabinet with two months' worth of alcohol to see the Laguerres through their frequent dinner parties. And then, in early March, the cable from New York arrived: "André Laguerre to take the post of assistant managing editor at *Sports Illustrated*. Please be in New York in two weeks."

What Nathalie Laguerre had not been privy to was a late-night walk in the Tuileries Garden, Luce and Laguerre candidly discussing one man's company and the other man's life. It seems likely at this time that Luce pressed the issue again and, because he so rarely gave direct orders, asked Laguerre whether, if he was needed, he could bring him to New York to help out with the struggling magazine.

And to that, André Laguerre could only have said yes. "There were only two people in his life that he truly admired. One was General de Gaulle and the other was Harry Luce," said Nathalie Laguerre. "If either of those two asked him to walk on his head, he'd have done it."

Frank White knew his old friend was disappointed, but he also recognized the special bond that existed between Laguerre and Luce. "I can't tell you how much, or why Luce was such a fantastic figure in Andre's life," White once said. "André was a very cynical guy. He was another sort of alter-ego type for Harry, but Harry didn't understand him. Not many of us did."

Years later, James would take credit for the idea to bring Laguerre over to the States, but none of the staff at *SI*—or higher up at Time Inc.— deemed that plausible. "It was very much Harry's idea to get André in there," said Heiskell. "I do remember being surprised myself, because I remembered André as a great bureau chief, and as a de Gaullist. I was brought up in France, so I had a lot of great conversations with him. But I thought of him as a political character, totally. An expert on national affairs. I hadn't known the *Racing Form* side of André Laguerre. I knew the other André, and a very impressive André he was. Not half as awesome as he would be later."

Around the company, many were surprised by Laguerre's acceptance of the job. But by the time he and Nathalie—then eight months pregnant—prepared to leave for New York, Laguerre had his assignment. Much had changed since the war. He was a husband now, and an expectant father (Michele Laguerre would be born four weeks after the Laguerres arrived in New York). And after years of reading international newspapers for Cardinals scores or sneaking off to the track between political assignments, he now would have a chance to merge his love of sports with his love of journalism. In a note to his London staff, he explained his decision: "For the past twenty years . . . I have been covering mostly politics and international affairs, where mediocrity is unfortunately and too often the best way for a man to get ahead. There is no place for mediocrity in sports. I'm looking forward to working in a field where a striving for excellence and a dedication to performance count so much."

# CHAPTER 6

# "ALL THINGS TO ALL PEOPLE"

## On Monday, April 30, 1956,

Sid James sent a memo to the staff announcing a pouring that afternoon "to meet and welcome André Laguerre, who will officially be installed in his new job come Thursday." The pourings, (company-sponsored cocktail parties on the office premises), were a ritual part of the Time Inc. culture. The staff had spent much of the interim since the March announcement speculating about the new addition.

"What's he like?" Creamer asked Tibby in late April.

"He's a Frenchman," said Tibby. "He's tall. He has dark hair and wears dark suits. And a white shirt and dark tie. And his wife was a Russian princess."

With that description, Creamer envisioned a "very sophisticated, European, French count—I thought of this elegant man—I could see the perfect cuffs, you know, the marvelously tailored suits. And then this French baker shows up. Much more sophisticated than any French count ever could've been."

Laguerre exuded a confident, hard-nosed élan. His quiet assurance was poles apart from the glad-handing peppiness of James; staffers quickly realized that they'd just met their next leader.

"I don't want to say anything critical about James; he was very good to me," said Creamer. "But he had this sort of bouncing energy—every issue we put out was the best issue ever. It was always hectic. Sid was really a man for the present. Laguerre had more of a sense of the future and of the magazine's relationship in the world and the economy and so on."

Laguerre didn't make any big statements, attempted no power grabs. He took his remote office without grumbling and even suffered other chippy indignities (Tibby would forever pronounce his first name "Anndray") with composure. Laguerre's mere presence brought an element of resolute calmness to the floor that hadn't existed before. It also set the stage for the next, and most painful, part of *SI*'s evolution, from an uneven, class-conscious magazine emphasizing sporting leisure to a spectator sports–intensive newsmagazine.

"They had to make this magazine—had to make sports—important," said Roy Terrell. "André is different from these guys. First, he's a brilliant man and a better journalist and so forth. He also had a love of sports, although he knew much more about international politics and things like that—he was a great expert in certain fields, but he didn't really know that much about sports. But he cared about it; he realized, 'This is important,' and he listened to people who did know something about it."

And while Laguerre was neither insubordinate nor deceitful, it was apparent that he expected, and intended, to lead the magazine one day. "I think everyone felt it and knew it," said Nathalie Laguerre, who with André often joined Sid and Agnes James for social occasions. "He and Sid were very polite and nice, but I knew he wanted to go in there and do it his way. It's difficult putting a man like André into a position where he wasn't in charge."

● ● ●

Even as Laguerre's posting was the talk of the fourth floor, Time Inc.'s executives were more preoccupied with the dire results on the advertising side. Ad pages weren't merely falling short of projections, they were mocking them. Simply stated, the business side's eagnerness to be all things to all advertisers resulted in an incoherent sales strategy. The *SI* ad staff was arguing, to advertisers who usually bought space in highbrow magazines like *Esquire* or *Sunset*, that there was a new leisure class to be captured in the sports magazine. To advertisers who regularly staked out space in *Fortune* and *Business Week*, *SI*'s salesmen characterized the new magazine's readers as upwardly mobile and preoccupied with business. To outdoor advertisers who typically bought space in *Sports Afield* and *Outdoor Life*, the ad staff pitched the *SI* reader as a hearty outdoorsman. They argued nearly the opposite when trying to secure advertisers of women's products, contending that the magazine was for the whole family and, furthermore, that women were really the ones in most American households who made subscription decisions. A number of these claims might have been true, but they couldn't all be true, and the advertising industry sensed *SI*'s desperation.

Robert Cowin, among the first to see the need for a clearer focus on hard sports, was growing increasingly frustrated with James's optimism, oblivious as it was to all logic, evidence, and prevailing trends. He'd shown James several foreboding reports and surveys, but the managing editor seemed unperturbed. One morning in 1956, Cowin brought another grim circulation report into James's office.

James sat at his desk, with his hands clasped in front of him, smiling. "How's it going, Bob?"

"Not very good, Sid," Cowin said gravely. He'd decided this time to bring just a single sheet of paper, showing the indisputable fact that subscribers were not re-upping in the way that *SI* needed. They were dissatisfied with the magazine. It was dire news for a magazine trying to build a loyal following. "I want you to look at this," he said, sliding the piece of paper across the desk.

James took it, looked at the paper for a few seconds, crumpled it up, and threw it in his wastebasket. And then he clasped his hands back in front of him, smiled again, and asked, "Is there anything else?"

The editor had also been ignoring the critiques of Bill Scherman in promotion. As early as 1955, Scherman had sent Howard Black an analysis of single-copy sales, showing that "the best-selling covers are those which have on them a leading personality of the season's major sport or sports," rather than "esoteric" sports like mountain-climbing, fencing, horse riding, or skin diving. And an April 1956 memo on "Why Subscribers Cancel" noted that nearly half of the 265 subscription cancellations in the past year complained about a lack of major sports coverage. "The majority of people who gave a reason for canceling *SI* claimed that *SI*'s main interest seemed to be with sports out of the reach of the average reader." In the words of one reader, there were "too many safaris, bull fights, birds, and fashion."

Newsstand sales dropped and ad revenue was again falling far short of projections. With all of that, James went down to Bermuda for *SI*'s third annual ad sales convention in May of 1956 and opened his speech by noting happily, "Success is a many-splendored thing."

• • •

Haphazardly, new talent was flowing into the magazine. When Roy Terrell went to Evanston, Illinois, in the spring of 1956, to cover the NCAA basketball tournament, he spent much of his time with Tex Maule, who by then was writing a sports column for the *Dallas Morning News*. Maule was eventually hired that October to become the magazine's pro football writer. For the first time, the pro football preview earned a cover billing, with a note inside that the sport's "emergence as a truly national game was dramatized from coast to coast Sunday afternoon when CBS telecast the first four of a total of 63 pro games it will send to the country's television screens this autumn." Maule wouldn't begin a regular pro football column until 1957, but for the first time, the magazine had a staff writer who was primarily associated with the pro game. Maule joined Terrell as another Texan proponent for more and better-focused coverage on football. He also delighted in teasing Andy Crichton about the level of football in the Ivy League, claiming that Abilene, Texas, high school could beat both Harvard and Yale on the same afternoon.

Rising through the reporter's ranks within *SI* was an eccentric young writer named Gilbert Rogin, who had been hired in early 1955 on the clip desk, fresh from college and a military stint. Back home in New York, he was still living with his parents, Russian Jews who had emigrated to America as children. An aspiring short story writer who rechanneled his talents to journalism after a failed attempt at painting, he was clearly a major talent, and began vying for a staff writer position. He wasn't the only one on the way up. Shortly after Laguerre's arrival, sports-savvy staffers took an increased role. Staff writer Jeremiah Tax brought a thorough grounding in pro and college basketball. Among the reporters, Les Woodcock, Bill Leggett, and Walter Bingham all solidified the magazine's baseball coverage.

Another new byline in 1956 belonged to a little-known Harvard graduate and Barnard College professor named George Plimpton, who was struggling to start a new literary magazine called the *Paris Review*. Plimpton had been recommended to Sid James by Whitney Tower, who had known him through Manhattan social circles for years. Tower suspected that Plimpton, despite his lack of major magazine writing experience, could fulfill one of James's wishes: to get an interview with Harold Vanderbilt, the successful defender of the America's Cup, inventor of contract bridge, Vanderbilt family heir, and all-around sportsman. Tower knew that Plimpton and Vanderbilt had been close in college, and he made the pitch when he saw Plimpton on a weekend train out to Syosset. The untested writer was grateful for the interest and agreed to take on the assignment. He came back with a sprawling piece, one that James ran in four installments in the fall of 1956. It marked the beginning of a unique and fruitful writing career for Plimpton. No freelancer in *SI*'s history would ever be more closely identified with the magazine.

And later in the decade, in a rare coup, *SI* outbid *Time* for the services of Ray Cave, the assistant city editor of the *Baltimore Evening Sun*. With a military background and a classical education—he graduated from the great books program at St. John's College in Annapolis—Cave was a crack journalist and a natural leader who would, in the early '60s, move onto the editing track. The sum of the the the new hires and promotions was to give *SI* a better grounding in spectator sports. The magazine wasn't yet ready to make hard sports its number one priority, but it was finally reaching a point where, adhering to group journalism tenets, it wouldn't be embarrassed.

With much of the free world expressing outrage over Soviet reprisals in Hungary, *SI* began its coverage of the start of the Olympic games in the December 3, 1956, issue. Laguerre led the *SI* delegation down to Melbourne, where he was joined by Roy Terrell and photographers John Zimmerman and Dick Meek.

Laguerre's lead piece in the December 3 issue quoted IOC chairman Avery Brundage's vow to continue the games regardless of the political situation. Laguerre then noted that "the athletes as well as those enjoying their efforts have so far been notably successful in dissociating their minds from the dangers which plague the universe. That may be an ostrichlike attitude, of course, in which case I can only report that it is very pleasant in the sand down here." But far from ignoring the situation, *SI* had already begun to get in the middle of it.

It began with a call in late November to Whitney Tower from the Hungarian Olympic patron Count Ante Szapary (his wife was Tower's distant cousin), who told Tower that a substantial portion of the Hungarian Olympic team wanted to defect, and hoped to do so through *Sports Illustrated*, leaving it to Tower to make the necessary arrangements. Within 48 hours, Henry Luce had received an audience with Secretary of State John Foster Dulles. Furtive plans were made with Juan Trippe, head of Pan American Airlines, to have a plane waiting at Melbourne Airport. At the height of the Hungarian intrigue, James and Laguerre, speaking by phone, were reduced to using code to communicate. ("How many rolls of film do you think you'll be bringing back?" "It should be about 25 or 30 rolls.")

At the conclusion of the games, 33 members of the team voted to defect. They were ushered from the village and flown to safety on the Pan Am jet detached specially for the mission. "Luce wanted to add something extra to the package," recalled Tower, "so he and Sid James made it known as the Hungarians were on their way to a New York City welcoming reception on the Rockefeller Center ice rink that all defecting Hungarians would be guaranteed jobs in the U.S."

Laguerre's summary of the bizarre events, "Down a Road Called Liberty" in the December 17 issue, explained how the Hungarians, with a little help from *SI*, outwitted the Soviet secret service, and found their way to the United States. The piece would provide a crucial element of legitimacy to *SI*, earning the magazine the Overseas Press Club of America award for the "best magazine reporting of events involving person, places or things outside the United States" in 1956. It also won the staff some respect within the building.

But as the magazine's second full year drew to a close, there was still little good news from the business side. Though circulation had increased in 1956 to 600,000 and the ad department brought in more than 1,100 ad pages (up from 737 the previous year), the magazine was still losing money far beyond the third-year projection. In a letter to Larsen, Luce made the success of *SI* "Time Inc.'s No. 1 publishing job for 1957. Real success may be briefly defined as putting *SI* in a position to come close to breaking even in 1958. Close to breaking even in 1958 may be defined as having a deficit in 1958 of not more than 10 percent of the gross."

By this time, the fiddling with the format had become manic. James was bouncing ideas off promotion, trying to come up with "a bright bullseye phrase or slogan or gimmick or idea that exactly fit this magazine and/or could be used to characterize it or promote its interests." Among those considered: the portmanteau "ENTHUSIACTIVE" to describe *SI*'s readers; or, even more labored, a series of spots built around the rhetorical question, *Who killed Whistler's mother?* "Obviously, it is sport or *Sports Illustrated* that killed Whistler's mother," wrote James. "The rocking chair is gone and she is indeed out on the golf course and all sorts of places pleasuring herself and otherwise extending her active life."

On December 17, 1956, Laguerre sent a confidential memo to the staff, adding a dose of reality to the incessant conceptualizing: "One of our most important 1957 resolutions is to keep a tougher eye on the content of the magazine. . . . In 1957 the ante is being upped for all of you. It will no longer be satisfactory to have an attractive lay-out, a snappy head and 'coverage' of a must event or person . . . Each story must justify itself by its writing and—more important—by its sheer journalistic value."

A couple weeks later, Laguerre, in a memo to James, began to show irritation that he'd been made to sit in on another series of lengthy discussions about emphasis on news vs. feature pieces, hard sports vs. "quality sports": "[i]n the end, I threw these notes away, having arrived at the startling journalistic conclusion that our most important editorial aim should be to have better stories. . . . *Time* will never publish as much foreign news or medical news as some publications, but we should acquire the same unquestioned authority in relation to sport that *Time* has in relation to 'serious' news."

While the discussion about focus continued, the Kentucky Derby provided the magazine an unexpected highlight in 1957. Early in 1954, during dry runs for the yet-to-be-titled magazine, someone had borrowed the idea of photographing the birth of a thoroughbred (a portfolio first executed by the Dell incarnation of *Sports Illustrated*, in 1949). The shots of the young colt named Iron Liege weren't published in '54, and languished in *SI*'s vaults until the winter of 1957, when Whitney Tower observed that the horse had an outside chance to run in the Kentucky Derby. The portfolio finally ran in the February 25 issue, under the title, "The Baby Started Out 9,066 to One." On the first Saturday in May, the 8 to 1 longshot won by a nose, after Bold Ruler's jockey, Bill Shoemaker, mistakenly stood up in the saddle at the sixteenth pole, thinking it was the finish line.

But 1957 was also marked by embarrassments. When the February 4 issue—with a cover shot of yachtsman Hugh Schaddelee—hit the stands, *SI* was in for ridicule both within and outside the building. The cover caption butchered his name, spelling it "Shadelee." Later that year, Tex Maule spent weeks working on a cover feature, about the powerful Oklahoma Sooners, winners of 44 games in a row. He produced a 1,000-line story (about 6,500 words) on Oklahoma's winning formula, titled "a+S+x+f+b = INVINCIBILITY." James loved it and slapped the cover line "Why Oklahoma is Unbeatable" on the November 18 issue, which hit newsstands November 14. Two days later, Notre Dame ended the streak, upsetting OU, 7–0. The morning after the game, James showed up to the office with a smile on his face, informing a dubious Creamer that "we can use this to our advantage!"

• • •

As James continued trying to put out a magazine that fit Larsen's and Luce's contradictory expectations, Laguerre became the center of the magazine's internal resistance movement, which often gathered at the Three Gs on 48th Street (what *SI* promotions man Robert Fisler described as a "particularly ecumenical watering hole"). Even suburban stalwarts like Creamer and Crichton began to spend time there, stopping by for long lunches and taking a couple nightcaps after work. One Saturday evening, Crichton showed up late to the house of his brother, the novelist Robert Crichton, who took one look at him and said, "I finally know what the Three G's stands for: Going, going, gone." But it was a time in America when public drunkenness was accepted. A three-martini lunch wasn't a figure of speech, it was a fact of life. "It got ugly," recalled longtime promotion director George Trescher. "Everybody drank so much those days—everybody had three-martini lunches, then wondered why we were screaming at the help in the afternoon."

As with other Time Inc. magazines, the alcohol-addled afternoons were part of the *SI* culture. Barbara La Fontaine, who would later become one of *SI*'s first female staff writers, was working for Andy Crichton as a secretary in 1957 when Dick Johnston invited her to lunch. "When I got there, he had ordered martinis," she said. "And I had never had a martini. At the time I had the weird notion that red wine sobered one up, and I asked if I could have a glass of red wine. Dick bought the bottle, put it into his coat pocket and we went back to the office. I remember tottering into Dick's office and saying, 'You only have to think, but I have to type.' One used to be able to go up to the medical department and ask to lie down in a small dark room. One used to do so."

It was inevitable that, even in the hard-drinking world of Time Inc., Laguerre was going to become something of a drinking legend. One night in 1959, he and Jerry Tax set out for an All-Star game in Pittsburgh. They met in Penn Station for the train, Tax with an overnight bag and pajamas and a book he was reading. Laguerre brought his briefcase from work, containing two quarts of scotch, which were consumed en route, as they stayed up through the night talking about the magazine and the world. When they arrived in Pittsburgh, Tax recalled, "We left the station and took a cab to the hotel, where some of our writers were staying, met them, and had some beer. Then we went to the ballpark, and had some more beer there, and watched the game. When it was over, we walked back to the station, because we decided to get something to eat on the way back. We stopped at about 15 different bars and never got anything to eat. Drank all the way there, drank all the way back, and my wife damn near shot me when I got home."

• • •

In December 1957, Luce was hosting a dinner party for several executives at his winter home in Carefree, Arizona. Over dinner, someone asked Luce why *SI* wasn't yet showing bottom-line improvement.

Before he could answer, Clare Luce, from the other end of the table, spoke up.

"I'll tell you what the trouble is," she said. "It's trying to be all things to all people—fashion, cooking, outdoors—it's a mélange."

Harry Luce usually invited his wife's dissent, but on this occasion he glared at her across the length of the table. She continued anyway.

"You gentlemen must realize that it is the wife who makes the financial decisions in the household. And what she wants is Charles Goren's bridge column. And you'd best give it to her."

Perhaps Luce was glaring at Clare because her view was already one of the "mélange" of different viewpoints that *SI* was trying to satisfy. She had argued that the bridge expert Charles Goren should have a weekly column, and the department was installed. Luce, convinced that he needed to appeal to female readers, had organized a monthly lunch with four prominent women (they received $500 a month as a consulting fee) to give him ideas about how the magazine could better appeal to women. The Bonnie Prudden series—a recurring column of pictorial exercise instruction—would come from this klatch, which was led by Laura Z. Hobson, author of *Gentleman's Agreement*.

On January 23, 1958, Laguerre had lunch with Hobson, sending a report to Luce that afternoon ("She claimed a woman's right to exaggerate on occasions, which I would be the last to deny . . ."). He closed the letter by repeating his suggestion "that we ought to have a first class woman journalist on the staff."

Later that year, on August 11, 1958, Clare Luce made the cover of *SI* for her "further adventures in The Heaven Below," the second piece she wrote for the magazine about skin diving. The joke around the office that fall was that if any readers wrote in saying they enjoyed Mrs. Luce's article, a form letter would be sent announcing that their subscriptions were being terminated: "You're not our kind of reader." When she met Laguerre at a dinner party one night, the first thing she said after the introduction was, "Ah, yes, *Sports Illustrated*. The only good things in it are Charles Goren on bridge, which I suggested, and my articles on skin diving." Laguerre smiled gamely, held his tongue, and took another deep drink.

• • •

The first sign of the magazine speaking with consistent vision about spectator sports came in the spring of 1958. In the baseball preview issue, Roy Terrell took a studied, sanguine tone about the move of the Brooklyn Dodgers and New York Giants to Los Angeles and San Francisco. "The national pastime has finally become national in scope as well as name," he wrote, adding that "most of the tears which flowed into Gowanus Canal and temporarily threatened commerce on the Harlem River actually came from New York baseball writers who suddenly found themselves on the verge of becoming statistics in the recession." This was in stark contrast to the apocalyptic musings of Tibby, who wrote about the moves extensively in Events & Discoveries. The same issue featured a "State of the Game" essay from Creamer, forecasting heightened popularity for the sport and dismissing the shibboleths about its demise.

But page flow was still a problem. Devoting a color section in the front of the book to Spectacle—which couldn't possibly be topical because of the long lead time that color required—and the mass of unrelated photos in Wonderful World only served to prohibit the magazine from covering news in a coherent, striking visual fashion. The structure also hampered flexibility. After Arnold Palmer's rousing Masters win in '58, the story received just five paragraphs and three pictures in a condensed News of the Week section that ran with the Baseball Preview. The Masters, in fact, only shared the front page of that abbreviated section with, among other items, news of the Oxford-Cambridge boat race.

There seemed little urgency, in those years, to cover late-breaking stories. One of the reasons Palmer's Masters win got such short shrift is that for Herbert Warren Wind, writing on deadline remained a major ordeal. A year later, Gwilym Brown wrote the news story on Art Wall's Augusta victory, with Wind weighing in a week later. "We'd always have to give him a week off, because he'd come back from a tournament with a runny nose, a cold, just a disaster," remembered James. In his cramped, smoke-filled offices at *SI*, Wind would dictate his stories to secretaries. Barbara La Fontaine, for one, grew to dread the hours in Wind's hot, non-air-conditioned office, where she more than once nearly fainted from the heat and smoke.

Football coverage became more thorough, though it too was plagued by annoying inconsistencies. After the death of Herman Hickman, Laguerre argued that *SI* should create its own "expert" in college football (just as it had done with Maule in the pros), rather than hiring another celebrity author who would merely require more collaboration and rewriting work. But James was convinced that the celebrity angle helped the magazine's profile and single-copy sales, so Red Grange—a man who had last been in organized football as the coach of the Bears in 1938—was called in to make college predictions. After a strong year as the lead college football writer in '58, Terrell had to step aside for Grange to write the bowl previews.

In 1959, James had staff writer Alfred Wright, an elegant Yalie and globetrotting husband of Joan Fontaine, covering college football. Wright showed up in the second quarter of a Notre Dame game in South Bend one day that season and ran into Robert H. Boyle, who had moved to the company's Chicago bureau and was reporting the game for *Time*. While Boyle focused on the field, Wright seemed bored.

"I think Potter Stewart is going to become the next Republican presidential candidate," said Wright during a Notre Dame drive late in the first half.

"Why is that, Al?" asked Boyle, still watching the game intently through his binoculars.

"Bones hasn't had a president since William Howard Taft. It's bloody well time."

At the half, Wright turned to Boyle and said, "I find this game rather boring. Would you like to cover it for *SI* as well?"

"I can't, Al, I'm here for *Time*," explained Boyle.

"Oh, too bad," said Wright pleasantly, collecting his things. Before leaving he nudged Boyle and said, "Bob, as far as I'm concerned, college football ends at New Haven, and it doesn't pick up again until Palo Alto." That pretty well crystallized the magazine's view of college football in the '50s, although Terrell had tried to break through the East Coast bias.

The first issue of 1959 showed that the magazine was at least moving toward an understanding of the importance of pro football. The lead news story was Maule's account of the 1958 National Football League championship game, accompanied by the dramatic photographs of Hy Peskin and Arthur Daley. Decades later, the Baltimore Colts' 23–17 overtime victory over the New York Giants would be seen as the delineation between pro football past and future, and James Michener would muse that "the symbiotic relationship between pro football and television is awesome; it really is made by the Gods." Terrell had known this for much of the '50s, and throughout the early years of the magazine, he and Maule were in the forefront of those pushing for more pro football coverage. To its credit, *SI* recognized the significance of the '58 title game instantly. "Never has there been a game like this one," Maule wrote in his lead. In his usual dry, spare fashion, he recounted the key elements of the game, the way the "pressure and all of the frenzy of an entire season of play was concentrated on the misty football field at Yankee Stadium."

The headline for the story originally read "The Greatest Football Game Ever Played," but when Laguerre saw the page proof, he changed it. He wasn't one for myriad grammar rules, but in little more than two years in America, he'd grown weary of the media's indiscriminate use of the word "great." So the main headline became "The Best Football Game Ever Played" (although the jump subheads, on the second spread and the back of the book where the story ended, both slipped through as "Greatest

Game"). The sequence of photos in the layout was odd; Peskin's now-classic end zone photograph of Alan Ameche, sprawled in the end zone as the crowd poured onto the field, ran two columns wide with the story's conclusion, in the back of the magazine on page 60.

After the story had been written and edited, as the core staff was preparing to leave the building, Roy Terrell sidled up to Maule and said, "You know, Tex, that was a marvelous football game. But I know it wasn't the best football game ever played, and you know it. The best football game ever played was the 1940 A&M–Texas game."

For once, Maule didn't argue.

• • •

Later in 1959, Luce chose Hedley Donovan, editor of *Fortune,* to be his eventual successor. When Donovan left his post at *Fortune* that September, it was to work under Luce and learn journalism at the highest levels. Early in what he would characterize as his tenure as "Apprentice Luce," Donovan proposed that he spend a couple months tracking *SI,* a magazine whose prospects he was much more skeptical about than his boss. "My own view was that the magazine was not as good editorially as Luce thought," he wrote, "and that I was a more natural reader of *SI* than he was and probably a better judge of ways it might be improved."

In Donovan's memoirs, he remembered James as "a genial man with picture sense and good newsdesk reflexes—and a cheerfully uncritical view of his magazine. The magazine was publishing some first-class photography and reporting, but this was intermingled with many a journalistic embarrassment. There were mystifying headlines, odd typographical stresses, banal pictures given too much space, outbreaks of cliché, the cutesies, the tasteless."

In an early 1960 memo to Luce, Donovan weighed in with his tempered view: "The estimated financial results [a $2.3 million loss in 1959] strike me as approximately just. I find considerable encouragement in the fact that *SI,* with all its painful shortcomings, can even come as close as it does to making money. But let's not say to the editors of *SI,* 'How can *SI* be made even better?' That isn't really the situation. This is not a very good magazine."

Donovan wasn't the only one reaching that conclusion. James's effervescent personality had worn thin with many of his subordinates. While his enthusiasm was infectious, his lack of empathy and vision had become a problem. "Sid was a tremendous second-guesser," said photo editor Gerry Astor. "'Why didn't you do this? Why didn't you do that?' And,

Jesus, if an airplane was delayed, he would scream at me, 'Why did you use that airline?'"

"I liked James okay," said Roy Terrell. "I just had this—it's nothing to be proud of, but I'm Scots-Irish, and a marine—and I had a certain contempt for people who couldn't do things right. So I had that feeling for Sid always. He's a good old guy, but he's just blundering, and flopping around and doing the wrong things." Jack Olsen, the workhorse *Time* writer who came to *SI* in '59, concurred, seeing James as "all image, all surface. He's a nice enough guy, big laugh, big handshake, but I never saw a speck of editorial talent and he brought in three or four people that were equally talented and caused a lot of trouble in the early days."

He might have been speaking of Tibby, who by 1958 had acquired a half-dozen writers working full-time to help him compile the weekly turgid ramblings of Events & Discoveries, which he would inevitably shape to fit his own arch style. "The typical headline for every item was always 'Now in November,'" recalled Bill Leggett, one of the reporters detached on the thankless detail. "'The leaves have turned gold and Yale is playing Harvard.' It was absolute bullshit, pumped out every week. Out of all the copy that was produced, there would probably be seven items, all of which ended up reading like 'Now in November.' And Jack had no news sense whatsoever. We'd start out every week with this huge meeting of maybe 14 people to get this goddamn section going. It never closed on time. And Laguerre hated it. Because when the writers would go to the Three Gs, they would start to say something and you could just see him cringe: 'I don't want to hear about it!'"

Tibby's writing in E&D occasionally lapsed into the genuinely bizarre. The second item in the January 6, 1958, issue—"Sport in Space"—noted that as the Atlas rocket was circling overhead, a Florida sunbather rose from his chaise longue to cheer the rocket on: "Whether or not this vocative body-English contributed materially to the first successful flight of the Air Force Atlas may never be known, but, in a time of pedagogical argument over the relative values of science and sport, it offers a healthy suggestion of interdependence. The lion's share of responsibility for the world's future may now rest with those once dismissed with a snort as greasy-grinds, but the competitive spirit summoned up by a nation's cheerleaders still packs a propulsive wallop as potent as that of any lab-distilled fuel."

Laguerre, unhappy and restless with a wait that was taking him into his fourth year as assistant managing editor, wrote Luce a long, stern letter early in 1960. He had grown restless with James's incessant glad-handing, casual lack of focus, and blithe disregard for the specifics of magazine-making. "He said he wanted out if he wasn't going to be given this job," said Leggett. "Laguerre was frustrated because he was doing the right thing but it wasn't getting him anyplace. *SI* still wasn't making money and it didn't look like it would ever turn the corner."

After the 1960 Olympics in Squaw Valley, Laguerre grew even more impatient. At a supper in Manhattan one night, with Nathalie and *SI* photographer Jerry Cooke, he seemed to be nearing a decision.

"I've been waiting in the wings for four years," he told Cooke. "If I'm not the managing editor by Rome [the site for that summer's Olympics], I think we'll just go home to Europe."

Finally, in March 1960, Laguerre walked into Dick Johnston's office and closed the door. The simple act alone communicated the gravity of the visit.

"Look, I'm going up to talk to Luce, and tell him I think it's time for a change. I wanted to find out if you're with me or against me."

Johnston and Laguerre were never close friends. Their styles were diametric opposites: Laguerre lived to be with the boys and remained loyal to Nathalie; Johnston lived to be with the women, and the conspiratorial pleasure he took in talking with most any female puzzled the man's man Laguerre. But at the core, the two men respected each other.

"It's time," agreed Johnston. "I'm with you."

And that was it. Laguerre went up to Luce's office and was unusually blunt, even for him. "If you're going to make me managing editor," he told his boss, "let's do it."

Luce, who anguished over top-editing changes, asked for a few days to figure out how to best make the move. Publisher Art Murphy, who had succeeded Harry Phillips just a year earlier, made it easy on Luce, offering to move out of the publisher's job and suggesting that it would be the perfect place to install Sid James.

In the meantime, Jack Olsen confided in Johnston that he was getting ready to go back to *Time*, having had his fill of James's leadership. "I've had it with this shit," said Olsen over drinks. "This guy doesn't know dick about writing or anything else—he's a lightweight little shit who surrounds himself with people like Ezra Bowen, and they're all full of shit. These guys are in the ascendancy."

Johnston said, "Jack—*do not go*. Do—not—go."

The next week, Luce invited Laguerre to dinner on the 47th floor, and formally offered him the job. Donovan recalled Luce emerging from the lunch in which he promoted Laguerre as "somewhat shaken. After he offered Laguerre the job, and André accepted, all of which took five minutes, neither of them, Harry told me later, seemed to have anything more to say—an unprecedented vacuum at the Luce lunch table."

Recalling the transition decades later, James seemed blissfully unaware of the magazine's calamitous first years. "The only thing I know was that our circulation went up, up, up, up; it never went down," he said. "It never went down. It never took a dip! Nor did our revenue, even our advertising revenue. And this notion that we were going bankrupt was just a lot of nonsense. Hell, we had a great cash flow."

While James surely had faults as a managing editor, his devotion to the magazine was complete, and he was ever vigilant in guarding the church-state split between editorial and advertising. Further, his personal enthusiasm and unstinting determination—nearly heroic in its imperviousness to outside criticism—created an environment in which *SI* could survive. That it would prosper later without him was clear. What was also clear is that the magazine might not have survived the decade if it weren't for the sheer force and volume of James's indefatigable optimism.

But now, in April 1960, André Laguerre was taking over. *Sports Illustrated* had found its leader; now it would find itself.

# CHAPTER 7

# "HEAVY WATER"

## 1960 was a watershed year

for American sports. The legend of Arnold Palmer was solidified with his stirring U.S. Open charge at Cherry Hills. At the Summer Olympics in Rome, America got its first glimpse of a light-heavyweight named Cassius Clay. On the 23rd ballot, the National Football League elected an obscure new commissioner named Pete Rozelle. The year brought the death of NBC's Friday night fights and the birth of Lamar Hunt's American Football League, which envisioned a country, and television market, big enough to handle eight more professional football teams. And on September 17, an ABC television producer named Roone Arledge supervised his first live telecast, of the Alabama-Georgia college football game. With the theatrical elements that Arledge brought to the telecast—field-level microphones, roving cameras, close-ups not only of action on the field but coaches, fans, and cheerleaders off it—televised sports would enter into the modern era.

*Sports Illustrated* was crossing a threshold, as well. In addition to naming a new managing editor and publisher, the magazine closed its first "fast color" cover, a shot of Jim Beatty winning the 5,000 meters at the Olympic trials on a Friday, slightly more than 48 hours before the July 11 issue closed. In its first major departure from its original "class magazine" strategy, *SI* dropped its basic subscription price from $7.50 a year to $6.75, and circulation neared the 1,000,000 mark. *SI*'s profile was increasing: John F. Kennedy was spotted at the Los Angeles Airport en route to the Democratic National Convention with an issue of *SI* under his arm. And shortly after his election, Kennedy put together some notes— with the help of Laguerre cohort Joe David Brown—on "The Soft American," urging the population to face the Red menace by getting in shape.

In February 1960, *SI* had become the first magazine to move into the gleaming new Time & Life Building, on 50th Street and 6th Avenue. The editorial staff had the 20th floor to itself, figuratively and literally a level above the business division, on 19. The skyscraper had three interior elevator banks, providing a maximum number of office window views around the perimeter of the fat, rectangular floorplan. It also had the luxury of air conditioning, an amenity that the old Time & Life Building lacked.

After waiting four years to take control of *Sports Illustrated*, André Laguerre wasted no time in putting his mark on the magazine. There were no large staff meetings, no big speeches, none of the ostentatious inspirational tactics that had been such a part of James's repertoire. Instead, he calmly set about making a series of long overdue changes.

His promotion wasn't announced until the May 2 issue, but *SI*'s transformation began immediately after Luce gave him the job. With the April 18 issue, Scoreboard—the dry recap of results from the previous week that had traditionally followed the contents page—was moved to the back of the book, shortened and renamed For the Record. In the rapidly growing sports pages around the country, national results were being reported much more thoroughly anyway, so Scoreboard had outgrown much of its early usefulness. The name change was necessary because in the same issue, *SI* debuted Scorecard, a two-page notebook of harder-edged opinion and observation that replaced the haughty ramblings of Events & Discoveries. Rather than Tibby riding herd on seven different writers, Laguerre assigned a single senior writer to coordinate the column, and write most of its items (encouraging occasional submissions from other staff members). Scorecard was placed in the front of the book, where the title made thematic sense as an opening section. With the elimination of the picture feature Pat on the Back, the final department in the magazine was the letters section, The 19th Hole.

Laguerre's biggest organizational change was a shuffling of senior editors' responsibilities. Instead of assigning editors to oversee different areas of the magazine, he reorganized them by sports. One senior editor was expected to know baseball, another was assigned college football, another was given skiing and the Winter Olympics. Laguerre saw specialization increasing in sports, and wanted his senior editors to bring more expertise to the copy they handled.

A month after taking over, Laguerre sent the staff a typically terse and carefully worded one-sentence memo that read: "Will editors and writers please make a point of not quitting work without saying 'good night' to Dick Johnston or myself—preferably Johnston." The note also underscored the clear distinction that Laguerre was making between his assistant managing editors, placing Johnston as his first lieutenant. While Laguerre might change a line or two of copy in his final Monday morning readout, Johnston would for the most part be the final authority on editing —what would be referred to within the office as "the blue pencil"— reflecting his status as the best line editor at the magazine. Conversely, Jack Tibby's role was reduced, with Laguerre giving him a variety of administrative chores and installing him as the liaison to new publisher Sid James and the business side.

Laguerre also relieved Jerry Snyder of his duties as art director, replacing him with a young graphic artist from *Life* named Dick Gangel. In Gangel, *SI* would find the pefect design interpreter for Laguerre's editorial vision. Snyder had embodied the essence of old-school design sensibilities; his cover choices were static reveries, almost musty in their lack of force or drama. By contrast, the ruddy-faced, rosy-cheeked Gangel was an elegant visionary, with experience at commercial art studios and a brief tour at *Esquire* magazine. He loathed the artistic gimmickry of mainstream American magazine design, having been raised on a more sophisticated European view. A pilot in World War II, Gangel had an air of toughness and discipline rarely seen in an art director. He had little patience for theories of typography and space, yet possessed a coherent vision of how design elements could translate a journalistic idea. "Gangel was a modernist," said Creamer. "He just knew what was au courant, and he started designing the magazine that way."

Gangel walked into the art department on his first day, introduced himself to assistants Harvey Grut and Marty Nathan, and announced that his first priority was to find a new cover logo, to replace the stale, nearly antique look of *SI*'s logotype, largely unchanged since its inception. He quickly did away with the cluttered, superfluous elements in *SI*'s internal design as well.

The redesign was put on hold in August, as *SI* prepared for the Summer Olympic Games in Rome, to which Laguerre devoted an unprecedented amount of space. The August 15 Olympic preview included eight pages of color, and eight pages of charts sizing up the medal prospects for every event. The light-heavyweight division in boxing included the note: "Teen-age Cassius Clay, who has been called another Patterson, was the only American to score a knockout in the Olympic trials. The chances are he will have more trouble against the Europeans, some of whom have had as many as 200 fights." When the Games started, *SI* devoted 43 pages over three issues to cover the event more completely than ever before. The lead writers for *SI*'s coverage were Jack Olsen and Tex Maule, who returned from Rome invigorated and inspired. (They'd both picked up copies of *Lady Chatterley's Lover*—still hard to find in America—in an Italian bookstore and, as Maule would remark later, were suitably impressed: "After that, we can write anything!") Rome marked the beginning of a playful, enduring friendship between the two men, who had a running bet over who could publish the most books. In Maule's 1961 fiction debut, a football novel for teens called *The Rookie*, a young quarterback is duped into a damaging interview by a cagey writer named "Jack Oslen."

• • •

In September, Laguerre returned his attention to the evolution of the magazine. In a memo to Luce, he argued that the protracted discussion about the magazine's direction and focus needed to stop. He was weary of Luce and Larsen's reluctance for *SI* to demonstrate a hard-sports bent, "as if it were somehow desirable to conceal the fact that we are a magazine about sport in the first place." He asked Luce for his support in cutting back on the general departments—cooking, fashion, travel, etc.—so that he could beef up the magazine's news focus:

> There have been times when our general material has not been general enough, yes, but to increase the quota would be to out-general ourselves; the result might or might not be a successful magazine, but it would not be a sport magazine. Should there, on the contrary, be more "hard sport" and less of the other? Many readers and many of our staff would say yes. They resent it when they think we are overloaded with fashion or the recreations of the wealthy. They share in the sport mystique; some of them regard sport as an art form, and most of them as more than recreation; there may be some immaturity in their attitude, but these people have the flame which makes any journalistic enterprise interesting, and with which we tamper at our peril.

While Luce was restrained in his reaction to the memo, Hedley Donovan was in Laguerre's corner, writing later that, "Andre's kind of mind was just what was needed to cut through some of the softness and sloppiness in the magazine, but beyond that, he had a broad journalistic imagination and an especially perceptive view of the way TV (whatever it might do to other publications) was going to help *SI*."

Television was changing the rules of magazine journalism, especially for mass-circulation weeklies. Andrew Heiskell, who in 1960 was promoted from publisher at *Life* to chairman of the board of the company, left with pangs of worry over his old magazine. Heiskell sensed that much of the power of *Life*'s photojournalism was being muted by the moving pictures on the nightly news. Though the impact on *Life*'s bottom line hadn't been felt yet, it would be shortly.

But Laguerre—who just four years earlier had been so uncertain of the new technology that he pulled Walter Bingham aside and sheepishly asked him for a recommendation of what kind of American television he should buy—sensed a different set of forces at work in the field of sports. Newsstand sales had been unusually high in the weeks after both the Winter and Summer Olympic Games, and had also enjoyed similar spikes after the previous two National Football League championship games. That seemed to argue against the conventional wisdom that televising an event diminished interest afterward. In time, it became clear that national television coverage actually enhanced the appeal of *Sports Illustrated*, creating a desire among readers to learn more about what they had watched. And that realization, subtly but profoundly, would shape Laguerre's two great technical innovations at *Sports Illustrated*: the redesign he engineered in the fall of 1960 with Gangel, and his push toward "fast color," the obsession that would occupy him through the rest of the decade.

The long-overdue redesign addressed many of the magazine's graphic—and editorial—weaknesses. Under James, *SI* often lacked a clearly marked news opener and grouped other features (Events & Discoveries, Spectacle) right behind the lead item. This tricky coordination of elements was further hampered by Snyder's jumbled design. Laguerre and Gangel quickly organized a structure that separated the magazine into these components:

- *The news leads*, three or four news stories, led off the week's coverage, with the lead story always running at least four pages. Followed by news stories of lesser significance, these pieces moved toward the middle of the magazine.
- *The "feature well,"* the center area of the magazine, generally included three less time-intensive stories, which closed earlier than the news stories. These could be profiles, previews, or illustrative or pictorial portfolios, often running past the center of the magazine. (On most magazines, the feature well referred to all nondepartment pieces, but at *SI* the term was used more specifically.)
- *The columns*, as they were called internally, or departments, as they were listed on the contents page, came next. These were shorter stories, about specific sports, usually with a hard-news edge. With the departments, Laguerre had the luxury of making news judg-

ments through both space allotment and positioning. The big college football game of the week could play in the front, as a news lead, while a significant, but less important game, or a profile of a lesser-known star, could lead off the college football department, with the week's national wrap-up, the traditional Football's Week, folded in behind that lead story.

• *The bonus piece*, SI's showcase for its most literate and accomplished writing, anchored the back of the magazine. Laguerre viewed this last piece as crucial. The bonus piece, 52 weeks a year, would provide a longer, literary-minded takeout on some person in or aspect of the sports world, often running between 6,000 and 8,000 words, sometimes longer.

Bracketing the stories would be the contents, the Letter from the Publisher, and Scorecard in the front of the book, and For the Record, Faces in the Crowd, and The 19th Hole in the back. There was also space at either end for "advance text" or "regional text," essays on various aspects of sport ("Yesterday," "First Person") that were carried only in regional or zoned editions created by SI's ad staff for upscale and niche advertisers.

Putting Scorecard in the front of the book and eliminating Spectacle set the stage for the design changes that followed. With the October 17 issue, a new, more modern logotype appeared on the cover, a product of Gangel's tinkering. A graceful italic sans-serif typeface, much lighter than its predecessor, began appearing on captions and department folios in December. And the year-end issue brought the first glimpse of the new body copy typeface, with Gangel discarding the knobby Bookman font of the '50s for a smoother, more sophisticated Times New Roman. Between the cleaner look and more logical organization, SI was finally able to demonstrate a sense of order within its pages.

"Up until that redesign, I could no more tell you where things appeared in the magazine, or why—nor could anybody else," said Terrell. "There wasn't any consistency. I just knew it wasn't very attractive sometimes, was kind of confusing sometimes. But I probably never could have come up with a concept like André and Dick did."

Besides the new cover design, the October 17, 1960, issue featured another significant arrival. Against some of the best sports photographers in the world, a 17-year-old delicatessen delivery boy named Neil Leifer scored a coup, getting the single "fast" color shot that SI ran of the World

Series, as well as another black-and-white shot on the second spread. Photo editor Gerry Astor had been nervous about using Leifer, knowing he was underage. "In the back of my mind was, what happens if he drops the camera on somebody? What is going to be the insurance problem for this magazine when it comes out we're using child labor in something like this?"

Leifer's improbable ascension was a tribute to hard work. Astor had met the pushy, precocious kid while he was delivering sandwiches for his uncle from the Stage Door deli (taking his tips in rolls of film). Leifer had learned the craft of photography, from the age of 12, at the Henry Street Settlement, which catered to activities for the heavily Russian and Polish populations in the Brooklyn area. (Two other *SI* shooters, John Iacono and Manny Millan, came out of the same program.)

Leifer became a star on a talented staff that embraced Laguerre's push for more and faster color. "He seemed to listen to us more," photographer John Zimmerman said of Laguerre. "You could go into André's office and talk to him about stories and things. He loved horse racing, so he would say, 'Gee, I like this idea,' and he would tell you what he'd like to see, and you'd tell him what the problems were and what compromises you'd have to make. He'd really *understand*, and expect to see what you told him he could get, not something that he expected that was impossible."

Zimmerman spent much of his career redefining what was possible, becoming the first photographer to put a camera inside the goal at a National Hockey League game. After Zimmerman brought up the idea, Astor made a request to the New York Rangers' icekeeper, who looked in the NHL rulebook and found nothing expressly prohibiting it. A remote wire was buried two inches below the ice surface and frozen over prior to the game at Madison Square Garden, running from the camera to Zimmerman's seat behind the goal. That portfolio, "A Breathless View from the Hottest Spot on the Ice," ran in the January 15, 1962, issue, and was followed three weeks later by "The Ubiquitous Hands of Mr. C," the first action photography from behind a glass backboard at an National Basketball Association game, with eight pages of Wilt Chamberlain in action against the Los Angeles Lakers. It closed with a classic photograph that filled up both pages of the spread (a "double-truck" in magazine parlance) of Chamberlain smiling while dunking.

There were still major technological hurdles, mostly centered on light for indoor events. The most common film at the time, Kodachrome, had an ASA rating of 10 (the weekend photographer of today would typically use nothing less than 100), meaning that much of the light for pictures had to be manufactured, a costly, cumbersome procedure requiring mammoth strobe lights. "We had eight packs in four corners of Madison Square Garden," said Zimmerman. "That's 32 packs, and they weighed 80 pounds apiece. Plus the converter you had to have for them, which was another 80 pounds, so you've got 36 times 80 pounds. It used to take at least a day, with two guys or three guys scrambling around working with electricians, because you didn't have enough power by plugging into any accessible outlet. You had to have 50-amp-lines running to the equipment."

The flash of the strobes was accompanied by a disconcerting popping noise, more like an amplified crunch, that some found distracting. Few athletes complained about the lights (although Pancho Gonzalez wouldn't allow their use for indoor matches on the pro tennis tour of the early '60s), but television's representatives hated it, and started fighting for exclusion of strobes, which often burned out the frame of the very moment of action they most wanted to get on instant replay.

"When they became aware of the problem, that's when they really tried to put the kibosh on it," said Zimmerman. "I must say, if I were a TV producer or a network president, I would agree with them."

Ever cognizant of the emergence of television, Laguerre pushed to make SI's coverage more topical. In an era of brinksmanship, he was making an art form out of the late close, catching an event on a Sunday night or even, improbably, a Monday, holding a scant few pages in the front of the book open until the last conceivable moment. It was an area of journalism that was only being explored at the mass weeklies, and Laguerre and his crew were charting its outer limits.

The breakthrough came March 13, 1961, in Miami, with Gilbert Rogin's story on the third Floyd Patterson–Ingemar Johannsen fight. It would be the first Monday night event to make it in the same week's magazine, with Patterson knocking out Johanssen in a sloppy six-round fight. Creamer would recall that the issue was "closed in a photographer's shop in Miami and sent directly to the printer in Chicago, as we didn't have time in those more primitive days to follow normal communication paths. Laguerre and Johnston and Gerry Astor looking at the photos being developed in the photo shop. Rogin sitting sideways in a tiny cubicle between the front of the store and the lab area in the back, with people constantly passing back and forth right behind him, writing the story page by page and handing each page to me as he finished. I'd go over it, catch a typo or two, hand it to Johnston, who'd make only the most minor changes and hand it to Laguerre for a quick read before we sent the stuff on to Chicago by the telex we'd had installed. The story was almost literally perfect, written to fit in an immense hurry in inadequate space in a cacophonous room. We sent photos and story on to Chicago, and 36 hours later, when the train Margaret and I were returning to New York on stopped in Washington for a few minutes, I found the magazine on the newsstand, complete with story. It seemed magical, and it was such a good story."

The one drawback was that the photographs were still in black and white. Printing "fast" color was prohibitively expensive (with overtime charges running up to a quarter of a million dollars per page to process a color photograph shot 36 hours before the magazine closed) and still time consuming, relative to black and white. Sitting with Gangel one night after a close, Laguerre shook his head and said, "My good man, we just have to find a way to do this faster."

● ● ●

While a new formality was observed around the office, both morale and productivity improved. "Laguerre said to me once that the important thing was that we have fun," remembered Robert Creamer. "His idea of the job was something you worked at during the morning, and you went out and you had a few drinks at lunchtime, and you talked about it. And after work, you'd stop to have a drink or two and talk about it. And maybe at dinner you might have somebody there who was in sports. And on weekends, Laguerre didn't turn it off and on—it was part of his life, a very European attitude."

Laguerre's office became the focal point for all of the work at the magazine; his liaison to the rest of the staff was his omnicompetent secretary Ann Callahan, who began working for him as a temp out of the Time Inc. secretarial pool in 1956. A pretty brunette with an incandescent smile, Callahan was also a student of human nature, especially when it came to Laguerre. On Monday mornings, when he was doing the final readout on pages, she would summon writers and editors for consultations, with a short, bright phone call: "Come down, please." Occasionally, she'd gently redirect staffers intent on asking for raises or airing complaints, counseling, "Today's not a good day." What made Callahan extraordinarily valuable was that, in an environment full of journalists who loved to gossip (which is to say, journalists), she was reliably discreet. Waiting at Callahan's desk to see Laguerre one December day, Walter Bingham asked casually where the *SI* Christmas party was being held that year. "I'm sorry, I can't say," Callahan replied. A flustered Bingham explained, "Ann—I . . . I don't even *want* to know. I'm just trying to make conversation."

Lunches were long, usually held down at Laguerre's "local" of choice, the Three Gs. Every day at lunch ("He'd just drink, but we'd try to sneak in a bowl of minestrone," said one writer), every evening after work, and most Sunday nights, while waiting to put the magazine to bed, Laguerre would hold forth at the Gs. One of Laguerre's constant companions was the prolific veteran writer Morrie Werner. The old-timer had been hired because of his proud journalistic legacy (he'd written dozens of books, including definitive biographies of both Brigham Young and P.T. Barnum) and because, simply, Laguerre felt his presence boosted morale. Like Laguerre, Werner was conversant in a breathtaking array of topics, from the latest important novel or political movement in Europe to the fifth race at Belmont Park or the relative merits of blended scotches. At lunch, they'd drink and talk and drink some more, ribbing one another mercilessly, out of affection as much as competition. And after work they would return, for another round or four, until the time came for Laguerre's limo driver to take him home for dinner.

In the weeks of constant but purposeful change that marked the fall of 1960, Laguerre also sent another memo, this one a relatively voluminous three-paragraph effort, addressed to the staff writers:

1) During the last couple of weeks I have been aware of a "let-down" psychology in some areas. Some slipshod stories, marked by repetition and tired writing, have been turned in. They simply make for more work by yourselves and the editors. Some other stories have plainly not been thought out in advance. Please understand there is no law against thinking by writers.
2) [Text editor] Percy Knauth is not getting a flow of suggestions for what we call the bonus, or long text, piece. This is a pity. Recently, the very best long text pieces have more than once been contributed by staffers (Olsen and Terrell, for instance). I should think you would be anxious to get your name over a long story like this, and this particularly applies to writers who are not assigned a regular beat. Please do something about it.
3) Writers, and especially departmental writers, should consider it a duty to make suggestions [for Scorecard]. I have never been in a place of refreshment with more than two of our writers without being witness to (and occasionally participant in) an argument. Please pass some of this contentiousness on to Mr. Werner.

While Laguerre's rebukes were pointed, he was in truth beginning to assemble his sort of staff, one with a blend of experienced, knowledgeable editors and writers (like the veteran workhorse Olsen, who happily stayed after Laguerre's promotion) and young, talented staffers who could also move smoothly between writing and editing duties.

While his staffers were developing a rich affection and healthy respect for Laguerre, freelancers such as George Plimpton, who knew him more casually, were often awestruck by his impassive manner. Plimpton used to refer to Laguerre as "Heavy Water," the isotope used to construct hydrogen bombs. But he flourished under Laguerre, finding a sponsor for his interest in participatory journalism. Plimpton had been a fan of the *New York Daily News* sports columnist Paul Gallico, who would steep himself in the tradition of the game, finding it unseemly for a writer to criticize a player for striking out if he had never seen a major league curveball seem to dive toward his knees at the last possible instant. Plimpton envisioned a slightly different reason for his participation. He wasn't a sportswriter by trade, only an intensely curious fan. His primary goal was to relate to the average reader *what it felt like* to step in against the best in the world. The baseball preview issue of 1961 brought a bonus piece that would mark the start of Plimpton's participatory tradition with *SI*. "Dream of Glory on the Mound" was a 1,000-line piece, the first of his forays onto the field of major league play. The episode turned into an Everyman's dispatch from, as Plimpton's friend Ernest Hemingway would put it, "the dark side of the moon of Walter Mitty." At a post-season All-Star game in Yankee Stadium in the fall of 1960, *SI* gained clearance for Plimpton to pitch to the entire National and American League lineup. To coerce the two sides into playing along with the journalist, *SI* posted a $500 prize to be presented to the side that produced the most hits. Introduced by the Yankees public address announcer as "George Prufrock of *Sports Illustrated*," Plimpton improbably retired three of the first four N.L. all-stars he faced. But a 23-pitch confrontation against Ernie Banks (there were no umpires calling balls and strikes, so hitters could wait for a pitch they liked) sapped his energy. Plimpton's story ran to widespread acclaim and even imitation. In the June 24, 1961, issue of *The New Yorker*, Roger Angell wrote a send-up of the piece, in which the magazine *Sports Illusory* paid $1,000 to a scrub pitcher with literary aspirations to spend a day on the staff of the magazine. The success of the book led to Plimpton's wildly successful participatory football book *Paper Lion*, which had its genesis as an *SI* bonus piece three years later.

The end of the summer of 1961 saw two of the best, and most widely quoted, bonuses in the magazine's history. The first one, "This Is Cricket," ran August 28, a product of Roy Terrell being freed from beat reporting to write fewer, but longer, stories. It wasn't the first time *SI* had taken on the subject; in early 1955, James had coaxed Paul Gallico out of his self-imposed sportswriting retirement to write about cricket, but his effort for *SI* seemed strained and superficial. Terrell's take, by contrast, was much more clinical, although informed by a subtle wit. Early in the piece he suggested that "[t]he first thing an American should do is accept the fact that a great deal of what his countrymen have written about cricket is true. In this way he can subdue his mirth early and concentrate on technique." By absorbing not just the sport's rules but also its conventions, Terrell was able to compare and contrast it smartly with baseball. The piece was an example of *SI* at its anthropological best, widening the horizons of its readers, striving toward a greater understanding where other magazines might be satisfied with simple ridicule. Further examples came from Olsen, whose memorable bonus on English soccer, "Six Dreary Days, Then Saturday," ran in 1963.

Less than a month after Terrell's piece on cricket, *SI* published Gil Rogin's "12 Days Before the Mast." Rogin's game stories and profiles often displayed an excessive reliance on long columns of unremitting quotation. But writing in the first person, he could use many of the same techniques that would shortly earn him praise as one of the best short fiction writers of his generation. He had volunteered for a Plimptonesque assignment, as a crewmember in a long-distance yachting race. Marvelously illustrated by Gangel favorite Marc Simont—the sketch of Rogin on the opening spread made him look like a brooding, childish Nixonian caricature—the piece began:

> The ruts and tracks of life are made early, and mine never led to sea, so I don't know what others lose and find there. . . . What can you say about the sea? "High interiors and kelpy bottoms"? Chekhov said that you can say nothing significant about the sea except that it is big. But the sea is also—out of sight of land and off maps—perfectly round. Sailors call it the round locker. Traveling, one remains in its center as though fixed with a pin. . . .
>
> "Niner. Niner," we cried as the Kenyon, the nautical speed indicator, showed nine knots. I was known as Toots Kenyon, ludicrously got up in flannel pajama bottoms beneath Bermudas as though dressed for a roller derby—all my other clothes were soaked—for my feet were always in front of the Kenyon, that round idol.

Later in his life, working as an editor, Rogin was heard to ask about a story, "Is this funny?—I don't have a sense of humor." But "12 Days" showed a gift for self-effacement, with Rogin poking fun at the foibles of the distinctly unadaptable modern urban animal.

The rest of 1961 included several breakthroughs: Jim Murray, in one of his last pieces for the magazine, wrote an affecting travel diary about life on the road with the Los Angeles Lakers ("A Trip for Ten Tall Men"). Gangel began using an eclectic blend of modern artists, less literal than anything *SI* had featured before, including the wry French painter André François, who executed an affecting, impressionistic portfolio on hockey. Jack Olsen documented "The Pool Hustlers" in the same year that Paul Newman's *The Hustler* was released. And in a story that made headlines in newspapers across the country, Ray Cave helped break open the latest point-shaving scandal in college basketball, at St. Joseph's University ("Portrait of a Fixer," May 8).

In little more than a year, Laguerre had redesigned the magazine, beefed up its news coverage, established an oasis for literate feature journalism, and provided a forum for his best writers to speak seriously on any subject even tangentially related to sport. Laguerre's changes were being noted with unusual enthusiasm from above. One of Hedley Donovan's critiques in 1962 noted that a recent issue seemed to him "one of the most readable and attractive magazines that ever came out of this building."

*SI* was taking a lead in other areas as well. Laguerre moved with relative speed, considering the time and the company, in hiring and promoting women. Within months of taking over, he promoted Barbara La Fontaine (nee Heilman), who had begun as Crichton's meek but searingly observant secretary and, one day in 1960, shyly handed him a piece she'd written about crabbing. "The Crabslayer" ran almost literally without a touch of editing in the August 29, 1960, issue. Afterward, Laguerre called La Fontaine into his office and asked her, "What do you want to do?" After some protestations, she admitted she wanted to write. Buoyed by a serene, almost chirpy sweetness that some found unsettling, she was surprisingly perceptive about athletes. Red Smith called her profile of Sonny Liston the best ever written about the fighter, and her essays on racers—stock car champion Fireball Roberts, the versatile Mario Andretti—probed the psychology of the driver in ways previously unexamined. Two years later, he hired Liz Smith, who would cover fashion and the social side of sports for five years before moving on to a new career as a gossip columnist.

Another rising star was the quietly willful Patricia Ryan. Raised in a horse-racing family in southeastern Pennsylvania, Ryan graduated high school at age 16 and went to the Katherine Gibbs secretarial school in New York City, finding work a year later as a secretary at the Jockey Club at Belmont Park. Hired by *SI* in 1960, Ryan was sixth in a string of secretaries assigned to Ezra Bowen that year, but she persevered and got her break a year later. During a week when all the other reporters were on assignment, a jockeys' strike was called at Belmont; Ryan went to investigate the incident and her file ran, in Score*card*. The next week, Fitzpatrick asked her if she wanted to become a reporter. Ryan agreed, but only if she wouldn't have her pay docked. Reporters, at the time, were making less than secretaries.

On June 1, 1961, Sarah Ballard started working for the magazine. While others hired around her would enjoy greater public recognition, few *SI* employees ever had such a galvanizing effect on the office. A Stanford graduate who had grown up on the West Coast, she belonged to a generation of American women who came of age in the postwar era, stuck between a promise of new possibilities and freedoms, and the still-grim reality of secretarial jobs, unequal pay, and a culture that was occasionally hostile, and usually exploitative, toward women.

But Ballard was irrepressible. She succeeded despite the evident disapproval of Honor Fitzpatrick (who thought her skirts were much too short) and the benign neglect of Jerry Tax (for whom she would labor unhappily as secretary for more than a year). Her early proponents, pushing for her to get a shot at a reporter position, were Robert Creamer and Dick Johnston.

In addition to her professional assets, Ballard was a gifted flirt, and before her second marriage—to a young Associated Press writer named Nicholas Pileggi—her presence would have a near-seismic effect on the office. It wasn't merely that she was attractive; it was that her combination of intelligence, mischieviousness, and sexuality was unprecedented at the company. The veteran philanderers at Time Inc., used to quiet, bookish sorts or giggling sexpots, weren't quite equipped to deal with a combination of the two. One writer slumped down in a chair across from Honor Fitzpatrick's desk in 1962 and shook his head in a kind of stricken wonder. "I'm going to have to go back *out* on the road," he said, "if I ever want to save my marriage."

"She spent most of her time flirting, I think," remembered Fitzpatrick, with more fondness than disapproval. "She was the belle of the ball—she had some of them spinning."

Laguerre had changed the internal organization of the magazine, but he hadn't yet significantly altered the writing staff, and he wanted a fresh infusion of young, talented writers to complement the staff. The need was especially acute in 1962, since three of his most reliable writers were going to be unavailable: Gilbert Rogin left his staff job to go on contract, to devote more time to his short fiction (he would return in 1965, to edit Scorecard), and both Roy Terrell and Ray Cave had become senior editors.

In March 1962, *SI* brought in John Underwood, a talented, well-rounded writer from Miami. In May, a Princeton University graduate named Frank Deford was hired straight out of school as a reporter. And by the end of the year, Laguerre had summoned Dan Jenkins from Texas. Years later, Terrell would remark that the key to being a superlative writer at *Sports Illustrated* was a combination of talent, a thorough knowledge of the sport being covered, and hard work. "It's amazing how many good people, super people, had one or two of those qualities. But in my time, there were only three guys who had all three, who you really could almost build a magazine around—that was Underwood, Jenkins, and Deford."

Rogin had met Underwood at the Patterson-Johannson fight in 1961 and asked him to send his clips. In Miami, Underwood had worked under Stanley Woodward, during Woodward's painful, bitter exile from the *New York Herald Tribune*. Woodward's stentorian voice and stern style made an impression on the erect, dedicated young sportswriter. "He literally put up a list of taboos when he first really took over at the *Miami News*," said Underwood. "And at first, a lot of us said, 'How can you write if you can't use all these clichés?' all the things he would not tolerate." Underwood learned well, developing an unpretentious style, both graceful and crisp, consciously studious.

Deford's hiring was a happy accident. In 1962, the Ivy League pipeline into the Time Inc. office was still a force. Deford, just weeks away from his graduation at Princeton, arranged for a series of interviews to be coordinated by Princeton alum and Time Inc.-er John Titman. When Deford showed up at the Time & Life Building one April morning, he was sent up to Titman's office for a short pre-interview. The older man began explaining Deford's itinerary for the day, who he'd be meeting from each magazine, what to watch for at *Time*.

"Look, Mr. Titman," Deford interrupted. "I wouldn't work there if they offered me the job. This is a waste of my time and theirs."

"Well, who do you want to talk to?" asked Titman quizzically.

"The only one I'm interested in talking to is *SI*. *Time* is group journalism—that's not for me. *Life* is just pictures. And I'm not about to waste my time on [the house organ] *FYI*."

But Titman prevailed on Deford to at least see the men, giving him his informational folder—to present to each interviewer during the day—and sending him on his way. His first interview was at *Time*. After being asked to wait outside the magazine's personnel director's office, Deford sat down. And, because no one had asked him not to, he opened the folder. The first words he read, from Titman's evaluation, were "Not very bright."

"So now I'm feeling really pissed off," Deford recalled. "I come in to see the guy at *Time,* and of course he looks at the folder and then looks up at me like he's expecting some guy with, you know, straw coming out of his teeth. Right away, I'm pissed off, plus I don't want to be working here anyhow. And I said, 'I'm really not the least bit interested in working for *Time.* So, nice to be here, but I'm sorry I'm taking up your time.' Well, then the tables are twisted and now *he's* annoyed."

By the time Deford reached the 20th floor for his last interview, at *Sports Illustrated,* the word had made it through the building that a young interviewee had preemptively turned down *Time* and *Life* because he wanted to work for *SI.* He went to lunch with Jerry Tax and Ray Cave, who remembered him from Baltimore, where Cave had given the young copy boy an early journalism lesson after Deford misspelled Graham Greene's name while rewriting a press release. In the afternoon, Deford was brought back to 20 and ushered into Laguerre's office for a short interview. The magazine had just fired reporter Maury Allen and was desperate for a quick replacement. Deford was offered a job as a reporter-researcher before he left the building, and skipped his graduation ceremonies at Princeton so he could start work at *SI* as soon as possible. (In March, Laguerre had visited spring training, and treated Allen and several others to dinner. After returning from spring training, Allen made the fatal error of listing a dinner from the same night on his own expense account. Even in the liberal Time Inc. expense system, this was a fireable offense.)

As a rule, male journalists might be rugged, natty, or even striking, but for whatever sociological reason, they tend not to be movie-star handsome. Frank Deford was the exception. He was six-foot-three, with a shock of dark hair and a slyly confident smile (the Clark Gable mustache would come later), as well as a Baltimore upbringing that added to the air of debonair Southern gentleman. He might have been an actor or a politician, but he wanted to be a writer.

Deford, like Dan Jenkins, spent a happy childhood buffeted by circumstance. His grandfather had been the scion of one of the wealthiest families in Baltimore, where the Deford Tanning Company delivered leather goods to harbors up and down the East Coast, but wound up in financial ruin near the end of World War I. Deford's father, Benjamin F. Deford, Jr. , graduated from Princeton in 1926, and found a job working with Bell Telephone in White Plains, New York. Later, he moved to Richmond, Virgina and met the daughter of a prominent banker, the vivacious

Louise McAdams, whom he married in 1934. Two years later, Louise's father took over a Baltimore bank and Frank Jr. and Louise returned to Baltimore where, in 1938, Benjamin F. Deford III was born. He was the oldest, by more than a decade, of three brothers. His childhood echoed with hints of past wealth: rich families that his father knew, lavish oil paintings in the house, grand lawns to play on during the summers in Richmond. At the height of the depression, Frank Jr. tried to raise extra money through a fruitless chicken farming effort that led to longer hours and, eventually, more debt.

Although Deford's father never enjoyed much financial success, he sent all of his sons to private schools, and preached a personal code that held honesty above all. At Princeton, Deford was expelled for a year after being caught with a woman in his dormitory ("it sounds a lot more exciting than it actually was") and wound up taking another year off to put in his six months of military service. But by the time he got to *SI*, he was more mature and better traveled than most college graduates, possessing an unusual sensitivity to cultural privilege. And although he was still rough when he got to the magazine, it was obvious that he had considerable potential as a writer.

Meanwhile, Dan Jenkins, who had picked *Sports Illustrated* eight years earlier, was waiting, impatiently.

In 1959, Sherrod had left the *Press* to go to the *Dallas Times-Herald.* He took Bud Shrake with him, because he knew that Jenkins, not yet 30, was ready to be sports editor of the *Press.* Jenkins easily assumed the sports editor's duties and soon began stringing for *Sports Illustrated. SI's* chief of correspondents, Earl Burton, stopped in Fort Worth in 1959 and took Jenkins and Sherrod out to lunch at the old Baker Hotel in downtown Fort Worth. "How they hired writers is they would go out and see them in the field," recalled Sherrod. "And they would invite them to New York for a couple weeks so they could observe them, see if they blew their nose on their sleeve—sort of an audition." New York didn't appeal to Sherrod, nor did Burton's attitude. It was shortly after that that he began referring to the magazine as *Sports Elevated.* But Jenkins jumped at the chance, and went up for a glorious two-week tour of duty that year, putting in a fortnight at the old building. "I thought, *holy shit,* this is big time!" he said. "Are you kiddin' me? I'm a fuckin' stringer, I'm sittin' here lookin' out the window down at Rockefeller Center. I got a guy coming around to shine my shoes. I got a guy bringing me all the newspapers I want. I got people comin' around bringing me donuts and danishes and coffee every 30 minutes, and nobody around here *does* anything. Except go to lunch."

But even as he aspired to join the magazine, he was still outraged by its occasional lapses in news judgment. Shrake had driven to Baton Rouge for the monumental 1959 Ole Miss–Louisiana State game in which Billy Cannon would become a Bayou legend and, with just five minutes after the game to file his story, he wrote what Gary Cartwright would later call "the greatest deadline sports story I've ever read in my life." Back home in Fort Worth the next Friday, Jenkins was appalled to find a single page on the big game in the back of *SI*. "*One fuckin' page!* I'm waiting for *SI* to come out, and it comes out and they barely covered it. And I thought, if I ever work there, I'm changin' that."

That same year, an older, wiser Jenkins married for the fourth and final time, wedding his old high school and college friend, the recently divorced June Burrage. Burrage was a smart, blazing beauty who had done some modeling work in Texas and New York. "The first time I saw her," said Blackie Sherrod, "I thought she was the most beautiful woman I'd ever seen in my life."

By 1961, Jenkins had rejoined Sherrod, Shrake, and Cartwright, this time at the *Times-Herald*, where their irreverence remained, but the stakes were higher. Emboldened by a budget, Sherrod covered Texas authoritatively, but also sent his staff around the country to follow the top national sports stories of the day, developing one of the first non–New York sports pages with a truly national scope. That didn't prevent his staffers from constructing the occasional hoax, like the year they invented a Texas high school football team named the Corbet Comets, with twin star running backs Rickie Ron and Dickie Don Yewbet (the last name was a further-inside joke, a play on TCU coach Abe Martin's answer to most questions), who advanced to one of the nearly countless small-class state final games, without any readers catching on to the deceit.

At the 1962 Masters, Jenkins had lunch with Ray Cave, who expressed interest and said the magazine would be hiring him soon. A few months later, Earl Burton sent a routine note out to all the stringers. The magazine was assembling a story, to be written by Al Wright, about putting. They were looking for stringers to furnish one or two funny stories about putting, if they could. Rather than submit a file of anecdotes, Jenkins simply wrote the story, turning in a 3,000-word piece called "Lockwrists and Cage Cases" that was accepted in full and ran in the July 16, 1962, issue. The story, and Jenkins's initiative, got Laguerre's attention. It also brought one of the more dubious moments of fact-checking in the young magazine's history. Sarah Ballard was assigned to check the piece. "So I was talking to Dan on the phone, whom I didn't know, and he was referring me as a checking source to Bud Shrake, whom I also didn't know. And Bud, who I had probably awakened on a Sunday morning, just said, 'If Dan says it's true, it must be true.' And I thought, *Oh, my God—what would Honor do if she knew?*" When faced with such a problem, Ballard could only let it fly and remember what Andy Crichton would cheerily say when faced with an intriguing but unverifiable statement: "That fact is *too good* to check!"

After the piece, hiring Jenkins became a top priority. In November 1962, Jenkins got the call. It was late in the afternoon and he was sitting at the *Times-Herald* office when the phone rang. It was Laguerre, and he was to the point.

"Would you like to come on staff?" Laguerre asked.

"Uh, let me think about it for five seconds—yes," said Jenkins.

He went directly to the apartment complex where both he and Sherrod lived. Sherrod had stayed home from work that day, having caught a cold the weekend before. When Jenkins got there, jumpy, smiling, his boss instantly knew what was up. And he understood.

"Blackie," said Jenkins. "I hate to leave Texas, and the *Herald*, and I hate to leave you guys, but, you know—the Yankees just called."

# CHAPTER 8

# THE THIRD NEWSWEEKLY

In the spring of 1963, the Laguerres threw a dinner party at their Upper East Side apartment, inviting several of the new staff writers. Nathalie Laguerre noticed how fond André had become of his new additions, especially the garrulous Jenkins couple ("He was the rough and tough one; she was very sophisticated"). They brought out the Bell's 12-year-old scotch, Andre's favorite for special occasions, and after the meal, the guests congregated in the large Laguerre living room. Somehow the subject of parlor games came up. A few rounds of charades were played. Then Dan Jenkins, eyes bright with mischief, asked if anyone there had ever heard of the Bad Imitation game. It had been very popular with the dopeheads in Austin, he explained by way of introduction. Then he offered to demonstrate.

"Oh, God, no," said a mortified June Jenkins, rolling her eyes.

Jenkins slipped out of his shoes and, in full suit and tie, stood on his head, his stockinged feet up against the wall.

And he stayed there, his face getting redder and redder.

The audience was laughing at the visual incongruity, but couldn't begin to guess what it was exactly that Jenkins was supposed to be portraying.

After a few more seconds, Jenkins said, "Clue! Who does this look like in a Milan train station?"

There was a moment of silence. And then Laguerre, seated nearby on a couch, started a deep, long laugh, his stomach jiggling in successive peals of mirth. By now, Jenkins had come down off the wall and was faced upright again, so he could helpfully explain to those that hadn't caught on yet. "It's Mussolini."

"That brought down the house," remembered John Underwood. "Nobody played anything else after that."

Jenkins was an instant success at the magazine as well. When he arrived at the *SI* offices in February 1963, Laguerre took him on a tour of the place, then brought him back to his office, and asked him what he wanted to cover. Jenkins said he already knew that Al Wright was the main golf writer, and said he'd be glad to cover whatever events Wright didn't want. "But mostly," he added, "I need to write college football."

"Why college football?" Laguerre asked.

"I know more about it than anybody else. See, there's this thing out there called Number One. And we need to cover that. Not just the Army-Navy game and the Ivy League."

"Very well," said Laguerre. "You're my college football writer."

In truth, when Terrell became the beat reporter, *SI* had started to treat college football as more of a national sport, but Jenkins's criticism still had credence. The magazine had yet to cover the long season as a continually unfolding drama, a multi-act play toward a specific end, replete with significant elements of tragedy that would result in one team being coronated at the end of the season with the mythical national championship, a title as coveted as it was ethereal.

It proved to be an amazing year for Dan Jenkins. He and June had driven the 1,583 miles from Fort Worth to New York City in two days in January 1963, with their two-year-old twins Marty and Sally, and the one-year-old Danny swaddled in an improvised crib in the backseat. Dan and June were smart and well-educated but not worldly. Before arriving in New York, they had never seen bagels, had never eaten pizza. A year later, in the winter of 1964, they spent two weeks in a villa in Innsbruck, Austria, where Dan was covering the Winter Olympics. It was a heady ride for someone who, by his own estimation, "used to think Beaumont was an exotic dateline." And yet something about it seemed so inevitable, as if Jenkins had spent his whole life preparing for the move. "Dan, we used to call him Broadway," said Terrell. "Because from the minute he landed in New York, he was more of a New Yorker than anyone I ever saw."

The quality of writing at *SI* was steadily improving, and the consistently high quality of the bonus pieces brought attention to the magazine as a literary oasis. After the spate of hires in 1962, Laguerre was finally pleased with the composition of his staff. With a first line of Olsen, Maule, Jenkins, and Underwood writing (Deford, who began as a reporter, would develop later), and smart, committed editors like Terrell, Creamer,

Tax, and Cave working closely with them, Laguerre sensed the magazine now had the journalistic firepower to deliver on its promise.

The emphasis of the coverage had changed as well. In *SI*'s first three years, fishing ranked fifth, eight, and fourth among all sports in number of articles per year. By the third year of Laguerre's reign, it was relegated to second-class status, 13th among all sports. Basketball, which ranked 10th and 12th in 1954 and 1955, was never lower than fourth under Laguerre, who capitalized on its ascendancy in the spare winter sports schedule. Baseball would be first in number of stories in 12 of the first 13 years of the magazine, but pro and college football moved up steadily. Both would eventually pass baseball by the end of the decade.

The raw numbers were just as stark. *SI* ran 10 pro football stories (not counting departments) during 1955, 13 in '56, and 13 in '57. By the mid-'60s, the number would reach 30. College basketball was the subject of 24 articles in the two years 1956–57. In 1964–65, that number had increased to 63. The converse was also true; there had been 13 hunting stories in 1955, but just 3 in '62. There were 23 stories on general sporting fashion in 1955–56, but just 8 in 1965–66.

In a confidential letter to Luce dated February 23, 1962, Laguerre had written: "I'm developing a strong hunch that pro football is our sport. We have grown with it, and each of us is a phenomenon of the times. We gave it more coverage last year, but I plan to extend it this fall. It seems that our reader identifies himself more with this sport than with golf or fishing. College football is too diffuse and regionalized. Baseball in some quarters is considered old-fashioned or slightly non-U. Horse racing and winter sports have less broad appeal."

By 1963, the American Football League had proved its staying power, surprising the National Football League and television executives alike with its resilience (the AFL's seminal television deal, in which revenue was shared equally by all teams, had quickly been copied by the NFL). Despite the challenge, the NFL's popularity only continued to surge, even weathering the gambling scandal that led Pete Rozelle to suspend Alex Karras and Paul Hornung for the 1963 season (both had admitted to gambling on NFL games, though not those involving their own teams). Rozelle's decision was widely criticized at the time, but American sports was just emerging from a scandal-plagued period when the legitimacy of any result was open to question. In his April 29 piece, "Players Are Not Just People," Tex Maule defended his old friend Rozelle, arguing that players were rightly held to a higher standard of conduct. The magazine came back to the issue three weeks later, putting Hornung on the cover under the headline "The True Moral Crisis in Sport," with a John Underwood piece inside arguing that the increased money at stake, more than anything else, would challenge sport's ability to conduct itself honorably. "The purpose of sport is to offer recreation," wrote Underwood, "to lift men out of their humdrum experience and offer them exultation they cannot find in other pursuits. When profits become the only objective, sport dies. The name is retained, but it is a mockery. In death, it kills more important things than itself."

Underwood's starched-shirt moralism brought a brisk air of rectitude to the debates. He looked and acted more like a country lawyer than a sportswriter, and he wrote more like a professor, evincing a stern but rational tone that was all too rare in a field still dominated by holier-than-thou grandstanders and everybody-does-it cynics.

In the summer of 1963, Laguerre put both Jenkins and Underwood on the college football beat, where, within a few years, they would change his mind about the limiting regionalism of the sport. For the first time in 1963, *SI* chose a number one team at the beginning of the season, with Jenkins arguing in the college football preview that Texas "should finish the season undefeated, the strongest team of 1963." That it happened just like Jenkins said it would (Texas closed out its 11–0 season with a 28–6 win over Navy in the Cotton Bowl) would have been enough to ensure that his arrival was noticed. But Jenkins also contributed the year's most memorable bonus piece, a November 11 story titled "The Disciples of St. Darrell on a Wild Weekend."

The story had been percolating in Jenkins's mind since he got to New York. He saw a spot on the schedule in October of that year, State Fair weekend in Texas, when football fans in Dallas, with a little extra effort, could see four football games—three major college and one pro—within a 48-hour period. Jenkins's piece introduced a different sort of archetypal fan into the sporting literature, heretofore dominated by baseball disciples, Ivy League tailgaters, and urban basketball junkies:

Joe Coffman is a modern Texan. This means that Mary Sue is a pretty, loving and understanding wife, that his sons . . . are healthy and happy, that his business is successful . . . that his ranch-type home is comfortable, with all of the built-ins manufacturers sell these days, that he has a 1963 Oldsmobile Starfire and a 1962 Impala (both convertibles), that his close friends are mostly the ones he grew up with or knew in high school and college. Being a modern Texan also means that Joe Coffman might not recognize a cow pony if it were tied on a leash in his backyard, that he despises Stetson hats, that he likes cashmere sport coats, pin-collar shirts, Las Vegas, playing golf at Colonial Country Club,

Barbra Streisand ("Think she can't sing?"), good food, good booze, Barry Goldwater and, more than anything else, the Texas Longhorns.

Jenkins's piece followed Joe and Mary Sue Coffman and their friends Cecil and Pat Morgan as they attended all four games. Their weekend began at the Cotton Bowl Friday night, where SMU upset Navy. After the game, they went to a party in suburban Dallas, at an apartment where a stuffed moose head wore a name tag reading "Joe Don Looney" (the apartment, and the moose, belonged to Shrake and Cartwright). The next morning, just slightly hung over, the Coffmans and Morgans set out for the big game, Texas-Oklahoma:

> Cecil was plugging along nicely on the toll road when Pat reminded him that he was going 80 mph. The speed limit is 70.
>
> "Can't get there too soon," said Joe. "Got to go hear Hank Thompson. He's always singing on the fairgrounds at noon."
>
> "Yeah," said Cecil. "That's about like you common people from Fort Worth. You *lack* them hillbilly *sangers*."
>
> Said Joe, "Can't beat it. Drink beer, listen to old Hank and then warp the Okies. Perfect day. I had to have about $50 worth of that 5½ points."
>
> "Did you bet Joe?" said Mary Sue in a concerned voice.
>
> "I 'magine."
>
> Mary Sue looked out the window.
>
> "We're gonna warp 'em," said Joe.
>
> "Guarantee you St. Darrell's gonna drown 'em. Too much character. I don't care who they got. Joe Don Looney. Jimmy Jack Drunk. Anybody . . ."
>
> Mary Sue and Pat opened the beer and Joe and Cecil sang a parody on the hillbilly tune: *I don't care 'bout my gas and oil,/ Long as I got my Dare-e-ull Royal,' Mounted on the dashboard o' my car.*

The eventful weekend showed a different sort of football revelry to *SI* readers. There were none of the elbow-patched Ivy League niceties, no mentions of yachting or the Cape, and no ephemera. Football was at the center of the experience, not on its margins as it often seemed to be back East. It would set the tone for much of Jenkins's work that would follow.

King Football's psychic significance would be underscored two Fridays later, when John F. Kennedy was assassinated. While other publications scrambled to cover the unfolding events in Dallas, *SI* tried to decide on the proper response, a dilemma complicated by Pete Rozelle's decision, on Saturday morning, to go ahead with football games the next day. They wound up sticking with a Jenkins cover story on Roger Staubach, and defending Rozelle's decision in Scorecard.

It was only a week later, with a pall still hanging over the country, and the magazine receiving letters of outrage from readers who felt as though *SI* underplayed the assassination and went easy on the NFL, that Laguerre reached a difficult decision. He chose Rozelle as Sportsman of the Year, for bringing pro football to the big time and his handling of the Karras and Hornung cases. The decision was initially unpopular within the halls of *SI*, with Jenkins and others trying to talk him out of it. In retrospect, it was a visionary choice, an example of Laguerre grasping a reality long before it would become conventional wisdom. Football had eclipsed baseball in the national consciousness. The NFL's popularity was exploding, and Rozelle's leadership was a crucial reason. But there was still a hard contingent of older owners who dismissed the new commissioner as a slick, out-of-his-depth publicity man. The Hornung case put much of that talk to rest, but *SI*'s recognition would cap Rozelle's breakthrough year.

For Rozelle, *SI*'s significance was twofold. First, from the coverage of the 1958 National Football League championship game onward, "it treated pro football as it had never been treated." The Sportsman of the Year honor was approbation for an embattled executive. "It gave me more credibility with the old guard of owners," said Rozelle. "Suddenly I was no longer a 33-year-old kid commissioner."

And much of that was due to a magazine that, on some visceral level, was beginning to matter. Laguerre was aware of this, and in a statement he sent to an *SI* ad sales conference in 1963, he expressed *SI*'s purpose succinctly:

> Our editorial concept of what this magazine is trying to do is a simple one. First of all, we are trying to produce the best written and best looking weekly magazine in the world. . . . As for writers . . . I am particularly proud of a group of young writers who are in the process of establishing names, which, believe me, will be nationally famous for years to come.

With Laguerre pushing for late closes, demanding a higher standard in writing, pressing the edge of the envelope in fast color, *SI* was emerging as an innovative, groundbreaking magazine. And if no one else in the magazine industry took seriously Laguerre's professed goal to make *SI* "the best written and best looking weekly magazine in the world," it was becoming increasingly difficult to dismiss it as "merely" a sports magazine. And yet there was the incontrovertible nagging fact: nearing its ten-year anniversary, *SI* was still losing money.

• • •

In terms of both ad pages and ad revenue, *Sports Illustrated* had become by the early '60s one of the top 10 weekly magazines in the country. Its regional editions, which had been developed in the mid-'50s as a way to bring smaller advertisers into the magazine, were a hit, and the concept was spreading to other Time Inc. publications and beyond. For all this, it was still considered a failure, by many within the building, who had given up trying to figure out how to push the magazine into profitability, and by many in the industry, who viewed it still as a product of Luce's addled indulgence. Ad pages, which had slowly but steadily risen from 737 pages in 1955 to 1,908 in 1960, actually went down, to 1,831, in 1961. The next year they improved slightly, but still fell short of 1960 levels. The engine seemed stalled. In May 1961, nearly seven years into the game, *SI* was still losing money. Advertising director Pete Callaway and Sid James were clashing at every turn, and the ad staff was starting to choose sides. "So why aren't we making money?" wrote Scherman to Callaway. "We've got plenty of accounts, all right, but no volume. We can't make real money until we get the volume."

The crisis in confidence could be seen in the April 23, 1962, edition of *The Gallagher Report*, the gossipy but influential newsletter for advertising and media executives. The item read: "SPORTS ILLUSTRATED. Top management at Time Inc. worried. Time Inc. has invested $30 million in *Sports Illustrated* over the last eight years. *SI*, which had just begun to break even, is sliding again. In first quarter, off 9% in advertising pages. Carried 28,030 subscriptions in arrears during last half of 1961; otherwise would have missed its 950,000 rate base 16 out of 26 issues. Despite this, pushed rate base up to 1 million in January, 1962." *SI*, wrote Gallagher, "should be a bi-weekly." In summing up the sparse benefits to the company, it was concluded that the magazine had served as "a useful laboratory for regional editions" and "proved that Time Inc. was fallible, a healthy experience for any organization, particularly one with a 'supernatural' complex."

By late July, Luce decided to send Andrew Heiskell to investigate. Others had taken a closer look at *SI*, without much consequence. But in his understanding of both the editorial and business sides of magazine publishing, Heiskell was in many respects Luce's best man. Born in Naples, Italy, and educated in France and at the Harvard Business School, he possessed the sort of smooth, amiable assurance that came from being 6-feet-5, patrician, multilingual, and married to actress Madeleine Carroll. His affable demeanor masked a firmness and a brilliant marketing mind, which had helped him become one of the youngest publishers in the company's history, taking over *Life* at age 30 in 1946. In 1960, Luce had promoted him to chairman of the board of Time, Inc. Now Luce asked him to go down to *SI* and find out, once and for all, what the problem was. At once courtly and casual, Heiskell had a sense of perspective that many of the more insulated Time Inc.-ers lacked. He was perfect for the reconnaissance mission.

Heiskell wasn't unfamiliar with *SI*'s problems. After the promotion in 1960, he said he'd "spent the next four years helping Harry say to the board, 'We now have the answers. We're going in the black.'" But the answers hadn't been forthcoming. Luce told Heiskell to survey the entire magazine operation, from the editorial to the advertising, circulation as well as production. "I do remember that I had to be reasonably diplomatic because everybody else [on the 34th floor] had already tried to figure out what was going wrong. The feeling at *SI* was, 'Oh my God, one more.' And so I had to be very gentle in my approach to asking the questions, trying to find out what the answer was. So I spent a fair amount of time trying to find out what it was that they were selling."

On August 12, 1963, Heiskell sent a copy of his confidential memo to Luce's office. As Luce read the memo, paper close to his face, eyeglasses on top of his head, his eyebrows shot up, as they often did when he was presented with a new, compelling argument. Heiskell's case was persuasive, so much so that it seems inevitable, even self-evident, in retrospect. His memo opened by arguing that the magazine itself wasn't the problem, but noted gravely that because of the magazine's problematic advertising situation, "if it continues on its present course *SI* will be like the mountain climber who repeatedly thinks he has reached the top only to find the peak is still ahead and above." Heiskell then outlined the familiar problem: *SI* was in a weak position selling against more concentrated niche titles in the monthly magazine field. He concluded that in almost every situation, the magazine was scrambling "for that *last* buck," and that it needed to change its overall focus.

> Whatever may *have* been the rights and wrongs of sales strategy I urgently propose that we are now at the point at which a coherent sales approach is possible—and that can make *SI* an important factor in terms of volume and profits, though it may mean some category losses in the short run.
>
> I suggest (quite strongly) that *SI* concentrate on the following. . . .
> It should disassociate itself from the *Holiday, Esquire, National Geo-*

*graphic, Playboy* field and promote itself as one of the newsweeklies. The monthly leisure field simply doesn't supply enough potential ($) for *SI* and forces it into competitive battles it cannot win at a profit.

The Heiskell memo's simple recommendation, to scrap the previous sales approach and instead sell *SI* as one of the newsweeklies—competing directly with *Time* and *Newsweek* for advertisers—would have broad repercussions. Financially, it was the crucial final piece of the sales puzzle; *SI* showed its first annual profit (of about $50,000) in the calendar year 1964. "Don't attribute all the success to this little notion," Heiskell said. "The advertising success is also due in part to the fact that as an editorial entity, it became something that people applauded. Laguerre was doing his job brilliantly. I felt that he was doing everything he could as an editor to make it a success. It was not up to him to do the other." Journalistically, the newsweekly concept made perfect sense, since that was what Laguerre's magazine had become anyway. But the idea also demonstrated how far *SI*, and the company's conception of sports, had come in ten years.

It was left to Robert Fisler and others in the promotion department to come up with the best way to frame the new strategy. Fisler presented an ad committee with the idea at a morning meeting early in 1964. "We're going to bill *Sports Illustrated* as 'The Third Newsweekly,'" he explained enthusiastically.

"What about *U.S. News and World Report*?" Henry Luce asked. "It's the third newsweekly."

"Mr. Luce, with all respect—*U.S. News* isn't a newsweekly," said general manager Garry Valk. "It's a filibuster." It was also Fisler's idea to combine the magazine's initials to form a dollar sign, and put that on virtually every piece of correspondence that *SI* sent to advertisers. It would prove to be one of the most successful campaigns in the company's history.

• • •

Late in 1963, Roy Terrell was promoted to assistant managing editor and given "lead editing" responsibilities, helping Laguerre conceive story ideas and assign writers to them. And though Dick Johnston still held out hope of being the managing editor one day, the promotion made it clear that Terrell was the heir apparent.

Shortly thereafter, Terrell had been casting about for another staff writer, and asked Jenkins for suggestions. "I told him that Bud Shrake was the best sportswriter in the country who wasn't already working for us," said Jenkins. "I didn't mention that he'd been my best friend since

Paschal." Shrake was summoned to New York. He remembered his interview as "going to the bar and drinking with André. As far as I could tell, if you could stand there at the bar and drink with André, and carry on a conversation for several hours, and he found you amusing, you were in."

Three weeks after the first interview, Shrake arrived for his first day of work and took the elevator to the 20th floor of the Time & Life Building. "I remember the first thing I saw when I got off the elevator was people in the hall playing hockey. They had a tennis ball and they were using real hockey sticks—Jack Olsen was the goalie."

Shrake also saw that at *SI*, Laguerre's bar of choice had become something of an extended office, a place where Laguerre spent long lunches bouncing story ideas off his lieutenants, discussing breaking news, conjuring up different ways to approach tired subjects. It was also a place for the sort of esprit de corps that energized Laguerre. There was the infamous match game (a diabolical, nobody-wins-but-someone-loses elimination contest in which each participant hid between zero and three matches in his hand, then tried to guess the total at the table); the morbid Morrie Werner Dead Pool (in which Werner himself eventually participated); and the Jenkins-inspired Blight Draft (with every participant asked to name one person he'd most like to see come down with a fatal disease). Laguerre never instigated the games, but he presided over much of the madness with a drink and a smile.

"André wasn't much of a homebody," said Frank Deford. "He was very European, except that he didn't chase women. To go to the bars was what André wanted to do, and be with the boys. I'll never forget, one time he said to me, 'Frankie, one of the most important decisions a man must make is whether he's going to hang out with the boys or chase women; you can't do both.' Another guy at the bar, whose name I won't give you, had been married probably three times, said, 'Oh, now you tell me.'"

One night Laguerre was standing in the muted light of the Three G's, downing another J&B-and-water at the corner of the squarish bar while watching Werner agitatedly trying to explain to Tex Maule why Joseph Conrad was the single unsurpassed figure in 20th-century literature. For all his good company, Werner was easily angered, by no one so much as the snippy pipe smoker Martin Kane, whose crisp jibes always seemed to get under the old man's skin. While Werner and Maule's contentious discussion escalated, Laguerre leaned over to Kane and whispered something in his ear, bringing a devilish smile to the writer's face. After a few more seconds of Werner further expounding on the rarefied talent of Conrad, he paused for a breath. It was at that instant that Kane chimed in with the scripted comment: "Hey, Morrie, if Joseph Conrad's so fucking great, how come he doesn't write in Polish?"

Back at the bar, Laguerre took a puff on his cigar, tapped his empty glass on the countertop, and waited for another refill.

That spring of 1964, the Three Gs closed, necessitating a systematic search for a new bar. Shrake had just completed his first story for the magazine, and Laguerre summoned him. "I want you to find us a bar," he said. The rules for Shrake were simple. The new locale: 1) had to be close to the Time & Life Building; 2) couldn't be an "in" spot; 3) had to have some food service; 4) had to be a place women could go without being unduly bothered; 5) couldn't have a jukebox; and, finally and most importantly, 6) every fourth drink a person ordered had to be free.

Shrake spent ten days casing out many of the hundred or so bars within a three-block radius of the Time & Life Building, and finally settled on a viable candidate, whose casually relaxed atmosphere was a cut above the Three Gs. What worried him was the name: The Steak de Paris. "I almost didn't even suggest it to him because of the name," remembered Shrake. "But then I found out the owner was Belgian, so that made it okay." There was one other problem: the main bartender was Alsatian and thus, by connection in Laguerre's mind, a German. Laguerre couldn't abide a German serving him alcohol. So after a furtive discussion with the owner, a new French bartender was hired, and *SI* had its bar for the next couple of years.

"André drank scotch and water and he drank a lot of 'em," said Jenkins. "But he never got drunk. I don't think any of us got drunk—we just got brilliant. More good story ideas came out of the bar than anywhere."

Shrake would marvel at Laguerre's unerring nose for the good, off-beat story, and his persistence to pursue it even in the face of staggering expenses. "One time we were standing at the bar and he said, 'I wonder what's happened to all those sporting facilities in the Far East now that the British are pulling back east of the Suez Canal.' I, of course, didn't have a ready answer for that question. He said, 'You don't know, huh? Go find out.' 'When?' I asked. 'Now,' he said. 'How long have I got?' He said, 'As long as it takes.' In this case, it took about six months."

One morning in his first months at *SI*, a contrite, badly hungover Shrake showed up to Laguerre's office, with a confession.

"André, I've got to tell you something," he said. "I had a few too many cocktails last night, and I hired somebody to shoot the Patterson fight over in Sweden."

"Well, tell me, just who did you hire?"

"Frank Sinatra."

Laguerre looked at him evenly and surrendered to his deep, distinctive chuckle, "Hew, hew, hew," reserved for the truly absurd. *SI* did grant Sinatra a photo credential for the Floyd Patterson–Eddie Machen fight in Stockholm, becoming the first Time Inc. magazine to support his avocation. Sinatra would later shoot a championship fight, 1971's epic Ali-Frazier bout, for *Life*.

• • •

By the mid-'60s, the civil rights movement was fighting some of its battles on the fields of sport. A group of black players boycotted the American Football League All-Star game in New Orleans in 1965, after they were denied lodging at the hotel where white all-stars stayed. *SI* reported the story with a first-person account by white San Diego Charger offensive tackle Ron Mix, who wrote that he'd decided to join the boycott even though "I felt it would be wrong." Reader response was voluminous, demonstrating that much of *SI*'s readership was aware and engaged by the race issue, though the most pointed defense of the black athletes' cause came from Morrie Werner, whose letter was printed even though he was listed on the masthead. (That Laguerre chose to run it as a letter rather than in Scorecard, where such an item would have amounted to an editorial stance, was indicative of the sensitivity about racial issues that prevailed at the time.)

Much of the writing about athletes in the mid-'60s confirmed the general journalistic views that sportswriters shouldn't try to handle "real-world" issues. Against this backdrop, though, there was a group of *SI* writers at the time who were able to write about black athletes with rare lucidity. In a story about the newly transplanted Kansas City Chiefs in the September 16, 1963, issue, Jenkins gave a glimpse of black culture through the sly boasts of Chiefs' running back Abner Haynes. Two months later, Gil Rogin would collaborate with Bill Russell on an oral history ("Grown Men in a Child's Game"). In '64, Shrake would show the casual daily racism encountered by Buffalo Bills' star running back Cookie Gilchrist.

But the locus of all questions of race had become the Louisville Lip, Cassius Marcellus Clay. The 1960 Olympic light-heavyweight gold medalist had turned pro with significant fanfare, and *SI* had covered much of his career closely, including a long feature March 11, 1963, on "The Eleven Men Behind Cassius Clay," the Louisville business consortium that was bankrolling his pro career.

As the date for the February 25, 1964, championship bout between champion Sonny Liston and the audacious challenger Clay approached,

Laguerre made what seemed to be a curious decision. Few were giving the young fighter a chance against the sullen champ, whose veneer of invincibility was leading some to call him the greatest heavyweight ever. Liston was an 8–1 favorite, but Laguerre sensed a surging interest in the bout. *SI* devoted more space to previewing that fight than any non-Olympic event in the magazine's history. There were seven different stories over a one-month period in January and February, with reports from both camps, a diagram of the seating arrangement and ticket prices at the convention hall in Miami Beach, a review of the four men who had beaten Liston early in his career, and a first-person cover story in the February 24 issue, with Clay sitting on a mountainous stack of bills just outside a bank vault, the cover blurb reading, "My $1,000,000 Getaway." Clay's piece, "I'm a Little Special," gave him the opportunity to explain why other boxers nearly as good hadn't attained his level of celebrity: "And the reason for that is because they cannot throw the jive. Cassius Clay is a boxer who can throw jive better than anybody you will probably ever meet anywhere."

Because the fight was on a Tuesday, *SI* was prevented from covering it in the March 2 issue, but came back with two stories in the March 9 issue (subscribers would get their copies nine or ten days after the fight). Maule's analysis, "Yes, It Was Good and Honest," recapitulated the fight and showed a new respect for the new champ ("If Sonny Liston and Cassius Clay fight again, as they surely will, Clay probably will win again"). The second story was a profile piece, "The First Days in the Life of the Champion of the World," written by staff writer Huston Horn, who had been stationed at Clay's camp, and spent the next day with the rechristened Ali and Malcolm X, who told him that the new champ would "mean more to his people than Jackie Robinson," because while Robinson had been hailed by whites, Ali was "the black man's hero." While Horn seemed to agree with Malcolm X, the piece took pains to avoid mentioning that Clay had chosen the name Muhammad Ali. This would become an ongoing debate within the offices of *Sports Illustrated* (and many other publications) in the following years. Most sports pages in the '60s refused to call Ali by his new chosen name. For much of the balance of the decade, *SI* made a curious compromise, referring to the fighter as Ali and Clay interchangeably within stories, and without comment. By 1968, the style on first reference was to call him "Muhammad Ali (né Cassius Clay)." But it wasn't until 1967 that he was referred to as Ali on the cover.

The build-up to the second Ali-Liston fight would give the magazine cause for its most pointed writing on race relations to date. It came in the clean, burnished prose of George Plimpton, riding on "Big Red," the bus carrying Ali north from Miami to his Chicopee Falls, Massachusetts, training camp. The account of a portion of the trip, "The World Champion Is Refused a Meal," appeared in the May 17, 1965, issue. Plimpton's article (expanded in his boxing anthology *Shadow Box*) dramatized the relationship between Ali, still arguing a hard separatist line in race relations, and his trainer Drew "Bundini" Brown, an integrationist, as the bus stopped near the Florida-Georgia border for a meal.

> The restaurant had a screen door that squeaked and the people inside, six or seven couples sitting in the booths, looked up when Bundini and the others came in. He sat down at the counter, the reporters on stools to either side. The waitress looked at the group and put her hands together. The manager came out from behind the counter. "I'm sorry," he said. "We have a place out back. Separate facilities. . . . The food's just the same." Through the serving window the reporters could see two negro cooks looking out. "Probably better," the manager said with a wan smile. He talked at the reporters as if Bundini was not there. Bundini's face began working. The reporters could not look at him, so they began intimidating the manager, whipping furious words at him. He stayed calm, tapping a grease-stained menu against his fingertips. "In this county—Nassau County—they'd be a riot," he said simply. . . .
>
> Bundini said: "The heavyweight champion of the world and he can't get nothing to eat here." He spoke reflectively, and he spun around on his stool and stood up.
>
> The screen door squeaked again and slapped shut. The champion stood in the room, leaning forward slightly and staring at Bundini. He began shouting at him. "You fool—what's the matter with you—you damn *fool*." His nostrils were flared, his voice almost out of control. "I tol' you you ought to be a Muslim. Then you don' go places where you're not wanted. You clear out of this place, nigger, you ain't wanted here, can't you *see*, they don' want you, nigger. . . ." He reached for Bundini's denim jacket, hauled him toward him and propelled him out the door in an easy furious motion, Bundini so preoccupied that he offered no resistance. He stumbled out on the macadam as if he had been launched from a sling.

The piece detailed the sensitivity and caring at the core of Ali and Brown's relationship, as well as ending with a measure of redemption for the trainer. Plimpton's account dramatized not just the lingering racism that existed more than a decade after *Brown* v. *Board of Education* and a full year after the Civil Rights Act was passed, but what a corrosive, embittering effect this had on Ali and his camp.

The rematch itself, the one-round knockout on May 25, 1965, in Lewiston, Maine, was almost an anticlimax, but for the work of Neil Leifer and his camera, at ringside. Herb Scharfman and Leifer were both assigned to shoot the fight for *SI* that night. But in boxing, because there is such a small space for action, photographers are often at the mercy of fate. After Ali's quick right knocked Liston down, Leifer saw the shot of a lifetime developing before his eyes: the dizzy former champ lying pros-trate, gloves bobbing dumbly at the sides of his head while the angry champ, a picture of poised, potent power, stood above him angrily urging him off the canvas, his coiled, red-gloved fist imploring, the overhead strobes perfectly limning the smooth muscles of his frame.

"I just remember thinking to myself: *Stay there*," said Leifer. "*Don't get up*. It was perfect. It couldn't have gotten better. I knew if it went 14 more rounds, it wasn't going to end any more perfectly than it already had for me." Between Ali's legs, one can see the typical expression of the moment—three faces with mouths agape—as well as one look of stern, close-mouthed remorse. This last visage belonged to Scharfman who, even then, might have sensed that he was standing on the wrong side of history. The picture would become one of the most famous sports photographs of all time, the best-known image of the century's best-known athlete. None of this, of course, was going through Leifer's mind at the time. "In 1965, with Muhammad Ali, who could've imagined?! You thought here was a colorful, sensational, flashy fighter with a big mouth who would last a couple of years and, like all the other champions, someone will beat him and he'll be history. Ali became bigger and bigger and then the images became more and more important, and then it became harder and harder to get an image like that." The image, oddly, wasn't chosen as the cover shot; Laguerre went instead with an unspectacular shot from the brief period when both fighters were standing.

At the time, the question of whether the fight was fixed dominated postfight conversation, and the elusive nature of Ali's knockout punch only exacerbated the discussion. There were about a dozen *SI* writers at the fight; Rogin, Crichton, and Maule all had clear views of the short, sav-age right that snapped Liston's jaw around. Many other staffers were con-vinced it was a fix. "We got back to the office," remembered Shrake, "and Tex was demonstrating how Ali twisted his fist and got a karate move and all this bullshit." Shrake, unmoved, burst into Laguerre's office claiming the fight was fixed. He said the response he got was "the angriest I'd ever seen André."

The June 7 issue included three separate pieces on the fight. The lead

Scorecard item took much of the news media to task for its coverage in the aftermath, which "verged on hysterical." Maule defended the propriety of the fight: "Muhammad Ali, born Cassius Clay, retained the heavyweight championship of the world by knocking out Sonny Liston with a perfectly valid, stunning right-hand punch to the side of the head, and he won without benefit of a fix." Elsewhere in the magazine, a five-page portfolio of color pictures of the fight, climaxing with Leifer's soon-to-be-classic shot faced off against a reprint of Jim Murray's column. Murray had by then established himself, at the *Los Angeles Times*, as the premier sports columnist in the country. His closing hinted at what *SI*'s readers were just beginning to understand: "Whatever Cassius Clay is or believes in, he's all ours. Sonny Liston couldn't get close enough to hit him with a bucket of birdseed. It's going to be terrible on the ears, but Cassius is right back where you have to listen to him and he's coming in loud and clear."

• • •

No one guessed it at the time, but the nation's perception of *Sports Illustrated* was forever altered by a seemingly minor turn of events occurring between the two Ali-Liston fights. On a fall day in 1964, Laguerre summoned Jule Campbell to his office. For six years, Campbell had been an assistant to Fred Smith in the fashion department, and a personal favorite of Laguerre's. A deceptively demure, but fiercely self-reliant woman, Campbell had risen by outworking the competition everywhere she went, beginning as a secretary at *Glamour* and winding up as that magazine's accessories editor, before moving to *SI* in 1958, when Smith hired her to add a dose of youth to the magazine's stilted fashion spreads.

Laguerre had taken a paternal interest in Campbell; she was at once fond of him and a bit intimidated. "He was tough, very tough, and he made grown men quake," said Campbell. He liked me, and that scared me even more, because he singled me out." During the weekly Friday afternoon cigar run, Werner was instructed to pick up a few of the forbidden Cubans for Campbell's dad as well.

But on the day Laguerre summoned Campbell to his office, she was just another bright young reporter, who had distinguished herself more for her work ethic than any particular editorial contribution. When Campbell arrived, Ann Callahan showed her into Laguerre's office.

"Jule, my dear," he said, by way of greeting.

"Yes, sir?" Campbell said.

"How would you like to go to some beautiful place and put a pretty girl on the cover?"

More than three decades later, after the entire process of what would come to be known as the *SI* swimsuit issue had been debated and deconstructed by feminists, sociologists, subscribers, and sports fans, Laguerre's rhetorical question still stands as the perfect demystification of the entire process.

For years, Laguerre had been painfully aware of the editorial void that existed during the early winter months of non-Olympic years. In the fall of 1962, Smith had traveled with staff writer Art Kane to the Bahamas, to write a travel piece on winter getaways, and the following January, Laguerre placed an unidentified model on the cover, her head just emerging from the surface of the water, with the tagline "Away From the Resort Mob." A year later, the January 20, 1964, issue featured the waiflike model Babette March on the cover in a white bikini, with the headline "A Skin-Diver's Guide to the Carribean—Fun in the Sun in Cozumel." Inside that issue was a four-page color portfolio of four other swimsuits, which elicited little reader reaction. Laguerre had been unimpressed with assistant fashion editor Jo Ahern Zill's work on the issue, and even less enamored with the svelte but relatively flat-chested March. It was fashionable—this was the age of Twiggy after all—but Laguerre and Smith sensed that Campbell might be able to come up with something that was less imitative of a fashion magazine spread.

Campbell went to work on the assignment immediately, realizing instinctively that she wanted to get a different sort of model. "I went to California, because I thought we should use more natural kinds of women. And in California, they are bigger and healthier, and look more like beach girls. The girl who I chose to put on the cover still had her baby fat, and that was in the days when everyone was really, really skinny."

The young model was Sue Peterson, 18 years old when the shot occurred in Baja. When Campbell picked Peterson up at the airport in Los Angeles, Peterson's mother took her aside and said, "Mrs. Campbell, she has never been away from home before. I am trusting her into your care."

Laguerre assigned his tenacious senior writer Jack Olsen to write the travel piece that would accompany the pictorial. It was both a sensible and a sensitive assignment. Olsen, in the midst of an agonizing divorce, was despondent and Laguerre had grown concerned. He assigned photographer Tony Triolo to visit Olsen, with instructions to pilfer sleeping pills out of Olsen's bathroom. Laguerre thought that the travel assignment, to Cabo San Lucas, would be a way for Olsen to get away from his familiar four walls. By the time the issue—dated January 18, 1965—hit the newsstands, Olsen and Peterson were dating. She would move to New York, living for five months with Campbell and her husband Ron (a designer for *Fortune*).

The cover photograph was provocative. It showed the cherubic-faced Peterson smiling at the camera as she walked along the beach in a black-and-red maillot that didn't have any side panels. Inside that issue were three pages of color photographs, one of Peterson in a pink suit, and a single, startling black-and-white shot of a tanned Peterson, in repose on a beach, wearing a nude-colored body stocking under a white fishnet jumpsuit. The headline to Liz Smith's fashion story on swimwear was "The Nudity Cult."

Middle America blew a gasket. "Tell your cover girl Sue Peterson she is beautiful. I love her. I want to marry her," wrote one reader. Another simply wrote, "Sue! *Wow!!*" But for all the adoring male fans it garnered, the piece offended the sensibilities of a good portion of *SI*'s most loyal subscribers, many of whom had answered one of the ad department's early pitches for *SI* as a "family magazine." "Perhaps you do not know it, but nudity is more destructive to our youth than an atom bomb," explained one angry reader.

Laguerre was pleased with the response that the issue engendered, both positive and negative, and later in 1965 decided to send Campbell out to do another "sunshine issue" for the following January. Suddenly a trifle had become a tradition.

A few months later, Laguerre intervened again on behalf of his old friend Olsen. He called a young writer into his office and asked him to sit down.

"I don't want you dating Sue Peterson," he said.

The writer stared back at him, surprised at both the admonition and the fact that Laguerre even knew he was contemplating asking her out in the first place.

"But André, why?" asked the writer.

"Because Jack Olsen is in love with her."

The writer considered this for a moment. "Well . . . *I* think I could be in love with her, too."

"Yes," said Laguerre. "But Jack Olsen already is."

Olsen and Peterson were married in 1967. And while there was some skepticism among the staff, the marriage lasted. Thirty years later, they were still happily wed, living on Bainbridge Island, Washington, just across from Seattle.

• • •

*SI* was also breaking new ground in photojournalism, searching for a faster alternative to the traditional letterpress printing format, where it had for years been pushing printing techniques to the limit.

"With letterpress, you just had to wait for acid and metal," said Bill Gallagher, Jr., a production staffer at *SI* whose father was the head of production for *Life*. "And the very latest you could go, back in the early '60s, was one page of color, from Saturday afternoon. A college football game, the Kentucky Derby, whatever."

But Dick Gangel was exploring another avenue. At the time, a few monthly magazines were experimenting with offset printing, a means of printing through indirect image transfer that didn't require the long lead time of letterpress and, once it went to press, could produce copies at a faster rate. At the time, letterpress was the industry standard for weekly magazines, which had to tolerate the 24- to 36-hour lag time for striking color plates. But Gangel sensed that the speed offered by offset printing could outweigh its perceived shortcomings, and convinced Laguerre to experiment with it.

One September weekend in 1965, Gangel and Ray Cave were dispatched to Chicago to do a test printing, under deadline conditions, of four pages of offset color. They stayed up all Sunday night and caught a Learjet back Monday morning, At the end of the Monday staff meeting, Gangel stood up. "I would like everybody to note that Cave and I just produced this thing overnight," he said, presenting the color pages from a Sunday afternoon National Football League game. "This is what offset can do for you. You have to look at the cost, you have to look at the binding and all that, but this is what we can do."

The process was expensive and nerve-racking, but *SI* began using it later that fall. "Laguerre could spend money, if a thing was right, like a drunken sailor," said Garry Valk, who succeeded Sid James as publisher in 1965. "And that was always a source of friction. Tibby was caught in the middle. I'd always be on Tibby's back, saying 'You can't do this.' And Laguerre would be telling Tibby, 'I'll do what I want to do.' There was more of a schism between Laguerre and the business side than on other magazines."

By the fall of 1966, *SI* began to run four pages of offset color a week. What the staff would find, once it grew accustomed to the offset process (spoilage, due to unsatisfactory results, was nearing 40 percent in the first year), was that in addition to being faster than letterpress, offset was also both crisper and brighter. Red, which often seemed dull and diluted in the letterpress format, shouted with clarity on offset presses. "Get me some more teams that wear red," Laguerre would chuckle slyly (and by the end of the '60s, a few golfers got wise, wearing red on Sundays to improve their chances for cover billing should they win a major). The progression of fast color grew rapidly, from 38 pages in 1965 and 92 in 1966. By

1967, *SI* was printing more than 200 pages of fast color. Most important, the offset breakthrough allowed *SI* to finally merge the best color with the latest news, and the combination would guarantee a mass audience.

The use of offset meant that the magazine's use of color was limited only by its budgets and the weather, which could still keep film from getting to Chicago for closes. Logistical headaches popped up everywhere. Initially, the R.R. Donnelley printing plant in Chicago didn't have the equipment for offset printing, so *SI* farmed out the color pages to the Fawcett-Haynes Printing Co. in northwest Chicago. They also needed a lab to work over the weekend processing the color, and chose the ANRO Color Service, a small lab, located above the Blackhawk Restaurant on Wabash Avenue just south of downtown Chicago, run by a pair of precise World War II veterans, John Susan and Irv Rosen, who had been prisoners of war together at Stalag 17 in Germany. While Laguerre and some of his lieutenants would camp out at the Blackhawk, film from whatever event was closing late would be flown into Meigs Field just off Lake Michigan. There a car would whisk it to ANRO, whose modest three-room setup would serve as darkroom, layout room, and photo processing plant.

For the Monday, November 22, 1965, heavyweight title fight between Muhammad Ali and Floyd Patterson in Las Vegas, Ray Cave prepared a 70-page memo for Laguerre on the logistics of making the deadline. The rough-mannered, iconoclastic production chief Gene Ulrich then distributed a 19-page memo to his production staff, outlining every employee's responsibilities, by the minute. "The big memos were the reason we could get it done," said Bill Gallagher, Jr. "*Time* and *Newsweek* didn't know when most of their news was going to happen. We knew to the minute. And we'd say, 'Okay, we'll spend the extra $116,000 or whatever.' The numbers were huge, for the '60s anyway."

The pressures of the late closes were so intense that one production man actually died of a heart attack during a particularly grueling 30-hour siege at ANRO. The schedule was brutal because, when a late event was involved, *SI*'s core editing team was up much of Sunday night in Chicago, then had to rush back to New York City to read out page proofs on Monday morning. These expeditions were headed by Laguerre, who, even under the best of circumstances, had developed a paralyzing fear of flying. "You know, I don't travel very well," he'd say, before sneaking multiple flasks onto a flight (one of his favorites looked like a half-eaten sandwich).

Almost everyone involved would come away with late-closing war stories. One Sunday night, Gangel, Gallagher, and assistant art director Marty Nathan had their commercial flight from Buffalo to Chicago grounded in Cleveland because of a blizzard. Gangel located a private plane, but the pilot explained that he couldn't fly without another licensed pilot on board.

"I'm a licensed pilot," said Gangel, who had kept his license after the war. They left the Cleveland airport in a driving snowstorm without a flight plan, under cover of darkness, en route to Chicago. Nathan would remember flying so low that "you could see the street lights changing color." Nearing Chicago, the private pilot asked if anyone knew what Meigs looked like from the air.

"Keep flying along the lakefront," offered Gallagher. "It'll be on your left."

When radio contact with the Meigs tower was established, the tower warned that the previous plane had skidded off the runway. They landed. After deplaning, Nathan and Gallagher literally kissed the ground. Gangel was already steps ahead of them, looking for a cab.

"People did stuff like that because you didn't want to disappoint him," said Andy Crichton. "You just didn't want to let Laguerre down. We all did at some time, though."

But deadlines were always met. They were particularly crucial, in *SI*'s case, because of its already narrow window for newsstand sales (issues would arrive at most newsstands on Thursday and, because of the cycles of sport, would be old news by Saturday afternoon). Dick Labich, who worked as production manager for *SI* in Chicago during the mid-'60s, was continually astonished by Laguerre's awareness of the entire process of magazine making. "He was, as managing editor, as much concerned with newsstand delivery in Florida as he was with what his cover looked like," Labich said. "I never met anybody at Time Inc. in those days that was so involved with the entire distribution process." Jim McCluskey, who also worked in Chicago before becoming a Time Inc. vice-president in charge of production, used to marvel at the audacity of *SI*'s schedule. "Nobody was near *Sports Illustrated* in those days," he said.

• • •

The *SI* sales convention of 1965, held close to Harry Luce's Carefree, Arizona, home, had the feel of a valedictory. At the estate in Carefree, Luce would come as close as he would ever get to living the sporting life. He was under doctor's orders to exercise, and he often golfed at the Arizona Biltmore golf course, which bordered his property. He and Clare would also take morning swims in the heated pool, and occasionally play bridge at night.

The 67-year-old Luce had retired as editor-in-chief a year earlier, naming Hedley Donovan his successor. And at the time of the convention, Sid James was about to leave his publisher's job, to be succeeded by Garry Valk. Luce often went to *Time*'s sales gatherings, but hadn't attended an *SI* retreat in 11 years. But the '65 sales convention was a chance for him to publicly embrace the two men who had brought *Sports Illustrated* into being and, ultimately, profitability. He was joined by Laguerre, who, in an unprecedented move, even introduced his old journalistic mentor. After Laguerre's introduction, Luce rose to speak:

> First of all, I must make a remark about André Laguerre. During my career as editor-in-chief, all those years, my main single job was to pick a managing editor or to have a managing editor in sight. And I think it may be proper and fitting for me to say that the choice I'm proudest of, vainest of, is the choice of André Laguerre. . . .
>
> But I can't speak about André Laguerre without speaking about Sid James. I didn't so much choose Sid James: Sid chose himself. He chose himself at a time when the idea of *Sports Illustrated* was right down at the bottom of the floor. And to put it briefly: there wouldn't be any *Sports Illustrated* today if Sid hadn't said, "I'm willing to undertake it."
>
> Sid was the one who had the nerve and the enthusiasm to undertake what had already been proven to be an impossible job.

He went on to commend Jack Olsen's bonus piece on English soccer; Robert Boyle's jeremiad on the environment, "America Down the Drain"; and Gangel, who, he said, "comes pretty close to being a dream of an art director."

And then in closing, the press lion in winter said, "So may I then compliment you individually on a wonderful publisher, my dear friend Sid James, on a truly great managing editor, André Laguerre . . . And on behalf of Time Inc. may I give you a salute of well done, well done indeed."

Luce was in his twilight. But his last baby, after ten years and nearly $40 million in losses, was securely in the black.

# CHAPTER 9

# GLORY DAYS

One afternoon, a young reporter was standing with Laguerre at a bar called the Canton Village, drinking in silence and watching a local midday television show in which a pair of hosts were interviewing a famous French chef—renowned for making the best omelettes in New York City—who was preparing to open his own restaurant in Manhattan.

Throughout the lengthy interview, the hosts peppered the chef with questions, asking him how long he'd been cooking, who taught him, what his best dish was. At the end of the segment, as they signed off, Laguerre stood at the bar and shook his head.

"Bad interview," he grumbled. "All that and they never asked him the most important thing: Where do you get your eggs?"

Laguerre was rarely more effusive than that about his philosophy of journalism, but in the second half of the '60s, his unerring journalistic instincts would lead *SI* to new ground, where it would become more prominent than ever before.

The staff was paid poorly in comparison to other magazines within the building, but Laguerre evinced an almost otherworldly level of loyalty; there was a strong sense among writers and editors alike that they were bound up in something important. It was also clear that Laguerre shielded the staff from much of the executive-floor meddling that went on at the other magazines. "Laguerre protected you from *everything*," said Ray Cave. "It's like having a loyal commander in the field in the army. One that you just go anywhere with, because you know that he's going to keep them from getting at you—them being the people on your own side."

Sitting back in his chair, tapping his white stick against his desktop, Laguerre was prone to long, thoughtful silences. He agonized for months in 1966 before deciding to let Gangel shrink the cover logotype so that both *Sports* and *Illustrated* would fit on a single line. One day in the late '60s, while sitting and talking with Ray Cave about story selection, Laguerre stopped talking in the middle of a sentence to consider the matter further. Out the window of Laguerre's office, the clock atop the Newsweek building was clearly visible to those sitting in the chair in front of Laguerre's desk. So Cave waited and thought, keeping his eye on the clock as the silence dragged on. Twenty-two minutes after Laguerre stopped talking, he continued his point in midsentence and completed his thought.

Sometimes, the decision could come quickly. Creamer called Laguerre at home one night before closing a long bonus piece, having noticed that a sequence of drop caps, the enlarged capital letters at the start of a paragraph that provide some variety in long stretches of type, spelled out the letters S-H-I-T over several pages. Creamer didn't want the magazine to be embarrassed, but stopping the presses at that point would cost nearly $100,000. He presented the alternatives to Laguerre and waited.

"Go ahead and let it run," said Laguerre, after a few seconds of thought. "Most people won't even notice it, and those that do will be delighted."

And throughout that period, *SI* reflected Laguerre's worldly, inquiring eclecticism. *SI* was first a newsmagazine, but after devoting the first three or four stories and several departments to reporting the sports news of the week, the magazine had a three-story feature well and a lengthy bonus piece to move far-from-breaking news. The January 8, 1968, issue typified the eclectic story mix: it included the obvious lead piece, Maule's story on the 1967 NFL championship game between the Packers and the Cowboys, followed by Bud Shrake's story on the AFL championship game. But the same issue also featured a Charles Schulz pictorial essay on Snoopy golfing at the Bing Crosby pro-am, Curry Kirkpatrick's report from an obscure outpost of college basketball (where the predominantly black school Norfolk State was leading the nation in scoring), and the bonus piece, Jack Kerouac's memories of playing football at Columbia University.

Out in the heartland, *Sports Illustrated* was having a profound impact on sports fans, becoming as much a part of the weekly routine as the daily sports pages, Monday-morning quarterbacking, and the Prudential scoreboard show on fall Saturdays. Fast color made the covers more topical, and being chosen for the cover—despite recurring talk of the *SI* cover jinx—became proof of athletic legitimacy and, occasionally, a cause for hysteria. When Rick Mount was featured on the cover of the February 14, 1966, issue, 7,300 copies of the magazine were sold on the newsstands of his hometown, Lebanon, Indiana (pop. 9,523). On a national level, circulation more than doubled in the '60s.

*SI* under Laguerre was tailored to a world that embraced television, taking the measure of beautiful, charismatic stars like Muhammad Ali, Joe Namath, and Arnold Palmer. At a time when the depiction of sports in other magazines was often bombastic and overwritten (in *Esquire*, Thomas B. Morgan was cautioning about the "eerie parallel in the recent histories of U.S. politics and pro football"), *SI* had become the trustworthy source, at once informative and elegant, a bastion of authoritative sanity in a time of heightened anxiety. Maule's dispatches from the NFL wars were required reading for a generation of suburban professional sports fans who had retreated from drug culture and Vietnam debates to the comfort and protection of the television set in the den. Similarly, Frank Deford and Curry Kirkpatrick helped bring basketball to a truly national audience for the first time. With the very idea of the American dream being challenged, *SI* existed as both an oasis from the internecine societal struggle, and a bridge over the ever-widening generation gap.

The magazine's reach, in access, in attention, even in outrage, could best be seen in middle America. By 1966, when *SI* writers went on assignment, especially in college towns across the Midwest, it was big news. Writers would arrive at hotels and find their names up on the marquee; sports information directors went out of their way to curry favor. "There were several times when I was asked if I would like some female company in my room," said Deford. Covering the Midwest regionals in Wichita at the 1966 NCAA basketball tournament, Deford tried to talk with Texas Western coach Don Haskins, who brushed him off before he could even introduce himself. As Haskins was walking away, one of his assistants walked up to him and said, "You know, the guy you just blew off was from *Sports Illustrated*." Haskins turned on his heels and greeted Deford like a prized recruit. Later in the tournament, Adolph Rupp let Deford sit in the Kentucky locker room during the halftime of the championship game against Texas Western. It was there that Deford first became aware of the virulent racism that still existed in the Kentucky program. "Stop that coon; stop that big nigger," he recalled Rupp telling a player, though he couldn't write about it at the time because he'd gained entry to the locker room for background purposes only, and then only in the event that Kentucky won.

But no one had a larger effect than Dan Jenkins, partly because the events he was covering, big college football games and major golf tournaments, were tailored to big build-ups anyway. "When you heard that Dan Jenkins and *Sports Illustrated* were coming into town for a game, everyone got a bit more excited," said longtime Nebraska sports information director Don Bryant. Typically, Jenkins would arrive in town a couple days before an event, interview the coaches and a few key players during the day, and hold court at the hotel lounge at nights, picking up every check in sight.

In 1966, Michigan State and Notre Dame ripped through their early schedules undefeated, on course for a November showdown. The week prior to the game, reporter Gary Ronberg, a Michigan State alum, was sent to East Lansing to prepare a file on the Spartans. He had been regaling Jenkins, who spent the week back in South Bend, with stories about the splendors of the East Lansing campus.

Saturday morning, November 19, arrived cold and drizzly, with slate gray skies and a winterly chill casting a pall over the entire town. But Ronberg greeted Jenkins at the airport and insisted on giving him the full campus tour anyway, and so Jenkins silently went along. They finally wound up in the press box, where, looking out over the campus beyond Spartan Stadium, sipping coffee, Jenkins delivered his verdict to Ronberg: "Gary, I hate to tell you this, but it reminds me of Stalingrad."

The game, of course, ended in a controversial 10–10 tie, and *SI*'s coverage that week put the magazine at the heart of the debate. "Furor Over No. 1" read the red ribbon tagline above the *Sports Illustrated* logotype of the November 28 issue. And then, above a picture of an Irish back falling into a pile of Spartan defenders, there was the headline: "Notre Dame Runs Out the Clock Against Michigan State." Jenkins' lead story, "An Upside-Down Game," sent the Notre Dame campus into a fury:

Old Notre Dame will tie over all. Sing it out, guys. That is not exactly what the march says, of course, but that is how the big game ends every time you replay it. And that is how millions of cranky college football fans will remember it. For 59 minutes in absolutely overwrought East Lansing last week the brutes of Michigan State and Notre Dame pounded each other into enough mistakes to fill Bubba Smith's uniform—enough to settle a dozen games between lesser teams—but the 10–10 tie that destiny seemed to be demanding had a strange, noble quality to it. And then it did not have that anymore. For the people who saw it under the cold, dreary clouds or on national television, suddenly all it had was this enormous emptiness for which the Irish will be forever blamed. . . .

Put the No. 1 team, Notre Dame, on its own 30-yard-line with time for at least four passing plays to break the tie. A No. 1 team will try *something,* won't it, to stay that way?

Notre Dame did not. It just let the air out of the ball. For reasons that it will rationalize as being more valid than they perhaps were under the immense circumstances, the Irish rode out the clock.

The story prompted hundreds of letters to the *SI* offices, most of them coming from apoplectic Notre Dame fans. On the campus at South Bend the next weekend, students collected money to buy every issue of *SI* they could find, and burned 1,200 copies in the campus commons. A week later, after Notre Dame had ended its season by routing Southern Cal, Jenkins received another letter, representative of the general tone of mail from Irish fans, which read: "Notre Dame 51, Southern California 0. Go straight to HELL! You lousy son of a bitch!" He framed it and placed it on the wall of his office.

Jenkins was doing more than merely angering fans. His writing possessed an assured attitude and sardonic tone that would become the crucial final element in the emerging *SI* news story style. Jenkins's pieces combined much of Sherrod's wisdom, passed down while writing in an afternoon newspaper style, with the ability to render a strong point of view without using the first person. His stories read like a combination between a column and a game story, with more analysis than the former and more humor than the latter. Implicit in any of his pieces was that it was the definitive, last word on whatever event was being covered. And as demonstrated by the Notre Dame–Michigan State lead, he had an uncanny knack for the sportswriter's first rule, boiling down a week's build-up and an afternoon of action into the essential, pertinent elements.

"My interest in being a sportswriter coincided with the magazine when it was at its best, which was Jenkins, who I believed influenced sportswriting as much as anybody who has ever written," said *New York Daily News* columnist Mike Lupica. "The way he wrote leads. The way he got into a story, the way he put fun in it, and a point of view. I go back and look at stuff I wrote in college and it's hilarious; I believe that my style is quite different from Dan's. It wasn't when I was a kid. We were all tremendously influenced by him."

There was also an aura of the forbidden to Jenkins's stories, evidence of his surpassing skill as a reporter. He capitalized on *SI*'s unmatched access, spending time away from the locker room with coaches like Darrell Royal and players like Joe Namath.

"He was the best I ever saw at using a friendship to his advantage," said *Washington Post* sports editor George Solomon, who was writing college football for the *Fort Lauderdale Sun-Sentinel* in the late '60s. "I know a lot of people who say, 'I'm friends with Michael Jordan' or 'I'm friends with Joe Montana,' and it doesn't show. Jenkins was friends with a lot of them and used it to his advantage journalistically. He probably never betrayed a trust, but still was able to use it. I remember he did a piece on John McKay, when he was coaching at USC in his heyday. You just got a sense that McKay had him into the den looking at film, and you knew that you were going to get more from this story than, say, I could have done, and I was covering college football at the time. Anybody can be a pal to someone, but what good does it do you? But Darrell Royal put Jenkins into his inner circle, and then Jenkins brought that inner circle to the readers."

While other writers were tortured about what confidences to betray and what to keep, what to report and what to leave out, Jenkins instinctively *knew*. "I knew certain things didn't belong," he said. "What good does it do me to write that a guy got drunk last night? Or smoked a joint? Or spent some time talking to someone who would not be closely identified as his wife? That's not going to win me a Pulitzer. It's going to lose me a friend and a source. And what's it got to do with anything anyhow?"

And Jenkins's distinctive style would help to shape and inform the prose of those within the magazine as well. Plimpton would call him "one of the great writers of first lines that there has ever been," and many of the staffers at the magazine tried to match him, if not directly in style then in tone and attitude. That attitude, most closely reflecting Jenkins's persona, shaped the style of a generation of sportswriters, within the magazine and beyond.

• • •

As fast color came, *SI*'s photographic priorities, and its editorial emphasis, would change; the ascendant photographers in the late '60s were those who thrived on deadline pressure. Rather than a leisurely crowd shot of the previous year's Kentucky Derby, Laguerre now wanted the decisive shot of the Saturday afternoon race, and heaven help the photo editor who didn't assign the right man to do the job.

The magazine was a magnet for talented young photographers: Manny Millan specialized in basketball, Heinz Kluetmeier and John Iacono were accomplished generalists, veterans Richard Meek, Tony Triolo, and Jim Drake had the skills for the deadline stress. But two would stand out. One was Leifer, the deli delivery boy who had grown up into a single-minded fanatic, thrilling to the pressure of the shoot. The other was his antithesis, the handsome, laid-back Flemish-American prodigy, Walter Iooss, Jr. The two were doomed to be connected forever through their photographic rivalry, but away from the arenas, they were comically mismatched. The squat Leifer had developed a sort of headlong orneriness, to make up for all the times he'd been overlooked or ignored. Iooss, leonine and seductive, not averse to sneaking out back for some pot an hour before an event, was the quintessential long-haired, safari-jacketed shooter. He earned the envy of his competitors with his nearly miraculous ability to find the right shot, though many of the subjects he covered, like Ohio State football coach Woody Hayes, loathed him simply because of his rebellious looks.

Within the world of *SI*, Leifer-Iooss would develop into one of the classic journalistic rivalries of the era; wherever there was a big event, the two shooters were inevitably out front, vying for the perfect cover shot. During the 1967 NFL Championship game, the famous Ice Bowl at Lambeau Field, where the Packers battled the Cowboys in 13-below-zero conditions, Iooss and Leifer were battling the elements and each other. "I had had the best game I'd ever had and Walter had had the worst game he'd ever had," said Leifer, remembering Bart Starr's climactic touchdown sneak. "The end of the game, Bart Starr goes into the end zone, and in front of me moves the referee, and I've got the referee's ass, and Walter has a clean view of the touchdown, the first good picture he took all day, and the best picture of the game." When Gene Ulrich went to Meigs Field to pick up the color film late that night, the courier who delivered it still had icicles on his eyebrows.

But more than pride was at stake over cover photographs. Writers were naturally competitive as well, but they were on salary while, at the time, *SI* had no staff photographers. Photographers were paid a basic day rate, then paid bonuses for the pictures that ran in the magazine. The difference between getting four pictures and a cover and getting shut out, could be the difference between $1,500 and $150. Iooss was a master at the most innate skills of the sports photographer's trade, able to compensate for a lack of preparation with his instinctive talent at the moment of action.

"Walter would get to town the night before a game," said Leifer. "He'd invariably meet some beautiful lady at the bar. He'd be drunk, stoned, up all night, and he would arrive as the National Anthem was being played and he'd be punching his motor drive to get it to work because these things used to break all the time. I was in bed by myself, sober, early, and the first person at the stadium. I had thought about the backgrounds—*Is there a Marlboro ad that I want to keep out of the background?*—'cause Laguerre wouldn't run a cover if it had a big ad in the background. My equipment was in perfect working shape. And Walter held his own all those years. Says something about Walter. I don't think he ever put ten seconds of thought into it. He just never missed. At the beginning, you think of a little bit of it as luck. I probably thought a half-dozen times that Walter was a little lucky. After a while, you know it's not luck."

"It was war," remembered Iooss. "Neil was very aggressive—far more aggressive than I was, and he always had a way of getting covers. I remember the 1965 championship game, Browns and Packers, I dropped a lot of film out of my pocket. I'll never forget it—it still bothers me. Then something happens in the end zone and Neil's screaming, 'I got the cover! I got the cover! I even left room for the logo!' I just thought, *Neil, you bitch*. But when he said it, it was like, 'Jesus, he's probably got it.'"

Their approaches were different, but together, they would account for dozens of the most memorable photographs in the magazine's history, including about seven years' worth of *SI* covers. Their rivalry was never more pronounced than in big games; even though they were competing not only with each other, but also the best of *SI*'s other shooters, Iooss and Leifer traded cover shots over the first four Super Bowls. Iooss's Super Bowl I shot of Max McGee jogging into the end zone was answered a year later by Leifer's famous shot of Vince Lombardi being carried off the field by the Packers. In Super Bowl III, Iooss responded with an unforgettable image of Joe Namath, the quintessence of the nickname Joe Cool, squirting water into his mouth on the sidelines. Leifer got the cover the next year, with a shot of Len Dawson calmly taking a snap from Chiefs' center E.J. Holub as the Chiefs dissected the Minnesota Vikings in Super Bowl IV.

• • •

While the lead writers and the fast color were giving *SI* a newfound sense of journalistic urgency, the magazine continued to raise its profile in the literary community with its bonus pieces.

The summer and fall of 1965 would feature a half-dozen memorable bonus pieces, the magazine topping itself from one week to the next. Larry L. King wrote a requiem for middleweight legend Sugar Ray Leonard, "Sugar: Down But Not Quite Out," in the September 6 issue. Two weeks later, in the college preview issue, John Underwood weighed in with his analyticial argument of why "The College Game Is Best." The year-end double issue featured a unique bonus piece. "Then My Arm Glassed Up" was John Steinbeck's response to a Ray Cave query to write a piece for *SI*. Steinbeck wrote back that he couldn't write sports because he didn't know anything about it, but his reply was so lengthy and finely wrought that Cave recognized that Steinbeck's answer *was* his story.

The season also saw the first bonus piece from Mark Kram, who had been hired earlier in the year at Terrell's and Cave's urging. A talented sports columnist for the *Baltimore Sun*, he was quickly placed on the boxing beat, where he excelled. His portraits of fighters and the raconteurs on the fringe of the boxing game had a brooding gravity to them, but he could also marvelously evoke a sense of place, as he did in the August 30, 1965, issue on the Illinois State Fair in Du Quoin. A year later, he'd write lyrically about his hometown of Baltimore ("A Wink at a Homely Girl") as the Orioles prepared to play in their first World Series.

But Jenkins, again, was the writer who would most clearly delineate the new *Sports Illustrated* from the old. He had been contemplating for years a memoir of his fevered youth on the links of Goat Hills in Fort Worth. In the August 16 issue, Jenkins returned to the setting for "The Glory Game at Goat Hills," which opened with a wistful preamble about his youth, then described an American golf subculture about as far removed from John Marquand's genteel Happy Knoll Country Club as one could fathom. At Goat Hills, he remembered, there was "the very good chance that all of us would be in one hollering, protesting, club-slinging fifteensome," frequently engaged in some gambling aberration of the original game, such as playing the course backward, or "to every other hole, to every third hole, entirely out of bounds except for the greens (which meant you had to stay in the roads and the lawns), with only one club or at night, which was stimulating because of all the occupied cars parked on the more remote fairways." He mentioned some Goat Hills graduates who attempted to make the pro tour, and then he documented the series of events that sent him to journalism, recounting the details of his performance at a tournament called the Waxahachie Invitation:

> I know it was an unusually strong field one particular year because it took 70 to qualify for 30 of the 32 places in the championship flight. Unluckily, I shot 71 along with 11 others, so there had to be a playoff—swatfest, it was called—for the last two places. A playoff meant a gallery. Bad deal.
>
> We began swinging and nine players bogied the first sudden-death hole and were eliminated. (I envied them all.) One player got a birdie and was in. Two of us made pars and had to go another hole for the remaining berth or the privilege of being thrashed 6 and 5 the next day. . . .
>
> My opponent was a tall fellow named Shelby, and I did not realize

until a few years later that it was the same Carroll Shelby who raced sports cars. This might have been the thing that drove him to it. The crowd stayed—the ritualistic barbecue and dice game were still a good hour off—and it had no respect for either of us. As we stood on the tee, perspiring from fright, I heard someone say, "Who you want?" And the reply: "Aw, neither one. They both chili dippers."

Whatever Shelby did, I did better. He hooked, I hooked. He hit over the fence, I hit over the fence. The giggles trailed us endlessly. He got lost in the gully, I got lost in the gully. He landed in the bunker, I landed in the bunker. At one point I heard a man say, "Well, I been to the Dublin Rodeo, I've met the Light Crust Doughboys and I've stepped across the Mississippi where it ain't but a foot wide, but I never seen nothin' like this." Finally, perhaps through a bookkeeping error, I won the hole with a 10.

This exaggerated nonfiction was ascendant at the time—Tom Wolfe was defining the genre and Hunter Thompson would take it to a different realm years later in *Rolling Stone*—but it was nonetheless a groundbreaking advance in sports journalism, which was energized by the transfusion.

The next year found *SI* casting farther for bonus pieces. A doctoral candidate from Yale named Pete Axthelm traveled to Brazil to explain Pele's popularity to an American audience, and wound up on the staff; Jack Olsen wrote about his adventure, along with partner Ray Cave, at a high-stakes bridge tournament in Las Vegas; the fast-rising Frank Deford showed a gift for the profile piece in his feature on Arthur Ashe; John Underwood began a series on Alabama coaching legend Bear Bryant. Later in the fall, George Plimpton's *Paper Lion*, an expansion of a two-part bonus piece about his fall camp experience with the Detroit Lions, hit the bestseller lists. For the 1966 year-end issue, Laguerre devoted 27 pages to a bonus package on the emerging sports culture and stars in Africa.

• • •

In December 1966, the Steak de Paris closed, ending another era in the drinking history of the magazine. The bar was ushered out with The Match Game to End All Match Games, presided over by "Commissioner" M.R. Werner and "official scorer" Walter Bingham. Tex Maule lost, and wound up buying a round of drinks for nearly 40 people.

Another search was not needed, however, as the staff quickly gravitated to a just-opened bar on 50th Street, just off Sixth Avenue. Walking out the southwest door of the Time & Life Building, it was just two doors down to the Ho Ho, a Chinese restaurant and bar that would be *SI*'s unofficial headquarters for the balance of the Laguerre era.

It would also be witness to the magazine's greatest paradox over this period: as the drinks flowed, in multiples of four, and the lunches got longer and the expense accounts got fatter and the writers better-known, somehow the magazine kept getting better. For a while, at least.

The drinking occasionally began in the office. Johnston, in the Time Inc. tradition, had made pourings a regular feature of the *SI* edit cycle. Whether it was for a new employee reporting for duty, or a holiday, or to honor Bingham, Crichton, and Gwilym Brown running in the Boston Marathon or, in the words of Laguerre, "to deplore the occasion of Morrie Werner's 80th birthday," pourings were frequent, starting on 20 and usually continuing down at the Ho.

Alcohol also was a constant factor on hectic Sunday nights, when the long hours gave the 20th floor the look and feel of a campaign headquarters on election night. "There was a refrigerator outside my office, and I had the key," said Bill Gallagher, Jr. "We had six cases of beer in there and a case of soda. And I would open it up on Saturdays and Sundays at one o'clock, so the staff could get through the day. The liquor cabinet was up on the 29th, at *Life*. But it seemed that Bill Gallagher, Jr., had the key to the beer chest, and Bill Gallagher, Sr., had the key to the liquor cabinet."

Not that those looking for a drink ever had to look very hard. On a Sunday night, staffers walking into Dick Johnston's office could count on finding three things: Honor Fitzpatrick, sitting in front of his desk, going over copy; Johnston's girlfriend Connie Wood (who was Harold Hayes's secretary at *Esquire*) sitting on the couch; and, on the coffee table in front of the couch, an open bottle of Dewar's White Label scotch, there for anyone who wanted to partake.

Because Johnston and Laguerre had such differing sensibilities, the crowd surrounding each was vastly different, though there was some overlap. Around Johnston, the talk was less likely to involve sports.

"Dick didn't give a shit," said Jenkins. "He knew more about pornography than anything. He ran with a slightly different crowd, but everybody liked Dick. He was just an old *Life* guy who liked Laguerre a lot, and they got along. But rather than standing around the bar drinking with Laguerre and telling sports stories and ordering 5,000 J&Bs a night, Dick would rather be getting laid. Or going to a really good restaurant. He was great on expense accounts. He was the leader in the clubhouse at taking a researcher to lunch at Lutèce on company money."

Laguerre almost never drank in his office. And most of the senior editors were usually scrupulous about not drinking until the serious work was done: stories edited, headlines written, captions completed. But for much of the staff, this was a rule generally honored in the breach. Drunk or sober, almost everyone stopped by the Ho Ho afterward.

The Ho Ho was done up in a Chinese Emigrant Charmless motif, with plastic orange trees flanking the doorway, a partition of floor-to-ceiling plastic beads en route to the bathrooms, and, snaking around the pillar in the middle of the small stairway leading to the bar, a garish green dragon. "It looked like somebody had thrown a hydrogen bomb into the Ming room in Hiroshima," said Bill Leggett, mixing his nuclear metaphors. "That place hummed all the time. Henny Youngman used to go there—try to get around the idea of Henny Youngman and Laguerre being in the *same bar*. Somebody once said we only stayed there because all the bartenders looked like Braulio Baeza, the jockey."

And very quickly, they started calling it the Ho.

"Now the Ho was all right," said Andy Crichton. "It had been La Fonda del Sol, a very smart place. The Chinese come in, and there is nothing very smart about it—they're just turning over a lot of people with a cheap lunch, and no one's sitting at the bar. So we took over the bar, and that was fine for us, because some of us could get some soup or something delivered to the bar. André would be drinking the entire time, so at least we could get something to eat. Before we died."

Upon returning to New York from assignments, the writers would hurry to see Laguerre at the Ho, like Hemingway calling on Gertrude Stein in *A Moveable Feast*, to provide tales from the road. "When you came back from the road, he wouldn't want a report on your story or anything like that," said Jenkins. "He wanted to laugh a lot—so you'd tell him the funny things that happened while you were on the road."

Virtually every day at lunch and every evening after work, Laguerre would be accompanied by the steadfast Morrie Werner, whose job at *SI* seemed to consist of: 1) Selecting quotes for the They Said It section in Scorecard; 2) Accompanying Laguerre to the bar at lunch and after work; 3) Placing bets for Laguerre, Maule, and himself, often through Bill Gallagher, Jr., nearly every day, and 4) Buying cigars on Fridays for Laguerre, Crichton, Jule Campbell's father, and himself. Since Werner would have gladly done all but the first of these duties without pay, it was a pretty good job. But there was no resentment. The younger writers looked up to him; Jenkins and Shrake would press him for details of New York back in the '20s and '30s. Junior staffers would stop by his office and throw darts at his customized dartboard, with Richard Nixon in the bull's-eye ("If you hit Nixon, he'll die a horrible death tonight!" he used to tell staffers), or study the memorabilia on his wall, which included a sign that read,

"While your ancestors were dancing around campfires painted green, mine were Kings of Israel." Above all, Werner was a fount of both good cheer and righteous anger, living testament to the golden era of New York journalism. "We were all Morrie's children," said Pat Ryan. "Because he was by himself, he'd like to go out to dinner or something. So you ended up having an evening with Morrie where you'd drink with him and then end up putting him in a taxicab."

On a typical evening after work, Laguerre and Werner would be at the Ho, usually joined by editors like Crichton and Creamer. Many of the writers—Jenkins, Maule, Shrake, Tower, Olsen, Leggett, often Deford—would stop by if they were in town. Harvey Grut and Marty Nathan from the art department might be there as well, along with Art Brawley from production.

The drinking would continue well into the evening, with Laguerre bouncing ideas off his compatriots, and occasionally writing notes to himself on a bar napkin. Laguerre drank J&B and water at the bar, though he stuck with the English Bell's for special occasions or at the track. Regardless of the circumstances, he always tipped the same, to bartenders, coatcheck girls, maître d's: it was one dollar. In the Laguerre lexicon, there came a time to call for the final round. This was followed by The Bloody Final. "Then he'd say, 'Now we're going to have an ABF,'" said Marty Nathan. "For the longest time, nobody knew what that meant. It turned out it was the Absolute Bloody Final." One day, in the middle of one of those graduated send-offs, Shrake stood up from his barstool and fell drunkenly to the floor. "From now on," Laguerre announced, "the last drink of the night shall be called 'The El Shrake-O.'"

For some at the magazine, the daily processions to the bar started to take on a dark quality. Not everyone there could handle their alcohol, and there was frequently a price to be paid domestically. "It was probably a factor in breaking up my marriage," said Les Woodcock. "We just didn't come home when we should've. We drank at lunchtime. I wasn't the worst; there were lots worse. You spent more time with your researcher or your secretary than with your wife."

Shrake, like dozens of *SI* staffers, wound up in Alcoholics Anonymous. "André thoroughly enjoyed the camaraderie of the bar," he said. "Back in those days, one of the reasons I drank so heavily was that's *what you did*. The ones who didn't drink, you didn't fuck with them. They were not to be trusted. If you were not a hard-drinking guy, you didn't belong in our company. And we had a really good time. Looking back on it now, I can see that André was drinking himself to death."

"You were there because he had a magnetism that was just extraordinary," said Jack Olsen, a frequent drinking partner in the early '60s before moving to Colorado. "It wasn't as simple as sucking up to the boss. But you can't deny that we were doing it. I mean, if you had a chance to have a drink with the king every night, would you do it? We all damaged our personal lives to a certain extent. But he was an irresistible man. And Nathalie—one part of her hated all of us because we was keeping him away from home."

There was undeniable comfort and security in the rituals, but Laguerre never seemed to hold a grudge against those who didn't drink with the group. Terrell and Cave were his two top lieutenants in terms of determining story assignments and shaping the magazine (Johnston stuck to the line editing), and neither of them was ever seen in the Ho.

"I was a very good friend of Laguerre's," said Terrell. "But I also had a wife and some kids, and I went home in the evening. Some of the people who were in it early dropped out, because they said, 'This is no way to live. And this isn't the way we want to do it or have to do it.'"

But for years, it was the way it was done.

On February 28, 1967, Henry Luce died.

Even as they were returning from the memorial service, Nathalie feared for her husband's career. "I knew that this would change things. He didn't have that many friends upstairs—and he hated the business people—so the picture changed." Hedley Donovan had succeeded Luce as editor-in-chief in April 1964, but he had kept his distance from Laguerre, and acceded to Luce's wishes that *SI* receive clearance for more and costly increases in fast color pages.

They coexisted with reasonable harmony for a couple of years, but as Luce faded from the picture, Donovan began to resent Laguerre, less for his autonomy than for his attitude of entitlement to it. The picture was not brightened by Laguerre's behavior at the mandatory weekly managing editors' meetings that were a Time Inc. tradition. Something of a misnomer, the weekly gatherings were really held at the pleasure of the editor-in-chief, who would invite the four managing editors, and a few other key executives and top editors, to create a power lunch of a dozen or so each week.

"André would sit there glumly, never opening his mouth," said Andrew Heiskell. "Everyone else was talking, arguing with Hedley. André just sat there, and at the end just got up. In that sense, they didn't get along. André wasn't trying to get along with anybody. I think it's just André."

The talk usually focused on politics and culture, two areas in which Laguerre had expertise. But he hated the tone of the lunches, all politesse and pomposity; it wasn't where he wanted to drink or whom he wanted to drink with. "I was there once with Hedley, and everyone else at the table had spoken," remembered Jason McManus, then an AME on *Time*. "André said nothing. And Hedley said, 'Well, André, would you care to comment on this topic?' And André just said, 'No.' And that really made Hedley mad. Hedley finally quit fighting at the lunches."

In early March, Laguerre was talking about Luce with Mark Kram over the inevitable scotch and water at the Ho.

"Things will never be the same," he said somberly.

"What do you mean?" asked Kram.

"Luce had a commitment to writing. Despite his flaws, you knew he backed you up. He was for accidents. Accidents are going to happen less and less. Those people are going to take over."

Kram didn't have to ask who those people were.

• • •

At Houston's Hobby Airport, on April 24, 1967, Bud Shrake, driving a rented white Cadillac convertible, picked up Muhammad Ali and Bundini Brown as they stepped off their flight from Washington, D.C. It was indicative of the sort of access that *SI* enjoyed during the period that it was Shrake and *SI*, rather than Howard Cosell and ABC, who met Ali at the airport to squire him around Houston just four days before he would officially decline to enroll in the army. In "Taps for the Champ," *SI*'s eight-page lead story the next week, Shrake provided a firsthand glimpse of Ali's week, including his visit to the campus of Texas Southern University ("'Are you married?' Ali asked a girl. 'Yeah, man, I'm married to SNCC,' she answered.") and his refusal to be inducted. The story marked *SI*'s most pointed expression of support for Ali after years of vacillation and signaled that *SI* was finally beginning to engage the racial question.

Race had become a sore subject at the magazine, though Laguerre was, by all estimation, without bigotry. "He had that European colorblindness," said Olsen. The prevailing question, that plagued *SI* from the black players' boycott of the AFL All-Star Game to the threatened Olympic boycott in '68 in Mexico City, and beyond, was where to draw the line. How far did the magazine go in covering the political issues of the day? As a rule, Laguerre didn't want *SI* to be a standard-bearer for any cause, other than the sanctity of sports. He feared the fallout of alienating his readership by putting too many blacks on the cover of *Sports Illustrated*. Yet there were times that he fought against a more pointed institutional discomfort over race at the upper echelons of the company. A 1968 cover of Earl "The Pearl" Monroe silhouetted against a white backdrop elicited a stinging critique from Ralph Graves, who was serving a tour of duty on the 34th floor. Graves called it "one of the ugliest, most unappealing covers that I could recall ever having on one of our magazines." In a curt memo of response three weeks later, Laguerre informed him that it had been among the best-selling issues of the year.

"Donovan questioned early on whether we should have that many blacks on the cover," remembered Terrell. "Not necessarily because he was a racist, but from a business point of view. He said, 'Our readers are 99 percent white—are they going to buy these magazines?' And I think André, among other folks, pointed out to Donovan that sports fans don't see black and white like other people do."

But Laguerre remained aware of—and sensitive to—the perception.

"I remember having a conversation with him one time," said Crichton. "I said, 'André, do you realize that there was a time when it was the Irishmen and the Germans and the Italians? All the people getting kicked around the most are the toughest when it comes to playing these games. That's why the blacks are taking over. They've been kicked around plenty now. This is the one place they can get going.' He became more sympathetic to this, but he was still afraid."

Underwood and Olsen attacked the issue from a sociological perspective, while Kram and the young college basketball writer Curry Kirkpatrick did it by steeping themselves in the black experience, emerging as interpreters of black urban culture. Jenkins did it, as always, with humor, lampooning the logic of the bigots.

But Olsen was the writer that Laguerre trusted the most. Pointed and prolific, with a muckraker's tenacity evident on his compact face and enveloping eyes, he was a tireless reporter who set an example for hard work that the rest of the staff followed. For his efforts, he received more prestige assignments than anyone under Laguerre. Late in 1967, during one of his occasional visits to the city (he was by now living in Colorado with his wife Sue Peterson, just two years away from leaving the magazine to write books full-time), Olsen was called into Laguerre's office. Laguerre felt it was the right time to do a story about the state of the black athlete in modern society. By this point, the dichotomy between such "positive" role models as Floyd Patterson and Ernie Banks was being contrasted with a more militant vision, expressed by the likes of Jim Brown, Bill Russell, Muhammad Ali, and others. Laguerre sensed there was more to the story, and when he turned Olsen loose to do the investigation, the writer

unearthed a mountain of seething black resentment. He produced a monumental five-part series arguing that while white America blandly spoke of
all the good that sport had done for blacks, it was oblivious to the way the
system was exploiting blacks, and of the rampant racism that still existed
in all levels of athletics.

Laguerre recognized that the series would be groundbreaking, but he
also knew that it veered so far from the conventional wisdom of the times,
and of Time, Inc., that the entire project might be imperiled if Hedley
Donovan were to see it beforehand. So prior to publishing the explosive
series, Laguerre chose not to tell Donovan that it was running. At a managing editors' lunch in mid-June, Pat Ryan accompanied Laguerre up to
47. "Some reference to black athletes came up," she recalled. "I started to
say something about the series and I could tell by his look that Laguerre
didn't want it discussed. We maneuvered the conversation—the fact that
we were going to start a series about black athletes next week did not get
exposed." The magazine was so secretive about it that the upcoming series
wasn't even mentioned in the Next Week teaser on the contents page of
the June 24 issue.

Once all five installments were edited, Laguerre left to spend his
month-long summer vacation in France, confident that if he could get the
first section of the series in the magazine, Donovan would be unwilling to
pull back the rest. Ray Cave, who edited the series, left the morning after
closing the first part, and headed up to Maine with Pat Ryan.

"The Black Athlete—A Shameful Story" read the headline on the July
1, 1968, issue. David Noyes's illustration showed a close-up of a black man
behind a pair of dark Wayfarers. The first 16 pages of the news section was
given over to Part 1 of Olsen's story, "The Cruel Deception." It began:

> Every morning the world of sports wakes up and congratulates
> itself on its contributions to race relations. The litany has been re-
> peated so many times that it is believed almost universally. It goes:
> "Look what sports has done for the Negro."
>
> To be sure, there are a few fair-minded men who are willing to
> suggest that perhaps the Negro has done something for sports in
> return. Says George McCarty, athletic director of the University of
> Texas at El Paso, "In general, the nigger athlete is a little hungrier,
> and we have been blessed with having some real outstanding ones.
> We think they've done a lot for us, and we think we've done a lot for
> them." . . .
>
> You can hear these arguments any night of the week in the saloon
> of your choice, even in the *Negro* saloon of your choice. The cliché that

sports has been good to the Negro has been accepted by black and white, liberal and conservative, intellectual and red-neck . . . But Negro athletes do not agree. Almost to a man, they are dissatisfied, disgruntled and disillusioned.

Black collegiate athletes say they are dehumanized, exploited and discarded, and some even say they were happier back in the ghetto.

Black professional athletes say they are underpaid, shunted into certain stereotyped positions and treated like subhumans by Paleolithic coaches who regard them as watermelon-eating idiots.

A member of the University of Houston's coaching staff once made the mistake of telling Halfback Warren McVea, "I think this university's athletic program has been pretty damn good to you." McVea, a short, black artillery shell of a man, snapped back, "I think I've been pretty damn good to this university. I want you to remember one thing: you came to me, I didn't come to you."

Hedley Donovan spent much of Thursday morning, June 27—the day the issue hit the newsstands—in his 34th floor office, reading the first installment, and growing increasingly angry. He knew that Laguerre, already in France, had intentionally concealed the series from him, a deceit that amounted to direct insubordination. Donovan's long-stated rule was that as long as his managing editors told him what was coming, he'd try to stay out of their way. Donovan called the 20th floor, and asked for the editor of the piece, and was further infuriated when he realized that all the particulars, not just Laguerre, but also Olsen and Cave were out of town. Donovan was patched through to the affable but over-matched Art Brawley, a steady Laguerre drinking companion and the magazine's outdoors editor, who was performing Cave's normal duties that week.

A few minutes later, Brawley, who stuttered under pressure, called Cave.

"C-c-can you come down to New York?" Brawley asked when he reached him in Maine. "Hed-Hedley wants to have lunch."

"Art, I'm on vacation," said Cave. "Hedley wants to have lunch?"

"Hedley *really* wants to have lunch. And he wants you to come down and talk about the Black Athlete series. You have to come down."

That afternoon, Cave flew back to the city. On Friday, he and Brawley went to a private dining room on the 47th floor for lunch with Donovan.

There was little small talk. "I'm troubled by part one," explained Donovan, his flat Minnesota intonations conveying the gravity of his concern. "It just isn't right. And the thesis of the series is wrong. The reason it's wrong is that we *all know* that sport is a route up for the black in this society. It's one of the few ways they have of getting ahead. And what you in effect are saying is almost the opposite."

Cave was mindful to choose his words carefully. He knew Donovan was exquisitely sensitive to the civil rights movement, but he also knew that his conception of the black athlete's experiences was as limited as most Americans'. Donovan's idea of the typical black athlete pretty much began and ended with Jackie Robinson.

"Hedley, the story is right," Cave said firmly, like a logic professor explaining a new theory to a colleague. "Olsen is the best reporter we've got going in our part of the business. He might not be our most eloquent writer, but he is certainly the best gatherer of information. So, Hedley, what Jack Olsen says is right. You may not like it. You may not want it. But the one thing I'm not worried about is whether his facts are wrong."

Donovan, looking troubled, stared at his plate for a while, then let out a deep sigh. "Well, now, are you going to make it plain in the series that there are black athletes who are *not* being taken advantage of?"

"Of course," said Cave.

"Plain enough?" asked Donovan.

"Plain enough."

"You're totally confident that all the investigative work in the series is accurate?"

"Absolutely."

"Okay. Go ahead."

The rest of the lunch consisted of Cave trying to disguise from Donovan, without directly lying to his editor-in-chief, the fact that he had the other four parts of the series in his possession. "I certainly wasn't going to give him the whole batch," said Cave. "We were smarter than that. If we had sent it as a batch, then he would have the right to be truly pissed off."

"The Black Athlete" elicited over a thousand letters, the largest response of any story or series in the history of the magazine. The second part argued that many inner-city blacks were doomed from the moment they received their college scholarships, exposed to a culture shock on college campuses, viewed as little more than athletic chattel, and strongly discouraged from dating whites. The third segment offered a jarring analysis of the way racial enmity had fractured the campus of the University of Texas at El Paso, just two years after its all-black starting lineup led the school (then called Texas Western) to an upset win over Kentucky in the NCAA basketball championship and raised its profile nationwide. The last two segments were devoted to pro sports—the fourth being a general discussion of the inequity in pay and less-tangible benefits at the pro level, the last segment a lengthy dissection of racial tension on the St. Louis Cardinals football team.

At State College, Pennsylvania, Joe Paterno was preparing for his third season as head football coach at Penn State. He spent much of July in escalating anguish, reading one installment after another of Olsen's series. Paterno was already a different sort of college coach, animated by a genuine empathy for his players and a deep concern that football contribute to their attaining a well-rounded adult life. To him, Olsen's series was a bracing, terrifying wake-up call. When the football team arrived for fall practice in August, Paterno immediately called a meeting of his black players.

"I was astounded," said Paterno. "I could not believe the things that were going on. We did not have a lot of black kids at that time, and one of them I had was a kid by the name of Charlie Pittman, who turned out to be All-America [in 1969]. As soon as the kids came back, the first meeting I had, I grabbed the black kids on the squad and I sat them down and said, 'Look, I have the *SI* magazine. I just got through reading these things and I'm shocked and embarrassed. Are any of these things on campus? Do you guys have any kinds of gripes?' They said, 'No coach. We don't have that on this campus,' which obviously made me feel good, but I remember my reaction. That series had such an impact on coaching, on our whole social consciousness in this country that all of a sudden we were doing these kinds of things to people and exploiting them."

For the remainder of that convulsive summer of 1968, leading up to the Mexico City Olympics, Olsen's series had set the agenda for discussion about blacks and athletics. It would become the single most important piece in *SI*'s history, clearly changing the terms of the debate about the black athlete.

It would also cause a rift between Donovan and Laguerre that would never be healed. Donovan had always understood Laguerre's reverence for Luce, and felt awkward giving him orders. In a company where MEs enjoyed vast amounts of power, Donovan had granted Laguerre nearly total autonomy, based on his excellent performance and Luce's stamp of approval. But Laguerre's handling of the series demonstrated to Donovan a lack of trust. And from that moment on, he began to wonder if Laguerre had garnered too much power.

But Laguerre had spent his political capital wisely. Not only had he tactically outmaneuvered Donovan in placing the series in the magazine, he protected himself after the fact due to the sheer strength of Olsen's piece and the overwhelmingly positive reaction it received. And as he would later do with an investigative series about women in sports,

Laguerre had solved the question of how far to get into the political melee. In bonus pieces, profiles, and investigative series, *SI* would use the world of sports as a prism through which to view the larger world.

And for all the vacillation over covers and what name to use in describing Muhammad Ali, it could be argued that *SI* provided a more nuanced, fully dimensional view of black America than almost any other mainstream publication of its time. Much of this was due to circumstance: by focusing on athletes, rather than the political leaders that preoccupied *Time*, *Life*, and *Newsweek*, *SI* viewed blacks outside of a purely political context. It was a circuitous road to enlightenment: Americans who might never abide or understand Malcolm X learned to respect the militant pride of Jim Brown; those who didn't trust Martin Luther King came to revere Bill Russell (who, with a strong push from Jerry Tax, was named Sportsman of the Year in 1968).

But something else was apparent. The very things that were making sports such a fertile ground for *SI*—its increasing visibility on television, the way that real-world concerns were spilling over onto the field of competition, the increasingly large amounts of money at stake—were complicating the rules of coverage. With the contentious, politicized Olympics in Mexico City, sports would finally lose the carapace of sanctuary that had made it such a reliable respite from the brawling, protest-laden '60s. Social unrest was coming to sport, and so was big money. And *Sports Illustrated* would be changed like all the rest.

# CHAPTER 10

# "9,000 DRINKS AT THE HO HO"

Mexico City was a journalistic debacle for *Sports Illustrated*, its darkest moment in an otherwise glorious end-of-the-decade run, and a hint of the changing media landscape ahead. Bob Beamon's otherworldly 29' 2½" long jump, which shattered the world record by nearly two feet, earned just a single paragraph of coverage in John Underwood's lead story the following week. Lee Evans's record 400 meters and the black-gloved protest salute by John Carlos and Tommy Smith received similarly short shrift, and none of the stories made the cover, which announced "The Packers Are Not Dead."

For all his news sense, Laguerre seemed paralyzed and strangely unprepared for the tumult in Mexico City, covering it as though it were little more than the biggest sports event of two successive weeks. Predictably, *Life* and *Time* devoted more space to the protest and its attendant publicity. *SI* could argue that the political controversy was a mere backdrop to the larger Olympic story, but coming just weeks after the five-part series on The Black Athlete, the absence of a broader view seemed schizophrenic. Regardless, it still begged the question: One paragraph for Bob Beamon's jump?

Part of the problem was Laguerre's formula, which had served *SI* so well throughout the decade. On a regular basis, the News-Features-Departments-Bonus lineup was a sound one, providing a literary texture that other newsweeklies couldn't match while still delivering the most important sports news of each week. But what to do when virtually all the sports news came from one place? While *SI* gave the 1968 Summer Games nearly unprecedented lead treatment (12 pages in the first week's roundup, eight pages the next week), it still didn't come close to covering or reflecting the significance of the drama that unfolded in Mexico City. The mistake was in viewing the Games as a single event, rather than several major events occurring in one place. John Underwood and Bob Ottum (who wrote the second week's lead piece) were put in the hopeless situation of trying to wrap up an entire week's news and political turmoil in a few hundred lines. It couldn't be done well, certainly not to *SI*'s standards.

And with ABC for the first time offering daily live coverage throughout the Games, *SI*'s once-over coverage seemed particularly superfluous and marginalized, not much better than what U.S. dailies were providing, much sooner, to their readers. Roy Terrell sensed that if the magazine was going to excel with future Olympic coverage, it would need to devote writers and space to individual sports, getting behind and beyond the story that was being told on television, just as it did with big football and baseball games.

But *SI* rebounded quickly after Mexico City. Bud Shrake wrote a fantastical but prescient piece in the December 9, 1968, issue called "A Champagne Party for Joe and Weeb," telling how the Jets would go on to beat Oakland in the AFL title game, then upset Baltimore in the coming Super Bowl. Throughout '69, *SI* stayed on top of, if not a step ahead of, breaking news. Jenkins's profile of the rebel Joe Namath and his nightlife anticipated the rift between Namath and the league that resulted in the memorable June 16, 1969, cover blurb "Namath Weeps," in which a crying Broadway Joe announced his short-lived retirement. There was nothing as controversial as Olsen's series on black athletes, but *SI*'s special investigations were trenchant: Underwood wrote a major investigative piece on sneaker companies paying amateur athletes to wear their products, and Bil Gilbert's three-part series about the growing threat of drugs in sports brought the subject of anabolic steroids into the mainstream. In the year-end and decade-ending double issue, William Oscar Johnson (who had come to *SI* from *Time* a year earlier) began a series called "TV Made It All a New Game," examining the changes that television had brought to the world of sports. It would take the success of *Monday Night Football*, considered a risky proposition when it debuted in 1970, to convince the last of the skeptics just how central a role spectator sports was assuming in American culture.

• • •

By the beginning of 1969, Frank Deford had been at the magazine for six and a half years. He had started as a gifted but undisciplined reporter, prone to exactly the sort of mistakes that drove editors crazy. "What's wrong with this guy?" editor Jerry Tax would mutter to colleagues. "I don't have any hope for him." But the truth was nearly the opposite. Tax, forever sucking on hard candy, forever kvetching, was prone to exaggeration. He recognized that Deford could be a major talent, if only he could harness his use of language. Tax served as a patron to several young writers (Pat Putnam, hired in '68, referred to Tax as "my Jewish mother"), but none more so than Deford, whom Tax regularly edited on the basketball beat. "Deford was not a very good writer," said Terrell. "And Jerry edited Frank for years. Jerry would say, 'You can't do this, Frank,' and Frank would say, 'Well, you know what I mean.' And Jerry would say, 'Yeah, but I can't go along with every issue of the magazine and tell readers what you mean.'"

Deford learned quickly and spent much of the mid- and late '60s covering college and pro basketball with rare depth and insight. In 1969, he moved off the full-time basketball beat to concentrate on bonus pieces, starting an extended tour of the margins of American sport, defining the breadth of *SI*'s coverage as he went. That year alone, he wrote a piece about the enduring low-rent appeal of the roller derby ("Five Strides on the Banked Track," later turned into a book); the perennial success of the anachronistic Miss America pageant (which he also later expanded into a book); and the tale of "Little Irvy, the Only Twenty-Ton Traveling Whale." Deford had long been fascinated with the fringe of the American sporting life, the sideshow daredevils and minor league outcasts who passed through the Baltimore of his youth. Reporting on these characters and their surroundings as an adult, he took simple pleasure in the incongruity—the tall, dashing man in a sporty blazer surveying the vaguely sad carnival ground. In a short time, Deford became *SI*'s most reliable choice for an out-of-the-way (which meant, at the time, a typical) bonus piece or a penetrating profile. In Laguerre's complex story mix, Deford's pieces often served as a counterpoint to the harder sports coverage that increasingly dominated the front of the book.

Replacing Deford on the basketball beat was the eternally youthful Curry Kirkpatrick—Jenkins often referred to him as "my friend, the child writer"—who had spent much of his adolescence dreaming about working for the magazine. A sports junkie and *SI* subscriber from an early age, Kirkpatrick had been raised in St. Louis before spending his high school years in upstate New York, where he'd often sit in his father's car and listen to the radio broadcasts of three area colleges (Niagara, Canisius, and St. Bonaventure) with outstanding basketball teams. Fascinated by the rhythms and grace of the college game, Kirkpatrick matriculated to North Carolina, where he wrote sports for the *Daily Tar Heel*. He introduced himself to Deford at a North Carolina game and asked for guidance on how to apply to the magazine, and was hired shortly after graduation.

While Deford looked like a movie star and dressed the part, Kirkpatrick resembled nothing so much as a diminutive, slightly petulant British rock star, whose mod suits and designer glasses only exaggerated his baby face and fine, curly hair. His writing, influenced by both Jenkins and Deford as well as the New Journalism of the day, was an amalgam of one-liners, puns, and pop cultural references that managed to tap into the heady urban brew of college basketball. Kirkpatrick came along at just the right time, as the college game behind Lew Alcindor and then Bill Walton started to be a major television property. "Curry knew the black athlete slant," said *Washington Post* columnist Michael Wilbon, of his youthful days reading the magazine. "Nobody else in print did. Nobody. He was hip. Not middle-of-the-road or six weeks late, but hip."

On the basketball beat, Kirkpatrick surveyed largely different terrain than Dan Jenkins did on the football beat, although they would both spend considerable time on the UCLA campus. But while Jenkins's coverage took him to large state universities with generations of tradition, Kirkpatrick was pursuing the upstart basketball powers, which tended to be smaller, less prominent schools, from Marquette and Wisconsin–Eau Claire to Pan American and Lamar, where a few players could make a difference and where the emergence of the black athlete could more clearly be seen.

"He was the Tom Wolfe of sports," said Tony Kornheiser, who was writing about college basketball for *Newsday* when he met Kirkpatrick. "Curry used to walk around in *doe-skin pants*. Curry would walk into a gym, and everybody wanted to be near him, and there were nights in my life, walking the streets with Curry Kirkpatrick, I thought I was sitting at the table with Dorothy Parker."

Whereas Deford and Kirkpatrick grew into accomplished writers while working within the *SI* editing system, three other key writers from the period arrived fully formed.

Mark Kram was perhaps the most talented and certainly the most troubled of the group. Born George Melvin Kram, he'd been a star athlete in his Baltimore high school, and on Valentine's Day 1955 signed a professional baseball contract with the Pirates organization. But after a beaning in Burlington, North Carolina. that left him with recurring headaches, he was released barely two months later, eventually returning to Baltimore to pursue his writing career. He was an erratic but extraordinarily gifted writer, a hard-bitten literary dreamer inspired by the mordant wit of Mencken and the masculine worldview of Hemingway. "I always wanted to write like Edward Hopper painted," Kram said, and his essays had a component of tragic grandeur to them. He certainly suffered like Hopper; Bud Shrake called him "the most tortured writer I've ever known in my life."

Kram's personality often suggested a hibernating bear being roused far too early, but he was uniquely suited to the shadowy theatrics of boxing. At the same time, he was moody and wildly unpredictable in social situations, punching out a female researcher at one party and getting into a scuffle with Norman Mailer at another. One night, he drunkenly challenged Laguerre, a man he revered, to a bar fight, before Shrake and assistant art director Marty Nathan intervened and put him into a cab. But Kram was also fiercely loyal; he was a drifter who needed a cause, and in Laguerre he found it.

Kram's densely constructed boxing dispatches revealed much about how the real world was experiencing the sporting world, often using it as a proxy for its cultural wars. In his preview of the first Muhammad Ali–Joe Frazier fight, in 1971, he wrote:

> The disputation of the New Left comes at Frazier with its spongy thinking and pushbutton passion and seeks to color him white, to denounce him as a capitalist dupe and a Fifth Columnist to their black cause. Those on the other fringe, just as blindly rancorous, see in Ali all that is unhealthy in this country, which in essence means all they will not accept from a black man. For still others, numbed by the shock of a sharply evolving society, he means confusion; he was one of the first to start pouring their lemonade world down the drain.
>
> Among the blacks there is only a whisper of feeling for Frazier, who is deeply cut by their reaction. He is pinned under the most powerful influence on black thought in this country. The militants view Ali as the Mahdi, the one man who has circumvented what they believe to be an international white conspiracy. To the young he is identity, an incomparable hero of almost mythological dimension.

The fight, on March 8, 1971, at Madison Square Garden, represented a grand confluence of sports, culture, and politics, coming at the height of Black is Beautiful pride and regnant racial awareness. *Life* sent Sinatra to ringside to shoot the fight, with Norman Mailer writing about it. But always at the center of the drama was the genuine developing enmity between the two men, which Kram captured better than any writer at the time, or since.

"Oh that was an extraordinary night," Kram remembered. "Limos were three deep around the Garden. It was snowy; a strange March night. The sky was strange. This had been building up for a week, without even talking hype here. You didn't have to hype this fight at all, the way things are hyped today." What Kram couldn't have known was that there would be two more Ali-Frazier fights, each one marking a pivotal moment in his life, and the magazine's.

The year of the first Ali-Frazier fight, Laguerre made the last key hire of his tenure, bringing in Ron Fimrite, a sports columnist at the *San Francisco Chronicle*. Fimrite was an elegant stylist with a raconteur's charm and an encyclopedic knowledge of sports history. It made him perfectly suited for bonus pieces that revisited past legends (Hank Luisetti, Max Baer, and Jackie Jensen, among others), but he was also adept at news stories. He would go on to cover some of the biggest events of the '70s: O.J. Simpson breaking Jim Brown's single-season rushing record, and Hank Aaron breaking Babe Ruth's homer record. Laguerre was especially fond of him because of his cultured background and his San Francisco roots, but also because Fimrite seemed to make many of his most astute observations from a barstool.

While Deford, Kram, Kirkpatrick, and Fimrite showed the expansive possibilities of *SI*, it was Roy Blount, Jr.,'s misfortune to butt up against its limits. A major talent from the moment he was hired at the magazine in 1968 from the *Atlanta Journal-Constitution*, Blount was such an iconoclastic writer that he was fated from the outset to have problems with the *SI* editing gauntlet.

A Vanderbilt University graduate who grew up in Decatur, Georgia, Blount was a round-faced, whip-smart, slow-drawling paradox, a take-no-prisoners civil rights advocate and unreconstructed liberal who found pleasure in the very institutions—the elegiac traditionalism of baseball, the ritualized violence of football—that were being savaged by the left-wing deconstructionists of the period. His writing combined a southerner's acute awareness of family ties with a preternatural rapport with black athletes. At heart, Blount was a literary natural who arrived with an identifiable style. One of his earliest assignments was a profile of Johnny Bench, in which he observed: "For a catcher to rise up amidst his grotesque impedimenta as Bench does, cock his arm like a flash and shoot a ball out with enough velocity to beat a runner to second without either attaining appreciable loft or tailing off at the end is one of the wonders of cultivated nature. The only comparable thing would be a bear that really danced well."

Blount's bashful charm hid a contrarian's nature and a distinctive, uncompromising attitude about his writing. All these factors made it inevitable, perhaps, that he'd have more problems than other writers with the *SI* editing system. It was after writing a hockey story for Roger Hewlett (universally the least respected of *SI*'s senior editors) that he was first confronted with the corporate arrogance of the place. "I remember

Roger Hewlett saying, 'You give me the lumber, I'll build the house.' That really pissed me off. I never wrote for Roger Hewlett again. I just don't like to be fiddled with. It's like sending your kids off to school and they come back the same kids with different haircuts."

Writers like Jenkins often felt constricted by the language limitations at *SI*, but Blount was more hampered by the institutional bias against discursive essay writing. While Blount was still fighting to get his wry observations into the magazine, he was venting his excess creative energy on the *SI* bulletin board. As a first baseman for the *SI* softball team, he was the unofficial team reporter and could be counted on to lend a vaguely subversive air to the proceedings. One day he approached a member of the opposing team, the Strasberg Actors Studio, and offered a handshake during pregame warm-ups. "Pleased to meet you," he said. "My people have been Methodists for years." In those softball accounts, usually typewritten on the back of yellow legal paper, one could see the emerging humorist exploring his powers, writing for the sheer fun of indulging his own talent. Designed to be read by no more than a few dozen coworkers, Blount's reports showed an exaggerated display of southern chivalry, even omitting profanity. From his report on a 17–9 win over the Sapporon Film productions team, in which *SI* reporters Larry Keith and Stephanie Salter played starring roles, there was this:

> One of the things that has to be gotten to the bottom of before Tuesday's game can be seen in perspective is exactly what it was that Larry Keith said to their first baseman. According to Stephanie Salter, the exchange began as follows:
>
> "You guys are all a____les," said Larry. That much is clear. And right on the button. And also clear is what the first baseman snapped right back with:
>
> "Oh, and I guess you guys are athletes right down the line." *Then* comes the puzzler. Larry is said to have staggered the first baseman with this:
>
> "Well you guys are closer to being a____les than we are to being athletes."
>
> But that, surely, is not to say very much. No right-thinking person can fail to be glad that it served to squelch the A____les' first baseman; but even if you don't let your mind wander and start quoting Tennyson, "closer is He than breathing, / And nearer than hands and feet"—still you get a little confused over the thrust of that remark. I mean being closer to being a____les than we are to being athletes still doesn't place you within any kind of danger zone. You could be closer

to being a turnip than we are to being athletes and still carry on an intelligent conversation.

But "we are closer to being athletes than you guys are to being a___les" won't do either. It sounds like a compliment. Perhaps "We're closer to being athletes than you guys are to *not* being a___les" is closest to the mark.

Anyway, they were a___les. Especially their pitcher. No details necessary.

Throughout the first half of the '70s, Blount wrote perceptively about baseball and football, and chipped in with the occasional unforgettable bonus pieces on coon hunting or chewing tobacco or the world's oldest living lifeguard. That he didn't quickly become one of *SI*'s best-known writers was a failing of the magazine, not the writer. He and Laguerre never quite understood each other, though the editor would later select Blount for a plum assignment that would launch his book-writing career. After his marriage broke up, Blount moved to Manhattan and fell in with Jenkins, Shrake, Ballard, Iooss, Fimrite, and Salter. "Lots of staying up half the nights telling stories," he'd remember. "No supervision, no meetings, just get your story in on time. Seldom had to be at the office, and when you were there, someone was playing catch in the hall or running from office to office in a gorilla suit. A great job for a young man. I work a lot harder now, drink a lot less, don't smoke dope at all, get a lot more sleep, eat a lot healthier, and feel less lively."

• • •

For women at *SI*, the late '60s and early '70s marked a period of painful progress. The prolific Jack Olsen wrote a book in 1969 called *The Girls in the Office*, which consisted entirely of condensed transcripts of interviews with 15 different women, whose identities were concealed (all of them worked within the Time & Life Building). Olsen's thesis was that women were the victims of the new workplace, working long hours for low wages, falling into fruitless affairs with married editors who would within a matter of years dump them for younger women who would repeat the cycle. Olsen meant for the book to be a conscientious cry for justice, but most of the women on the staff found it a simple exercise in titillation. "It was bullshit," said one female editor. "That was just Jack being Jack. Seeing what he could stir up."

But at least some of Olsen's points seemed credible. While writers like Deford and Kirkpatrick clearly deserved their promotions to staff writer status, it appeared to many that chief of reporters Honor Fitzpatrick still favored male reporters, putting them on a faster track to writer-reporter jobs than equally talented females. Female reporters, almost without fail, got fewer assignments on the road. This was partly because of convention, partly because of practicality (women couldn't get in locker rooms), and partly because of an institutional bias. One exception was the Masters, where Sarah Ballard joined Jenkins, Ray Cave, Walter Bingham, and Mark Mulvoy in 1967, the entire *SI* contingent staying in a house that the magazine rented during the week of the tournament. At the time, the female reporter's position for *SI* on the Masters trip was roughly analogous to the Walter Brennan role in a John Wayne movie, with Ballard expected to do all the marketing and all the cooking, in addition to her reporting duties. On Thursday, she walked the golf course, did post-round interviews, walked back to the house to get dinner ready, and then cooked for the whole *SI* contingent. "And then, after I cooked dinner, Ray Cave said that he had a couple of friends coming by later, and they would like some dinner, and would I mind cooking some more?" said Ballard. "You know, just a couple of steaks and a salad or something. So Walt and everybody went off to play miniature golf, and I stayed there while Ray entertained Mark McCormack and John DeLorean, in the kitchen of this stupid house."

After returning from Augusta, Ballard mentioned the trying week in passing to Honor Fitzpatrick, who erupted. "My reporters are not to be used as cooks!" she shouted, complaining to both Johnston and Laguerre about the injustice. When Ballard returned to Augusta in '68, *SI* had hired a cook to work in the house for the week.

Change rarely occurred so swiftly, and some suspected that Laguerre's Old World French sensibilities were the problem. "André was not particularly fond of women," allowed Whitney Tower. But it was less that Laguerre was biased against women than that he simply seemed uncomfortable around most of them. *Time*'s Martha Duffy, one of the few females in Laguerre's inner circle of drinking partners at the Ho, felt that was due to his innate shyness. Pat Ryan, who was promoted four different times while working for Laguerre, had another explanation: "He believed that if you were going to play with the guys, you should play like a guy would—don't ask for any quarter. For instance, you'd stay up all night long and you'd be closing a story at eight o'clock in the morning. Laguerre would go home, take a shower, change his shirt, and be back at ten. And if you did the same, you had all the respect in the world from him. But if you were going to say, 'Oh, I can't possibly be in until four o'clock in the afternoon,' then you weren't going to have any respect. But that didn't matter what sex you were."

• • •

In 1970, a group of women filed a sex discrimination suit against Time Inc. A petition of support was passed around *SI*'s offices, and 23 women signed. When informed of this, Laguerre was reputed to say, "Do we have 23 women at *Sports Illustrated*?" Many women declined to sign. Ann Callahan said she hadn't seen any signs of sexism. Pat Ryan understood the impulse, but felt the protest was misplaced. Sarah Ballard, too, felt that she "didn't want a stew just for the sake of a stew, especially at that point in my life where I had been sweating it for so long." When a settlement was reached, and new procedures installed throughout the company, it led to what Ballard would refer to as Laguerre's revenge. "He did all the things he had to do in the way of promotions and everything, and I benefited from this," she said. "But not a single person he promoted had signed that or had anything to do with that petition. In a way, he won in the end."

In 1971, Laguerre promoted Ryan to senior editor, eventually moving her to the prestigious outside text editing position, in which she would preside over bonus pieces. The day he promoted her, he told her he'd give her a $3,000 raise, to $21,000 a year.

"It's not enough," said Ryan.

"What do you think is enough?" Laguerre asked.

"I should be making what a starting senior editor who is a man would get."

Laguerre harrumphed and called to Callahan in the outer office. "Annie, bring me my list," he said. After Laguerre pored over the salaries of senior editors, he raised Ryan's pay to $28,000 a year.

"He was probably the first ME at Time Inc. who had a functioning woman senior editor that *really was a woman senior editor*," said Ryan. "That wasn't just a name on the masthead, or someone covering fashion."

With the magazine's reputation growing in New York literary circles, Ryan ran an outside text department that could get virtually anyone in the literary community to write for *SI*. Freelancers like Larry L. King, Wilfrid Sheed, E.L. Doctorow, Thomas McGuane, and Jim Harrison were regular contributors. "I had no trouble getting a Bill Buckley or someone like that to write for the magazine," she said. "And certainly literary agents thought of it as very good writing. Did the *New York Times* know that it was? I mean, the *New York Times* didn't give a shit about sports."

Pat Ryan's relationship with Laguerre would remain close, and often quarrelsome, for years. One afternoon in the early '70s, he walked into Ryan's office and, in a single sweep, killed two of the bonus pieces she'd finished work on and accused her of not getting along with Betty

DeMeester, the only woman at *SI* who seemed intent on pursuing a drinking friendship with Laguerre. After scolding her, he turned to leave; Ryan grabbed her stapler and threw it at her boss as he was walking out the door. The projectile sailed past his shoulder, missing him by inches, and he kept walking.

"Nothing more was said," recalled Ryan. "You did terrible things to Laguerre. He did terrible things to you. But it wasn't carried over to the next morning."

Laguerre's relationship with Jule Campbell was just as close, but rarely as contentious. He immediately endorsed her work on the swimsuit issue, and told her not to worry about the negative letters and subscription cancellations that the issue annually garnered. From her first swimsuit issue, in January 1965, Campbell had been fighting the industry that viewed her as some kind of inconsequential interloper. When she called the powerful modeling doyenne Eileen Ford in 1966, to ask if she could get a model for the swimsuit issue, Ford scoffed. "She's with *Harper's Bazaar*. What makes you think she would work for *Sports Illustrated*?"

But Campbell, for all her twinkling, soft-spoken niceties, had a veneer of toughness about her. "I'm a Taurus—you don't do that to me twice." She vowed to stop using Ford clients, and start finding her own models. By 1967, she had fashioned a philosophy that ran against the prevailing New York-ironic-waifish trends dominating the industry. "I just look for a girl who seems the type my husband would like," she said in a '67 pub memo. "The girl has to look healthy, has to be the kind men turn around to stare at, has to have visible spirit and should be athletic."

One such model was Cheryl Tiegs, a Californian who exuded the sort of comfortable beauty that Campbell was looking for. When Tiegs made her first cover appearance, in the 1970 issue, she first saw the issue on the newsstands, and thought, "'Oh, I'm on the cover of *Sports Illustrated*. I might as well buy one for the collection.' And I went home, and that was the extent of the celebration. Nobody talked about it; nobody interviewed us." What *SI* did do, though, was use the models' names in Campbell's coy, flirtatious captions, providing them with a degree of identity that fashion magazines didn't. It was a minor point, one that was given little thought internally, but it had major consequences: *SI*'s most loyal readers were reading the cutlines, and writing in for repeat appearances by their favorite models, who were turning into stars in their own right.

The shoots themselves, at the time, were modest outings, with the model joined by Campbell (who handled makeup, if the model didn't do it herself), the photographer, and a photo assistant. "I remember, I thought I was overweight, but Jule always liked that," said Tiegs. "She always liked it if you sort of spilled out of the bathing suit. She was very encouraging and made me feel good about my body." Campbell wanted her models to feel sexy, but she was also very protective of their sexuality, stepping in front of a cameraman if she felt a pose was too titillating, and keeping close tabs on the models away from the shoot. "She was adamant about staying away from the women," said Walter Iooss, one of Campbell's favorite photographers. "She used to put herself in the middle; the girls on her left and me on her right. She was everywhere—it seemed like there were about ten Jules. You could never get away. I remember trying to find a secluded place with a model once and within minutes, I heard, 'Wal-lee . . . Wal-lee. . . .' It was like, where can you go?"

"She *did* keep her eye on the models and the photographers," said Tiegs. "Not to say that she could do it every minute."

In one sign of progress, Billie Jean King was the first woman to receive *SI*'s Sportsman of the Year award (which was called Sportswoman of the Year when given to a female), sharing the award with the Sportsman of the Year, UCLA basketball coach John Wooden, in 1972.

A month after that award was given, *SI* found itself in the center of a gender debate. The main player was reporter-writer Stephanie Salter, who had a keen eye, a vivacious nature, and potential that she wouldn't fulfill until leaving the magazine. During her four years at *SI*, she would acquit herself well as a perceptive baseball reporter, quickly be accepted into Jenkins's inner circle, fall in love with Fimrite, and wind up being the unintended center of attention at the 1973 Baseball Writers Association of America gathering. The stodgy BBWAA's annual dinner was a black-tie, blue-humor affair, full of fat stogies, long toasts, and profane wisecracks. Fimrite, Blount, and photo assistant Don Delliquanti went to the Americana Hotel for the 1973 dinner, and brought Salter along. More than one attendee recalled that she looked stunning that night, wearing a halter dress and the requisite black tie. The *SI* contingent sat together at a table, stood for "The Star-Spangled Banner," and was just getting to their fruit cups when a security guard was sent over.

"You're going to have to leave," the guard informed Salter.

"Why?" she asked.

"Because this is a stag event—it's males only."

"Is there someone I can speak to? I have a ticket, and I'm properly dressed."

Jack Lang, the autocratic secretary of the BBWAA ("the all-time sort of communist clerk," in Salter's words), was called over to the table. When Salter pleaded her case with him, showing him her ticket, Lang pulled out his wallet and started throwing money on the table, to refund the cost of the ticket.

"That's not the point," she said.

Lang, by now shaking with anger, threatened to call the police if she didn't leave. And in those few minutes, Stephanie Salter became a journalistic cause célèbre and a pioneer in the women's movement.

"Blount left with me," she remembered. "And this was a hardship for Blount. Because I think Casey Stengel was speaking, and Blount was dying to hear him. God bless him, he said, 'This is an outrage. I'm going with her. If she can't eat here, I don't want to.' Delliquanti went, too. Fimrite, of course, love of my life, said, 'I'll see you afterwards—I'll buy you a drink!'"

The *New York Times* reported the snub two days later, and Laguerre fired off a vehement letter to the BBWAA, leading to the eventual relaxation of the male-only rule. True equality in the locker room wouldn't come until later in the decade, and with decidedly more legal wrangling, but the BBWAA incident became a small victory for women sportswriters.

A more symbolic, more gratifying one came later in 1973, at the Billie Jean King–Bobby Riggs challenge match in Houston. Riggs had soundly routed King's contemporary, Margaret Court, in the first "battle of the sexes" just months earlier.

"Billie Jean King beating Bobby Riggs was the greatest thing that ever happened," said Ballard. "I was down there. You can't imagine why it was so important, now. It was a farce, but it was absolutely, terribly important, because Margaret Court had screwed up, you know, and it was embarrassing. And the thought that the same thing might happen to Billie Jean was just terrifying."

Ballard was the reporter assigned to the story, following King around while Curry Kirkpatrick, who would write the story, hung out with Riggs.

"It was the first time I ever felt there was actually sort of a fraternity of females in and around a sporting event," said Ballard. "Most of these people weren't actually in sports, but the fact that we had someone, that I wasn't the only one, for once, made it great. Grace Lichtenstein was there; she was doing a book on the women's tour at the time. And Nora Ephron was there, covering it for somebody. And I was there, and Susie Adams. Anyway, it was a big table, and Grace was holding the money—we were taking bets from the men, and they were all betting on Riggs."

The victory was a defining moment in female sports history, and back in New York, Walter Bingham, who was always good at headlines, wrote one of his best for Kirkpatrick's story: "Here She Comes, Ms. America."

•  •  •

By the beginning of the '70s, Dan Jenkins had become the magazine's most popular writer. His coverage of college football and golf had resulted in two anthologies, *Saturday's America* and *The Dogged Victims of Inexorable Fate*. He wrote regularly on golf's four majors and other important tournaments, and though he shared the college football beat with the excellent John Underwood, Jenkins was the first among equals, the "big-game collector" generally assigned to the most important games, like Southern Cal–UCLA in 1967, Texas-Arkansas in 1969 and Nebraska-Oklahoma in 1971.

But it was at Augusta, where he'd attended every Masters since 1951, that Jenkins first became a celebrity. Joe Marshall, who was a reporter at *SI* before moving up to staff writer, remembered a time in 1972 when he first became aware of the Jenkins aura. "We were all seated on the veranda there, having drinks; Dan was with us. First round was over, and Dan quietly got up and walked off, and I looked over and he was on the putting green with Jack Nicklaus. Nicklaus was one stroke off the lead and had gone through the press tent with the whole spiel—driver, four-wood, etc. Dan spent like five minutes with him. But I remember being so impressed that he could approach Nicklaus and that it clearly wasn't an interview. Nicklaus was leaning on his putter, chatting and smiling and waving, gesticulating with his hands. Jenkins was talking to him, and he was clearly getting a just-between-friends kind of view of what was going on. The rest of the reporters there would have killed for that kind of access. Dan had it because of who he was and the way he wrote."

It became a myth around Jenkins that he never walked the course, simply sat around the veranda at Augusta, or the clubhouse elsewhere, and waited for the tournament to come to him. "I know that when I went with Dan to golf tournaments," said Curry Kirkpatrick, recalling his early days as a reporter, "I thought that was how it was done, just sitting on the veranda and letting the story come to you. And I thought that simply because that was how Dan was doing it." Plimpton, who would invariably find Jenkins drinking in some lounge after a tournament or game, suspected that his friend "wrote his stories by osmosis."

Jenkins had developed some effective ways to maintain his bearings through all the drinking. In the evening, he'd usually order a cheeseburger and milkshake from room service, before going down to the bar. And then, once he sat down, he'd keep the coffee coming as well, rotating for hours and hours between J&B, black coffee, and Winstons. "By that time," said one colleague, "Pat Summerall would be passed out."

"The trouble with sitting around," wrote Shrake, "is that you never know when you're finished." Jenkins was the one who decided. Myra Gelband, who followed Sarah Ballard as the reporter for golf, learned a trick from golfer Dave Marr. At three in the morning or so, when she simply couldn't punish her body any longer and still hope to function the next day, she'd get up as if to go to the bathroom, and tell the table to order her another drink. Then she'd disappear.

"Four days on the road with Jenkins was about as much as my body could handle," said Iooss of golf tournament assignments. At the Los Angeles Open one year, Iooss got up to leave a table at 6:45 a.m. "Dan, I've *got* to go to bed," he said.

"What!?" protested Jenkins.

"Dan, it's quarter to *seven*!"

"Iooss, get out of here," Jenkins barked. "You're an amateur."

For years, Jenkins had been toying with the idea of a novel, partly because he realized that he'd never get rich on the nonfiction anthologies that he'd already published. His buddies Shrake and Cartwright had both written novels and, in fact, even Tex Maule was writing them. For years, all Jenkins had was a title, *Semi-Tough*, an expression from his Fort Worth youth, and the vague notion that it would be a story about football.

He finally wrote the manuscript in the summer before and the winter following the 1971 football season. In the summer of 1971, on a stopover in Paris, Jenkins left his briefcase, with the only copy of the half-completed manuscript, in Orly Airport, along with his wallet, his passport and all his money. Once he realized what he'd done, he went straight to Time Inc.'s Paris bureau, furious at himself and the world in general.

"Is the bureau chief here? Who's here?" he asked the receptionist.

"They're in a meeting right now," she explained.

"Well, the meeting's fucking *over*," he said, brushing past her and walking into the office of Fred Connors, an old friend of Laguerre, who was the bureau chief. "Hey! I'm Dan Jenkins from *SI*. I got a fuckin' problem and you people have to solve it—*right fuckin' now!*"

Connors, who possessed a measure of Laguerre's poise, stood affably to greet him. "Dan, I've been wanting to meet you," he said. "What's your problem?"

"The problem is I lost my fucking life, that's my problem!"

Jenkins explained and Connors went into quick action, contacting the embassy to arrange for another passport, then calling Orly, where the briefcase had already been turned into lost and found, untouched.

"It added five years to my life right there," said Jenkins later. "Just being fuckin' *pissed*, 'cause I had never done anything like that in my life. I never lose anything, I never go off and leave anything, and the fact that I had done it made me so goddamn mad at myself, I stayed mad for a year."

He finished the novel in Hawaii early in 1972. That spring, he showed a copy of the manuscript to Shrake. "I read it, and I advised him to tone it down," said Shrake, "to take out all the ethnic jokes, or at least to cut 'em way back, and to take out some of the needless profanity. And if he had listened to me, nobody would have ever read the book, probably. 'Cause then Dan went to his editor, Herman Gollob, and Gollob said, 'Bud doesn't know shit about it. Instead of doing what he told you to do, put in more profanity, more ethnic jokes.'"

Gollob, who bragged he was the only Jew to ever graduate from Texas A&M, had the right idea. Late that summer, just weeks before the book's publication date, Pete Rozelle spotted Blackie Sherrod in the press lounge prior to a Cowboys exhibition game and pulled him to a corner. "Have you read *Semi-Tough*?" the commissioner asked. Sherrod said he hadn't. Rozelle shook his head. "I got an advance copy and, damn, it's *pre-tee* damn good." He gave a grim smile, which communicated that he loved the book for its humor and hated it for what it might do to the image of his league. "I knew then, and by the way Rozelle shook his head, it was going to be sacrilegious at best," said Sherrod.

In October, a staffer drinking with Jenkins at the Ho mentioned Deford and asked, "Did you know that Frank is writing a novel about pro football?"

"Well, he better hurry," said Jenkins. "Mine's coming out next week."

Jenkins had already built up a large following in *SI,* and *Semi-Tough* wound up as a surprise hit, opening up on the *New York Times* bestseller list, where it stayed well into 1973. When Jenkins got the news, by phone from Herman Gollob, he was in Fort Worth, visiting his grandmother Sally in the house where he grew up. He went out to the porch, smoked a cigarette, and thought about how far he'd come from the typewriter in the kitchen.

*Semi-Tough* was conceived as the diary of an All-Pro running back during the week leading up to the Super Bowl. Those closest to Jenkins immediately recognized some familiar personalities in the novel. There was plenty of Jenkins himself in the main character, Billy Clyde Puckett, and Puckett's best friend Marvin "Shake" Tiller bore quite a resemblance to Bud Shrake. Much of Puckett's memories of high school and college days had the ring of truth as well. "Everything in that book actually happened," said Jenkins's old friend Don Matheson, "up until about page 150."

But it was the language—Jenkins unfettered for the first time to write exactly what he heard in locker rooms or out on the veranda—that was revolutionary. Roy Blount, Jr., had witnessed the same spirited biracial give-and-take in the Pittsburgh Pirates locker room, and found the novel bracing, freeing up writers to move closer to the complex, vulgar truth of the locker room environment. *Roots* author Alex Haley wrote Jenkins later, commending him on the novel and emphasizing that he understood the language wasn't racist. The book contained a scene from a team meeting unlike anything that had ever been in sports literature before, with the young white wide receiver Shake Tiller attempting to get his team's racial problem out into the open:

"Well, I'm not up here to talk about the world," Shake said. "All I want to make clear is, a nigger who plays football can whitewash himself by knocking down more sumbitches than knock him down. And when he knocks down enough, he'll look around one day and find out he's rich and famous. And then he can go buy a Cadillac and a big house and start fucking up a good white neighborhood—or whatever it is you guys like to do."

Shake grinned in order to let everybody know that was a joke. The spooks, I mean. Some did and some didn't. A couple of them just kept on standing around with their arms folded, staring down at the floor. As if they were listening to an assistant coach who was reminding them they had to quit stealing socks and sweatsuits.

Puddin Patterson said, "Say, baby, you don't have no idea what it's like to be black, you dig? So how come you standin' up there layin' out all this jive."

Some spook voice from the back of the room said, "Tell me somethin' *about* it."

And another spook voice said, "Two, four, six, eight. Texas gonna integrate."

Shake answered Puddin. "All I'm talking about is trying to be a good football team. Is that what we're here for?"

Puddin said, "We doin' a job, baby. You catch them balls and I'll block them folks. Ain't nothin' else to it."

From somewhere again in the back of the room, a spook voice said, "Say, Puddin. You know what a Texan is?"

Puddin half-turned around.

He laughed and said to the room, "Cat done told me it was a Mexican on his way to Oklahoma."

Reviews tended toward the rapturous. "His writing and his ear recall—there is no higher compliment—Ring Lardner, though in different times and different Americas," wrote David Halberstam in the *New York Times* Book Review. Larry L. King, in *Life*, concurred: "Jenkins smacks of Ring Lardner, is all, with scraps of Damon Runyon and maybe Kurt Vonnegut thrown in."

As Jenkins's star rose, his influence only increased. A month after the book was released, Jenkins wrote a story about Nebraska wingback Johnny Rodgers's performance against Colorado, observing that "if Johnny Rodgers is not this season's leading candidate (if not, in fact, the only candidate) then most of the voters must be planning on writing in the names of their cousins." Elsewhere in the piece, Jenkins argued that the media had overplayed Rodgers's run-ins with the law. Many thought the article was a deciding factor in the tight voting for the Heisman, with Rodgers and Oklahoma tailback Greg Pruitt the cofavorites. Upon accepting the trophy at the Heisman ceremony in December, Rodgers closed his speech by thanking Jenkins for the support: "He more or less broke the ice for me and got me kind of started. . . . I really don't know him well but I have a lot of respect for him."

Jenkins seemed to take it all in stride: the success, the reviews, even the six-figure royalty check that showed up in the mail later that fall. "Celebrity had yet to become a drag," said Salter, who witnessed much of the fun. "*People* magazine didn't even exist." Jenkins hit the talk-show circuit, chatting with Jack Klugman (subbing for Dick Cavett) and Ethel Merman one night, doing the *Tonight Show* with Johnny Carson another night.

When Jenkins's old friend and colleague Gary Cartwright visited New York in the winter of '73, he could see the book's impact. It was six years before anyone in New York City would hear of Gilley's or see *Urban Cowboy,* but Texas was already becoming a formidable cultural presence. At "21" and Clarke's, Toots Shor's and Elaine's, execs from the suburbs were patting each other on the back and saying they were semithirsty, then hailing the bartender to order a young scotch. It was a good time to be Dan Jenkins.

He had been at the center of *Sports Illustrated*'s social whirl for years, but with the novel, he would raise "sitting around" to a kind of inebriated performance art. "Let's start with the end of the week," he said. "You knew you had to get drunk Monday night; that was the end of the week. Celebrate the end of the week, or celebrate the big game you'd been to. Now you're off Tuesday and Wednesday, you can sleep, recover from the hangover, get some work done. Thursday's the first day of the week, so you're refreshed. You had to get drunk that night. You also had to get drunk Friday night. Saturday night you never went anywhere if you were home; you stayed home Saturday night. And Sunday night was usually a closing, which was hang around the Hoy Yuen [the popular dinner spot for Sunday closes]. Maybe your wife comes in, you go to dinner or something, maybe not. You're waiting for a story to close. You're escorting it through all those dangerous channels where something horrible can happen to it, because of idiots who gotta put their fingers in something, whether it was an editor or the copy room, or whoever."

Away from the Ho, Jenkins's two favorite spots were P.J. Clarke's and Elaine's. Clarke's was the base camp for several generations of midtown Manhattan drinkers (the setting for Billy Wilder's 1945 classic *The Lost Weekend*), a classic bar that Jenkins once described as "a landmark to the days when the Irish sang more often than they threw bombs." At Clarke's, Jenkins and Shrake were warmly greeted by maître d' Frankie Ribando, who had been seating them in the exclusive back room long before Jenkins was on the bestseller list. Then it would be "upstate" to Elaine's, where Jenkins and Shrake were favorites of owner Elaine Kaufman, who had made the Second Avenue and 88th Street establishment the exclusive choice for uptown literati. Jenkins had been moving in interesting circles for years; in the late '60s, he started spending time with his neighbor, a young New York actor named Robert Redford who looked him up for advice about a movie he was making called *Downhill Racer*. At Elaine's, he was a legend long before *Semi-Tough*, drinking late with writers like Irwin Shaw, Terry Southern, James Jones, John Carradine, and Bruce Jay Friedman.

"Dan Jenkins understood the secret of New York," said author Nick Pileggi, who was married to Sarah Ballard during the period and became a frequent drinking partner. "I don't know where he learned it or how he learned it, because most people don't. Even native New Yorkers don't learn it. The secret of New York is called whipout. Whipout is money and it's cash, and you take care of people who take care of you. As a result, there wasn't a restaurant, there wasn't a bar, there wasn't any place in New York where the owners and the maître'd's and waiters didn't throw people out of tables when Dan Jenkins walked into the room. And Dan Jenkins could sit there at that table and drink coffee all night long while other people were having cases of champagne sent over, and at the end of the night, his legitimate bill would come out to $30, and he would leave a couple hundred as the tip. He understood that you've got to cover the table; he knew how the city worked, and I always admired how he handled that."

When they weren't at Clarke's or Elaine's, the *SI* crowd often went over to George Plimpton's handsome apartment on East 72nd Street overlooking the East River. There were occasional parties at Shrake's, down in the Village. It was there on a Saturday night in 1968, with the full Texas contingent in tow, that Cowboy quarterback Don Meredith challenged Shrake and Plimpton to a pissing contest—off the balcony and across the street. "We stood on the rail and Meredith was *fantastic,*" remembered Plimpton. "He damn near reached the opposite curb. We were almost doubled over with laughter." Having seen Meredith's condition that night, most of the gamblers in the *SI* office bet on the Giants the next day. Meredith's first pass went several feet over his intended receiver, but he shook it off and the Cowboys won easily, 28–10.

● ● ●

Though alcohol was still the drug of choice in the late '60s, much of the staff had been experimenting with drugs. Taking speed was, of course, a good way to stay sharp for an all-night writing assignment so as to make a morning deadline, but it came with a toll. There were plenty of scenes like the one Shrake described in his novel *Strange Peaches*: ". . . when you take a lot of Bennies you don't always know what you are about to say. Now, in this Washington hotel hallway, I could feel my heart plunging through my back against the wall. I'd probably had fifty martinis and Scotches since I'd last tried to eat anything but an Almond Joy, and I was entering that strange, illusory country where soon I might hop sideways to avoid a man in a black leather cape, or catch from the edge of my eye the flicker of a creature that had not been there an instant ago. All I really wanted at the moment was to keep from patting any invisible dogs and get back to Dallas."

When it came to drug abuse, few could keep pace with the legendary Walter Iooss, Jr. With his athlete's physique, Serpico beard, and flashing eyes, Iooss possessed the tanned good looks of a virile Bee Gee. And every female from Jenkins's ten-year-old daughter Sally to the fully grown swimsuit model Cheryl Tiegs had a crush on him. He also had an amazing capacity for marijuana, making him popular with several colleagues and more than a few ballplayers of the era.

From the time Blount, Iooss, and Phillies star Dick Allen got high together while working on a profile on the slugger, Iooss and Allen stayed in touch, striking up a friendship. Iooss and his assistant Mike Ehret were waiting for Allen at the clubhouse before a 1969 game at Shibe Park. It was a twi-night doubleheader and Allen had asked Iooss to meet him beforehand. A half hour before the first pitch, a black Cadillac with tinted windows rolled into the players' area of the parking lot. The driver's side window slid down a few inches and Allen, his eyes little more than red slits, looked out.

"Walter, Walter . . . what time is it?"

"Man, it's five-thirty!" said Iooss. "What have you been doing?"

"Shit man . . . I thought I missed the game. I got pulled over for going too slow in the left lane. Don't leave me. Get me in the ballpark."

The rest of the afternoon would stay with Iooss for years. "So we go into the clubhouse. Everyone's on the field. As soon as he walks in, he asks the clubhouse guy for a Coke, a candy bar, an ice cream bar—everything to give it away. He says, 'And put on the Mighty Burner.' It was the very hot black DJ, Sonny Hopson, the Mighty Burner. He was dedicating records: 'My man, Number 15, Dick Allen.' So Dick's sitting there, chewing on everything sweet, the records are blasting. 'Licking Stick' by James Brown is on. And he says, 'Well, I've got to go out.'

"So now I'm sitting in the stands. It's the first inning. Dick steps up to the plate. First pitch comes and he bails out. Strike one. I turned to Mike, and said 'What did he bail out for?' Next pitch, bail out, strike two. Next pitch, bail out, strike three. He walks from the batter's box toward the dugout, looks up at me and he waves, like 'Come on.' The next thing I hear is the PA announcer: 'Dick Allen has been removed from the game with a sprained wrist.' So I wait for him to dress, and I'm standing outside the clubhouse in the street. And there he is. He's now in the chief of police's *car*! I said, 'Mike, he's *trying* to get arrested.' I'll never forget what he does next. He looks out with this huge Cheshire grin, holds his hand out, and he's got a rolled joint ready to light. He says goodbye to the chief and says, 'Follow me.' So we went on this 90-mile-per-hour trip to his home. And that was an unbelievable night of abuse. He was a wild boy, Dick."

Pot was responsible for one of the most infamous covers in *SI* history, the 1972 Iooss shot of Dolphin running backs Jim Kiick and Larry Csonka, the latter flipping off the camera. "Those two guys were so stoned," remembered Iooss. "I'll never forget Csonka saying, 'This is the longest walk I've ever made in my life.' They were out of their minds. All they did was laugh, and give me the finger, for the entire session. Obviously these pictures were shown to the managing editor, the art director, and everyone else. No one saw the finger, not even when they looked at the proof. You'd have thought they'd have gotten wise where virtually every picture someone had a finger up. But no one saw it. These things happen."

Rumors of Iooss's exploits filtered back to the office, where photo editor George Bloodgood, himself a reckless alcoholic, was aggravated. One day in the early '70s, Bloodgood came out of his office at the far end of the *SI* photo department and summoned Iooss with a foreboding stare.

As Iooss got up, he heard his colleagues giggling and oohing. Being summoned to Bloodgood's office, especially when he was ripped, was never fun. Iooss walked in.

"Close the fuckin' door," said Bloodgood.

"Oh, here we go," said Iooss.

Bloodgood stared dully at him, as if gathering himself for a definitive statement. "No more fucking pot smoking!" he said. "Do you hear? Look, everyone knows you do it. It's got to stop now. I can only back you so much. Laguerre? Terrell? Forget it. They're all going to let you dangle."

Then Bloodgood got up from his desk and walked over to his coat rack. He rifled around in his coat pocket and eventually pulled out a pill bottle, which he bobbled and dropped. The cap flew off at impact, spraying dozens of brightly colored pills across the floor.

Both men froze for a second. Then Bloodgood kneeled down and started scooping up the pills. After a moment, he looked back up at Iooss. "Ah, forget what I just told you."

In light of all this, it seemed odd that *SI*'s editors would send Iooss and Bud Shrake to Kingston, Jamaica, to cover the Joe Frazier–George Foreman fight in 1973, but they did. Kram had begged off—he was mortally afraid of flying—so Shrake was sent, along with George Plimpton, to cover the bout. While Shrake and Plimpton were ostensibly doing reporting to prepare for the fight, Iooss was hanging out with his old friend, jazz musician Les McCann, whose band was in Kingston for a concert. After four days of debauchery, Shrake and Iooss met late in the morning of the fight, Monday, January 22, 1973, and made a solemn pact not to drink any booze or smoke any pot after lunch.

But an hour before the main event, Iooss came to Shrake with an elephantine joint, and a proposal that they smoke it right away, and as fast as possible, thereby giving them time to regain their bearings by the start of the fight. "It'll wear off by then," Iooss assured him. Afterward, Shrake's only lucid memory of the beginning of the fight was Iooss catching his eye from ringside during the boxers' introductions and mouthing the words, "It hasn't worn off yet."

Foreman knocked world champion Joe Frazier down three times in the first round, with a savage series of punches. Iooss looked blankly at the scene and tried to snap as many pictures as he could. At the end of the round, he hit the rewind button on his camera and realized he didn't have any film in it. "That was the last bout that *Sports Illustrated* sent me to," said Iooss. "But I had one hell of a time." Somehow, Shrake managed to file 3,000 coherent words for the tight Monday night deadline.

Back in New York, while the younger staffers were doing the expected things with sex and drugs, the older generation seemed to be torn between trying to keep up or admitting their own mortality by opting out.

"Every institution was under siege," recalled Stephanie Salter. "You didn't believe in much of anything. I see some of the beliefs of that era, *Five Easy Pieces*, things like that, and I think, *No wonder*. What a time; and boy did it set the stage for Reagan. I've often described it as that rare, rare window of opportunity when everything was a green light for—not even experimenting, but having sex as just being the natural culmination of a halfway decent evening. There was this tremendous pressure on a lot of the married people, some of the older adults, that if they didn't engage in this stuff then they were totally uncool. There was something truly wrong with them, they were afraid to live, afraid to be free. *What's the matter?* Really, a virtue was rapidly turned into a vice."

The Ho was still the home base for the *SI* staff, but a new generation of staffers—more liberated, less cautious, more attuned to the times—was frequenting it. Salter had started running with Ballard shortly after arriving, and the two could often be seen in the late afternoon down at the Ho, leaning back in their barstools, knees resting against the padded bar. It was there that Salter learned to abandon her vodka and tonic for the more urbane scotch and water. From their chair, the two women (and others, like Chrissy Walford, Myra Gelband, Susan Adams) started their own clique. They even adopted a few of the male rituals. "I can remember a couple myself that really did feel like conquests," said Salter. "I wasn't mean to them. I was 22, 23, and knew I was in charge. I was making this happen, making some middle-aged guy's eyeballs spin in his head. If you take away the 9,000 drinks at the Ho Ho, I probably never would have done any of that. I guess I was supposed to do it at the time. I survived to tell the tale, so I look back on it very fondly. They're my war stories, my act of combat."

And so at *Sports Illustrated*, the period had the feel to it of a last bacchanal. As one writer remembered, "You'd sit at the bar down at the Ho, and hear people at the pay phone, calling some loyal spouse someplace saying they were going to miss the next two trains."

# CHAPTER 11

# LAST CALL

## As the new decade began,

André Laguerre's victory seemed complete. *Sports Illustrated* was culturally relevant and solidly in the black; it had revolutionized deadline journalism in the weekly newsmagazine field and, with the consistent excellence of the bonus piece, elevated the level of sportswriting to unprecedented heights. The magazine had become the cultural centerpiece of the rapidly expanding universe of sports, and Laguerre's fiercely loyal staff recognized that he was the man who had made it all possible. Yet for all his triumphs, Laguerre seemed more wearied than gratified. He had already overseen more than 500 issues of the weekly magazine, a punishing schedule even for a young, fit man. The ideas that flowed so freely through the '60s were less easily summoned, and the thrill of the late close had diminished.

Unusually quiet around his friends, often atypically sullen in the office, he was casting about for one last mission, a third act to complete his career. And for a time, he had it in his sights. While *SI* had established itself as the company's best-written, best-run magazine, *Life* was free-falling, losing ad pages and relevance with each passing week, a victim to the television boom. To Nathalie and his closest colleagues, Andy Crichton, Ray Cave, Morrie Werner, a few others, Laguerre confided his belief that he could save the dying magazine, though he never produced a printed plan to do so. "He would never go that far; he didn't need to," said Cave, who discussed it with him. "We both knew what he would have done with *Life*: taken it back to what it was, make it a news picture magazine, take it back to the franchise that abandoned it. It was a helluva magazine. I don't think Laguerre thought it would be difficult at all. I am sure that he never personally pressed his case."

In fact, he did the opposite, seeming to do all he could to antagonize

Hedley Donovan, frequently not taking his calls, occasionally avoiding the weekly managing editors' lunches, and maintaining an attitude of bored silence when he did attend. Recalling the chilly relationship between the management and Laguerre, Andrew Heiskell said that he and Donovan never really considered the possibility of putting Laguerre in charge of *Life*. But Cave found that inconceivable: "You would've *had* to consider it," he said. "I mean, here's your most successful managing editor. Running a picture magazine—he can illustrate it. And I think there's not a single doubt that Heiskell and Donovan had extensive conversations about it. Heiskell might say they didn't, but they must have. *They must have.* I mean *Life* was by far the company's biggest problem. How could you not look for any possible solution?"

But when Roy Terrell volunteered at a lunch meeting in 1971 that he thought Laguerre would be perfect for the *Life* ME's job, Donovan cut him off, refusing to even discuss the matter. After years of Laguerre's stony silences at managing editors' lunches, and the tactical brinksmanship surrounding the Black Athlete series, Donovan was disinclined to look to Laguerre to solve the company's darkest problems. The rift deepened, and when *Life* finally folded in December 1972, Laguerre further aggravated Donovan by refusing to take any of *Life*'s writers onto the *SI* staff.

"André didn't play by the rules," said Deford. "On the one hand, he was the most perfect company man who ever existed, because he believed in Time Inc. and what Henry Luce had created; he believed in the magazine and he sweated blood for it. But his idea of being a company man didn't include being a bootlicker."

His closest friends sensed that Laguerre was losing his edge, drinking more and taking longer to recover. Some traced it to Luce's death in 1967, others to the rift with Donovan over the Black Athlete series in 1968. In 1970, Charles de Gaulle died, just days before a trip to New York in which he'd planned to see his old friend and lieutenant. With the death of de Gaulle, the two great influences of André Laguerre's life had passed on.

And, through it all, Roy Terrell waited for his turn. Late in 1970, Terrell sat in Laguerre's office and confronted him.

"André, you know, you told me five years ago that you might be leaving soon. I've been assistant ME for seven years now, and I'd like to edit this magazine sometime."

"I can't do it right now," Laguerre said apologetically, explaining that the recent stock market downturn had darkened the family's financial future. "You'll just have to hang on."

Dramatically alienated from Donovan and the Time Inc. corporate leadership, and without Luce's support to back him up, Laguerre was losing his base of support. The Time Inc. executives found him unresponsive, while he found them meddlesome and distinctly unappreciative.

So he continued to make his daily trips to the Ho Ho, at lunch and after work. But by the early '70s, the process took on a grim purposefulness that hadn't existed before. The bar became a fortress, a last refuge from the corporate realities of a company that in Laguerre's mind had grown more bloodless and businesslike since Luce's death. At the Ho, one could imagine that the old rules still applied. The lunches grew longer, and Laguerre occasionally returned from them in no condition to work. "You wouldn't exactly go into his office at 3:30 and suggest a five-part series," said Ray Cave.

• • •

Many of the other editors were following Laguerre's lead, and drinking even more. For some, the charm was gone; the brutal schedule and daily hangovers were taking a toll. On November 1, 1970, Dick Johnston retired. He had grown to hate the fall grind of editing the rapidly declining Tex Maule's stillborn prose on tight Sunday night deadlines. Johnston longed to return to Hawaii, where he'd been stationed as a war correspondent. After receiving a sizable offer on his Manhattan apartment, he went to see Laguerre, who arranged for him to get a year's salary as severance. Then Johnston headed for the islands with his longtime girlfriend Connie Wood (Johnston and his wife, Laurie, had been separated for more than a decade, but never divorced).

"By the late '60s, so much of what was wonderful about New York was being lost," said his daughter, Elisa Johnston. "He also told me that drinking no longer did for him what it used to do. It no longer energized him. That was it, you see: my father was prone to depression; alcohol stimulated him. This whole notion of three-martini lunches and 'how did they get the magazine out?' That's one reason they *got* the magazine out."

The displays of public drunkenness became more common, not just by Laguerre but by such crucial support troops as photo editor George Bloodgood and production chief Gene Ulrich. Roy Blount, Jr., once recalled phoning an editor to ask about a headline and receiving a drunken, slurred response that was "all the more maddening for sounding so much like human speech." Andy Crichton was drinking more as well, and becoming notorious for sleeping past his Mamaroneck stop on the New Haven line train ride home. He'd often wake up in Rye and walk the three miles back to his house; for a marathoner like Crichton, it amounted to a good sobering stroll.

Terrell and Cave, the two highest-ranking editors who didn't regularly drink at the bar, sensed that the culture was dragging the magazine down, starting to hurt the product. But both were powerless to do anything about it. Then, too, Laguerre continued to show a remarkable capacity for recovery. Two different editors recalled one Sunday night in 1972 when he seemed sluggish and sodden at the bar, but roused himself for a readout on a late-closing story. Once up in his office, he took out his gold-plated pen and held it in his hand, which slowly hovered over the proof pages. He caught three small but crucial mistakes that other editors had missed.

But there were numerous other times when Laguerre returned from his lunch and Ann Callahan closed his door, letting him sleep for the rest of the afternoon. In Hawaii, where he still wrote occasional pieces for *SI*, Dick Johnston began getting up at five o'clock in the morning, telling Connie Wood that, "If I call after lunch, they won't even remember I called."

He had that right. One Monday afternoon that spring, Robert Creamer was nervously waiting outside Laguerre's office.

"Thank God you're back!" Creamer said. "Hedley Donovan has been trying to get in touch with you for five hours!"

He handed the message slip to Laguerre, who crumpled it up as he walked into his office and barked, "Tell 'im to go fuck himself."

A few moments later, Terrell showed up in the office, to check on a late-closing story. Creamer stood there as his revered boss slumped back in his chair.

"Ah, Terrell," Laguerre said, waving him in, a look of reckless remorse on his face. "You're one of my best men, and you're not worth a shit."

Terrell left. He didn't often deal with Laguerre when he was drunk, and in the latter years that meant he didn't often deal with Laguerre. One of the most valuable members of the staff, Terrell was suddenly spending more time on the periphery. He had been promoted to executive editor and given the "blue pencil" duties after Johnston's retirement, but the promotion meant that he spent less time working with Laguerre, and now Terrell seemed stuck in a suspended state of waiting.

"If you stay at number two for as long as Terrell did, you develop an amazing bitterness," said one editor. "Terrell felt that André should have left five years earlier. So Terrell sat there, basically at the prime of his professional life, playing number two. And when you're number two to André Laguerre, you're really number two."

"Terrell always said that he just wanted to be ME for five years," said

Walter Bingham. "He told me this one Sunday night. Roy's sitting there, and he had nothing to do. He said, 'I just want five years.'"

Laguerre was growing more distant, which made him that much more formidable. But beneath the veneer, the proud man was growing sad and sentimental. He had been surprised at how emotionally connected he was to his daughters. Sitting in the Ho with Jule Campbell one day, he told Campbell how much he enjoyed talking with his eldest daughter Michele and asked, "Do you think Michele will treat me one day the way you treat your parents?" The younger Claudine, born in 1964, received all the affection that the baby of the family might expect. André would walk with her in the park and spin tales about a special raccoon who lived in a rock in Central Park. In the morning, Claudine would awaken to small prizes under her pillow, furtively brought to her by her raccoon in the park.

It was also becoming more apparent by this time how dependent Laguerre had become upon those around him: Nathalie at home, Ann Callahan at work. Callahan had become an all-purpose aide-de-camp, doing much of his shopping for him on her lunch breaks and shielding other staffers from his office when he needed to nap after particularly long lunches.

For all his experience and education, Laguerre was not a resourceful man. When Nathalie and the girls would take a vacation, he was stuck. There was a lengthy session before one vacation in which Nathalie literally taught him how to boil water so he could make himself a cup of tea. "He achieved that, but that was all he achieved," she said.

She returned from a vacation in the summer of 1973 to the large apartment on Park Avenue, where a family housemaid was bewildered by André's behavior. "Mr. Laguerre—I don't know what he was doing," the maid said. "For a few nights he'd sleep in one bed, then a few more nights in another bed, then another bed." Nathalie was perplexed as well, until she discovered burnt-out light bulbs in two of the bedrooms. Then it dawned on her: *He didn't know how to change light bulbs.*

• • •

Laguerre's last stand really began in another magazine.

By the early '70s, Clay Felker was two decades removed from his time on *SI*'s experimental committee. He'd left Time Inc., gone to *Esquire* for a while, then founded *New York* magazine, turning it into a hip alternative to *The New Yorker,* actively covering print media with the same energy that the business press had long devoted to movie studios and television networks. When former *SI* reporter Sandy Treadwell pitched Felker on a story about the myth of Laguerre and the ascension of *Sports Illustrated,* he quickly commissioned the piece. *Life* and *Time* were institutions by then, but *SI* had never received a full overview in a national magazine. Laguerre, who loathed the idea of media reporting on other media—he referred to it derisively as "intramurals"—refused to sit for an interview with Treadwell, but several other staffers did. Among them was Dick Johnston, who took Treadwell's call out in Hawaii and talked at length, finally letting out his last measure of resentment for his longtime adversary Tex Maule.

"And Now for the Good News at Time Inc." read the story's headline in the January 22, 1973, issue of *New York,* facing a full-page black-and-white shot of Laguerre, smiling and holding a stogie, walking proudly to the Time & Life Building, quite likely from the Ho. The piece outlined Laguerre's critical and commercial success at *SI,* noted that he seemed less prone to suggestions than ten years earlier, and devoted space to his friendship with Werner. Then Treadwell wrote:

> Tex Maule's hold on the managing editor is more difficult to understand. Maule has for a decade been the most famous of *Sports Illustrated*'s writers and as one editor says, "His career would make an interesting minor, very minor, novel.". . . He is quite possibly the worst writer on the magazine, and yet he owns the professional football beat, the most widely read and important writing assignment in *Sports Illustrated*. On Sunday evenings during the football season the magazine mobilizes itself to rewrite Maule's copy. Contradictions are removed, paragraphs are juggled, and anecdotes are inserted. His original Western Union file is transformed under intense deadline pressure into an entertaining well-written story. Yet he maintains his beat year after year, not least because he is Laguerre's longtime drinking companion.

When the story was published, Maule was furious (he filed a libel suit against Treadwell) and Johnston was contrite ("André, I'm sorry," he explained by phone. "I didn't know he was going to print it all.")

Although Laguerre remained staunchly loyal to Maule, the writer's decline had become a major problem. An NFL loyalist to the core, Maule staked much of his reputation on the unquestioned superiority of the established league over the upstart AFL. After the Jets and Chiefs won Super Bowls III and IV, he took it hard. In the late '60s, pro football editor

Gilbert Rogin had taken to calling Maule's researchers to ask for their reporting files, in hopes of cobbling together a piece any way possible. In the fall of 1972, Laguerre brought Deford into the office to be pro football editor—and de facto rewrite man handling Maule's copy. "Never mind how the lawsuit turned out," said one editor. "Treadwell got it about right. By that time, Tex had just lost it."

Treadwell's piece also noted that the hijinks of the early and mid-'60s had dissipated. "Now the twentieth floor is very businesslike and there is little time for jokes and games." One game that continued, though, was speculation over who would succeed Laguerre. Treadwell explained:

> Eight years ago Roy Terrell, *SI*'s executive editor, seemed to be Laguerre's probable successor. "But Laguerre stayed on and eventually his candidacy outlived its probability," says one editor. Ray Cave, a thoroughly capable assistant managing editor, is the new front runner, but Cave's chances might also diminish with time. It is an accepted fact that Laguerre will have his job as long as he likes and will hand-pick his replacement. Last year, for the first time in his career as managing editor, Laguerre began to delegate authority and spend even more time in the Ho Ho restaurant, his favorite bar. "Twelve years is a long time to spend at the same job," says Johnston. "I think that he has become very bored with the magazine and that he'd retire tomorrow if he could transport the Ho Ho and his drinking friends to France."

From the headline to the details of Maule's decline to the intimations of Laguerre's power, the story didn't sit well with Hedley Donovan. In fact, he was growing increasingly impatient with Laguerre's isolated entrenchment. In 1972, he'd offered him a job as editorial director, the second-ranking position on the editorial side, behind only Donovan's own, but Laguerre refused. At the same meeting, Donovan told Laguerre that after another year or so, it would be time for Laguerre to step aside. Laguerre ignored him. It was the classic case of two powerful men keeping a frosty, embittered distance. While Laguerre had nothing to do with Treadwell's story, and while he could have done nothing to stop it, the piece implicitly challenged Donovan's authority, just weeks after the spat over Laguerre's refusal to take on any of *Life*'s writers. To make matters worse, by the time of the story, the two men were entering their fourth year of a protracted debate over Laguerre's desire to spend more money so *SI* could use color on the contents page.

After the Treadwell piece, a pregnant expectation fell over the magazine. "I remember seeing the headline and thinking, 'Oooh, we might have a problem,'" said Deford. "I think everybody was thrilled to see the recognition of a) Laguerre, and b) the magazine. Nobody cared for us. Nobody ever wrote about us. It was like we didn't exist. And particularly didn't exist in New York, where all those guys were masturbating each other. It was *maddening*."

An uneven summer for the magazine began spectacularly, with a three-part series by Nancy Williamson and Bil Gilbert on women in sports, expertly edited by the fast-rising Pat Ryan. Beginning in the May 28, 1973, issue, with the cover tagline "Women Are Getting a Raw Deal," it continued *SI*'s trend of coming down on the right side, albeit sometimes reluctantly, on the important issues. The series would win *SI* its first National Magazine Award, and document the effect of the federally mandated Title IX changes by the NCAA, presaging a generation of broad evolution in female athletics.

The same summer, when Laguerre summoned Roy Blount, Jr., and told him he wanted the writer to spend a season with a professional football team, Blount was the first to suggest focusing on the Pittsburgh Steelers. He headed out for the Steelers training camp in Latrobe, Pennsylvania, in late July, to begin work on a three-part *SI* series and a superb full-length book, *About Three Bricks Shy of a Load*, just over a year later. But beyond that, there were few of the shimmering idea stories that had carried *SI* through earlier summers. The staff, sensing a transition was imminent, was splitting into camps, with Jenkins, Deford, and many of the writers favoring Ray Cave, while Jerry Tax, Bob Ottum, and many of the editors sided with Roy Terrell.

As Treadwell wrote in his article, Terrell's influence seemed to be receding. He had been waiting to succeed Laguerre for more than a decade, and many thought the waiting and resentment had changed him. Terrell had always avoided the cronyism of the *SI* bar scene, but he seemed to grow more and more aloof. He took short lunches, didn't like being called at home to talk about the magazine, and, at just about the time Laguerre was tapping the bar for his first refill at the Ho, was on the train home to Port Washington, Long Island.

Many speculated that Donovan had grown fond of Ray Cave, who was taking an increasingly central role in the weekly operations of *SI*. Yet there was an element to Cave that made people uneasy. He was selectively reticent, didn't fall easily into the rhythms of casual conversation. Those who didn't know him well found him humorless. "Ray never changed to me," said Mark Mulvoy. "I used to play golf with Ray up at Stanwich. Boy, I'll tell you, there was *no* humor. I mean, Ray would hit a golf ball, put his head down, and go after the ball, just attacking the golf course. Playing golf with Ray was not a lot of fun, and working with Ray, in ways, was not a lot of fun. Although you respected him because he was clearly brilliant."

In early September of that year, Donovan called Laguerre into his office and told him that, effective February 1, 1974, he would no longer be the managing editor of *Sports Illustrated*. He had been managing editor longer than anyone else in the company's history, Donovan explained, and it was time for a change.

Laguerre returned to his office and summoned Roy Terrell. "I've been fired," he said, explaining that the news wouldn't be announced until Donovan had decided on a successor. Laguerre took pains to assure Terrell that, despite his close relationship with Cave, he hadn't reneged on his promise to recommend that Terrell get the job, almost wistfully evoking their earlier days of working more closely together. "Roy, we've been good friends, but even if we'd been a lot better friends than we had, I couldn't do anything more for you than I've done."

Later that month, Donovan surprised former *SI* publisher Dick Munro by thinking out loud about the question of whether Cave or Terrell would be the preferable successor to Laguerre. "Hedley, it's a no-brainer," said Munro. "Cave's clearly the more talented, energetic figure." Others gave him the same advice, but heeding Laguerre's recommendation, Donovan decided to give the job to Terrell.

On Thursday, October 11, 1973, *Sports Illustrated* staffers found a memo on their desks from Donovan, which led, "André Laguerre is giving up the Managing Editor's job on *Sports Illustrated* next February 1st." From the curious opening, the memo stated that Laguerre would begin a year's sabbatical in February. "A new Time Inc. assignment has also been proposed to him, but he may decide to pursue career interests outside Time Inc. In whatever he does, he will carry with him the immense respect of the *SI* staff and fellow editors throughout the company." The memo went on to announce that Terrell would be taking over.

The day of the announcement, Cave was called into the office of Ralph Graves, the editorial director and Donovan's number two man, and told that he, of course, had been the other candidate. The general feeling on the 34th floor, owing to Cave's potential, was that Donovan had made the wrong choice.

"Hedley told me that he gave Terrell the job and not Ray because this was Terrell's last chance, and Ray was young enough that he'd have another turn," said Jason McManus, who was working a stint on the 34th floor at the time. "It was one of the few things that Hedley ever said that I thought was just appalling. And for Hedley to give it to someone that way."

Reaction to the move was swift and dramatic. Tex Maule and Mark Kram both offered to resign. Former *SI* staffer Pete Axthelm wrote a story in *Newsweek* criticizing the decision, quoting one editor saying that "the current hierarchy can't understand that a journalist can be great by being different. They're at cocktail parties and country clubs while he's in the Ho Ho Bar on 50th Street with his cronies and he makes them uncomfortable."

Even the staff members who recognized that Laguerre was past his prime were furious about the way the matter had been handled. "The hard feelings came from the fact that he was treated so shabbily," said Frank Deford. "André Laguerre had saved *Sports Illustrated*. He . . . *literally* . . . saved it. They were ready to fold it, and there was a tremendous amount of pressure on Luce to fold it. And if Laguerre hadn't made it work, it would have gone out of business. And how much money has everybody made off that? No effort was made to give him his due. That was the bad feeling; it wasn't so much that André had been replaced."

Oddly, one of the few people on 20 besides Terrell who seemed to understand why Laguerre was removed was Cave, the Laguerre loyalist. He had befriended both Donovan and Graves and understood the executives' position. "You have to remember that he was a cantankerous son of a bitch in the eyes of the establishment," he said. "And that wasn't their misjudgment; that was true. He was offered a job, you know, on the 34th floor. The number two job in the company on the editorial side. You couldn't be offered anything higher unless Donovan said, 'I'm gonna quit; you can have it.' So what the hell? I was a little surprised that they would have done that. And that took a little doing. If I'd been Hedley, I would have just let him go. I mean, who needs this? He's kicked us in the ankle for ten years; let him make his own life. Also, he was given a year's notice. He could have rethought the notion of going to 34; he could have done a lot of things. But he didn't want to. Basically, knowing Laguerre, in these areas he gave no quarter. And if you live by the sword, you are probably going to die by the sword. And that doesn't mean that anybody was unfair. The inside perception about Laguerre's being fired I am sure would be that he was treated very unfairly. Because damn few of them have a real sense of his separation from the management of the company. And if they *had* a sense of it, they would have liked it."

Even after the repeated warnings and the advance notice, the day of the announcement was a shock to Laguerre. That afternoon, Marty

Nathan walked into Laguerre's office to find his boss sitting at his desk, tears rolling down his face. "Martin," he said. "They've dumped me."

He was a proud man being told he'd outlived his usefulness. "He was brokenhearted," said Nathalie Laguerre. "He never expected it. It came as a terrible surprise to him. For a very intelligent man, he was incredibly naive about office politics."

She realized, as well, that something had been taken from him that could never be regained. For the first time in his professional career, he viewed himself as a failure. The hangover was monstrous: long sleepless nights, punctuated by tossing and turning, and a single recurring nightmare, which lasted for nearly a year. He'd wake up in a sweat, calling out, "They fired me, they fired me," while Nathalie would flick on the light and try to calm him down. "André was such a committed man to his work," she reflected later. "I think that was really his personal life, too. It was just primordial."

• • •

In his nearly 14-year run as *Sports Illustrated*'s managing editor, André Laguerre had engineered a remarkable journalistic transformation. Under his stewardship, the magazine's business side prospered in ways that those who had been on the staff in the '50s could barely imagine. *SI*'s annual ad base grew from $11.9 million to $72.2 million, and its circulation grew from 900,000 to 2,250,000.

But Laguerre's most important contribution was also the most ineffable. The writers had created the new *SI* and lifted it to a new level. But the idea that sports journalism could somehow be associated with sophistication, that *SI* would be among the magazines read by intelligent people with a broad worldview—only André Laguerre could have made that possible.

At the beginning of his penultimate week as managing editor, he sent out a typically succinct memo, reminding his staff, "You know I want to avoid parties or any other farewell ceremony, but I hope everyone will be around to shake hands, or even buy me a drink. The thought I would like to leave you with is that together we created something; we created something successful that gave pleasure and maybe occasional inspiration to many millions, and, most of the time, we had fun doing it. That was no mean achievement. Another thing I know is that Roy can count on the same intense loyalty you gave me all those years, and for which I am more grateful than I can say. Take care of yourselves. A.L."

The final weekend, January 25–27, 1974, felt like an unusually muted

Irish wake. There would be something at stake in the end, with a Muhammad Ali and Joe Frazier rematch set for Madison Square Garden on the Sunday night of the close. Jenkins flew back from his post-football vacation in Hawaii to be there. At Laguerre's behest, Robert Creamer called Jim Murray and Jack Olsen to come for the final night's party. The somber vignettes played out over and over. That Friday afternoon, Pat Putnam walked into Laguerre's office to bid farewell. He put his hand across Laguerre's desk and shook it. "I'm not going to say good-bye," he said. "I'm going to say thank you." Both men had tears in their eyes.

The staff started drifting down to the Ho at about 11:30 that Sunday night, only to be told after just an hour that the bar was closing. No one quite believed it, but no one had made arrangements ahead of time with the bartenders Jimmy and Tommy. Sarah Ballard was furious, throwing a handful of dimes against the mirror behind the bar and storming out. By 1 a.m., the contingent moved to the Canton Village on 48th Street. There was an exquisitely mediocre vocalist there, and Marty Nathan and Harvey Grut got her attention during a break. At the opening of the next set, she sang "My Way" and dedicated it to Laguerre. He sat there with a drink in his hand, nodding his head.

The party eventually worked its way back to Laguerre's office, for more toasts and tearful farewells. At about four in the morning, Kram, who'd been in a miserable funk since Laguerre's exit was announced, produced his story.

Laguerre read it, and winced a little bit, as if to forestall a complete surrender to emotion. He then okayed the story and sent it out to be typeset. Readers of *SI* that week might have puzzled a bit at the conclusion of the piece, but around the office, many staffers thanked Kram for his epigrammatic send-off. His story of Ali's dogged victory over Frazier ended like this:

> "How old those two fellas?" a lady in a gold fur asked, leaving the Garden.
> "Thirty-two and thirty," said a man next to her. "Frazier's thirty."
> "My, myyyyy. He looks sooooo old."
> So he does. And there is a French phrase that tells a lot about what many thought after seeing him: "To say good-by is to die a little."
> He was a singular man—and also a fighter.

# CHAPTER 12

# THE LONG ISLAND MAFIA

On Thursday, January 31, 1974, Roy Terrell became the third managing editor in the history of *Sports Illustrated*. Trim, purposeful, cheerful but businesslike, Terrell was an anomaly, a man dramatically out of step with his cultural surroundings. While other staffers were experimenting with drugs in the '60s, he was experimenting with travel photography. Long after other staff writers and editors grew jaundiced and stopped being fans, Terrell spent Sunday afternoons and Monday nights in front of the TV, as wrapped up as ever in the serial drama of the NFL. While others on the staff drank at the Ho and fell into multiple infidelities, Terrell headed home to his wife Charlyne, the woman he'd been with since high school.

After ascending to the position he'd long coveted, the one that he felt was rightly his, Terrell confronted the vast array of personnel problems that demanded his attention. Many of Laguerre's cronies had prospered and hung on without particularly distinguishing themselves, especially in the later years. There were numerous writers who hadn't been producing (*Time* expatriate Ray Kennedy, a genuine talent, suffered from an agonizing case of writer's block). Others, like Tex Maule and Bill Leggett, the magazine's lead writers for pro football and baseball, were clearly on the decline. At the same time, expense account abuse at the magazine had gotten out of hand. Many of the editors were less vigilant, many of the writers less accountable, many of the researchers less sharp than they ought to have been.

Alcoholism, long accepted as a matter of fact throughout the company, was finally being viewed as a problem. Terrell couldn't fire everyone, but he moved quickly to bring the most excessive cases in check and to send the message that continued indiscretions wouldn't be tolerated. Almost instantly, the culture of the magazine changed. While many writers and editors still gathered at the Ho, it was no longer the locus of the editorial events at *SI*. "Basically, Terrell resented Laguerre's style," said Mark Mulvoy, who worked first as a hockey writer and later as a senior editor under Terrell. "It inhibited Roy, and the minute Roy took over, bar sales within the vicinity of the Time & Life Building dropped by 82 percent. Justerini and Brooks probably had to lay off the night shift."

If all that weren't enough, Terrell was replacing a legend. He hadn't fired Laguerre, but more than a few staffers couldn't forgive him for taking his place.

A cadre of staffers would argue, immediately and for years after, that Ray Cave would have been the better choice. But Cave would have faced many of the same problems, and found it necessary to make many of the same painful corrections as Terrell.

"God it was terrible," said Bill Leggett. "There were people who hated Roy Terrell who didn't even know the man. Because he was the man who was given the job of replacing a legend. They say you can't replace a legend in sports; well, Roy did. Some people were very tiny about it."

It might have been the best job in the country, and Terrell often referred to it as such. But under the circumstances, it was surely one of the most difficult. Disliked by some of his writers, dismissed as uncooperative and unimaginative by the business side, unable to establish the sort of environment he wanted without deep resentment, he found himself in a quagmire.

His smile hardened and he moved doggedly forward.

• • •

Few vices were indulged with more consistency or pervasiveness than expense account abuse. Any purchase under $25 didn't require a receipt, so $24.99 became a popular expense account figure for all manner of lunches, cab rides, bar tabs, and midmorning breakfast interviews with the ubiquitous all-purpose source "Jock Strapalino." For years, Laguerre had kept the salaries low, and subtly encouraged the staff to make it up on the expense account. This they did. Maule boasted that the expense accounts helped him finance his Sutton Place condo. Alfred Wright came back from the British Open one year with a four-figure expense for a shooting stick. When he got to the bar the following Thursday, Laguerre greeted him with a chuckle. "Well, old man. I'm very curious to see that fine shooting stick of yours."

"I remember financing a Christmas simply by getting money with some jive story," said Roy Blount. "But eventually, I did have to write a story; I mean, I didn't steal the money, but I did borrow it in advance to pay for my children's Christmas."

Not all of the expenditures were so high-minded. "Curry Kirkpatrick's the one that elevated expense account writing to an art form," said one staffer. "Curry was so clever. He didn't advertise, but he just sort of told us that every road trip, he would figure out some way to make a major purchase out of his expense account—and I mean something big, like a new suit or a piece of leather luggage. And it always got put, deftly, as something or somebody he dined with, so that he really padded his income tremendously by his expense account."

So while it was both inevitable and necessary that Terrell do something to curb expenses, it still came as something of a shock when he did. The memo, dated April 13, 1974, was titled "Expense Account Abuses," and noted that the staff had already exceeded its travel and entertainment budget by more than $50,000. "Of the expense accounts turned in during the past three months, the very best that can be said for some of them is that they are abusive; at the worst, they are fraudulent . . . It is a deplorable situation that will no longer be permitted to exist."

There was little doubt that one of the main people the memo was directed at was Dan Jenkins, who for years had served at golf tournaments and football games as the unofficial ambassador of *SI*. Two weeks before the memo, he had run up a $2,200 tab at Joe's Stone Crab, dining with June and two other couples. For years, Creamer had sensed an "unspoken antagonism" between Terrell and the Texans. "I don't know this for a fact, but I think Roy resented the impact they made, the attention they received. Here he'd been working for years to get people to recognize that *SI* could do hard sports and do them well. He did it quietly, efficiently, effectively, and then here came these extrovert newcomers. People noticed them. They hung around the right joints, were big hello guys."

A few weeks after the memo, Terrell called Jenkins into his office and tossed the writer's latest expense account across the desk.

"Redo these," he said. "If you're going to live like King Farouk, you're going to have to pay for half of it yourself."

For a moment, Jenkins just stared at Terrell incredulously.

"Roy, what's that got to do with *journalism*?!" he asked. "Shouldn't you be thinking about what's gonna be on the cover? I did my expense accounts the same way I've always fuckin' done 'em."

"Well, you can't do them that way anymore. This is ridiculous."

"I *spent* the money!" protested Jenkins. "I didn't buy apartments with it. I entertain. I spent it—I think I should."

The chill that developed after the meeting would remain through the rest of Terrell's tenure at the magazine. The editor felt that Jenkins didn't appreciate his position. And the writer felt that Terrell had lost perspective.

"That's when I realized that Roy was more concerned about being a CPA than he was about putting out a good magazine," said Jenkins. "Roy was one of those guys who went out and did his job and didn't spend much money. Deford never spent any money; he didn't entertain. When I would spend $200 on a dinner at the Beverly Hills Hotel, Frank would be at Denny's or something. It was just a different attitude about things. I didn't try to be the biggest spender around there. But I'm told that I was."

"You couldn't resent Dan," said Terrell. "He was a big-time spender, and he did spend the money, but there were obvious things that had to be fixed. I mean, here we had guys like Deford who never put down a nickel on their expense account. I admire this man. Look, I cheated a little on my expense account, and I wouldn't blame someone else for doing a little bit, but this flagrant, absurd thing—it was an insult to your editors."

• • •

In the magazine, Terrell's tenure began promisingly. From his first issue, dated February 13, the *Sports Illustrated* cover logotype appeared with an outline, the first change in the cover design since Gangel had shrunk the words to accommodate both on a single line in 1966. More important, he took advantage of the increased color pages to provide more coverage of weekend events, which had occasionally been neglected or turned into departments in the '60s, when *SI* had only four to six fast color pages a week. He also improved the quality of the writing on the most important beats, choosing Jenkins and Fimrite to replace Maule and Leggett as the lead writers on the pro football and major league baseball beats respectively.

The cover of the sixth issue was the first in a three-part series adapting Robert Creamer's biography of Babe Ruth, *Babe: The Legend Comes to Life*. The exhaustive, definitive work received spectacular reviews and brought Creamer some notoriety unusually late in his career (he would retire within a decade). Jonathan Yardley, in the *Washington Post*, called it "the best biography ever written about an American sports figure." In two of the next four issues, *SI* exhibited its newfound flexibility, providing color for two Monday night events. The first was the 1974 NCAA basketball championship, with North Carolina State defeating Marquette (though the cover was justly devoted to the Wolfpack's scintillating double-overtime win over eight-time defending national champion UCLA two days earlier). Two weeks later, when Hank Aaron broke Babe Ruth's all-time home run record on a Monday night, Ron Fimrite was there to cover it. That Thursday, Aaron could be seen holding the ball aloft on the cover of the April 15, 1974, issue, with the simple headline: "715." A week later, *SI* came back to the event with a bonus piece by Plimpton, who had been following Aaron around since the end of the 1973 season.

Fimrite's baseball coverage was consistently strong, but Terrell's decision to put Jenkins on the magazine's biggest beat, pro football, was less successful. Jenkins was congenitally unsuited for the NFL. Pete Rozelle's domain was based on uniformity: no hip pads sticking out, no tearaway jerseys, nothing on the field of play to differentiate Kansas City from San Francisco or Miami or Minnesota. For a man who'd become famous for illuminating the unique regional enclaves of college football, it was a deadly change. It didn't help that, after *Semi-Tough* and the two succeeding novels, *Dead Solid Perfect*, about the life of a touring professional golfer, and *Limo*, written with Shrake, about television, he wasn't working on the job as hard as he once had. Though he would continue to be *SI*'s best-known, best-read writer throughout the '70s, Jenkins lost a measure of enthusiasm switching to the pro beat.

"I hated covering pro football," Jenkins said. "I got pissed off at the zebras. They kept fucking up everything they touched in pro football. It made me realize that pro football wasn't near as important as college football. Still isn't. Never will be. I never understood how they could take the greatest pass receiver in the world, put him in the pros, and teach him how to drop passes. Or teach great running backs how to fumble. It's roulette, or something; there's something *wrong* with it. I've never been able to get to the bottom of it. You know what it is? They don't feel any kinship to where they are. They'd be just as happy playin' in another city. There's no team there."

Terrell's ascension to managing editor required other moves. The first one, promoting Ray Cave to executive editor, was an easy call. Then Terrell, with some reluctance, promoted the legendarily eccentric Gilbert Rogin to assistant managing editor. Terrell was impressed with Rogin's line-editing skills and mastery of the English language, but he didn't feel he was a team player. "Roy Terrell told me once, 'You'll never get anywhere in this company unless you read the magazine you work for,'" recalled Rogin. "Well, I never read it. I knew all that stuff. I was out for myself. Why should I read it? I knew it all. What did I need to know about? What do I care about Washington State's football team?"

It would fall to Rogin to be the blue pencil, Dick Johnston's old job, traditionally the last line of editing responsibility. But then Terrell continued to edit copy behind Rogin, as vigorously as he had when he was executive editor. This extra layer of editing, which eventually became known as the red pencil, brought the magazine closer to the Time Inc. norm of group journalism. *SI* writers now routinely had their copy picked over by four different people: the fact checker who researched the story, the senior editor on the writer's beat, Rogin's blue pencil, and Terrell's red pencil. "I can remember my big shock after Roy took over," said senior editor Walter Bingham. "Suddenly, copy that you were editing went to Rogin or Cave, in the beginning, blue pencil. Cave was a heavy editor. Suddenly, there's all this red all over the place. There's no doubt that the heavy editing took place under Terrell."

Oddly enough, the best line editor at the magazine—one who brought an element of empathy to the process that even gifted editors like Rogin, Crichton, Ryan, and Cave couldn't match—was Bob Creamer. But Creamer had been judged not tough enough by Laguerre. Terrell shared this opinion, and was often dismayed by his good friend's lack of focus. "Bob was the most compulsive procrastinator I have ever known, and not nearly tough enough to be a good assistant ME," said Terrell. "He was easily diverted from the task at hand, any task, by the chance to talk about his hometown of Tuckahoe, by watching girls walk down the hall, by food, drink, discussions of Tuckahoe, discussions of the works of James Joyce, discussions of Willie Mays, the girls in the office, his wife Margaret, the Little League game in which his kids, or for that matter, anyone else's kids, were playing, the chance to tell someone about Tuckahoe, the chance to talk to anyone about anything."

Terrell also disapproved of the behavior of some of his other senior editors. He bridled at Crichton's occasional lapses in attention, such as his habit of doing crossword puzzles during the Monday planning meetings. Walter Bingham, who had been at the magazine 20 years and had proved himself an adept editor as well, was also passed over for a promotion. It didn't help that Bingham was a seasoned prankster who loathed the sober mood of the new regime. Forever typing up phony corporate memos ("due to the success of the ninth floor cafeteria, the hours of operation henceforth will be 9 a.m. until 7 p.m. daily. To compensate for the extra hours each day, the cafe will close down on Saturdays and Sundays"), Bingham was eventually humbled when one of his forged memos, signed by corporate executive Robert Steed, was intercepted and shown to Steed, who marched into Terrell's office demanding an explanation.

Bingham retreated to the Ho and spent the rest of the afternoon in the bar.

Terrell eventually settled on his best friend at the magazine, assistant managing editor Jerry Tax, as his most trusted confidante and right-hand man. Generally well liked, but transparently mindful of the prevailing political winds, Tax rode with Terrell and senior editor Bob Ottum on the train in from Port Washington every day (Hedley Donovan rode the same LIRR train). The wizened Werner once referred to Tax as "the Cecil B. DeMille of meals with ketchup," and Olsen and his cronies used to love to switch Tax's Valpolicella with cheap red wine when he went to the bathroom at lunch. But Tax had made some profound contributions to the magazine. He'd been on the forefront of recognizing basketball as a sport meriting national attention, and had taken a central role in developing several writers, none more successfully than Frank Deford.

Terrell was seeking Tax's counsel in much the same way that Laguerre sought Johnston's, but the effect was different. Laguerre and Johnston belonged to completely different social groups, while Terrell and Tax stuck together. Quite suddenly, the leadership of the magazine seemed to consist of a two-man cabal that took the train in together in the morning and left together in the evening. Over drinks one night at the Ho, Jenkins dubbed them the Long Island Mafia.

It wasn't a surprise when Ray Cave left the magazine. Cave, ever the good soldier, was too professional to let being passed over for the top job at *SI* affect his performance, but also too ambitious to easily fall into the role of Terrell's understudy. In 1976, Hedley Donovan moved him to an assistant managing editor's job at *Time* where a year later, he would beat out Jason McManus for the managing editor's job, succeeding Henry Grunwald. Cave's periodic stints at top-editing *SI*, usually during Terrell vacations, had earned the attention of Donovan for their audacity and dramatic presentation.

After Cave left, Terrell promoted Tax to executive editor and hired Ken Rudeen to be assistant managing editor. It was a decision he soon regretted; while Rudeen could work fast, he never seemed to assert any leadership ability and his remaining 20 years at the magazine seemed to exist in a void. He was, in the words of one editor, "a perfect example of the Peter Principle, someone promoted beyond their capabilities." Rudeen's real problem as an editor was a pronounced generation gap. When Curry Kirkpatrick made a reference in one of his basketball stories to reggae icon Bob Marley, the perplexed Rudeen brought the draft over to another editor, and asked earnestly, "What in *hell* does this have to do with Charles Dickens?"

Terrell, Tax, Rogin, and Rudeen were all hard-working and jovial, but they didn't spend much time with the writers and didn't spend any time at the Ho. So the natural antagonism between editors and writers, often assuaged over drinks in the Laguerre regime, quickly became more pronounced. In the summer of 1976, Tax sent a memo to the *SI* writing staff. The infamous document was reprinted in the *Village Voice* (Donovan was furious, both that it was written and that it had been leaked) and, twenty years later, Shrake still had a copy of the memo framed in his office. While it didn't have the desired effect, Tax's memo served to draw the lines more clearly between writers and top editors:

It seems to me high time the members of the writing staff of *SI* faced the realities of their situation. With the *rarest of exceptions*, they:

1. Never have even the slightest notion what stories will appear in the magazine each week until it is published, and couldn't care less about it.
2. Never make suggestions for stories that *should* appear in their magazine.
3. Spend much of their *working* time at home contemplating their navels or dreaming up ways to augment their incomes with outside jobs.
4. Kick like steers when tracked down and asked to take assignments which do not tickle their fancy.
5. Bitch and grouse when asked to take assignments two weeks in a row.
6. Never volunteer for routine, bread-and-butter assignments which must be fulfilled, like "Pub Memo," various "Weeks," etc.
7. Drag out over weeks feature-writing assignments that should be accomplished in days.
8. Turn in stories in an illegible, garbled up typescript that is an insult to their editors.
9. Generally take the attitude that when they are not called by an editor and given an assignment they have no responsibility toward the magazine, though this condition may last for weeks.
10. Consider their expense accounts the ideal vehicle to adjust their salaries to the level they feel they deserve.

Finally, and most remarkable of all, most would agree to the truth of these 10 points—but believe that's the way things should be.

The memo would further strain relations between Tax and the writers, as well as increase the suspicion among some that Tax, whom Werner once described as "a Jewish puritan," was exercising undue influence on Terrell.

But one reason the staff writers were harder to control was that they were becoming harder to find. John Underwood had been the first to go, returning to Miami late in the Laguerre regime. He was followed shortly by Fimrite to San Francisco, Shrake to Texas, and Joe Jares to Los Angeles. The dislocated staff writers "began to get a stranglehold on the magazine," said Cave. "And suddenly they're living all over the goddamn country. You can't run a magazine having your key staff members essentially behaving like freelancers. They don't contribute anything. You want them around. You've got to talk to them."

• • •

Laguerre was gone, but his specter remained. Kram, increasingly disheveled and increasingly unreliable under the new regime, stalked around the office in a kind of angry daze. "I hate this fucking place," he'd grumble to one of the reporters. "What's in it for me? What can I gain? I don't want to put myself into it anymore. Why do I want to write another story? Even if you didn't like a story, with the Old Man around, he'd give you an idea or two, get you involved in it. Then you had a full head of steam. But now . . ." His voice would trail off. He'd pick up a book from a reporter's shelf, riffle through it, and put it back. Then he'd rummage through a garbage can, searching for a magazine, then start muttering again. "I hate this fucking place."

For all his bruising bluster, the combustible Kram was a bundle of insecurities. After an emergency landing on an international flight in the late '60s, he had developed a paralyzing obsession with his own mortality that worked its way into every aspect of his work.

The extent became clear one Friday afternoon in the early '70s, after a wrestling story by Kram ran in the magazine. Andy Crichton received a call from an assistant sports information director at the school Kram wrote about. "I don't know if I'm talking out of place here," the caller said. "We didn't particularly like the article written about us, but that's all right. You have your rights. But it was signed by Mark Kram, and we prepared for Mark Kram to get here and, you know, he never came."

"Wait a minute," said Crichton. "Repeat that—you mean to say Mark Kram never showed up there?"

"No, we never saw him the entire week."

"Well, did anybody show up?"

"Yeah. Some guy named Herbie Ade."

A chill ran through Crichton. He knew Ade, knew he ran with Kram, and knew of Kram's phobia of flying. He hadn't known that Kram had been sending him out on stories, then paying him and making up the expenses on his expense account. The mere act of sending someone out to do the legwork for a story was hardly in itself a heinous crime. It was, in fact, one of the cornerstones of group journalism. On the other hand, Ade was hardly the sort of frontman the magazine wanted representing it at far-flung locales. Called the "Great Impostor" by one *SI* staffer, Ade was "the sort of man who would, at a party, claim to be a gynecologist, insinuating himself to women, counseling them about their particular maladies." Whatever his skills as a reporter, Ade saved Mark Kram from his greatest fear. But with Laguerre gone, Kram's fears multiplied: he would be swept up in sudden panic attacks, accompanied by profuse sweating, trembling, and disconnected speech. But flying remained his paramount fear, prompting him to take ships to Europe and trains whenever he could around the United States.

There were no ships to Kingston in 1973, when Foreman crushed Joe Frazier, so Kram didn't go. And he passed up, to his eternal regret, the epochal Rumble in the Jungle, Ali's startling upset of Foreman in Kinshasa, Zaire, in 1974. When Ali and Frazier announced their third meeting, in the Philippines in the fall of 1975, Kram knew he had to go. The Thrilla in Manila would become the final chapter of perhaps the greatest sports rivalry of the century. Terrell played it up, running a cover story on the two fighters, with a tuxedo-clad promoter Don King, still new on the fight scene, standing between them.

When the fight came, Ray Cave was filling in for Terrell, who was on vacation. He encouraged Kram to go and the writer finally agreed, provided he could fly with Ali. They met at his training camp in Pennsylvania, then flew together to Chicago, Los Angeles, and Hawaii.

On the last leg of the flight, from Honolulu to Manila, Kram looked forlornly out the window at the vast expanse of ocean below. For much of the flight, Ali, who was scared of flying himself, was sitting behind him and taunting him. "All that ocean out there, Mark Kram!" Ali teased, shaking Kram's seat. "Dark, dark, sharks! You goin' down now! You goin' down my friend, you goin' down!"

Kram, sputtering with laughter, responded, "If I'm going down, you're going with me! You're gonna make a better meal for a shark than I will!"

By the time the plane landed, Kram was, in his own words, a nervous wreck. George Plimpton recalled of Kram's harrowing journey that, "when he finally deplaned in Manila, someone remarked that 'nothing got off but a fluff of dandruff.'"

But the trip would be worth it. The event would bring out the best in Kram and change his life. He met a college student at the Manila Hilton on his first night in the city, and was immediately smitten. After three days, he realized that, whether on assignment or not, married or not, he was falling in love with her. While the other writers—Plimpton, Red Smith, Dick Schaap, Peter Bonventre from *Newsweek*—were drinking around the bar, Kram was sneaking out of the Manila Hilton past the 10 o'clock curfew under martial law, on his way to forbidden and genuinely dangerous assignations with his new lover (whom he would eventually marry).

The fight was held on Wednesday morning, October 1, 1975, in Manila, and Ali retained his title in a furious hour of battle that would rank as one of the greatest heavyweight fights of all time. Kram delivered his story two days later, opening with a description of Ali at the dinner held in his honor that Wednesday night at the Malacanang Palace. Kram's lead set the scene at the palace, mentioning that Imelda Marcos filled the plate for the weary champion as nearby candles flickered across his face.

The maddest of existentialists, one of the great surrealists of our time, the king of all he sees, Ali had never before appeared so vulnerable and fragile, so pitiably unmajestic, so far from the universe he claims as his alone. He could barely hold his fork, and he lifted the food slowly up to his bottom lip, which had been scraped pink. The skin on his face was dull and blotched, his eyes drained of that familiar childlike wonder. His right eye was a deep purple, beginning to close, a dark blind being drawn against a harsh light. He chewed his food painfully, and then he suddenly moved away from the candles as if he had become aware of the mask he was wearing, as if an inner voice were laughing at him. He shrugged, and the moment was gone.

A couple of miles away, in the bedroom of a villa, the man who has always demanded answers of Ali, has trailed the champion like a timber wolf, lay in semi-darkness. Only his heavy breathing disturbed the quiet as an old friend walked to within two feet of him. "Who is it?" asked Joe Frazier, lifting himself to look around. "Who is it? I can't see! I can't see! Turn the lights on!" Another light was turned on, but Frazier still could not see. The scene cannot be forgotten; this good and gallant man lying there, embodying the remains of a will never before seen in a ring, a will that had carried him so far—and now surely too far. His eyes were only slits, his face looked as if it had been painted by Goya. "Man, I hit him with punches that'd bring down the walls of a city," said Frazier. "Lawdy, Lawdy, he's a great champion." Then he put his head back down on the pillow, and soon there was only the heavy breathing of a deep sleep slapping like big waves against the silence.

Time may well erode that long morning of drama in Manila, but for anyone who was there those faces will return again and again to evoke what it was like when two of the greatest heavyweights of any era met for a third time, and left millions limp around the world. Muhammad Ali caught the way it was: "It was like death. Closest thing to dyin' that I know of."

For 15 years, *SI* had been moving in a specific direction—toward not just reporting or covering an event but distilling it, capturing its essence and presenting it in a compressed, lyrical image of deadline literature and photojournalism. Upon reading Kram's piece for the first time, Cave sensed that this, finally, was the apotheosis of the form. *SI* had seized the moment before: with Jenkins at Norman, Oklahoma, on Thanksgiving Day, 1971, for the Game of the Century between Oklahoma and Nebraska; with Fimrite on hand for the drama of Henry Aaron's 715th homer. But those events had felt constricted in their layout and execution. Jenkins's piece on Oklahoma-Nebraska was a truncated gem, running less than four pages, not even making the cover; Aaron's feat was a freak of timing that left Ron Fimrite just 30 minutes to file his story. But here it was all coming together; Cave ran the pictures big and ran more of them, taking full advantage of the time and technology at hand. The opening spread included the eight-page story's title, "'Lawdy, Lawdy, He's Great,'" and a pair of nearly full-page Leifer pictures, of the bruised, battered faces of Ali and Frazier after the fight. The cover headline read "The Epic Battle."

What would make Kram's writing all the more remarkable, after the fact, was that he'd missed so much of the color that went on after the fight, including the dinner at Malacanang Palace. But he had Leifer, who was everywhere, and he got some notes from Peter Bonventre, covering the fight for *Newsweek*. Whatever he did, and however he got it, Kram found the insight to conjure up a story that Bill Veeck, among many others, would call the best sports story ever written.

But within a year, Kram fell into financial trouble and seemed to take another slide. He would seal his own fate with a January 3, 1977, piece on Don King's televised heavyweight "box-off," to determine a new champion in the wake of Muhammad Ali's professed retirement. "There are American champions to be made—honestly," wrote Kram. "The last word is so important; the champions here cannot be made in the back room, they must be made in the ring." The problem was that the box-off was far from honest. It was a jury-rigged, King-controlled effort (and a successful one at that) to assure himself a piece of the next heavyweight champion. Through his old boxing connections, *SI* staffer Robert H. Boyle heard complaints about the tournament and, eventually, numerous rumors that Kram was on the take from King.

By this time, investigative reporter Mort Sharnik was hearing many of the same rumors. Rogin, a longtime Kram detractor, refused to edit Kram's copy and pressed hard for his firing. Terrell was inclined to take Rogin's criticism with a grain of salt. "Gil's dislike of Kram far predated the events [surrounding the box-off]," said Terrell. "How much the friction between Rogin and Kram was due to a strong personality conflict and how much to Rogin's expressed contempt for Kram as a writer, I don't know. Strangely enough, Tax felt much the same way about Kram's writing, always insisting that Mark's style was pretentious to a fault. I didn't agree, obviously; I thought Mark Kram was a heck of a talent."

But Terrell allowed Rogin to at least investigate the case. Rogin called in Sharnik and the company eventually hired a private investigator, who tapped Kram's phone and even tried to draw him into a conversation and admission of guilt over drinks one night at Gallagher's. Try as they might, the investigators could never conclusively prove that Kram had taken a payoff from King. But there were plenty of other allegations that were confirmed. He had demanded one-half of Dr. Ferdie Pacheco's $2,200 fee for excerpts from his book in the November 8, 1976, issue of *SI*. He had received money from powerboater and Benihana restauratuer Rocky Aoki, shortly after a piece on Aoki that ran in the March 1, 1976, issue. Inevitably, there were also several allegations of Kram sending others in his place to cover stories, then writing them later at his home.

When confronted with the allegations, Kram panicked, denying everything. In his flustered state, he claimed that he hadn't taken money from any of the men. (Kram maintains today that the money he received from King, which he says totaled $10,000, was for a development deal for two different boxing movies, and the money from Aoki and Pacheco was for ghostwriting.) Later, Kram would lament his behavior, admitting to leading "an unexamined life" during the mid-'70s. At the time, he called Laguerre and requested a hasty meeting. At a park bench in Central Park, they met and Kram outlined the charges against him. Laguerre had only one piece of advice: get a lawyer.

The May 2, 1977, issue of *SI* included a story by Boyle exposing the box-off, noting that an unnamed writer at *SI* may have been "on the take" as well, and the magazine was "investigating the allegations against the staffer." On May 13, Kram was fired for gross misconduct. Because the charges of his involvement with King could not be proven, they were not listed on the document outlining the terms of his firing sent to the Newspaper Guild.

Twenty years later, Rogin said he didn't remember any of the details of the investigation of Kram, a lack of recall that Terrell found preposterous. "My God, it was Rogin and Sharnik who came to me with the allegations in the first place," said Terrell. "Knowing their feelings toward Kram, and never having previously heard about any of this, I may have indicated a certain skepticism, but they were very convincing. I called in Tax to listen, too, and Rogin and Sharnik went through it all again. At that time I might well have asked them to go get some additional proof, so in that sense I could indeed have assigned Gil to investigate further. Anyway, they came back with the details; I called Kram in to face the charges before Tax, Rogin, and myself; and then I fired him. Mark Kram, a poor lost soul."

Kram's firing was bracketed by two key defections. Roy Blount, Jr., left to pursue a freelance career in 1975. *Three Bricks Shy of a Load*, published in the summer of 1974, had raised his profile, and he left the staff the following summer. By 1978, Shrake would leave as well, turning in his resignation shortly after receiving an assignment to cover the Junior National Rodeo Finals.

It wasn't merely that Terrell would lose three of his best writers in Blount, Kram, and Shrake. It was also that they were three of the magazine's most distinctive voices, versatile and literate, capable at once of good reporting and evocative journalism. Good people would replace them and talented writers would continue to be hired throughout the history of the magazine, but never again would *SI* have so diverse and accomplished a group of voices.

• • •

Rather than leaving Time Inc. immediately, André Laguerre had been persuaded by Hedley Donovan to spend six months in London to examine the feasibility of a European version of *SI*. In the fall of 1974, Laguerre submitted to Donovan a proposal for a European edition of *SI*, to be launched in England, with a greater focus on soccer, cricket, tennis. It would serve as a wide-ranging European bureau that could, in turn, punch up *SI*'s international coverage at a time when the global village of sport seemed to be coming together.

But when Laguerre presented his proposal to Donovan, it was summarily rejected. Publisher Jack Meyers (who had succeeded Munro as publisher in 1974) had been initially enthusiastic about the idea, but ultimately felt it wouldn't be financially practical. "It was a very well-written proposal," Meyers said. "It just wasn't worth funding. That's when Laguerre thought we'd sent him over on a wild goose chase, because he really worked on it." The magazine was, in the mid-'70s, making less than $10 million a year and would have needed more than that to get off the ground. Meanwhile, the company had been weathering the recession, and pouring millions into the launch of *People Weekly*. In that environment, *SI International* never had a chance.

Laguerre finally left Time Inc. early in 1975, to become the editor and publisher of *Classic*, a glossy, bimonthly horse magazine that covered the entire equestrian world, from thoroughbreds to show horses. It seemed an underfunded, quixotic mission from the start, but the devotion to Laguerre was so complete, that many *SI* staffers quit their jobs and invested some of their own money in the launch, just to work with him again. The full-scale procession to *Classic* included Whitney Tower, Tex Maule, Andy Crichton, and Les Woodcock. Even Sandy Treadwell, in the process of being sued by Tex Maule over his article in *New York*, signed on. (Laguerre was such a conciliatory presence that Maule and Treadwell, both working for *Classic* at the time, shared a cab ride to court on the day of the libel hearing, before settling.) At *SI*, Meyers and Donovan were more upset about the defections than Terrell, who viewed it as an overdue clearing of deadwood. When Meyers floated the idea of revoking Laguerre's pension (on the grounds that *Classic* was a competing venture, and a breach of his retirement agreement), Terrell dismissed it out of hand.

Suddenly, Laguerre and his coterie were together again, going from their midtown Manhattan office to a nearby bar, at the Long River Chinese restaurant, except on Mondays and Fridays, when he'd head over to Canton Village and meet his old *SI* cronies. Ann Callahan, who had stayed on to be Terrell's secretary, would stop by. *SI* copy desk chief Betty DeMeester was usually there as well. But the job itself was a mockery of the old life. *Classic* was a handsome journalistic success, but the bimonthly publishing schedule lacked the urgency that Laguerre thrived upon, and he spent more time than he wanted to in trying to figure out how to balance the books. And as DeMeester began spending more time with Laguerre, the old crowd, even such *Classic* stalwarts as Crichton, Tower, and Maule, spent less time at the bar.

By 1978, it was clear to all that Laguerre had slowed down. After he announced his retirement, naming Crichton his successor, he called Crichton into the office to talk with him about the job.

"Now there are certain things you must always do," Laguerre said softly, reaching into a drawer and pulling out a manila folder. "You must always get the monthly reports from the publisher, about circulation and advertising revenues. You must—"

And then he stopped. He shuffled through the papers and slumped in his chair, with a look of weary resignation. He hadn't received such a report for nearly half a year.

Crichton looked down at his old boss and felt his eyes water.

"I suddenly realized he was totally out of control of things. I wondered, What am I taking over here? What's left? It turned out I was absolutely right. It had been out of control. Things should have been done before that hadn't been done. He just wasn't on top of it."

*Classic* went under within a year.

• • •

In 1977, four years after Stephanie Salter crashed the Baseball Writers Association of America annual dinner, *SI* became involved in another gender-based controversy, again in baseball. Melissa Ludtke, a Wellesley College graduate who had played basketball and rowed during her college years, had succeeded Salter as the magazine's second baseball reporter. Ludtke had been on the beat for two years when, the day before the beginning of the 1977 World Series, she found Dodger manager Tommy Lasorda walking through the runway toward Yankee Stadium, and asked him if she could gain access to the Dodgers locker room if she needed to conduct postgame interviews. Lasorda referred her to Dodgers team representative Tommy John, who said he'd take a vote of players that night. Ludtke went home, without telling Jim Kaplan (*SI*'s other reporter), or Ron Fimrite or even Peter Carry, the bright, prim Princeton grad who had recently moved up to senior editor. The next evening, just hours before Tuesday's game one, Tommy John gave her the good news. "Well," he said, "I will not tell you that it was unanimous, but there was a majority that said that it's fine with them if you come into the locker room if you need to, to do interviews."

In the fifth inning of the first game of the Series, Ludtke was sitting in the auxiliary press box when she heard the p.a. announcer call her to the main press box. She was met there by the frowning Bob Wirz, a representative from the commissioner's office who told her that she would not under any circumstances be allowed to enter the locker room.

"And he gave two reasons at that point," said Ludtke, "one of which was that the wives had not been consulted in this decision, to which I think I replied, 'What decision have the wives ever been consulted in, in baseball?' The second one was the fear that the baseball players' children would be ridiculed by their classmates in classrooms if this happened, and obviously they weren't going to let it happen. So that was it."

Or so she thought. She went again the next night to Yankee Stadium for game two, and still didn't tell anyone about it. When she got into the office on Thursday morning, her phone rang early. It was Peter Carry.

"*What* has been happening at Yankee Stadium?!"

Carry had heard about the incident from former *SI* writer Jane Gross, who herself had broken the pro basketball gender barrier in the ABA two years earlier when she simply asked, and was granted, permission to go in the locker room after New York Nets games. Carry felt that in this instance the commissioner's office was taking an antediluvian, as well as legally untenable, position. Exhibiting the sound judgment that would quickly make him a fast-track favorite to be managing editor one day, Carry urged Terrell to make a case out of it and he instantly agreed.

The legal complaint, Melissa Ludtke and Time Inc. against Bowie Kuhn, Commissioner of Baseball, Leland MacPhail, President of the American League of Professional Baseball Clubs, et al., was filed in U.S. District Court on Decenber 29, 1977. Affidavits were taken for the prosecution from Merv Hyman, Pete Axthelm, Mike Lupica, Jane Gross, and Murray Chass of the *New York Times*. While *The New Yorker*'s Roger Angell wrote a sensitive, penetrating overview of the Ludtke case the following spring, he was in the minority; just as they had four years earlier with Salter, many of the hidebound elders of the baseball-writing fraternity turned against Ludtke.

Time Inc. won the case, with Federal Judge Constance Baker Motley ruling on September 25, 1978, that the ban on females was unconstitutional. By the time of the decision, Ludtke was newly married, writing under the byline Melissa Ludtke Lincoln. She didn't go to Yankee Stadium the first night the doors were open, wanting to avoid the inevitable circus atmosphere that ensued. Yankees manager Bob Lemon's sole words to his players on the subject were, "Oh, by the way, there's going to be some funny-looking reporters in here tonight." The commissioner's office fumed (the subsequent appeal failed; a three-man appellate court upheld Motley's decision 3–0), but a blow had been struck for progress. Kuhn sent a memo to the other clubs informing them that they were not affected by the rule, but Ray Kennedy, in his Scorecard item in the October 2 issue, stated the obvious. "It appeared that Kuhn hadn't gotten the message: The times they are a-changin'."

• • •

But for all the headlines Ludtke made, Cheryl Tiegs made more.

In the fall of 1977, Jule Campbell and Walter Iooss flew to Brazil to shoot the swimsuit issue for the following January. By this time, Campbell had turned the swimsuit issue into an *SI* institution. A reliable newsstand hit in January or February (usually the week after the Super Bowl story), the "sunshine issue," as Laguerre took to calling it, had become a cherished, if somewhat guilty, pleasure for many of the magazine's two million subscribers.

What happened on the Brazil trip, though, would bring the swimsuit issue to an entirely different realm of popularity and controversy. For swimsuit issue shoots, Campbell and the photographer often worked with two different models at a time, and in the fall of 1977, on a particularly overcast day off the Rio Negro at Manaus, Iooss was shooting Tiegs and a Rubenesque Brazilian woman named Maura de Carvalho. As the light waned late in the afternoon, Iooss was taking shots of de Carvalho, from behind, as she was kneeling in the surf. Campbell was sitting in the boat with an increasingly impatient Tiegs. "She was becoming very annoyed, just fidgeting," Campbell remembered. "So I went to Walter and said, 'Walter, let's take a picture of Cheryl now and we'll send her back.' And he said, 'No, no, don't interrupt me.' So a few minutes later, I came back and I said, 'Look, just take a snapshot and we'll send Cheryl back.' So he turned around because I had disrupted him and he said, 'All right.'"

Tiegs had donned a suit that was not destined, for all its popularity, to turn up on many beaches around the country. It was a white fishnet maillot, with a panel of white fabric below the waist, but nothing but fishnet through the chest area, meaning that Tiegs's breasts, in fact, her nipples, were plainly visible. Then Campbell suggested she get wet, "'cause I thought if her skin glistened at least we could get some highlights. It wasn't, 'I'll see more if the suit's wet.' And so she kind of dipped down in the water, her hands are just hanging at her side, she's not even posing. She was like, 'Walter, let's get this over with.'"

"We'd gone down a tributary of the Rio Negro, and it was just a gray day," remembered Iooss. "All sort of gray, the water was gray, there was this huge dead tree. So I'm occupied with this girl with an ass to die for, and Cheryl was getting disturbed. She could get disturbed if the attention wasn't toward her. And I guess it was her turn to shoot, too. I remember speaking to her afterward; she felt so ill at ease. There was no place to put her hands."

The shot, which Iooss would describe later as "the worst picture in the entire Brazilian layout," wound up going last in the tray of 69 Kodachrome slides that Campbell showed to Terrell. "If you show more than that, the eyes glaze over and the attention span is gone, the excitement's over," she explained. "So anyway, at the last minute, I just kinda stuck that in the back. I don't know why. The presentation was all over, it was the last picture, and it was kind of, 'Okay, wake up,' never thinking it would run."

It ran.

The January 16, 1978, issue, with Tiegs's fishnet shot inside, earned a record number of letters, far surpassing the highest prediction in the office's annual guess-the-number-of-cancellations pool. Campbell said she first realized that the picture had caused a furor when she heard "thousands of people calling and wanting to cancel their subscriptions or say I was a perv or something." The evocative power of the photograph was undeniable. But it's likely that the sensation wasn't prompted solely by the visibility of a beautiful model's breasts in the pages of a reputable American family magazine. Rather, the stir was heightened because the breasts of a *familiar* beautiful model had been exposed. Tiegs, who'd graced her first *SI* cover in 1970, had become something of a household name to its readers. And for years, Campbell's suggestive captions implicated readers in the illusion that they were getting to know the models. Now they felt they were seeing one disrobe.

Years later, many would point to the furor over Tiegs's fishnet shot as a seminal event, representing no less than the dawn of the supermodel era. The picture caused an explosion in Tiegs's already prosperous career, noted author Michael Gross in his industry tell-all *Model: The Ugly Business of Beautiful Women*: "In rapid succession, she posed in a pink bikini on a poster that knocked Farrah Fawcett-Majors off the walls of the rooms of several million adolescent American boys, announced a deal to write a book on beauty, and signed what was reported to be a $2 million contract to appear on ABC."

Others in the modeling business saw Tiegs's shot as a defining moment: "If there had been any doubt before that modeling was, like everything else, about to lose its virginity (or illusion of virginity) in the '70s, the January 1978 *Sports Illustrated* swimsuit issue put an end to it," wrote Stephen Fried in *Thing of Beauty: The Tragedy of Supermodel Gia Carangi*. "The uproar caused by one picture of Cheryl Tiegs reinforced the new truth that the way *straight* men perceived fashion models would determine the future of the business."

It was this last fact that would become crucial. Suddenly Jule Campbell, the hard-working fashion outcast whom Eileen Ford had brushed off in the '60s, was Jule Campbell, supermodel tastemaker, whom Ford was now catering to. She had earned the respect of virtually everyone in the industry. "Is she available on the 14th?" Campbell asked Ford about one model in 1979. "Well, if she isn't, we'll see that she is," Ford said.

All that remained was for the right marketing minds to come along and heighten the issue's profile further. But while the end of the decade wouldn't mark the height of its profile or profitability, Tiegs's fishnet shot probably marked the last time that a photograph in *SI* carried the capacity to truly shock its readership. There was no place for the magazine to go from there, without resorting to full frontal nudity, which was never an option. The sensibilities within the culture had changed to the point that the titillating flesh in *SI* increasingly became part of the fashion/beauty mainstream.

"The only thing that went downhill were the letters to the editor," said Barbara La Fontaine. "The horrified mothers and scandalized ministers carried us for the first years, but the world being what it is, our readers did not continue to be sufficiently appalled."

• • •

One day in 1977, La Fontaine found herself in an elevator with Terrell, who was looking particularly blue.

"How are you finding the job?" she asked him.

He looked down and grimaced, answering more directly than he per-haps intended. "It's not really been what I thought it would be," he said. "I don't think I'm going to hang in there for very much longer."

Privately, he admitted to some of his friends and colleagues that after 11 years as the heir apparent, some of the fire had disappeared when he finally got the job. "Maybe it doesn't mean as much to me as it once did," he told corporate editor Bob Lubar. "That's just a fault of my character that once I got there, once I did it for a while, I had no great challenges."

It showed in his disposition, and in his schedule.

"Terrell came in a little late, 9:45, and sometimes he was headed home by 5:15," said Mark Mulvoy. "Except on Sunday nights; then Terrell and the gang would all go to the House of Chan. It was an easy life. As an editor under Terrell, I could play golf at 6:15. I could get nine holes in a night. That was the magazine he ran, and it didn't hurt the bottom line of the magazine. It was just a different mindset, you know. The two or three hours that Laguerre would spend at the bar, from 1 to 3:45 or something like that, Terrell would have had a sandwich, been back in the office at quarter to two, and been editing copy."

Like James, Terrell wasn't one for all-night closes. Rogin's dominant memory of the era was of his furiously editing a late-closing football story while Terrell stood impatiently in his office doorway, waiting for the piece so he could sign off on it and go home. "I'm dancing as fast as I can, Roy," Rogin would say.

But more than anything else, for Terrell, the reasons for staying in New York were growing increasingly dubious. He had grown weary of the input of editorial director (and former *Life* editor) Ralph Graves, who, at Donovan's urging, was coming to 20 every week with a critique of *SI*. "I *know* what's wrong with the magazine; I edited the goddamned thing," Terrell would complain to Creamer. "And his magazine *folded*, and he's telling me what's wrong with *my* magazine!" Terrell had enjoyed many of the duties associated with the ME's job, though he was consistently frustrated by intransigence both below him among the staff and over on the publishing side. And personally, Terrell was growing disenchanted with the way that money seemed to be changing the rules at every level of sport.

In mid-December 1978, with all that in mind, Terrell sat down and typed a letter of resignation to Donovan, a man to whom he'd grown closer in the years after becoming editor.

> For almost 40 years I have been earning a living, raising and educating a family, pursuing a career, and now I am tired of getting up and going to work every morning. I want to go fishing instead.
>
> 1978 was an exceptional year for *Sports Illustrated*, yet I find myself only quietly pleased with our triumphs and success and only mildly stimulated by the thought of future challenge. . . .
>
> I am less and less enamored of those constant and pervasive New York irritants—crowds, noise, filth, bad manners, miserable winters, exorbitant taxes, etc.—and I would prefer to live the rest of my life somewhere else. . . .
>
> My mother is 83, my father 84, and both are declining rapidly in health. I want to spend more time with them before they go. My children are growing older much too fast, and I would like to spend more time with them, too. Actually, I haven't seen all that much of my wife in the last five years, either.
>
> And finally there are the many things I want to do . . . many are at least mildly adventurous, and some are physically demanding, involving boats and oceans and mountain trails and streams. I must get started on them while still relatively young. . . .
>
> It would be presumptuous of me to assume that you will attempt to try to talk me out of this decision, and therefore it would be doubly presumptuous of me to counter your (imagined) arguments here.

Donovan was stunned by the resignation, writing later that, "I thought I knew Terrell quite well personally . . . But I found I didn't really know him after all."

After fruitlessly trying to talk Terrell out of the resignation, Donovan reluctantly accepted it, then asked for a few months to determine a successor. Terrell agreed to keep the announcement under wraps, and in fact didn't tell anyone but his wife about his decision.

While it was inevitable that Terrell's editorship would be viewed as a transitional one, it had its share of highlights. At the Montreal Olympics in 1976, he broke out of the grab-bag of round-up coverage that hampered the magazine's past Olympic coverage, assigning a different writer to every sport and devoting virtually an entire issue on reporting the final week's results. He championed some key investigative series, most notably Underwood's ground-breaking writing on violence in football and the prescient Ray Kennedy–Nancy Williamson series on money in sports. He emphasized pro and college basketball to a degree that Laguerre never had. At a time when sports was in a convulsive period of growth, Terrell started giving more consistent coverage to upstart sports leagues like the American Basketball Association, the World Hockey Association, the World Football League, the North American Soccer League, World Team Tennis, and even the International Volleyball Association. The coverage of the ABA, primarily by basketball beat writers Peter Carry and John Papanek, would be a crucial element in the maverick league's survival. And *SI*'s two covers, one in 1974 and the other in 1976, would help make a superstar out of Julius Erving, the last athlete to attain that status without the benefit of television exposure.

Internally, he stanched the flow of expense account abuses, served by example and by action to curtail the alcoholism so common at the magazine in Laguerre's twilight days, and generally moved the magazine toward a smoother-running, more news-oriented schedule. Even those who revered Laguerre granted that Terrell, at the very least, demystified the editorial process.

Within 25 years of arriving in New York, Terrell had done all he'd wanted to do in the world of journalism. And now he could go down to the Florida Keys and enjoy the unhurried life that had for so long eluded him. Unlike virtually every other managing editor in *Sports Illustrated*'s history, Terrell never looked back.

"He just wanted to go fishing," said Deford in 1996. "And that's what he's done. The most amazing thing about Roy: all those people at Time Inc. who can't ever give it up, and Roy walked out of that office, and he never gave it a backward glance. I thought that was fabulous. Everybody else hangs on by their fingernails, you know? But he just walked out of there and said, 'Bye-bye.'"

Ultimately, though, Terrell would retire as the most misunderstood managing editor in the magazine's history. He left feeling as though he'd spent the best years of his career waiting to take over the magazine, only to find himself in a thankless position once he finally assumed control.

"God, what pressure," said Creamer. "I believe Roy tried to be decent and friendly with the business people, but I think he also felt in conscience that he had to keep fending them off, that he had to maintain editorial independence and do things the way he felt they should be done. But he didn't have Laguerre's clout. André took a money-losing magazine and turned it into a big profit-maker. Terrell had no reputation; he was a rookie, and he had denigrators like Cave and others, bad-mouthing him from the start. Nor did he have Laguerre's political acumen, that artful skill in dealing with both friends and antagonists. Laguerre liked the term 'Jesuitical'; the Jesuit order is legendarily the master of subtlety, guile, getting things done without seeming to. Roy was straight-arrow, open and direct, often too direct."

• • •

Nathalie Laguerre had hoped that the 1978 Christmas season would cheer up André. He had finally retired, on December 12 of that year, after a last stand at *Classic* that left her racked with concern. Arriving home at 6 or 7 o'clock during the fall, Laguerre would often slump into his easy chair, put his hands to his face, and confess to his wife, "I can't make it, darling. Please give me some strength." Seeing a man that strong in such a weak condition was difficult enough. But she knew that his health was worsened by his stubbornness. His fear of doctors was both irrational and complete.

He was drinking, by now, largely to keep up appearances, in a vain attempt to sustain the morale of his troops. At home, he'd go to bed by ten and sleep until three in the morning. Then, restless and wide awake, he'd turn on the television, and by the light of the set, tuned to the Western movies that he loved, André and Nathalie Laguerre would talk.

On December 30, Robert Creamer went to an upscale liquor store in Manhattan and bought Laguerre the largest, most expensive bottle of scotch he could find. The next afternoon, he walked up to the Laguerres' apartment building and, shivering with emotion, handed the doorman the bottle and told him it was for Mr. Laguerre. The note attached was short and sentimental. "I know I've always been a disappointment to you," wrote Creamer, who apologized for not rising higher at the magazine, thanked Laguerre for his influence, and wished him a happy retirement.

Just a few days later, *SI* staffer Betty DeMeester mentioned to Creamer that Laguerre had shown her the bottle. "See, Betsy," he said. "See? They haven't forgotten me."

On the morning of January 18, 1979, a bitterly cold Thursday, the phone rang at the Laguerre apartment at 9:30. It was Andy Crichton, already in crisis as *Classic*'s new editor.

"André, we've got a real problem here," Crichton said. "I'm going to have to let Tex Maule go. Because I haven't got the money to pay him a salary. I can pay him for pieces, but I can't keep him on salary. I may have to do the same with other people, too. Can we have lunch, down at Long River?"

"I'll be there," said Laguerre.

It was what Laguerre had been fearing for years, that men who had moved to *Classic* out of loyalty to him would now have to lose their jobs. Feeling weary and crestfallen, he bundled up in a trenchcoat and headed out in the frigid weather. Crichton, looking worried, was waiting for him at the restaurant. The two men talked around the problem for a while, until the point when Laguerre's eyes narrowed in concentration. "You can't let Tex go without letting Whitney go," he said, in a deep, forceful voice, exuding an air of the old authority. "You can't treat one one way and one the other."

"Well, I'm glad you said that," Crichton said, visibly relieved. "That was going to have to be the next thing I was going to have to do, I figured."

The rest of the lunch was spent sorting out the glum details. Afterward, the two men shook hands at the corner, and Laguerre turned to walk down to a fish market, to buy fresh fish for dinner. By the time he got back to the apartment it was almost 3 o'clock. He was chilled and short of breath and experiencing chest pains. Nathalie greeted him at the door, a quizzical look on her face.

But he shook off an immediate explanation. "Darling, it's too horrible. Let me rest and I'll tell you about it later."

"Go upstairs now," she said. "I'll get you a cup of hot tea."

When Claudine got home from school, she hurried upstairs to see her father, ecstatic over a good grade on a math test. The instant she walked into her parents' bedroom, she knew something was wrong. Her father was chalk white and sweating, lying across the foot of the bed, his feet still on the floor.

"Daddy, are you okay?" she asked.

"I just don't feel very well, sweetheart; I just need to lie down for a while."

She trusted him for a bit, and gave him her news. But she could tell that this was something more than one of his normal spells.

"Shall I go call Mommy?"

"No, no," he said, more softly now. "I'll be fine."

He didn't look fine, and Claudine quietly rushed downstairs to get her mother. As Nathalie headed upstairs, the panic in her eyes shook her daughter further. Nathalie straightened him out on the bed, loosened his tie, and tried to make him feel better. But by then he was barely conscious. Claudine rushed to the elevator and ran outside, the snow coming down in relentless waves now, and on that bleak gray afternoon, the sobbing 14-year-old ran up and down 71st Street, knocking on the doors of doctor's offices, hysterically trying to find someone to come and tend to her father. When she returned, the police cars and an ambulance were there, and André Laguerre was dead.

Dan Jenkins was in Miami, preparing to cover the Super Bowl, when he got the news the next day. That night, Jenkins took everyone in Miami that had known Laguerre, some 20 journalists in all, from Pete Axthelm to Phyllis George, to the Jockey Club for a memorial dinner. Jenkins wasn't much for toasts, but on this night, he made an exception. "Here's to André Laguerre," he said, lifting his J&B and water. "He didn't think of himself as Harold Ross or Clay Felker. He was just a guy, who, well—everybody that ever worked with him will tell you that he was the greatest man any of us ever knew." He put the $2,000 dinner check on *SI*'s tab, because, he said later, Laguerre would have wanted him to.

The memorial service was held on the following Monday at St. Patrick's Cathedral. Memory bends toward its intended direction, so it's impossible to establish whether the cathedral was nearly full with mourners, or whether it seemed particularly cavernous because it was half-empty. But what those that came to pay their respects would be talking about years later was Andy Crichton's eulogy, delivered in his strong, heartfelt Yankee intonations:

> I will be brief—not, however, as brief as André would have liked. That private man—with so many friends—would have preferred to leave unnoticed. "Hew, hew, hew," he might have chuckled in that low, almost inaudible voice, and turned and left, flicking an ash from his cigar and managing somehow to look like Charlie Chaplin, Groucho Marx, and

Sydney Greenstreet, all at the same time—the game over and, on the whole, a satisfactory one, played by the rules, some of them of his own making. "Risible," André might have said. It was his favorite word.

André seldom talked about himself. Who knows, for instance, what his politics truly were? Conservative-anarchist one friend suggested. Moderate-terrorist said another. Probably all of these. André had a profound disrespect for the easy answer. He might have understood better than any of us what we are all about—what forces stir us and drive our societies.

And maybe that was why this unsentimental man was so sentimental. I think he saw his life as one of protection, protecting himself, as any prudent man would, and Nathalie, Michele, and Claudine, but more than that, preserving what was good in this world, and for us—saving us from ourselves and from the awful errors he knew we were going to commit, and in fact, did commit when his vigilance relaxed, which was not often.

I was with André on his last day. We met, not surprisingly, at the bar. Not just any bar, but the bar, the bar that was settled upon only after long and serious research—and which satisfied Andre's criteria: unfancy, inexpensive and illogical.

The topics at first were light: the story, that delighted him, of his reception by Clare Luce after a long time: "Well, André, the same old pixie, I see." "Hew, hew, hew." Next, a defense of spy novels. Surely, André, no such people exist whose knowledge is Holmesian, whose memories are faultless, whose awareness of all things around them is numbing. "Yes, there are," he said, fixing the doubter with that stern, almost intimidating gaze that—in a corporal 37 years earlier—demanded attention, and probably started André on his way to us.

André had come out on a raw, cold day, when maybe he knew that he should not have. He was, as ever, performing a duty for a friend. When he had digested the problem—interrupting for details that penetrated the cant—he spoke, authoritative now, his voice bass and forceful. In few words, he laid out the solution—the pixie no more, rather, the serious man that, at bottom, André always was.

"Compassionate," a friend said. "You must use the word compassionate." Yes, but it was something else. André was brave. He dared to think, he dared to counsel. He dared to have the friends he wanted, to care for them—and to carry their burdens somewhere in the fast, mysterious middle of him. He dared to lead.

Publicly, André would have hated the word compassionate. And, of course, he would have edited these words—severely.

His admirers gathered that evening, and in the alcohol-sodden, senti-mentality-streaked night, they told stories and reminisced. The ones who'd already left were reminded of what they'd left behind. And those still at the magazine were reminded that it would never be the same.

They were also reminded of how quickly his star had faded at Time Inc. Nathalie Laguerre received a dozen polite, carefully worded notes from Time Inc. executives, but the company made no effort to properly eulogize Laguerre, and in the *New York Times* the next day, the death of a Lee Harvey Oswald lookalike got bigger play on the obituary page. When Robert Creamer wrote his obit for *SI*'s publisher's memo the following week, using the very sort of reserve that Laguerre would have appreciated, many staffers thought it was an insufficient response. It had become clear to Laguerre's followers that he would be as unappreciated in death as he had been in the last stages of his life. And it angered them.

It was at that precise moment that the Laguerre myth, already formidable, would begin to expand. He would loom even larger in memory than he had been in fact. Years later, Dan Jenkins said, "Laguerre told me three things when I started out. One, I couldn't receive too much hate mail to suit him. Two, I couldn't spend too much money on the road. Three, if any editor jacked with my copy, he would have him killed or fired, my choice." Whether Laguerre actually said this remains a matter of some debate. But it was indicative of the way Laguerre's leadership made his writers *feel*.

What they must have sensed, by then, was that it was never going to be that way again. "I think part of my problem is that I had no frame of reference," said Frank Deford, 17 years later. "I just came out of college. I'm sort of thinking, 'Every boss I ever have will be larger than life.' Here I am, 56 years old, and I'm still waiting for the next André in my life. I didn't really understand what I had until I lost it. I keep waiting to be saved by another Laguerre."

# CHAPTER 13

# SWEAT SPORTS

## One lazy Saturday morning

in the mid-'70s, Bob Creamer stepped out of the elevator and onto the 20th floor of the Time & Life Building. Creamer, universally liked, was a brilliant kibbitzer, able to needle with the best of *SI*'s sharp-tongued writers. As he strolled down the hallway toward his office he could hear the staccato, slightly baleful sounds of Gilbert Rogin explaining to a young writer what was wrong with his story.

"There's a horseshit editor," Creamer said merrily as he passed by Rogin's office, never pausing to break stride as he moved down the hall.

Rogin looked up, vaguely disturbed, and wheeled his chair toward the door. "I'm a good editor," he yelled out after Creamer. "I'm a horseshit *person.*"

Odd things pricked the ego of Gil Rogin. Raised in New York City by overprotective, Russian-Jewish émigré parents, Rogin had grown into a brilliant paradox around whom no one at the magazine was fully comfortable. He was a brooding, self-absorbed sensualist who cared little for the rules of decorum and was often awkward in social situations, yet he was fascinated with the vast power marshaled by editors who played by the corporate rules and worked their way up the masthead at Time Inc. Giving up his *SI* writing career in the '60s, he'd chosen to devote himself to the editing track, writing short fiction on the side. To the people who knew him best, Rogin was a tortured genius with a spaniel's loyalty and a doberman's bark. He'd literally be foaming from the mouth one minute, calling a longtime colleague a motherfucker, then professing his love for the same person the next. To those who didn't know him well—and this group included many in the Jenkins sphere—he was simply weird.

Among Rogin's compulsions was his all-consuming need to swim one hundred laps in a regulation-sized pool every day of the year. The exercise—he wouldn't use his legs—built his chest and biceps to nearly hypertrophic proportions. That exaggerated physique, combined with his flickering eyes and throaty, abrupt voice, gave him a somewhat menacing countenance. His elaborate rituals prompted Walter Bingham to remark that Rogin would be "the easiest person in the world to assassinate. He does the exact same thing every day." But for Rogin, these routines weren't routine at all. "I'm my own defensive coordinator," he would say, explaining that his habits were a way to defend his scarred soul against life's incursions. "Order keeps the black dog at bay."

Few questioned his brilliance; John Underwood once told Joe Marshall, "The rest of us only *think* we're writers. Rogin *is* one. Go read '12 Days Before the Mast.' If you want to read writing, the stuff that the rest of us do doesn't count. It can't hold a candle to it." Jack Olsen, who playfully called Rogin "The Bard," felt he was "the one authentic genius in the history of *Sports Illustrated*." Once Rogin became an editor, he was among the most respected in the building, taking several young writers under his wing. Roy Terrell thought of him as "the best pencil editor in the magazine's history," and others marveled at the things he could do to copy.

At the same time, Rogin's sensibilities were wildly inconsistent and his opinions often veered toward the arbitrary; he seemed to take every story personally, screaming in anger if a writer's style didn't suit him. And for all the talent that he granted him, Terrell didn't quite trust Gilbert Rogin, didn't feel he had the right temperament to be a managing editor. So when he sat down with Hedley Donovan early in 1979, Terrell did more than just recommend his old friend Jerry Tax. He also made clear to Donovan his deep reservations about Rogin. "I just thought he was mentally unbalanced," he'd explain later. Former *SI* publisher Dick Munro was more pointed: "I can see Roy kind of lying awake at night saying, 'Can I turn this suddenly-about-to-become-a-very-successful-magazine over to a lunatic?'"

But there were no other obvious candidates. Terrell's other assistant managing editors were Tax, who at 63 was already too old to realistically contend for the appointment, and Ken Rudeen, who lacked either the vision or the will for the job. Two who would have been viable choices, Ray Cave and Pat Ryan, had moved on (as well as moved in, together, after Cave's divorce), both winding up with top editing jobs at other Time Inc. publications, Cave at *Time* (in 1977) and Ryan at *People* (in 1982).

Terrell argued to Donovan that Tax should be given the job for "a couple years," serving as a transitional appointment until Rogin showed sufficient maturity or another candidate, perhaps the workmanlike Peter Carry, emerged from the pool of senior editors. But Donovan didn't like provisional hires, and didn't share some of Terrell's reservations about Rogin, whose eccentric habits and uncompromising commitment to the magazine were viewed with a kind of bemused affection on the 34th floor.

So on a brisk March morning in 1979, at the Snowbird resort in Utah, Rogin received a call from Hedley Donovan's secretary, Trudy Lance.

"Hedley wants to speak to you," she said.

*Why would Hedley be calling me?* Rogin thought. *Maybe he's coming out to Snowbird. Maybe he wants to know the snow conditions. Maybe someone died.* And then Donovan got on the line.

"Gil, Roy is resigning, and I'm making you the managing editor."

The shocked, gleeful Rogin thanked him profusely before hanging up and then began gesticulating wildly in celebration. He dashed out to the balcony, with its majestic view of the mountains, and jumped up and down with his hands thrust over his head. "Yippee!" he shouted, like a child who'd just won a house of toys. When he saw his girlfriend, Jacqueline Duvoisin, in the resort cafeteria a half hour later, he was so excited that he sputtered out the news in nonsensical half sentences; for the first several minutes, she had no idea what he was raving about.

Response to the hiring was generally positive, though there was a sizable minority who thought the appointment could only mean trouble for the magazine. One Time Inc. executive told an *SI* staffer that the hire was all wrong, and that Rogin "ought to be off in a corner somewhere writing a novel." Honor Fitzpatrick, by then retired for nearly a decade, recalled that she "almost died" when she heard of Rogin's promotion. "He's just the wrong kind of man," she said. "He was an inventive, creative, impossible little jackass, like all writers are, if you will please forgive me, but they are. They're hopeless as human beings. Gil Rogin, a dreadful little wretch, but a fine writer."

Within the small, cultish world in which short stories were widely read, Rogin had emerged by the mid-'70s as a fiercely gifted writer. John Cheever, once introduced to Rogin at a gathering, greeted him perfunctorily and then, after making the connection a few minutes later that he'd just met *the writer* Gilbert Rogin, went back, apologized profusely, and told Rogin how much he admired his work. At the Masters in the early '70s, Walter Bingham ran into fellow New Englander John Updike and chatted with him. "And give my regards to Gilbert *Row-jin*," Updike said, mispronouncing his name. "He plows a lonely furrow."

For all his successes, it seemed that Rogin often obsessed on his failures. He couldn't shake his difficult collegiate days at Iowa, when he aspired to be a painter only to realize that he didn't have the discipline for the craft. After a stint in the army, he transferred to Columbia and returned home to live with his parents, where he stayed until he was 25. He grew up with a profound sense of foreboding, a man whose dark, hard shell concealed a vulnerable soul. His close friend and writing protégé Kenny Moore once joked that Rogin measured the worth of a dictionary by finding out how many new synonyms it had for the word "sorrow." After a brief engagement to *SI* staffer Barbara La Fontaine (then Heilman), Rogin married, in the '60s, a woman who worked in the permissions department of *The New Yorker*. The subsequent divorce, separation, and the mysterious death of his stepson were portrayed, with nearly autobiographical faithfulness, in the novel *Preparations for the Ascent*, an achievement in both interior fiction and self-revelation. It would also present the Human Dynamo, his girlfriend Duvoisin, in thinly veiled form. When *Preparations for the Ascent* was published in 1980, many of the staffers at *SI* were thankful for its window into their boss's obsessions:

> Albert's number is thirty-two. In the morning, he counts silently to thirty-two before getting out of bed—or to sixty-four or to ninety-six; in certain situations multiples are admissible. (Albert weighed one hundred and ninety-two pounds until recently, when he went on a diet. Alas, one-sixty is beyond reach.) Going to work, he chooses the subway exit where thirty-two steps lead to the surface; these he ascends with uncharacteristic jauntiness. At his desk he downs his cup of coffee in thirty-two rapid, intense sips. Before retiring, he does thirty-two sit-ups, thirty-two push-ups, reads thirty-two pages and turns out the light.
>
> Now, making love to the Human Dynamo, Albert executes one hundred and twenty-eight strokes.
>
> "I can see you moving your lips," she says midway.

Just months after *Preparations* was published, to positive reviews, Rogin turned two new short submissions in to Roger Angell, the fiction editor at *The New Yorker*. Angell passed on them, and suggested he try another tack. "You're repeating yourself," he told Rogin. The small criticism seemed to shatter Rogin. He simply quit writing.

Fifteen years later, Rogin was still wounded by the critique. "Motherfucker! You can call him that! He *is* a motherfucker! He killed me! I don't even know whether he knows it. Writers, as full of self-esteem as I am, we're still fragile psyches because we're dependent on such a little market, a tiny market, for quality fiction that pays anything. That was what I wrote about and that was me and he wanted me to be somebody else for some obscure reason. He was a smart-ass and he's not a very good writer in my book either. You know, I'm a good person. I used to go to his house and parties and things. He killed me. He's probably totally unaware of it." Presented with Rogin's accusation, Angell was plainly bewildered. "I certainly had no intention of hurting Gil Rogin," he said. "I wanted him to write more."

Others simply wondered what had happened. When text editor Myra Gelband queried Updike about a golf piece in the early '80s, he wrote back to politely decline, but made a point to ask, "How come Gil Rogin isn't writing any fiction anymore? He's a genius at short stories." When she handed Rogin the note, he averted his eyes. He couldn't even think about it: the pain was too fresh.

• • •

At the first Monday meeting of the Rogin era, the new managing editor announced his intentions. "I want to stress my determination to concentrate on sweat sports," he said.

"Could you define sweat sports?" asked Walter Bingham.

"The two footballs, the two basketballs, boxing, baseball, and track and field." He also announced that he would put a greater emphasis on late-breaking news, with a vision of *SI* as "the first 24-hour newsmagazine" or, alternately, "the *Time* magazine of sports." This was an odd aspiration; *SI*'s writing had long ago outstripped that of *Time*, which in 1979 was being edited by *SI* alum Ray Cave, who had been promoted in large part to bring the staid newsweekly a measure of *SI*'s fast-color urgency, journalistic sharpness, and design savvy.

In fact, many editors thought the influence of Cave's brief top-editing stints at *SI* could be seen in Rogin's issues. Lead stories, almost always four pages before, began to run at six and even eight pages. Special event stories like the Super Bowl or the first Sugar Ray Leonard–Roberto Duran title fight, which might have gotten six pages in past years, grew to 10 and 12 pages. And Rogin brought a sense of the visually dramatic. When the USA hockey team scored its surprise gold medal in 1980 at Lake Placid, Rogin ran a cover picture of the team celebrating after defeating the Russians, without any cover headline. The picture and the moment spoke for themselves.

Rogin's fascination with the visual would prove a mixed blessing. "I was stunned when Gil was the one who decided he was going to be the art director at the same time," said senior editor Bob Brown. Rogin took a more active role than any managing editor before him, often sketching the dummy layouts himself. It didn't leave much to do for the eminent, influential designer Dick Gangel, who, after barely a year under Rogin, called assistant Harvey Grut into his office and said, "Harvey, it's all yours."

Gangel's departure marked the magazine's greatest design loss ever. For 20 years, he had given it a unified design, eclectic but cohesive, sophisticated without being elitist. The Gangel-inspired photo and artistic portfolios (they were called "acts" within the building), which would make frequent use of illustrators like Arnold Roth, Donald Moss, Michael Ramus, Marc Simont, and Robert Grossman, were brilliantly conceived departures from the static photo spreads of *SI*'s Spectacle days. In short, he achieved a style rare for any American magazine, much less a mass-market newsweekly.

Grut labored admirably in his new job, but he was no match for his predecessor and was replaced in 1983 by the equally ineffectual Rick Warner. In place of Gangel's apt touch, *SI* could offer little beyond more pictures, increasingly crisp and increasingly uniform. And while Rogin had a good picture sense, he had a famously eccentric inability to grasp what was and wasn't possible in photography. Photo editors and assistants would smirk at one another in the eerie glow of the color room during slide shows, when Rogin would find a picture with a small flaw and protest, "Why is that guy's arm in the way?! Can't we get his fucking arm out of there?!" Rogin also lacked Terrell's intuitive understanding of the sports landscape, resulting in photo choices that were often handsome but beside the point. In 1980, Kansas City Royals' third baseman George Brett wasn't on a single cover, despite dominating headlines with his summer-long run at the .400 mark. And after North Carolina won the NCAA basketball title in 1982 on freshman Michael Jordan's jump shot with 16 seconds to play, there were no pictures of the shot, or even Jordan, either on the cover or in the six-page lead story that ran following the game.

The use of more space for more pictures meant less space for the stories themselves, as writers and subeditors found to their frustration week after week. "Suddenly you've got stories that were written to 340 lines that have to run at 220," said Bob Brown. "It's 7 o'clock at night on Sunday, and you haven't got time for the writer to do anything with the thing, so bam!—there you go. I thought that Gil would have been far more defending of the writer's efforts, in that he's an excellent writer himself." Editors began to take issue with Rogin's wholesale cutting. A 400-line story (about 2,500 words) was constructed far differently than a 220-line piece, and cutting a good long story didn't always result in a good, or even lucid, shorter story. "What the fuck do we care!?" Rogin told an assistant more than once, a smile curling to his lips. "We've got a great picture!"

"I always wondered if Rogin subconsciously didn't like good writers, because he envied them," said one Time Inc. executive. "Now, I have no reason to know that, but they didn't flourish when he was managing editor, let's put it that way. Gil didn't reach out to try to get outside writers to do things."

The sense of esprit de corps that had survived through the Terrell era, and the attendant level of civility, clearly declined. "Gil was this complete anomaly," said one writer. "Capable of such discriminating thought on one hand and yet, in his day-to-day life, still very much trapped in the anal stage." He did much of his editing in the bathroom, and his hour-long morning sessions with the *New York Times* became legendary. Staffers waiting for a decision were sometimes told that "I think I can decide after I take a dump." Rogin, in a room full of editors, would often unleash loud, bleating farts, accompanied by a gleeful, almost manic smile. Only the perpetually composed secretary Ann Callahan, who'd stayed on after Terrell retired, seemed unfazed. "You pig," she'd say, and walk back into her office.

Power seemed to make him unsteady. Shortly after being hired, he went on what one senior editor described as a "reign of terror," quickly firing photo editor John Dominis and his assistant Don Delliquanti. (Years later, Rogin would say that firing those two, along with staff writer Coles Phinizy, were his greatest regrets.) Another infamous tantrum had Rogin scattering slides everywhere, leaving photo editor Barbara Henckel literally crawling on the floor to pick them up. *Washington Post* staffer and Pulitzer Prize–winning author Jonathan Yardley was regularly writing reviews of sports books for *SI* when Rogin took over, but after Yardley declined a request from Rogin made through staffer Linda Verigan to review *Preparations for the Ascent* in the *Post*, the piqued Rogin announced that Yardley would no longer write for *SI*. "He would be like a little child, throwing fits over little things," said one reporter. "We would all be standing around him, watching him edit, and he'd see a line he didn't like, and would throw the whole story out. He would just start screaming, even if he didn't like one word."

"I thought he was going to be terrific, as he had been as an AME," said Sarah Ballard. "I think certainly his taste in writing remained good and he cared about that stuff, but he became such a madman that . . . he was just crazy, I think. Just nuts. He was always eccentric as hell. From the time when he was a young man, he was everybody's favorite eccentric at the magazine, but he was also brilliant and talented and all those things. But the crazy part took over, I think, when he became ME, and he became power mad."

For all the anguish that his behavior caused, it was hard to question the financial results. A manifold increase in color pages helped *SI*'s profits double within Rogin's first three years as managing editor. Because of that, the company's new editor-in-chief Henry Grunwald (who succeeded Donovan in the summer of 1979), gladly indulged what he referred to as "Gilbert's little eccentricities."

• • •

In the years after André Laguerre left, *SI*'s bottom line continued a slow and steady gradual growth, turning a profit of $17 million in 1979. A year earlier, Kelso Sutton had replaced Jack Meyers as publisher. The diminutive, occasionally acerbic Sutton was well trained for the post, having spent part of the decade as corporate circulation director for all the magazines. While *SI* was solidly profitable, neither Sutton nor former *SI* publisher Dick Munro, who took over as Time Inc. president and CEO in 1980, felt it was operating at its maximum earnings potential. During his six-year publishing tenure, Meyers raised subscription prices from $12 to $20. Sutton pushed for even higher circulation revenues, jacking up the price from $20 in '78 to $36 a year in 1980. It was a two-pronged strategy, meant to increase revenue while at the same time weeding out the least desirable, lower-level demographic elements in the magazine's subscriber base. But what happened next was nearly unprecedented in magazine history. After an initial bit of resistance to the price hike, *SI*'s circulation actually went up, a trend that tended to confirm the belief of those on the editorial side, that the magazine's relationship with its readers was exceptionally strong. The statistical anomaly of subscription rate hikes bringing more subscriptions, despite little in the way of value-added bonuses or throw-ins to sweeten subscription solicitations, would be the central factor in *SI*'s spectacularly bright financial picture in the early '80s.

Sutton also moved, tepidly at first, into two other areas that would later have a huge bearing on *SI*'s profile. With the 1980 Winter Olympic Games in Lake Placid, New York, *SI* signed on as a corporate sponsor, at a fee of $100,000, though its presence was hard to distinguish in the blizzard of 342 corporate sponsors involved in the Games. It was under Sutton, as well, that *SI* started to vigorously promote its annual swimsuit issue, sending out media releases that alerted television stations and newspapers that the annual rite of winter was imminent. The new approach was testament to the newsstand success of the swimsuit issue. The 1978 issue, with Tiegs's controversy-courting fishnet, had sold an extra 50,000 copies on the newsstands, a huge spike for a title that had averaged sales of 79,000 a week on newsstands for 1977.

Considering *SI*'s broad successes, Sutton and others were surprisingly skittish about the imminent start-up of *Inside Sports,* a monthly sports magazine from Newsweek, Inc. and the Washington Post Co. The venture had tested in selected markets with a charter issue in 1979, then launched in the spring of 1980 with the editorial side headed by former *Rolling Stone* managing editor John Walsh, a brilliant iconoclast who commanded Laguerre-like devotion from his small, loyal staff. Walsh was a man of disconcerting physical stature, a brawny, intense albino who was legally blind. But he was also an editor with a large Rolodex and a reputation for surrounding himself with bright editors and talented writers. There would be only one direct defection from *SI* to *IS*—staff photographer James Drake left to be Walsh's photo editor—but the new magazine's masthead of contributing editors read like a who's who of *SI* alumni and magazine-writing bigfoots: Pete Axthelm and Roy Blount, Jr., both signed on, as did Thomas Boswell, Kenneth Turan, the novelist Pete Dexter, and a precociously talented Philadelphia newspaper writer named Gary Smith. The tough, uncompromising journalism promoted by Walsh would earn the respect of many longtime *SI* readers, some of whom felt the new magazine had the better writing. By printing on *Newsweek*'s presses, Walsh was able to secure a quick turnaround time, so that his monthly could operate as a topical magazine, with near-weekly deadlines. This often gave *IS* an edge in newsstand sales, as when *Inside Sports'* Duran-Leonard fight preview far outsold the similar issue of *SI* on newsstands in the summer of 1980.

The gist of the *IS* promotional campaign was that the new magazine was going to stick to serious sports. No kayaking, no mountain climbing, nothing but a group of literary-minded writers attacking the four majors, as well as significant minor sports like boxing, golf, tennis, and auto racing. It seemed preposterous that an established weekly newsmagazine like *SI*, which celebrated its 25th anniversary in 1979 with a circulation of 2.1 million and ad revenues in excess of $120 million, as well as annual operating profits of nearly $20 million a year, would be spooked by an underfinanced monthly that was just coming on the scene. But magazines are like nations; when they have no direct competitors, they are prone to invent them. Rogin had planned to enlarge the magazine's news component anyway, and the *Inside Sports* launch simply provided a clearer financial reason to do so. "I got the impression that *SI*, which did all these wonderful stories outside the beltway, now all of a sudden felt like it had to be more inside the circle," said John Underwood.

*Inside Sports* would lose $12 million in its first year and would be sold off by the parent company in 1983. Years later, even such higher-ups at the Washington Post Co., like Katherine Graham and Ben Bradlee, wondered if they hadn't pulled the trigger too soon. "They never should have fooled with it," said one Time Inc. executive. "They fudged. They know that. The losses—you're going to lose money for five years, and they couldn't take it. Their profit margin wasn't high enough on *Newsweek,* which was struggling at the time. But if it would have worked, then you could have taken it to a biweekly. And then you've got a player."

But *Inside Sports* had affected *SI.* It hastened the biggest technological change during the Rogin era: the manifold increase in color pages. In 1979, half of the magazine's edit pages were still being printed in black and white; within four years, *SI* became the first full-color newsweekly in the world. The change occurred quickly, most noticeably in football, where *SI* took full advantage of the technology. The January 11, 1982, issue included 24 pages of coverage on nine bowl and playoff games, all in color.

• • •

By the time of Rogin's promotion, Frank Deford had become the most eagerly anticipated byline at the magazine. Just as Dan Jenkins's style had revolutionized the news story in *SI,* forcing everyone who came after him to try to do something to match the brilliance of his indelible leads, so did Deford transform the very nature of the bonus piece, turning it into a psychographic high-wire act that, at its best, was at once readable, informative, and edifying.

Television was doing more personality coverage in the '70s, but rather than demystifying the sports heroes of the age, TV often simply added to the myth. It set the stage perfectly for Deford's insightful takes on the most famous and controversial figures of the era. He was aided by his powerful sense of empathy, which allowed him to elicit perceptive insights from athletes and coaches who had long been conditioned to speak only in platitudes. The '70s found him moving to the top of his form, writing brilliant tennis leads at the year's major events, devoting himself to bonus pieces the rest of the year. In 1975, he wrote about the shadowy career of tennis great and closet homosexual Bill Tilden; a year later, he traveled to Japan to visit Japanese slugger Sadaharu Oh. In 1978, a week before the U.S. Open, Deford profiled Jimmy Connors. "Raised by Women to Conquer Men" examined the way Connors's personality flowed from his aggressive playing style, attacking the tennis ball while it was still on the rise, and then showed the strategic limitations of the style as well as the misery that aggressive approach brought to his personal life. The piece infuriated Connors, who wouldn't talk to *SI* at the 1978 U.S. Open. But four years later, Deford was at the Palm Court of the Plaza Hotel in New York when a stranger recognized him.

"I'm a friend of Gloria Connors," he said. "I just want you to know how much Gloria appreciates that story you wrote on her son."

Deford was stunned. "Get out of here."

"No, at first she hated it," the man said. "But then she came to understand how right you were. It helped her a great deal."

The work had been remarkable anyway, but what made it particularly noteworthy were the conditions under which he wrote it. For years, Deford and his wife Carol had been coping with their daughter Alex's terminal illness, cystic fibrosis. Late in 1979, she took a turn for the worse, dying on January 19, 1980.

Throwing himself back into his work as a way to battle his grief, Deford would produce over the next five years a body of feature work unmatched in the magazine's history. Rogin would routinely send him out to draw profiles of the biggest, most provocative figures in sport; each year, it seemed, Deford wrote a piece or two that would become the most quoted essay on a giant of sport: in 1980, it was Pete Rozelle; 1981 brought his penetrating cover story on Indiana basketball coach Bobby Knight; 1982 found a fresh take on Alabama's Bear Bryant; in 1983, he would write the definitive Howard Cosell profile.

In August 1982, while working on the Bryant story that would run later that year, Deford got on a plane in Birmingham, en route to Atlanta to catch his connecting flight back to New York City. On the seat next to him was the sports section from the *Jackson* (Mississippi) *Clarion-Ledger*. A writer there named Rick Cleveland had written a piece about an obscure football coach named Bob "Bull" "Cyclone" Sullivan, a postwar legend at the tiny east Mississippi junior college in Scooba. As Deford read about it, he saw another mythic figure, but one who had never been celebrated, the flip side to Bryant.

It became the spark for the memorable cover story "The Toughest Coach There Ever Was," which ran in the April 30, 1984, issue. Deford's portrait of Sullivan began with a collection of bizarre anecdotes and memories (one of Sullivan's players, upon seeing a plane crash near the practice field, said his first thought was that the Russians were invading America and had decided they needed to take Sullivan out first). With the same empathy that animated his piece on Knight, Deford presented a forgotten American archetype, a hard but fair man who never got the chance to demonstrate his vision on a larger stage. The piece would help Sullivan get elected to the Mississippi Sports Hall of Fame.

Under Rogin, Deford became the anchor of the magazine, the writer around whom the rest of an issue was built. His prose was a graceful mixture of storytelling and subtle (sometimes not so subtle) psychoanalysis. His conclusions were peppered with conversational phrases, like the kindly narrator completing a moral fable for the rapt listener, often lapsing into a voice to bring about a sort of dramatic pause. "Now, you see, we are talking about discipline," he would write midway through his portrait of Bobby Knight. And by this time, Deford's style was set. When he came to do a bonus piece, he wasn't looking for the easy answer. If Jenkins was the best at capturing the crucial angle on a game in his deadline writing, Deford was just as accomplished at capturing the crucial angle in a life.

"Deford is Mount Olympus," said the *Washington Post*'s Tony Kornheiser, one of a generation of "takeout" writers who followed his lead. "Deford's Monet. There's a whole lot of people trying to paint, and they do pretty good work, and then Deford would come out with a piece, and people would go, 'Monet.' He's the best ever at the takeout—there's nobody within one hundred miles of that guy."

• • •

While *SI* was fixated on the threat of *Inside Sports,* the world of sports was undergoing its biggest change in a generation. On September 7, 1979, at 7 p.m. Eastern time, a new cable network called ESPN debuted, becoming the world's first 24-hour, all-sports television network. *SI* had dabbled in television without success, and at the time was focused on shoring up its dominance of the magazine marketplace. But cable television would forever change the sporting universe the magazine was covering. With ESPN's nightly news show "SportsCenter" and the Cable News Network's nightly 30-minute wrap-up "Sports Tonight," in-depth sports news and highlights became more widely available than ever before. Suddenly, *SI*'s exhaustive national roundups in the college football and college basketball sections seemed less relevant.

There was also the nagging sense that the balance of power in the media world was now tilting sharply toward television, and in this matter, ESPN's debut was only a symptom in an ongoing trend. Increasingly, television and not print media was setting the terms of coverage. The change could best be seen at indoor events, where, just as the magazine's color capability was growing, the environment in which it could shoot color was deteriorating. By 1981, *SI*'s routine request to use strobes at the Super Bowl (held indoors at the New Orleans Superdome) was nixed by NBC, which wouldn't tolerate the numerous flashes that might distract television viewers. It left photographers shooting inside the dome in natural light, leading to darker and, in the opinion of most, less aesthetically pleasing pictures. A *Wall Street Journal* story in 1981 noted that when *SI* ran a photo of Earl Campbell on the cover of their 1980 pro football preview, the picture taken inside the Astrodome was so dark that a graphic artist had to sketch in facial details of Campbell. "His eyes were a little close together," said Rogin, "but that's the kind of thing only his mother would know."

While reshaping the look of the magazine, Rogin was also reshaping the staff. Kenny Moore, the eloquent long-distance runner from Eugene, Oregon, who finished fourth in the 1972 Olympic marathon, had been freelancing throughout the '70s, developing his style under Rogin's tutelage, before becoming a staff writer in 1980. Also taking a larger role was staff writer Douglas S. Looney, who'd worked as an investigative sports reporter at the middlebrow national weekly newspaper *The National Observer* in the '70s. Tax and Terrell had both been impressed with his work on that paper, and felt he could add a harder edge to the coverage of *SI*. Looney came into his own with a series of sardonic, unsparing investigative pieces in the early '80s. The most significant one came in the spring of 1983, when he went to Norman, Oklahoma, to do a piece on Marcus Dupree, for the college football preview issue that fall. Looney had called OU sports information director Mike Treps a few days before coming to Norman, and announced he'd be down. But then, a day later, Treps called back with an odd message: "It is not in the best interests of our football program at this time to promote Marcus Dupree for the Heisman Trophy." Looney knew a good story when he was being steered away from one, and went down to Norman anyway.

When Looney got to his office, Treps said, "We're not helping you on any story on Dupree, and I told you not to come and you're here anyway. You're on your own." It was then that Looney, slightly bemused, slightly bewildered by the snub, walked outside and encountered Dupree. The two men had met before and after exchanging greetings, Looney informed Dupree of his intent.

"I'm here to do a story on you," he said.

"Great," said Dupree. "I've always wanted to be in *Sports Illustrated*."

"Well, you're fixing to be in *Sports Illustrated*. But you should know all the facts: Coach Switzer does not want me to do a story on you."

"Huh?" said Dupree, looking perplexed.

"I'm just telling you what they told me."

"Why not?"

"Well, what Switzer says is you don't practice hard. You don't work hard. You're sort of a detriment to the team, and even the other black players don't like you."

Actually, Treps had given him the last piece of information. Switzer never spoke to him for the story. After the story ran, Switzer said he had tried several times to reach Looney. "I don't have any recollection of that at all," Looney said. "Obviously, there are people I don't call back. I don't profess to have a perfect record in phone callbacks, but guys like Barry Switzer, I always called back. There isn't any reason I wouldn't call back Barry Switzer." (Switzer, however, was never quoted directly in the piece, lending credence to his contention that his calls were never returned.)

Dupree was on the cover of the June 20, 1983, issue, with the headline "Clash of Wills at Oklahoma," and the subhead "Heisman Hopeful Marcus Dupree: Can He Coexist With His Coach?" The Looney piece would start a storm of critical investigation into Switzer's program and would lead Switzer to the belief that *Sports Illustrated* had played a crucial role in his downfall at Oklahoma.

Rogin's most important hire on the football beat came in the pro game, where senior editor Mark Mulvoy had been pushing for a specialist to back up Jenkins, who would move off the beat in 1980, to concentrate exclusively on golf.

Rogin felt the pro football coverage missed an Xs and Os expert like Maule, preferably someone who could write and was willing to do the legwork required to stay on top of the growing, ever-changing NFL. Mulvoy had just the man in irascible *New York Post* columnist Paul Zimmerman, a beat writer for more than a decade, a former offensive lineman at Stanford and Columbia, and a man truly obsessed with professional football. Zimmerman had written the cogent *A Thinking Man's Guide to Pro Football* in 1969, but his mania predated that. During one of his first locker-room assignments for the *Post,* following the Browns-Packers championship game at the end of the '65 season, Zimmerman (still playing semipro football at the time) got involved in a long conversation with Fuzzy Thurston and Jerry Kramer on the Packers' offensive line audibles. So enraptured, in fact, that he missed talking to Bart Starr and Paul Hornung.

Zimmerman's mastery of football minutiae was staggering. During the game, he would keep a visual game chart, with different squiggles denoting pass, run, or punt, his tiny script indicating the ballcarrier or receiver. He'd also record: a defensive chart, in which he would highlight good plays by defenders (not necessarily just tackles); an offensive line chart, which would note successful blocks; a cumulative statistical summary, recording individual statistics for attempts, completions, carries, and fumbles for each team (the *New York Times'* Jerry Eskenazi said, "I don't believe Paul has ever believed a press release"); a chart on punters, including elapsed hang-time, distance and return yardage, coffin-corner efficiency, and, at the end of the game, the average hang-time for each punter. For fun, he would time the National Anthem.

"He is a sick fuck," said one editor at *SI* with a measure of affection. "But we need him."

Zimmerman, christened Dr. Z by Mark Mulvoy, was exactly the sort of plain-spoken, unspectacular reporter that other writers enjoy disparaging. But his understanding of the intricacies of line play provided a deeper view into the workings of the pro game than even Maule's best work. Zimmerman's detail-laden reports would guarantee him a loyal following at *SI,* though never much respect from his colleagues or editors. His story on the San Francisco 49ers' dramatic NFC title game win over the Dallas Cowboys in the January 18, 1982, issue provided an example of Zimmerman at his best. Walter Iooss, Jr., got the cover shot, of Dwight Clark's game-winning fingertip catch, high in the back of the end zone, while Zimmerman's piece dissected Joe Montana's closing drive with lucidity and depth. It was the best story written on one of the best NFL games ever played.

In addition to Zimmerman, Rogin was hiring a group of accomplished writers, many of whom had been influenced by the magazine during its Laguerre-era heyday. The new cast included:

> •Alexander Wolff, who had grown up with a passion for basketball and *Sports Illustrated.* Years later, he would still remember a picture of "Pete Maravich's foot anchored on a drive and his ankle at this impossible angle." After two years at Princeton, he spent a year in Switzerland, playing basketball for a third division club team, waiting impatiently for his *SI*s to arrive. Naturally gravitating to the prose of Frank Deford and Curry Kirkpatrick, Wolff would come back to Princeton intent on a writing career. Before his graduation, he'd written the playground hoops ode *The In Your Face Basketball Book,* and got an *SI* reporter's job straight out of college.

•Rick Telander, an All–Big 10 safety from Northwestern who had worked on a freelance basis for the magazine for years, debuting with a 1972 piece called "Football Like a Rose," about his failed tryout in the summer of 1971, with the Kansas City Chiefs. Like Moore for track, Telander was a journalist and contemporary athlete who had come of age after Mexico City, more attuned than most of his predecessors to the way black culture was becoming a dominant force in major sports.

•Franz Lidz, an eccentric essayist who would be destined, much like Blount, to never quite fit into the ever narrowing *SI* style. When Lidz proposed an *SI* story in 1981 about his uncle Harry, a man convinced that he was a world champion boxer in nine different weight classes, three different editors passed before he finally showed it to Rogin, who not only ran it but also insisted that he be its only editor. Out of the article came the genesis for Lidz's critically praised memoir, *Unstrung Heroes,* later adapted into a motion picture.

•Gary Smith, the formidably talented takeout writer who rejected his first offer to come to *SI*, remaining loyal to Walsh in the dying days of *Inside Sports*. He finally came on after the original incarnation of *IS* went under, and John Walsh resigned, in 1983.

Though the new hires were uniformly gifted, most of them had been deeply influenced, even pointed toward journalism as a career, by the *SI* of the '60s and '70s. They inevitably displayed less of the unruly variety of writing styles that the magazine nurtured in earlier incarnations. There was simply less new ground to be broken. But the most important change was one of dynamics. In the '60s and early '70s, writers worked, drank, and gambled side by side with their editors. By the '80s, they hardly knew them.

• • •

The phone rang in text editor Myra Gelband's office.
"Hello."
"Who wrote *The Duchess of Malfi*?"
"Webster," she said, and before she could ask why, she heard a dial-tone. She looked at the phone quizzically for a moment, then dialed Gil Rogin's office. He answered.
"This is Gil."

*Time* circulation man Robert Cowin, whose November 1950 memo suggested that Time Inc. "could put out a sports publication so far above and ahead of anything being published today that demand would be overwhelming."

Before going on to a Pulitzer Prize–winning career as a columnist for the *Los Angeles Times,* Jim Murray helped get *SI* off the ground.

Blackie Sherrod disciples Dan Jenkins and Bud Shrake at the *Fort Worth Press,* early morning, circa 1954.

At the party to celebrate the first issue, Time Inc. editor-in-chief Henry Luce stands between *SI*'s first managing editor, Sidney James, and publisher H.H.S. "Harry" Phillips, Jr.

Notorious raconteur and crack word editor Dick Johnston, spending a day at the bullfights in Mexico, flanked by his wife Laurie (left) and Natalie Wood.

Clockwise from above: Holding forth in the lay-out room, Sid James talks to the troops, circa 1955; André Laguerre, arrives at a friend's wedding in London in November 1953, less than three years before Luce summoned him to work at *Sports Illustrated;* more than 10,000 readers wrote in for "membership cards" to Happy Knoll Country Club, the site of John Marquand's satirical series of pieces poking fun at the manners and mores of the upper middle class.

THE EDITORS OF SPORTS ILLUSTRATED
EXTEND GUEST PRIVILEGES AT

**HAPPY KNOLL**
*Country Club*

TO _____ HENRY R. LUCE _____

signed _____ *Roger Horlick*
FOR THE BOARD OF GOVERNORS

Two quiet, proud men: Roy Terrell and Roberto Clemente, before a game in the summer of 1962.

The immensely talented, immensely eccentric Gil Rogin, interviewing a young contender named Floyd Patterson in 1959.

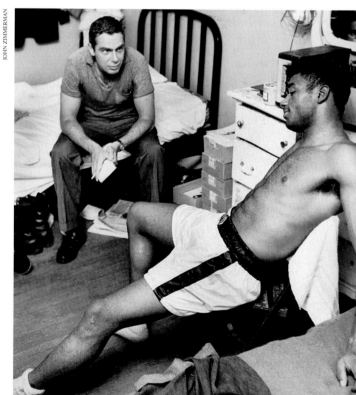

Above: Ray Cave, who would rise to executive editor at *SI,* before becoming managing editor at *Time.* At right: For more than ten years, Tex Maule was the magazine's best-known writer, capturing for *SI*'s avid readership the passion and complexity of pro football.

J. CONSENTINO

GEORGE BLOODGOOD

The precocious Neil Leifer, at Cleveland's Municipal Stadium for a 1961 game between the Browns and the New York Giants.

JOHN IACONO

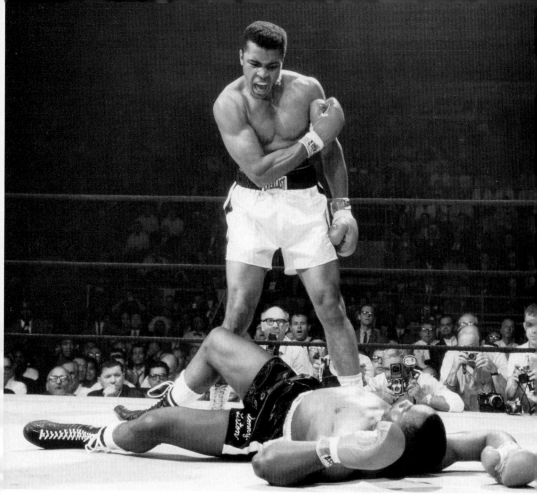

Neil Leifer's classic shot from the second Ali-Liston fight in Lewiston, Maine. After snapping the definitive shot of the century's definitive athlete, Leifer's only thought was directed at Sonny Liston: *Stay there.*

Trusted Laguerre drinking partner and longtime horse-racing writer Whitney Tower, pictured with his horse Carry Back.

Secret weapon Dick Gangel, who in Luce's words "comes as close to being the perfect art director as anyone I can imagine."

At left: George Plimpton, sharing a moment with friend and temporary teammate Joe Schmidt during the scrimmage that was the centerpiece of Plimpton's *Paper Lion*, one of a series of Plimpton's participatory pieces for *SI* that Ernest Hemingway described as "the dark side of the moon of Walter Mitty." Below: Jack Olsen, Laguerre's most trusted writer, whose groundbreaking five-part series "The Black Athlete" served as a wake-up call for the complacent leaders of sport in 1968.

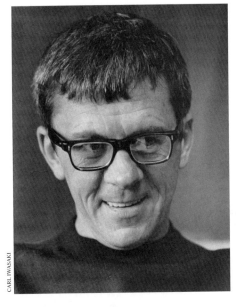

Morrie Werner—liaison to bookies, head of morale, wizened elder, and faithful drinking companion—makes his daily visit to Laguerre's office, picking him up for lunch. (Note Laguerre's white stick next to the clipboards on his desk.)

**COCKTAIL LOUNGE**

Above: Laguerre's official portrait, shot in 1973. "You can have five minutes," he told famed portrait photographer Arnold Newman, but he relented when Newman responded that "General de Gaulle gave me an hour." At left: Detail from a postcard from the Ho Ho, the Chinese restaurant and bar that served as *SI*'s satellite office from 1967 through Laguerre's last days at *SI* in early 1974.

The annual Crichton Bowl, in the early '70s at Mamaroneck Park. Back row, from left to right, Roy Blount, Jr., Sandy Treadwell (who went on to become the secretary of state in New York under George Pataki), Mike Del Nagro, Larry Keith, Mark Mulvoy, Ron Fimrite, and Andy Crichton. Front row, Curry Kirkpatrick, Walter Bingham, Les Woodcock, George E. Curry, and Gwilym Brown.

Relaxing after a Crichton Bowl, Robert W. Creamer (foreground) and Andy Crichton. For decades, they were the marrow of the magazine. Crichton followed Laguerre to *Classic* in 1975; Creamer retired in 1984.

Dan Jenkins, outside his favored haunt, P. J. Clarke's, around the time of *Semi-Tough*'s release in 1972.

Arthur Ashe and Frank Deford sitting in a festival tent during a tournament in South Africa in 1973.

The formidably talented Mark Kram, whom Bud Shrake called "the most tortured writer I've ever met.

The eternally buttoned-down John Underwood, the first of *SI*'s key staff writers to move away from New York.

Walter Iooss, Jr., is joined by a group of photographers and writers at an *SI* party in the late '70s. Clockwise from lower left: Tony Triolo, Jim Drake, John Iacono, Iooss, Herb Scharfman, Curry Kirkpatrick, and photo assistant Anthony Donna. John Papanek is peering over Scharfman's shoulder.

Clockwise from above: Gil Rogin, in his element—in the managing editor's office—in 1980;
perpetually underestimated Mark Mulvoy in
1983, long after his "Duke of Discount" and
"Prince of Polyester" days; Rogin's right-hand
man and heir apparent, Peter Carry.

The swimsuit issue, a novelty created under Laguerre, became *SI*'s best-known issue by the '80s. At left: *SI*'s Svengali of swimsuit shoots Jule Campbell, adjusting Elle Macpherson's suit. Below: The 25th anniversary of the *SI* swimsuit issue was a fateful moment for Frank Deford, his last appearance at an official *SI* function. Deford and his daughter Scarlet are flanked by, from left to right, models Elle Macpherson, Rachel Hunter, Maria del Carmen von Hartz, and Kathy Ireland. Just days later, Peter Price would call Deford about becoming editor of a proposed national sports newspaper.

Managing editor John Papanek presents Michael Jordan in 1991 with the replica of the Greek amphora given annually to *SI*'s Sportsman of the Year. Jordan was still on speaking terms with the magazine at the time.

At left: *SI*'s crack college basketball writer Alex Wolff, on a story about Auburn's natural wonder Charles Barkley in 1984. Above: Gary Smith, interviewing the grandfather of Yasuhiro Yamashita for a bonus piece in the 1980s.

Above left: Steve Rushin, with Gary Davidson—one of the subjects of his epic "How We Got Here" piece—at the 40th anniversary dinner. Above: William Nack and his muse— the legendary colt Secretariat. Left: Winners Chris Berman and Rick Reilly, with Reilly's son Kellen, at the 1995 National Sportscasters and Sportswriters Awards dinner.

Mark Mulvoy chatting with Bill Clinton at Congressional. The golf talk—and golf outings— increased during Mulvoy's second term as managing editor.

Daniel Okrent, reclining in his *Life* magazine managing editor's office, pre-bake-off.

Bill Colson in Central Park on Independence Day, 1995, one of his few days off during his trial in the bake-off.

Design director Steven Hoffman and Bill Colson, working in *SI*'s layout room.

"Why did you ask me that?"

"Because I knew you would know," he said in an exclamatory near-shout.

And there was another dialtone.

This was how business was conducted during the Rogin tenure: at breakneck speed, with inexplicable stops and starts. By 1980, Rogin had turned the ME's office into a sort of mad scientist's laboratory, often conducting meetings while lying on the floor, using his occasional outbursts as a sort of bizarre performance art.

Working with him most closely was assistant managing editor Peter Carry, whom Rogin was clearly grooming to succeed him one day. In the absence of Dick Johnston, Carry was the only editor who could be trusted to be vigilant about the finer points of grammar, to referee the debates that Jenkins called "the comma wars."

"He's a great idea man and a great administrative editor that way," said one respected editor of Carry. "But I think he's a dreadful copy editor. When you're an editor, you get the sense of omnipotence, that you have to do things. Rogin did an awful lot of editing and chopping when he was a copy editor. And I think Peter copied him doing it, whether consciously or unconsciously. Laguerre was a very sparing editor. He thought it was counterproductive if you edited writers too much; it made them lazy, he said. Whereas if you accepted what he did, maybe pointed out a few things, a guy would take personal pride in his work and work harder. But Rogin couldn't keep his pen off the paper. And neither could Carry. That meticulous nit-picking editing just destroyed writers' morale, editors' morale, everybody."

William Nack, the former *Newsday* columnist hired in Terrell's last days, was a careful, conscientious writer who suffered over every word. Nack was a pronounced throwback, a writer who would have been a natural playing the match game and tipping back scotches with Laguerre and Werner. Like those writers from earlier days, he bridled at the level of line-editing meddling. "When I got there, the editing was done wearing lobster bibs—there was blood all over the floor."

The core of conscientious editors had vanished, and the quality of prose in the magazine was suffering for it. But there was something else: the institutional memory was disappearing. There'd been a huge turnover since Laguerre left, and more writers had moved out of New York. In correspondence to his old friend Art Hill in the summer of 1981, Robert Creamer noted that 71 people, or almost precisely half the staff, had left the magazine in the space of seven years. Contemplating the ramifications left Creamer feeling "bereft." He continued:

My trouble is, I have little feeling for the magazine anymore. I get along with Gil Rogin, but I simply don't know or understand what he's doing or what he wants. As you know, I admire his writing. He's a serious writer, with a great respect for the art. But as a managing editor he constantly emphasizes illustration; the word is definitely inferior to the picture. Whenever we get a piece of copy, the first question is: how do we illustrate it? "I won't run this unless we have good pictures." Good copy sits around waiting for what Gil feels is the proper art (pictures or paintings) and sometimes dies of age. . . .

And it's not just that. A writer sent us three pretty good short pieces. Rogin liked one, rejected the other two. The writer was curious to know why the one was accepted and the other two rejected. That is, what made Gil like the one piece, not the other two. I absolutely could not tell him. I can't anticipate what Gil will like. Or what he won't like. Or why. The writer used a word to describe what he thought Rogin's decision-making was: "Capricious." I guess so. Although "capricious" means, I think, willful, or shallow, or unfounded. I'm sure Rogin thinks deeply about the magazine and about what he wants. Maybe the better word to describe him is "impulsive." Zip! this way. Zap! that way. Boom! let's do this.

Laguerre spoiled me. He was so blessedly rational, logical, purposeful. He thought ahead, had the broad view, understood (far better than I ever could) how this week's cover or last week's story affected next September's cover or next November's story coverage. He related things; he could be subtle; he could wait.

Rogin can't wait. It's right now all the time. I find it confusing and distasteful.

Creamer's feelings were shared by many of the veterans on the staff. Carry was one problem, and Rudeen seemed to lack much feel for writers. And rising through the morass was the unlikeliest of comers, the bombastic Mark Mulvoy. Among the changes that Terrell made in 1978 was to move Mulvoy back from the hockey beat to a senior editor post. He'd asked to come off the road in 1976, growing increasingly tired of the travel and the growing generational gap between himself and the athletes he was interviewing. Mulvoy drifted back into writing a year later but, on Memorial Day, 1978, he collapsed while golfing, suffering from a pinched nerve in his lower back. That brought Mulvoy back to the editing side permanently, and that summer he cut a deal with Terrell so he could have Saturdays off, both to spend more time with his children and make the rounds at his beloved golf courses.

Under Rogin, Mulvoy prospered, as an all-knowing sports nut, with a much better grasp of the terrain of major sports like football, baseball, and golf than anyone else in Rogin's inner sanctum. And yet, the day in 1981 when Rogin made Mulvoy assistant managing editor, he seemed almost amused at the prospect, walking down the hall to share the news with the staff. "You won't believe what I just did!" he said to a senior editor. "I just made Mulvoy an assistant managing editor!" Someone asked why. "I don't know!" Rogin said, laughing and moving on.

For all his strengths, Mulvoy was still regarded as something of a mendacious buffoon by a sector of the old guard. They remembered how out of place he seemed when he arrived in New York, how overmatched he was when compared to the writing talents of Deford or Kirkpatrick. John Underwood heard the news on a trip into the office a few days later. He went directly into Rogin's office.

"Gil, what are you *doing*?" he demanded.

Rogin held his palms out. "He's really all I've got."

"Well, if that's true," said Underwood, shaking his head gravely, "it's a shame."

# CHAPTER 14

# "KICK IN, YOU SON OF A BITCH"

*For I have always lived violently, drunk hugely, eaten too much or not at all, slept around the clock or missed two nights of sleeping, worked too hard and too long in glory, or slobbed for a time in utter laziness. I've lifted, pulled, chopped, climbed, made love with joy and taken my hangovers as a consequence, not as a punishment. I did not want to surrender fierceness for a small gain in yardage. My wife married a man; I saw no reason why she should inherit a baby.*

—JOHN STEINBECK, *TRAVELS WITH CHARLEY*

It was quiet by then, no sound but for the ringing in their ears and the clinking of busboys clearing off tables. A hint of early morning light was creeping through the windows of the Absinthe House Bar on a corner of Bourbon Street in New Orleans. Dan Jenkins sat where he'd been sitting for most of the previous eight hours. Roy Blount, Jr., an oversize grin on his face, was resting his head on his arms crossed on the table. Pete Axthelm, wiping his eyes from the latest round of laughter, smiled sleepily. His friend Max McGowan was sitting back in his chair with a bemused expression on his face. And June Jenkins, ever the trouper, had her head on Dan's shoulder. It was six in the morning, Super Bowl Sunday in the French Quarter. The more eager of the newspaper reporters in town, many in the city for their first look at the extravaganza, would be rising soon, getting set to run down for breakfast and get out to the Superdome. But Jenkins and his crew hadn't gone to sleep yet. And as he looked at the empty glasses and mountain of cigarette butts on the table, Dan Jenkins did that rarest of things—he conceded.

"I'm fuckin' out," he said to no one in particular. "I've *got* to go home. I've had 50 J&B and waters, I smoked six cartons of Winstons, and we got a fuckin' game in eight hours. I've got to go to bed."

No one said anything for a moment.

"I didn't realize," said McGowan, "that we all came down here to try to quit smoking."

Businessmen have conventions, college students have spring break, sportswriters have Super Bowls. For Jenkins and the *SI* crowd, the game had become the backdrop for a weeklong debacle of media overkill, redundant parties, and long nights of bodily abuse.

McGowan, the quick-witted former SID at Marquette and longtime research assistant and sidekick to Axthelm, was a frequent visitor to the big events. It was at one of the NFL's huge cocktail parties that Jenkins was escorting a drunken McGowan from table to table. At one table, where Frank Gifford and Caroline Kennedy were seated, Jenkins introduced McGowan, who extended his hand across the table, lost his balance, and overturned a couple of glasses.

"You'll have to excuse my friend," said Jenkins helpfully. "He hasn't eaten yet."

From the day in the sixth grade when his grandmother had pulled a typewriter out of the attic, Jenkins had followed his journalistic muse, which had led to these weeklong extravaganzas, bigger than the Olympics, bigger (to Jenkins's lasting resentment) than college football, bigger even than the World Series. But not—in his mind—more important. And it was this cognitive dissonance, so much emphasis being put on something that had lost the purity and drama and fear of the best sports events—that made Jenkins sullen and sentimental, testy and restless. So he went along and tried his best to laugh.

"Dan was clever and certainly a guy who could instigate a lot," said McGowan. "He was the instigator on the playground, but never the guy to get into major trouble, you know?"

The big events were also the place where Jenkins was faced with his legacy. A generation earlier, a group of young, sardonic sports reporters had come of age in New York City, all of them idolizing the hard-bitten columnist Jimmy Cannon, who dubbed them the Chipmunks and was decidedly ambivalent about their devotion. And so it was with Jenkins, who after two decades at *SI* had become a pressbox legend, an idol to a new wave of young, talented, irreverent sportswriters. At the Super Bowl and at the majors in golf, they'd come to sit at his table and pay homage: Mike Lupica and David Israel from New York, Tony Kornheiser from Washington, Rick Reilly from Los Angeles, scores of others. They just wanted to say they'd sat with Dan. But it was never enough. It was clear that many of them wanted, more than anything, to be him. Sooner or later, someone would want to tell him how much his writing had meant to him as a kid. And it was this, maybe, that made Jenkins so cantankerous. He'd just turned 50 in December 1979, and was not yet ready to be the Grand Old Man of anybody's games. And then to have to sit and listen to one of them gush, well, they should have read Hemingway: "We still went under the system, then, that praise to the face was an open disgrace."

And yet these men, with strong egos all, were so completely in awe of Jenkins that they felt they had to say *something*.

"I tell you a funny thing about meeting Jenkins," said Tony Kornheiser, a charter member of the generation of sportswriters who grew up on Laguerre's *SI* (the 12-year old Kornheiser had a letter printed in The 19th Hole in December 1963). "A lot of people idolize Jenkins. A lot of my friends—Mike Lupica, David Israel—they idolized Dan, and I idolized Dan. And so what happens, when you go to dinner with Dan, all of us who idolize him start doing his lines. Dan just sits there. Dan doesn't say anything. And then in the middle of dinner, Dan will say something, one sentence, maybe even one word, and it will just kill everybody. I wonder if it was torture for Dan to go out with us, because we were all acolytes. We were trying overly hard."

Few were trying harder than Reilly, a precociously funny writer from Colorado who'd gotten a staff job at the *Los Angeles Times* at age 24. "I was so in awe to sit with Dan Jenkins," he recalled of their first meeting, at the 1984 British Open. "We'd sit there and drink black coffee and eat those pork pies. Ever heard of those? They were horrible, but he was eating them, so I ate them."

Unlike so many of the sporting legends they covered, Jenkins was just as awesome up close.

"He was playing in a whole different ballpark," remembered Mike Lupica. "I sat next to him at Augusta; I saw what it was like. I was only writing a thousand-word newspaper column. He's writing whatever he was writing there. The Winstons would go down. The only time he'd get up was to get another cup of coffee or have Myra or somebody go get it for him.

Then I'd read him in the magazine and say, "How the hell did he do that?' It was like watching Nicklaus make some 40-foot putt. Every Sunday."

But toward the end of his six-year stint on the pro football beat, Jenkins was partying more and enjoying it less. He'd always been a world-class drinker, but his drinking had increased. Many of his friends were growing concerned that his lifestyle was genuinely hurting him. In journalistic terms, though, the crisis was even more profound: he was losing interest in his main beat, pro football. Throughout the '60s and early '70s, he'd been sustained by the sheer gravity of the moment; he could maintain the brutal writing pace because he *wanted* to be in Tuscaloosa one week and Ann Arbor the next. And he'd spend his magazine weekends, the Tuesday and Wednesdays, working on bonus pieces and his fiction. Sally Jenkins remembered, as a child, "falling asleep to the sound of my father's typing and waking up the next morning to the same sound." Now it was all different. There were very few Games of the Century in pro football in the late '70s, only a whole lot of Baltimores at New Englands. And while he'd kept a respectful distance from Roy Terrell, his relationship with Gil Rogin was acrimonious. Rogin thought Jenkins was a lazy prima donna, in his words a "fucking gag writer." Jenkins saw Rogin as a sybaritic gnome, who as a writer was guilty of the inexcusable sin of pretentiousness.

So Jenkins went to the office less, worked on outside projects more, went down to six Super Bowl games and tried to enjoy himself. An essay he wrote in the mid-'80s for *Playboy* provided a window into his typical Super Bowl week:

> None of us in the press look back on any great Super Bowl plays. We look back on that night on Bourbon Street when two of our members got into a bidding war for a fetching flower girl, and the winner watched her go down on room service for three days. We look back on the network pal who couldn't finish the job he had started with a tattooed debutante and shouted to an associate waiting to be next, "Gimme a break, I gotta read the fucking instructions!"
>
> We look back on the colleague who left the site early one week and then called back long distance to say, "Did we have fun last night? I've got a goddamn fish in my pocket!"
>
> And we look back with extreme fondness on the woefully hungover author who swallowed a capsule to assist him with his deadline story in the Miami press box and, 30 minutes later, still staring at a

blank page in his Olivetti, was heard to yell, "Kick in, you son of a bitch: you've never taken this long before!"

The Olivetti belonged to Jenkins, and the unprecedented writer's block was a combination of several factors: lack of interest, lack of sleep, lack of a sympathetic editor, and a heavy heart.

The trouble had started the week of Laguerre's death in 1979. Jenkins had called New York, asking to have the Time Inc. corporate jet flown down to Miami to transport the *SI* crew to the Laguerre memorial service the morning after the game. When this was denied, Jenkins was left morose and sullen. The game didn't improve his mood much. The Pittsburgh Steelers beat the Dallas Cowboys, 35–31, in the most competitive Super Bowl yet, but one that Jenkins (along with several other writers) was convinced had been decided by field judge Fred Swearingen's interference call against Cowboy cornerback Bennie Barnes, who was tightly covering Lynn Swann early in the fourth quarter of a game the Steelers were then leading by only 21–17. Jenkins had always believed the credo that a writer should find the angle he wanted in a story and then beat it to death, and in writing about a game he felt was ruined by Swearingen, he did just that. At the time, Mark Mulvoy was the senior editor handling pro football and Rogin was the blue pencil editing the piece. They tore up Jenkins's story and did a complete rewrite. It ended with a long quote by Bradshaw, summing up his day, "I just tried to go out there and win a football game," and then Mulvoy's idea of a wry kicker: "Which he did—and how." Jenkins went into a blind rage when he saw the finished article four days later.

"Mark's always been a bull in a china closet," said Joe Marshall, who was also writing pro football at the time. "He had a thousand ideas. Mark wasn't afraid to put a piece of paper in a typewriter and type a new lead. I was lousy at leads; I don't blame him for thinking he had to fix them. But I didn't like his any better than mine."

William Nack came to *SI* later that year, and was stunned when he heard the story about the Super Bowl rewrite. "When I found out that Mulvoy had to write the story, or rewrite the story, I thought, *Gee—rewriting Dan Jenkins? Wow*. Especially by a guy who had a reputation as not a very good writer."

Jenkins was tired of the travel, tired of the deadlines, tired of Mulvoy's editing, and tired of Rogin's complete lack of interest in golf. There had been five golf covers in Terrell's last full year, 1978, but Rogin could be counted on for only two a year, the winner of the Masters and the winner of the U.S. Open. In 1980, at the clubhouse at Baltusrol in Springfield, New Jersey, where Jack Nicklaus would win the

U.S. Open, Jenkins sat with Blackie Sherrod, who sensed that his old friend wasn't enjoying himself. "I'm going to make it to twenty years and I'm fuckin' out of there," Jenkins told him. "And I'm taking the furniture with me—they've got a hell of a retirement plan." That summer, he begged off the pro fooball beat. At the time, Jenkins's energies were clearly scattered: he was still on staff, was an established best-selling novelist, was writing screenplays with Shrake for Hollywood producers, and had even considered, with his friend Pete Axthelm, a television show of sports commentary.

"Are you glad to be done with that?" Creamer asked Jenkins one day, after he'd just finished a novel.

"I kind of miss the characters; they do whatever you want them to," said Jenkins wistfully. "But I finished the novel and there was this very beautiful woman standing next to me. And I asked her, 'Do I know you?' and she said, 'Yes—I'm married to you.'"

In the fall of 1980, June Jenkins initiated a trial separation. It was a wrenching period, and when they reconciled a few months later, Jenkins vowed to take life a little bit easier. This was a hard thing for a man who'd been taught by Sherrod "to put my soul in a pickle jar if I ever missed a story, got beat on one, or lapsed into a Fitzgerald-Hemingway coma and got too pretentious in a lead." But finally, he was learning that even if he did relax, he would still be a best-selling novelist, still be the magazine's most popular writer, and he and June were still living in their beautiful Upper East Side condo. He was in a dangerous position: that of a comfortable sportswriter.

Jenkins's byline ran less frequently in the magazine in the early '80s. Rogin resisted all but the most important golf coverage, and Jenkins hadn't written a bonus piece since the 1978 cover story on the making of *Semi-Tough,* the movie.

"Jenkins's routine stuff was a hell of a lot better than most writers' career best, but it was still routine, and Rogin resented that," said Creamer. "And the plain truth was that he wasn't working as hard as he had in the earlier years. None of us were. Rogin wanted Jenkins to act like a young writer trying to prove himself—work his ass off. Rogin was probably also pissed off that Dan's book had become a runaway bestseller while his own books, which I loved, were lucky to sell 5,000 copies."

• • •

After Kelso Sutton left the publisher's chair to become head of the Time Inc. Publishing Group in 1980, he was succeeded by veteran ad man

Philip Howlett, who brought a cautious, polished professionalism to the job. Howlett's first shock, in 1981, came in a meeting with Los Angeles Olympic Organizing Committee chairman Peter Ueberroth. The slick head of the L.A. games had vowed to avoid the financial debacle that befell Montreal in 1976. He also made clear that he intended to make better use of corporate sponsors, using fewer and charging them more. After 342 sponsors had generated $7.8 million at the 1980 Lake Placid Games, Ueberroth coaxed $200 million out of 98 sponsors for Los Angeles. Howlett knew the price of sponsorship would be going up, but he wasn't quite prepared for how much. In 1980, *SI* had paid $100,000 to be the "Official Magazine of the Winter Olympic Games." To have the same role in Los Angeles, Howlett learned, would cost $4 million. Howlett discussed the terms with his two top aides, associate publisher Don Barr and general manager Bob Miller. But *SI* had no real choice. With the insurgency of *Inside Sports*, it couldn't risk providing the competitor with Olympian legitimacy. They had to go for it.

It was a decision they never regretted, and one they knew they could afford. The trio had mapped out a financial model that would turn *SI* into a legitimately big business by the mid-'80s, with an emphasis on asking the reader to pay more for the magazine. And the readers proved, again, more than willing to do so. In the first half of the '80s, the subscription price rose from $36 a year to more than $52, generating more than $133 million in subscription revenues alone. Suddenly, a mature 25-year-old magazine that had been making between $10 and $20 million a year in the late '70s started showing breakthrough profits. In 1984, the magazine would make more than $50 million.

But they had to spend money to make money, and nothing was more costly than going to an all-color format, a move that Howlett feared would be prohibitively expensive. Rogin understood well the emotional connection that *SI*'s readers had with the magazine, and he recognized the way color photography of an event they'd watched could transport them back to the moment (he called it "the savor factor"). General manager Bob Miller argued that the industry was heading in that direction anyway. And in an impassioned plea in front of Time Inc. executives, Rogin compared *SI*'s current mix of full color and black and white with a major network telecasting only the first and fourth quarters of the Super Bowl in color. Finally, vice-president Jim McCluskey, who'd worked with SI during many of the hectic late closes in Chicago in the '60s, suggested in 1982 dropping the basis weight of the paper, to save money on both paper and postage (where the Postal Service charged by weight). With that as a hedge against the extra cost, Howlett finally agreed to move to all color.

As so often happens, the big change camouflaged a crucial detail. Editorial director Ralph Graves had been urging Rogin to use "pull quotes" (an enlarged version of a key passage or quotation) in feature stories. Rogin considered it an ugly, superfluous affectation, often a sign of an art director's creative bankruptcy. And since Rogin was, de facto, the art director, his position was firm—he didn't want pull quotes.

"Okay then," said Graves. "Then you've got to start illustrating every page."

A guiding principle would soon ossify into an unbreakable rule. In the short term, this simply meant that bonus pieces and long features had more pictures. But two things emerged from that trend. First, news stories got shorter, because the pictures took up more space. Second, bonus pieces got shorter as well, because, as Rogin explained, "We ran out of interesting pictures. It was repetitive and stupid."

The adjustments didn't seem important at the time, but they would be the beachhead on which the design elements of *SI* would stage their assault on writing. Every page needs an illustration. *The illustrations get repetitive. The solution is simple: Fewer pages, fewer repetitive illustrations. Fewer words.*

But the change went through, and with the September 5, 1983, issue— "Oh, Those Huskers!" exclaimed the cover, following Nebraska's 44–6 thrashing of Penn State in the inaugural Kickoff Classic—*Sports Illustrated* became the first American newsweekly to go to an all-color format.

"We were a little nervous about that," admitted Howlett later. "I think we all kind of felt that when somebody made the jump, *SI* was the logical choice. We looked at this thing and we thought, 'What magazine in the world is more suited for all color all the way through the magazine than *Sports Illustrated*? This is its world. There are a lot of things at *Time* that lend themselves to black and white, are almost better in black and white— Bosnia or Rwanda or any of these things may be better that way. I remember Gil Rogin was so sure that we were going to fight him, and was so delighted when we were as enthusiastic as he was that we should go ahead and do it. There's a lot of cachet in being able to go out and say you're the first magazine to have color throughout the book."

But Time Inc. was not a company renowned for its vision in the mid-'80s. Just as *SI* capitalized on one opportunity, it wound up passing on another. Months after *SI* went to all color, Texaco, which had recently bought out ESPN's parent company Getty, put the cable sports network up for sale. The energetic young executive Bob Miller had just taken over for Howlett as publisher, and he urged Time Inc. president Dick Munro to make a bid for the network. ESPN hadn't made much of a dent in the national consciousness yet, but Miller liked its potential. He felt it could be bought and renamed, perhaps as the *SI* Channel, and it could become an electronic conduit to the magazine. Ex-*SI* publisher Kelso Sutton, by then the head of the publishing group, was also in favor of it, but couldn't get the approval to make the purchase. ABC finally bought it for $237 million.

"We could have *had* ESPN," said Sutton. "I remember being in a meeting with Gerry Levin, and both Gerry and I were keen on buying ESPN. There were a lot of other things going on in the cable business at the time; we were acquiring cable subs, we were making big capital investments. Cable was growing like crazy, which is another reason why sports grew."

Time Inc. had just acquired Temple Inland, the East Texas paper company owned by board member Arthur Temple. "So when it got down to sitting down and doing strategic plans and stuff like that more at the corporate level," remembered Sutton, "there was always this big debate: 'Who's going to get the capital?' The cable company wanted more capital to go out and buy more systems. The paper guys wanted to build more paper machines. Some of us wanted to do things like buy ESPN. In retrospect, we should have pushed it a lot harder than we did."

It didn't seem that important at the time. Even in the world of mass-market magazines, there are very few billion-dollar mistakes being made. *Rolling Stone* ignoring the potential for MTV was one. *SI* passing at buying ESPN would turn out to be another.

• • •

If Dan Jenkins wasn't having much fun, Gil Rogin sure was. At a 1980 event at the Corcoran Gallery, where Rogin was standing with a drink, gazing out on the crowd in a three-piece suit, looking a little like a demented Gay Talese, a man in a dinner jacket came up to him and shook his hand.

"I'd trade jobs with you any day," the man said.

"I don't know," said Rogin. "What do you do?"

"I work in the Senate," said the man, whom Rogin would describe later as looking like a "superannuated chorus boy."

Rogin searched the man with his eyes. *Is he a head page? A sergeant at arms?*

Finally, he gave up. "What do you *do* in the Senate?"

"I'm a senator," said the man. It was Larry Pressler of South Dakota. Rogin laughed, but said it was no deal. He already had the best job in the world.

Shortly after taking over as ME, Rogin called his protégé Kenny Moore in Eugene, despairing that a Nike running shoe called the Sting, a blaring, suede and nylon contraption of bright orange and electric green, was being discontinued. He asked if Moore could get him a lifetime supply before they went out of production. Moore made a call to Nike headquarters and acquired the last six pairs of size nine Stings in stock. "I was going to send them to him," said Moore, "and then [text editor Myra Gelband] said, 'Wait, don't you see the possibilities here?' So what she did was take all the boxes and dump out all the shoes and make three boxes of just right-footed shoes and three boxes of left-footed shoes, which she took custody of. I presented the other three to Gil: 'These are the last three pairs on the face of the Earth; you have to ration them.' And he said, 'I will. They're going right home into the closet. It'll be years before I even get to the first pair.'"

Three years later, on one of his rare trips to New York, Moore was sitting in an office at *SI* writing about Alberto Salazar's 1982 New York Marathon win when Rogin came into the room, yelling loudly. "You can't defy fate!" he bellowed. "When something's discontinued, it's really discontinued! You can't store up against a malevolent future!"

Then Rogin went into a detailed description of his day: at his girlfriend Jackie Duvoisin's insistence, he finally threw out his original five-year-old pair of ragged Stings, and eagerly went to his closet to get his first pair from the supply Moore had procured, only to find that first one box, then the other two, all had pairs of right-footed shoes. "See," Rogin repeated dourly, "you can't defy fate. Everything that's good is discontinued." After enjoying his mentor's exquisite misery a few minutes more, Moore retrieved the other three boxes and marched into Rogin's office, explaining lovingly, "See Gil, sometimes your fate is planned for you."

Unbeknownst to Rogin, someone else was planning his fate as well. In the spring of 1983, he was called up to the 34th floor for a nine-month tour as an assistant to Henry Grunwald. The tradition of bringing a managing editor up to the executives' floor was part of the grooming process at Time Inc., less a hint of an imminent promotion than an inculcation process in which editors were exposed to the executive perspective. It was also a tradition, in the event of such absences, to give two or three different editors a chance to edit the magazine. The three men selected to edit in Rogin's absence were the three AMEs at the time, Peter Carry, Ken Rudeen, and Mark Mulvoy. Carry was the obvious heir apparent, Rudeen the out-of-the-loop veteran being given a ceremonial turn at the wheel, and Mulvoy, the lightly regarded darkhorse, a narrow-minded sports fan who seemed to lack the right stuff.

Carry went first, editing the magazine in the spring of '83. Another product of the magazine's Princeton pipeline, he'd come to *SI* in the mid-'60s, and stayed in touch with the magazine even while he was serving his military duty (even to the point of coming back to work at *SI* during his leave). In the '70s, he was a serviceable basketball writer, but his love for the language pushed him toward the editing track, where he'd become Rogin's understudy. Carry looked every bit the office dandy, preferring braces and bow ties long before they were in style, and long after they went out. He was also a fanatical wordsmith deemed too literal by many writers. "The worst word editor was Carry," said Ron Fimrite. "You'd have some rhythm going in your story and then he'd throw in some extra facts. He was great for getting a lot of facts in the story. You'd lose everything you were trying to get out of it. He was a fact loader."

During the three months of Carry's tryout for the ME's job, many thought he assumed a bit too much of the old military tone. He'd be curiously defensive when asked for the reasoning behind his decisions, and would snap at writers and editors with the slightest provocation. Bingham posted a sign above his own typewriter during the period, which read "He's Not Angry." "That's my reminder," he explained to fellow staffers, "that when I talk to Peter, he's not really pissed."

For all that, there seemed little doubt that Carry was going to be the man for the job. He went through his 13-week stint like a golfer with a six-stroke lead heading into the last round of the U.S. Open, concentrating on playing the course true to form, and not making any mistakes. "It looks just like Rogin's magazine," said one editor during the stint. "I guess that's the idea."

Rudeen's late summer trial was more of the same, a steady following of the Rogin formula. His one departure came when he placed, at Rogin's request, Howard Cosell on the cover of the August 8 issue ("The One and Only" read the headline), for Deford's bonus piece on the most controversial broadcaster in the country.

"The American Dream is usually portrayed as the vision of an abjectly poor kid," wrote Deford in the Cosell profile. "More often, though, the kids most determined to move up are those on the fringes of middle class comfort, those who can see the next rung on the ladder, not merely imagine it. Such was Cosell as a boy." And such was Mark Mulvoy, who the very week the story ran was preparing his all-out assault on the next rung at *Sports Illustrated.* Few of his peers viewed him as managing editor material, but that didn't bother him much. He had a plan.

Mark Mulvoy was the oldest of five children, born August 16, 1941 —exactly 13 years before the date of *SI*'s first issue—in Dorchester, a lower-middle-class neighborhood in south Boston, where the Mulvoy family lived on a street of 20 houses that counted 72 children, almost all of whom went to the Catholic elementary school St. Mark's. His father, Thomas Mulvoy, a first generation Irish immigrant, began working at the Boston Post Office in 1937. Three years later, Tom Mulvoy and his bride Julie moved into the two-decker on Lonsdale Street, where they paid $36 rent to the owners and upstairs tenants, Father Thomas Ford and his two sisters. When the Mulvoys moved out of the house in 1973, the rent was still $36 a month.

It was made clear to the Mulvoy boys that they were going to find a higher station in life than their father. They were expected to go to college and they were expected to work, just like Tom Mulvoy did virtually every day of his life. When he wasn't working as a mail sorter at the post office, he'd drive a Brink's truck or sell Blue Cross Insurance. Tom Mulvoy learned at an early age that for a man who wanted to work hard enough, there was always an angle. He got to bowl for free because he kept the bowling averages for all the participants in the church bowling league.

Mark was known as an inveterate sports nut and, within the house and throughout the neighborhood, by his nickname of Skippy. When there was time, he'd head down to Boston Garden, where a kindly old usher would let kids sneak into the arena for games, provided they got there 90 minutes before game time. He'd sit up in the rafters and watch the Celtics and his beloved Bruins, quickly becoming an expert on sports. When he was confirmed in 1954, Cardinal Cushing, the Archbishop of Boston, asked him what he wanted to be when he grew up. "A sportswriter," he said. That was not the thing that Cardinal Cushing wanted to hear, but his parents guessed it was just a phase.

A year later, when Skippy Mulvoy turned 14, his father worked a deal to send him off to caddy camp in Hyannisport, so that the next summer he could bring some money to the family as a caddy. Within two years, Mark and his younger brother Tommy (20 months his junior) were spending six days a week during the summer walking or hitchhiking to the Wollaston Golf Club in nearby Quincy. There they were exposed to a completely different world than the one of Dorchester double-shifts. They caddied for doctors and lawyers from Milton and Quincy. More than just impressed with the people and the surroundings, Mark Mulvoy was *inspired*. He used to caddy for Dick Gleason, a worldly bachelor in his thirties with a big car and an attitude. They'd get to the 18th hole and Gleason would say, "Four more swings and a Heineken." Mulvoy smiled and vowed to himself that someday he could belong to Wollaston Golf Club. And then he'd be drinking Heinekens.

So he worked harder than any of the kids in his class. While at Boston College, he wrote a sports column in the school newspaper called "Skipping Along." He also walked across the street to the *Boston Globe* and applied for a job in the sports department. When he didn't have a shift at the *Globe,* he started hanging around the Boston College sports information director's office, volunteering his help wherever and whenever he needed it. In the summer before his senior year, he got sent out to pick up *Sports Illustrated* reporter Merv Hyman at the airport. Hyman was in town working on *SI*'s college football preview issue, and the kid made an impression upon him. They kept in touch and in early January 1965, just six months out of college and a few hours after returning from his military duty, Mark Mulvoy was hired as a reporter at *Sports Illustrated*.

He wasn't close to being ready.

It's difficult to exaggerate how lightly regarded Mulvoy was by many of his colleagues on the staff when he started at *SI*. In an environment where spiky bon mots and clever comebacks were the rule, Laguerre and his cronies promoted a sort of cosmopolitan eclecticism. Most of the young reporters were well-to-do college grads who'd done some traveling, or else they were preternaturally talented writers. Mulvoy was out of his depth, and he knew it the day he started.

But Mark Mulvoy was nothing if not persistent. When he got to New York, he moved, along with fellow reporter Gary Ronberg, into the infamous apartment building at 435 East 65th Street. It was known as "The Stew Zoo," the stuff of legend among the sort of New York sporting types who knew where Giant running back Tucker Fredrickson's all-night parties were held.

Deford remembered Mulvoy, and Ronberg's excitement at getting an apartment at the notorious building. "They were gonna fuck their brains out," he said. "Well, they both married like the first stewardesses they met! It was so funny, Jesus! He started taking out Trish, and Gary started taking out whoever he did; I can't remember her name. You had to be amused by Mark then, because he was harmless. And everybody would laugh at him. 'The Duke of Discount.' Always! 'Look, if you go here, you can get four shirts for $36.' Aw, damn. Everything was a deal; he was giving everybody a deal all the time, always talking about how he was saving money. Drives [Deford's wife] Carol crazy. Every time he'd meet her, somehow the subject of money would come up right away. It wasn't enough to say what it cost, but he always had to get a deal on it, too. 'I got this.' Just *so* tacky."

His early days at *SI* were marked, more than anything else, by his boundless ambition. Months after arriving, he jumped at the chance to work with Jack Nicklaus for his instructional series. Staffer Gwilym Brown was growing tired of the assignment and went around the office asking reporters if they knew anything about golf. "Yeah! Golf! I invented it!" Mulvoy blurted. Suddenly, he was off to Columbus to meet the Golden Bear.

A few years later, when Laguerre pulled Brown back from London, where he was operating as *SI*'s one-man London bureau, Mulvoy bounded into Laguerre's office just hours after the news broke.

"André," he said. "If you need someone to go to London, I'll volunteer."

Laguerre looked at him thoughtfully and said, "No, Mark, you're much too valuable here. We need you here for hockey."

Moments after Mulvoy left, Laguerre was shuffling through papers. "I dislike the British," he said absently. "But I don't dislike them *that* much."

On the road, Mulvoy took after his father and found an angle. Some even took to calling him "America's Guest," the nickname originally given to George Low, the legendary gadfly of the PGA tour (profiled by Jenkins in a 1964 bonus piece). He quickly discovered the best ways to take advantage of expense accounts and hospitality suites. Throughout the '60s and early '70s, he even finagled a way for his brother Tommy to make a few all-expenses-paid spring training trips with him. In the '70s, Mulvoy wrote extensively about hockey and pro football, hopping between writing and editing, plowing through as-told-to books on his vacations and off-seasons, making enough money to afford a move to Westchester County. It was where the golfers lived.

For Mulvoy, the transparent desire for money was a manifestation of a larger search for power. He never again wanted to be just another kid from Dorchester. "I thought he was an opportunist and a self-aggrandizer," said one reporter of Mulvoy, "and he couldn't do it with the panache of Curry Kirkpatrick, who was exactly the same thing. Mulvoy was shrewd and clever and not deep. Not an intellectual. Not a poet. Not a great ear. I think he's one of what probably proliferates in American journalism now, which is a pretty shallow guy who's fast on his feet. Will do almost anything that he's been asked to do, and he won't fall on his sword for anything. I *really* like him, obviously."

Morrie Werner used to joke that a person couldn't insult Mulvoy—he just didn't *get* it. And whatever credentials he might have hoped to achieve as a big thinker were lost the day he showed up at the office, after moving into a new house in Rye, and asked his fellow reporters if they happened to have any extra books they didn't want. The Mulvoys needed something to fill up the built-in bookshelves in their new house.

Because there was such a reservoir of ridicule built up toward Mulvoy, many didn't see his real strengths. In addition to possessing an encyclopedic knowledge of sports, he had the wherewithal to orchestrate the breaking of major stories. Mulvoy played a key role in John Underwood's spectacular 1982 cover story in which NFL veteran Don Reese admitted to his cocaine habit. It required nearly a dozen trips, shepherding Reese into and out of detox centers, up to New York for depositions, all so *SI* could break the story. Throughout the process, Mulvoy was aware not only that the story could be big, but that it was winning him potential points with Rogin.

Mulvoy had taken a genuine interest, much more so than any of the other writers, in the business aspects of magazine publishing. He golfed with many of the ad reps. He had almost a savant's mastery of mock-ups, the list of which pages in a particular issue would be given to editorial and which would go to advertising. Mock-ups were one of the most complicated elements of the magazine-maker's art, beholden to arcane rules about placements (for instance, at least six pages of separation had to come between the car ads, and there were often a dozen in any issue). Mulvoy had, by 1983, already learned more than Rogin about how to manipulate mock-ups to the greatest editorial advantage.

Mulvoy was also, for all his bluster, a rapt, facile student of office politics, possessed of his own Machiavellian instincts for survival. He correctly recognized that Carry and Rudeen were editing in a conventional manner. So he made his trial a departure, running bigger pictures, using more double-truck photo spreads to take full advantage of the magazine's color capabilities. There was a breathless quality to many of the issues— six of Mulvoy's 12 covers had headlines with exclamation points, but they were different.

And his restless energy led him to a cover that would define his tryout.

Preparing for his last issue, he was looking for some way to further differentiate his trial period from Carry's and Rudeen's. Lying in bed at night, tossing and turning, searching for ideas, he finally hit upon one. Mulvoy sat up in bed, turned his bedside light on, and dialed up the number of Laurel Frankel, *SI*'s picture researcher.

"Laurel, get Jim Brown!" he said.

"Uh, Mark . . . it's two in the morning."

"It's only eleven on the West Coast."

By noon the next day, Jim Brown, the NFL great who had been grumbling about coming out of retirement to preserve his career rushing record, had agreed to pose in an Oakland Raiders jersey. He was scowling from under the *SI* banner the next week. "JIM BROWN" read the cover headline. "You serious? A comeback at 47? Hey! You're Just What the Borrr-ing NFL Needs!" One editor remarked that the only real surprise was that the headline didn't end with "—and How!"

At the time, no one felt that the editing trials would have much immediate impact. Successful MEs at Time Inc. magazines could typically expect an eight-year run, and Rogin clearly wanted to stay at least that long.

But the Brown cover was the talk of the Time & Life Building the following week, and Mark Mulvoy knew he'd made a statement.

• • •

When Rogin returned from his nine-month stint on 34, he seemed even more eccentric, more explosive, more unpredictable, than ever before.

He was back in his office in early December, in time to name the 1983 Sportsman of the Year. It was a wide-open field. The Associated Press had awarded its male athlete of the year award to sprinter–long jumper Carl Lewis, who was dominating the sprint distances and casting meaningful glances at Bob Beamon's record. AP chose Martina Navratilova as its female athlete of the year, on the strength of her winning three of tennis's four majors, including Wimbledon and the U.S. Open. The Sullivan Award, which went to the top "amateur" athlete of the year, went to hurdler Edwin Moses.

So more than few eyebrows were raised when Rogin selected medium-distance runner Mary Decker as Sportswoman of the Year. The first female to win *SI*'s award since Chris Evert in 1976, Decker was a defensible choice—she'd been outstanding at that year's world championships—but she'd hardly swept her events in the way Lewis and Moses had theirs, and she was far from being the dominant athlete in the sport, as Navratilova was. (In fact, UPI gave its female athlete of the year award to another track and field star, East German Jarmila Kratochvilova.)

The Decker announcement was greeted with nods and winks within *SI*, where Rogin's infatuation (some called it an obsession) with Decker was the source of more than a few jokes. It had long been clear to most of the staff that Rogin was "entranced by watching her run, watching her move," as Kenny Moore put it. Another writer recalled watching Rogin, on a visit to Eugene, having a look of almost beatific devotion as Decker rounded the University of Oregon track during her workout. "People generally felt that he was a little too obsessed with her," said track reporter Anita Verschoth.

"Everybody laughed behind his back," said Deford. "He'll do anything to get into her pants." Others were sure he already had. Franz Lidz recalled writer Craig Neff telling him that he'd witnessed Rogin and Decker "making out" on a couch in Eugene that year. (Neff would say later that he'd only heard rumors of such an incident.) And at the *SI* annual ad sales conference in 1983, in the resort town of Silverado, California, two *SI* salesmen said they'd seen Rogin leaving Decker's bungalow late at night. She'd been invited as one of the celebrity speakers, along with Joe Montana and other athletes. "Yeah, but Gil wasn't visiting Joe Montana in the middle of the night," said one attendee.

"Gil just couldn't see it," said one editor, with a measure of sadness. "He just didn't understand that this was an ethical issue and that he was jeopardizing the prestige of the magazine."

"I don't want to comment on that," said Rogin about the allegations of an affair with Decker. "It's nobody's business who I have relationships with and who I don't have relationships with. What really disappoints me the most about this whole thing is that anyone who would think I would let any personal thing, either hatred or adoration or anything in between, of any athlete, male or female, influence my editorial judgments about *SI* doesn't have a fucking clue who I am. And I don't care what these people think 'cause they're fucking stupid. They should know me by now. Journalism to me is almost a religion and whether I fucked Mary Decker or whether I didn't fuck her, nothing ever influenced me to what I put in that magazine."

The office talk was just starting to wane in the summer of 1984, when on successive trips to Los Angeles, for the Olympic track and field trials and then the Summer Olympics themselves, Rogin's behavior grew increasingly erratic.

At the U.S. Olympic trials in June, Rogin was near the press row close to the track when Decker failed to qualify for the U.S. team in her best event, the 1,500 meters. Down by the infield fence where he had moved to get a closer look, Rogin suffered a full-scale meltdown. "You fucking CUNT!" he screamed at Decker. "How could you fucking quit like that?!" The outburst took place well within earshot of the national press corps and several athletes, prompting Anita Verschoth, the veteran track and field writer who was *SI*'s main contact to Olympians, to bow her head in wordless anguish. Hours later, *SI* writer Bill Leggett got a call at his home in New York. "My God," said one of his friends in the press. "Your managing editor's just disgraced himself."

At the Olympics, Rogin fired two photo department members, then hired them back within hours. He was making bizarre story choices in the magazine: after Mary Lou Retton won the all-around gold in women's gymnastics, Rogin led the news section the following week with a 15-page Olympic swimming story.

And then there was Rogin's most celebrated conflict of the summer, one that many staffers had long predicted. From the day Rogin got the job, it was clear that he and Dan Jenkins didn't understand each other, much less like each other. In his writing and in his editing, Rogin fostered a certain kind of sensitive journalism that wasn't Jenkins's metier, elevating adept writers like Kenny Moore (who "made every track athlete sound like Dostoevsky," complained Jenkins). And after Jenkins quit football to devote himself to the golf beat in 1980, he was writing exclusively about a sport totally foreign to Rogin.

"You know, he said he wasn't going to change anything and his door would always be open," said Jenkins. "I don't know what happened. Gil was never really a journalist. He was a decent word editor. He wasn't horrible like some of them. He was a brooding, deep, literary type guy. He described me to somebody as a 'casual writer.' I was 'too casual.' I didn't 'know anything about commas'—I mean, I didn't! That was *the point*! I lost a few comma wars early; I knew I wasn't ever going to win them, so why worry about it? I worried about content; if they changed content on me, I went crazy. But that didn't happen often."

It began to happen more often in the early '80s, when Mulvoy became the senior editor for football (and later a blue pencil as AME) and John Papanek came off the basketball beat to become the senior editor for golf. Papanek had first noticed Jenkins's decline in 1980. Walking with Nicklaus during the dramatic final round of his U.S. Open win at Baltusrol, he'd returned to the press tent with pages of notes, gleaned from overheard conversations and small events that had occurred among the eclectic gallery. Jenkins's story employed little of Papanek's material and seemed, to Papanek, strangely flat. While on the golf beat, he coaxed a few rewrites out of Jenkins, most notably at the 1984 Masters where Ben Crenshaw won his first major.

"Gil was a recluse and weird son of a bitch," Jenkins concluded. "Did not inspire any kind of loyalty, and it was like he didn't want anybody else to be able to write well. We didn't get along much. I'd stay away from him. And by that time, I'm a book author. He thought of himself as a fiction writer, and I'd gotten lucky with *Semi-Tough* and stuff, and that pissed him off. I was pretty much a prima donna by then, although I never shirked an assignment, but I couldn't get a golfer on the cover, couldn't get any golf in the magazine. He thought it was a stupid corporate sport."

Privately and not so privately, Rogin and Mulvoy were saying out loud what was on a lot of other staffers' minds. Executive Ralph Graves compared Jenkins covering a golf tournament to Theodore White covering a political convention: "People were interviewing *Dan*."

"I think Dan was not really sweating, or working as hard as he had in the past," said Papanek, who began to doubt the vaunted Jenkins method of covering a tournament from the clubhouse or veranda. "When he didn't go out before, he had more guys coming in. Then, I think fewer guys came to him because guys were younger, and they didn't know Dan so well. He wasn't part of the crowd as much as he had been years earlier. But I certainly think there could have been ways to get Dan to take a little more pride, make a little bit more effort, in the work he was doing. And perhaps that is what Rogin's job should have been as managing editor, rather than the perennial angry screaming tirades of threatening his job, and those sorts of things." The tirades, significantly, were never personally directed at Jenkins. Editors and reporters took the brunt of Rogin's rage, until the 1984 British Open.

Seve Ballesteros rallied for the win and Jenkins wrote the story, on the usual tight deadline. As with much of his later work, it included more exposition about the importance of the event, and fewer instances of behind-the-scenes observation and anecdotage that had marked his earlier work. Papanek had made the trip over to St. Andrews and had no problems with the piece. "I got the story, read it—I think it was edited in New York by someone else," he remembered. "I wasn't really involved, so I didn't know anything. Nobody called, nobody told me from New York that this story wasn't acceptable and needed to be rewritten and what the fuck was Dan doing and how dare he. I got none of that."

But the piece was eviscerated, severely rewritten, again by Mulvoy. According to Mulvoy, Jenkins's original story left Rogin in such a rage that he wanted to fire Jenkins on the spot, only to be talked out of it by Mulvoy himself. Instead, Rogin decided that he would put him on probation. But first he went to the publisher, Don Barr. "I knew there would be an uproar, because both Jenkins and Shrake are so sold on themselves,"

Rogin said (an odd reason, considering Shrake had left the magazine five years earlier). "So I checked with the publisher to see whether he was of value to advertisers and he said absolutely not. Mulvoy said go for it. I was a very compulsive person, but I didn't fire him. I had no intention of firing him. Never crossed my mind. I was sort of punishing him, putting him in detention or something because he was driving us crazy."

When Jenkins got back to the *SI* offices the next week, there was a memo in his mailbox from Rogin, informing him that he was being "benched" from the year's final major, the PGA Championship at Shoal Creek. "It said I'd really let him down, that I'd sloughed it off," Jenkins said. "He missed every subtlety in the piece. He said 'You're concentrating on books and movies and not giving us your best work. I'm going to have to think a long time, long and hard, if I want to keep you on as the golf writer.'"

Anyone who knew Jenkins slightly knew what his reaction to such a note would be. "I went fucking crazy. I told my wife, 'I'm not gonna work for that cocksucker anymore!'"

That weekend, Jenkins wrote a short note of resignation that would become legendary within the halls of *SI*. "I'm going to relieve you the worry about what to do with your golf coverage," it said, "because I shan't be writing that for you anymore." He quickly signed column deals with both *Playboy* and *Golf Digest*; both publications had been courting him for years.

The news of the resignation, and the events that led up to it, would cause the biggest storm at *SI* since Laguerre's exit. Even longtime admirers of Rogin felt he'd botched it. "Gil was just dead wrong, and Gil should have been strung up," said Jerry Tax. "That loss was about as staggering, from my point of view, as the magazine has ever suffered. It never should have lost Dan Jenkins. He was synonymous with this magazine."

But the damage had been done. "They all started calling me," said Jenkins, "and they were saying, 'Oh, you can't do this, You can't do this.' And I said, 'Fuck you, fuck you. I'm outta here.' So then all my pals from the magazine, we started to get drunk together. I stayed on until the end of the year on salary, but I didn't hit another lick. I'd just go to the offices and open my mail."

And Jenkins and Rogin never spoke again.

Rogin would continue to be perplexed, years later, by the significance that others placed on Jenkins's exit. "He seemed intransigent about it," said Papanek of Rogin. "He always seemed not to give a shit about what anybody thought, or what Dan thought, or how Dan felt, or how anybody at the magazine felt, or how any reader might feel not having Dan Jenkins at the magazine anymore. As far as Gil was concerned, the guy lost it. He didn't care anymore, he had no pride, he wasn't working hard and he was insurgent and impudent and good riddance."

At the heart of the matter was the simple fact that, while others had coaxed compelling writing out of Dan Jenkins, Rogin didn't seem to want to try.

"Dan responded, like all writers, to affection and admiration and things," said Sarah Ballard, who along with Walter Bingham was Jenkins's closest friend still at the magazine. "And he got a lot of that from Laguerre. With Gil, I think he was crippled to some degree, psychologically, by the pounding. I think it may have been just getting older, too. But Dan used to do his best work with one hand tied behind his back. And he began to get a little nervous. He began to lose a little bit of confidence and I think Rogin probably had a lot to do with it. And Mulvoy, too. Mulvoy just had to destroy people. He's been doing it forever. And he took on Dan, and I would have bet my life that he couldn't do it to Dan, but I think he did."

Jenkins's exit confirmed what many had long suspected: that the balance of power had decisively shifted from writers to editors. Jenkins was one of the last of *SI*'s front line of writers who still lived in New York. Those days of drinking and banter and camaraderie between writers and editors were gone. "The atmosphere began to change with the spinning off of writers to other cities," said Ballard. "It began with John Underwood and then Bud Shrake and then Ron Fimrite. Take the writers, take the talent and the brains out of the place and you're left with . . . drones, as Dan would say. Not that there weren't some very ordinary writers before. But take these guys away and you don't have a lot left. It was just a good magazine, after that point. It wasn't the place that had been so much fun."

• • •

Rogin's behavior seemed more uneven than usual throughout 1984. But what his staff didn't know was that he was caught in a corporate double-bind in which his skill as a magazine-maker was in danger of costing him the very job that he so loved. Both Grunwald and corporate editor Jason McManus were impressed with his raw brainpower, mental acquisitiveness, and editing skills. In a series of long consultations, they agreed that Rogin was the only editor in the company with the necessary qualities to save Time Inc.'s flagging science monthly *Discover*.

During the spring of 1984, Grunwald lunched with Rogin several times on the 47th floor, broaching the subject of moving into the *Discover* job. But Rogin was sincere in his belief that he had the best job in the world, and he resisted at every turn. "He'd ask me to go and I'd just say no," Rogin said. "I fought him all the way—I had all these fallback positions. I'd be the editor of both. I'd be the supra-editor of both. Every way I could think of to get out of this. I didn't want to go and then he finally said, 'I insist.' And I realized I had no option."

Rogin was crestfallen. *Discover* publisher Jim Hayes recalled later that Rogin spent his first few months on the new job telling everyone, including potential advertisers, that he didn't really want to be there, that he'd been "ripped from the breast of *Sports Illustrated.*"

Rogin would leave *SI* with an uneven record. While the annual profits of the magazine had tripled during his tenure, from $17 million a year to more than $50 million, the nature of the magazine had changed. While some writers, like Deford and Moore, prospered under him, others, like Jenkins (and George Plimpton), were neglected and cast out. In essence, Rogin's role was to bring *SI* into an all-color age, where pictures often took precedence over words. And from here, there was no going back.

In late September 1984, just days after getting the news that he'd have to go to *Discover,* Rogin was called into Grunwald's office. The editor-in-chief was sitting with McManus. He was curt and to the point. He looked across the desk at Rogin and said, "We're thinking that we're going to name Mark Mulvoy the new managing editor. Are we making a mistake?"

"No," Rogin said, head bowed.

Rogin was torn, happy for Mulvoy but stricken over what the move meant to Peter Carry, whom Rogin had assured, on many occasions, would get his endorsement as the magazine's next ME. He didn't know how to break the news to Carry that he hadn't recommended him for the job. Ultimately, he never did tell him.

And so on Thursday afternoon, September 27, Grunwald summoned Mark Mulvoy to his office and offered Mulvoy the job as managing editor of *Sports Illustrated.* The raw, unpolished kid from Dorchester had risen to the top of one of America's premier magazines. And he'd earned it—he had a chance, and he seized it.

That afternoon, beaming, he was walking down the halls, telling people he'd just gotten the job. "I was pleased," said Creamer. "Mulvoy really had energy and drive, and I was really fed up with Gil."

The staff was shocked and Peter Carry, who walked into something of an ambush when he was called to Grunwald's office the same day and "congratulated" on his promotion to *executive* editor, the number two job, was crushed. But the contest had been fair and Mulvoy ("last going in, first coming out," said one executive of the process) had emerged the winner.

What his peers only sensed then was a difference that would be made manifest later. For decades the top editors and writers at *Sports Illustrated* had been distinguished by their wide range of interests, their sophisticated sensibilities: Rogin had his fiction and his perfectionism; Laguerre had his war and his renaissance eclecticism; Jenkins had an imagination spawned in Hollywood myths and Texas lore; Deford had a literary gallantry and a fascination with American ephemera. But Mark Mulvoy had only sports. He didn't read books, didn't have hobbies, and couldn't remember seeing "more than one or two" motion pictures during his high school years. Mark Mulvoy was a pure product of the world of sports, and little else.

And soon, *Sports Illustrated* would begin to reflect his sensibilities.

# CHAPTER 15

# THE BIG PICTURE

As he turned over his dream job to his unlikely successor, Gilbert Rogin's parting advice to Mark Mulvoy was succinct: "Don't fuck it up."

But Mulvoy had waited too long for that to happen. For years, he'd observed the life of a managing editor, the choices made, the problems faced, the power possessed. Now he intended to make changes and to consolidate his power in ways that Rogin didn't and that Terrell wouldn't. And though Mulvoy knew there could never be another André Laguerre, he wanted his vision of the magazine to dominate *SI* as completely as Laguerre's had.

In this, he would eventually succeed.

"I think what Mark brought to the magazine was a sort of daring new sense of confidence," said Bill Nack, who would clash with him frequently in the years ahead. "Mark is not afraid of his viscera. Many guys are; they act only with their head. Mark was not much of a writer, but he had a writer's sensibility, where stuff really comes from. Adlai Stevenson once said, 'All the great decisions in life are made by the viscera; the mind merely ratifies it later.' And Mark seems to have an understanding of that."

Coming early, staying late, Mulvoy was a fount of energy, generally heard before seen. Within the halls of *SI*, his voice became ubiquitous, the pushy, south Boston scrappiness still evident in his high, reedy accent. Those who knew him had learned to live with his repetitive use of clichés, like "No way, Jose" and "That's the way the cookie crumbles." But while Mulvoy often spoke in clichés, he had a more cultivated visual sense than any of his predecessors. He intuitively understood that it was a waste of *SI*'s design power to run small, detailed color pictures. Like showing an epic movie on a small television screen, the scale compromised the effect.

So his first change was to pick only the most evocative pictures and run them larger, not just with double-truck spreads on the news lead but with full page and page-and-a-half pictures throughout. It gave the magazine a bolder, more vibrant look, making a more forceful statement than Rogin's busy style. which could include ten pictures in a four-page story.

In coverage, Mulvoy modified and further narrowed Rogin's field of interest. The new ME was interested in the six core team sports—pro and college football and basketball, major league baseball and hockey—as well as big events in golf and tennis. Compared to Rogin, he cared little about track and field, swimming, or boxing. But the bigger change involved the magazine's sensibilities. For decades, there had been a dissonance between *SI*'s story mix and its reputation among average sports fans. In 1972, long after *SI* had shed its most effete and arcane sporting leisure elements, Jenkins would joke in *Semi-Tough* that *SI* was "a slick cookbook for the two-yacht family." Another ten years later, long after the time that the magazine had stopped venturing so far afield, newspaper columnists persisted in mocking *SI*'s perceived hauteur. "This is a publication easily impressed by expensive projects," wrote Blackie Sherrod in 1982, "such as diving for the elusive ermine in far-off Bonwit Teller's and egret-watching from Princess Grace's balcony." In that sense, the magazine's sophisticated eclecticism, refined by Laguerre and sustained in large part by Terrell and Rogin, was both admired and mocked. But because Mulvoy's interests and experiences were so narrow in relation to his predecessors', he was less comfortable with the writerly bonus piece on cricket, or the annual news lead on the NCAA lacrosse championship. Mulvoy was more like the typical American sports fan, whose own interests had narrowed in the television age. "Mark's genius is that he *was* our reader," said writer Steve Wulf. "And he was able to translate the content of the magazine into what our readers wanted to read. If he wasn't interested in something, then by and large our readers weren't going to be interested."

Mulvoy would find justification for these decisions with the help of modern research, relying to a greater degree than ever before on readership studies and focus groups. Every time a writer groused about the average bonus piece being cut from 12–13 pages to 9–10, or the narrowing of *SI*'s coverage, Mulvoy would trot out the readership numbers. Those surveys showed that the discursive, off-track features that many longtime *SI* readers cherished—Mark Kram writing on the Flying Wallendas, or Roy Blount, Jr., discussing the humble opossum—didn't score high, weren't read by nearly as many readers as a news story on a football game. What the surveys couldn't measure, of course, was resonance. Often the stories with the lowest readership levels, like the sprawling bonus pieces or quirky features, wound up staying with readers long after the game stories were forgotten. In the January 26, 1981, issue, the best-read article was Paul Zimmerman's Super Bowl preview. But a decade later, the only thing the issue was remembered for was Deford's oft-quoted profile of Bobby Knight, "The Rabbit Hunter." That wasn't the sort of thing that readership surveys could easily identify.

Stories about the outdoors were sharply proscribed, to the point that hunting, fishing, and environmental issues virtually disappeared from the magazine. "If it didn't have a green on it and a flag in it, it wasn't the outdoors as far as Mark was concerned," said one editor.

Through years of cocktail parties in Westchester County and hundreds of rounds at Apawamis Golf Club, Mulvoy had much more of a grounding in business than many of his colleagues at the magazine. It wasn't a coincidence that his conception of *SI* in the mid-'80s was similar to what other businesses, especially movie studios, were doing at the same time. It was an era in which studios were using sophisticated test marketing to help make movies more palatable, and in which presold blockbusters were counted on to show huge opening weekend grosses. With Mulvoy, the emphasis was on newsstand sales, which were almost completely dependent upon who was on the cover. Newsstand sales, always closely monitored at *SI*, began to take on a greater importance, far out of proportion with the 4 percent of circulation for which they accounted.

"Everything was eventually done by the numbers," said Deford. "A football player sells better than a hockey player; therefore, this week, we put a football player on the cover. A football player in action sells better than the portrait of a football player; therefore, we put the action shot on the cover. We'd never have a painting of a football player, because a photograph sells better. A Cowboy sells better than a Cardinal. Just bring it down to the ultimate . . . but you can't do that every week. And that's what was happening."

The narrowed story mix and more commercially conscious covers would help ensure that the magazine would continue to make record profits. And that, in turn, would continue to guarantee the benign neglect from the 34th floor. Neither of the top executives on 34 cared much about sports. Editorial director Jason McManus, who had direct oversight duties of *SI*, was a baseball fan and little else. And when a friend of Henry Grunwald's was asked to name the editor-in-chief's favorite sport, he replied, "Opera."

For the first time in the magazine's history, the managing editor was a more knowledgeable and more avid sports fan than anyone else on the staff. And he also had the coin of the editor's realm: story ideas, a precious quality, especially in the years after staff writers left New York. Mulvoy had a unique skill for packaging stories. Immediately, the season previews were more cohesive and more resonant. Where senior editors had too often fallen into the habit of assigning stories on whatever team was hot— this week the Hawks, next week the Knicks—Mulvoy knew sports well enough to make other connections.

And he knew how to generate news with covers. The cover of the 1984 college basketball preview issue was shot in the Oval Office, with Georgetown coach John Thompson and All-America center Patrick Ewing flanking President Reagan. A few months later, Mulvoy arranged for a portrait of baseball commissioner Peter Ueberroth and Willie Mays and Mickey Mantle, the two legends who were allowed to renew their formal relationship with major league baseball under his leadership.

But the change was more than just superficial. The college basketball preview issue in 1984 included a John Edgar Wideman essay on the much-maligned, oft-misunderstood John Thompson. For the year-end double issue that wrapped up the Olympic year 1984, Mulvoy ran a 20-page story by William Oscar Johnson on Seoul, host of the '88 Summer Games. Mulvoy reenergized the magazine, assigning staff writer Jack McCallum to the pro basketball beat, where for the rest of the decade he wrote compellingly about the Lakers-Celtics rivalry and the emergence of Michael Jordan as the league's next transcendent star.

"What Mark brought to the magazine was his own energy, his better understanding of sports, which Gil had lacked a little bit," said Deford. "Gil was like a first-generation immigrant trying to catch on. Mark was old family; he *knew* sports. He had a lot of good ideas for stories. I always thought that was his strength."

So although he was viewed as an intellectual lightweight by many of his writers and, by all accounts, didn't read anything longer than a bonus piece, Mulvoy brought a sense of purposeful urgency to *SI* that hadn't existed, really, since the early '70s. "Mulvoy has a lot of strengths," said Ray Cave. "People tend to work on Mulvoy's weaknesses instead of his strengths. He kept the magazine very hard-sports oriented. Also, more than any of the editors except Laguerre, he felt it had a sense of social purpose. He really worked hard on having *Sports Illustrated* cover the problems in sports. If you're going to be a sports fan, you can't just go to the games; you've got to understand that sports have changed a lot. Mulvoy was able to keep up with that."

And yet, it was inevitable that he would alienate many of his veteran writers. Those who valued the magazine for its sophistication were fated to loathe Mulvoy's more mainstream, reportorial approach. They also resented his longtime habit of criticizing one staff member while talking to another; Mulvoy had become notorious for giving hollow compliments laden with subtly denigrating jabs on the back end.

"Nobody's ever done anything to suit him," said Jenkins years later. "That's how he got where he is. But I knew that; I just thought it was laughable, because he never had any talent. He was a terrible writer, he was a horrible editor, and he was an expense account thief if there ever was one. That didn't make him any different from a lot of people." Even Jenkins, though, allowed that the magazine received a bracing dose of energy in Mulvoy's early days. "It was more lively under Mark. Mark would at least make a decision. It might be wrong, but he would fuckin' make one."

Mulvoy had expected some of this criticism, but what surprised him at the time was the way that he was condemned for his machinations on behalf of Rogin. When Mulvoy called Dan Jenkins a month after his resignation, June Jenkins, in a rare act of rancor completely out of character, told him to fuck off and hung up the phone. Some of Mulvoy's biggest critics were still in the building. William Oscar Johnson used to sit in his office late in 1984 and talk loudly to other writers about Mulvoy's faults. "He's got the attention span of a gnat," he'd say, loud enough to be heard down the hall. And Mulvoy, who possessed an almost bizarre fascination with his critics, would hear. His insecurity became legend. Unlike Rogin, though, he'd become politically adept enough to conceal much of the rancor, or express it more selectively. And, as he'd done for decades, he continued to work harder than almost anyone around him. Calls would come to photo editors and writers at all hours of the night. If Laguerre's favorite mode of communication was over drinks at the bar, Mulvoy's was over the phone. It was a different style for a different age. But it wasn't without its triumphs.

• • •

Early in 1985, text editor Myra Gelband called special contributor George Plimpton in to meet with her and Mulvoy. Plimpton had been largely ignored during the Rogin years, another result of Rogin's curious lack of affection for accomplished writers. (Just months earlier, Rogin had suggested, to Gelband's dismay, dropping Plimpton from the masthead.) With the new regime in place, she wanted to bring Plimpton back into the inner circle.

Because *SI* had an April 1 publication date coming up in 1985, Gelband had suggested to Mulvoy that Plimpton do a piece on various sports-related April Fools' pranks. But as Plimpton and Gelband and Mulvoy sat in the managing editor's office, going over notes from other reporters and files from stringers, they came to the conclusion that most of the jokes played on April Fools' Day were of the had-to-be-there variety.

Then Mulvoy volunteered a suggestion. "Why don't you do your own April Fools' story?"

Plimpton's blue eyes sparkled with the mischievous possibilities of the suggestion. Within minutes the trio had concocted the idea of an eccentric, mysterious baseball player.

"What if we have him coming from Appalachia?" suggested Plimpton.

"What if we have him coming from *Harvard*?" suggested Gelband, knowing that his alma mater was sure to send Plimpton off on a fit of creativity. He left Mulvoy's office energized, walking out of the Time & Life Building into a driving rainstorm, walking all the way back to his Upper East Side apartment, lost in the infinite possibilities of his pending invention. Over the next few days, Plimpton constructed "The Curious Case of Sidd Finch."

By late January, he returned with a story, and Mulvoy called his friend Frank Cashen, president of the New York Mets, who agreed to play along with the prank. When *SI* readers opened the April 1, 1985, issue, they found a bonus piece whose lead was sure to pique their interest: "The secret cannot be kept much longer. Questions are being asked, and sooner rather than later the New York Mets management will have to produce a statement. It may have started unraveling in St. Petersburg, Florida, two weeks ago, on March 14, to be exact, when Mel Stottlemyre, the Met pitching coach, walked over to the forty-odd Met players doing their morning calisthenics at the Payson Field complex not far from the Gulf of Mexico, a solitary figure among the pulsation of jumping jacks, and motioned three Mets out of the exercise."

Plimpton then proceeded to introduce the shrouded, inscrutable character of Sidd (short for Siddhartha) Finch, a Tibetan philosophy student who played the French horn and who was a source of intrigue for the Mets, due to his superhuman ability to throw a baseball 168 miles per hour. Photographer Lane Stewart had recruited a Chicago junior high school teacher named Joe Berton to play the part of Finch, and he was brought to St. Petersburg to take part in the veristic photos, with the help of a few Mets. Mulvoy, Gelband, and Plimpton all agreed that the story needed to be played straight throughout. Gelband had the idea to make the first letters of the words in the subhead spell out "Happy April Fools' Day." So she went home one night and sketched the secret message out, making it all the more effective by hewing to *SI*'s arch, knowing style:

"He's a pitcher, part yogi and part recluse. Impressively liberated from our opulent life-style, Sidd's deciding about yoga—and his future in baseball."

"My deal with Jason McManus at that time was he didn't want any surprises," said Mulvoy. "In other words, if the magazine came out and there were any surprises, he was in deep shit, because Grunwald would say, 'What's this goddamn thing in *SI*?' The magazine came out. And a lot of people went ballistic. Bob Miller, the publisher, was fearful that maybe we were duping the reader, and the advertiser, and everybody was upset. McManus was all over me because I pulled a fast one. And within three days the tide turned completely. Everybody wrote columns about what a wonderful spoof it was."

Grunwald was in Arizona, attending a *Time* ad sales meeting and suddenly, on Thursday afternoon, March 28, found himself fielding questions about the story. When it hit the newsstands that day, the prank found not just readers but other news organizations falling for the hoax. The *St. Petersburg Times* sent an investigative reporter to the Mets training camp. Plimpton was traveling at the time, but at about two in the morning, the *New York Times* tracked him down by phone. An angry writer from the sports department demanded, "It's a hoax, isn't it?" "Of course," said Plimpton sleepily, wishing later that he would have prolonged the ruse.

When Grunwald saw Mulvoy in the lobby of the Time & Life Building a few days later, he pulled him aside and smiled. "Mark, I don't know if I would have had the courage to run it myself, but I'm glad you did." Mulvoy, remembering it later, saw it as a validation of his editorship. "If that had gone the other way, who knows what the hell would have happened? But you know, reader reaction was very positive and let's face it—I mean, Sidd Finch became a book. Revived Plimpton's career by the way."


But Mulvoy needed his own star writer, around whom he could build his new version of the magazine. Laguerre had Jenkins. Terrell had Underwood. Rogin had Deford. Mark Mulvoy found Rick Reilly.

Reilly belonged to a generation of American boys who had grown up with *SI*, been shaped by the magazine and its worldview. Growing up alienated from an alcoholic father who called him Retardo, Reilly became an approval-starved class clown in high school, who got much of his best material from the pages of *Sports Illustrated*. When Reilly was 12, he crawled down to the edge of the stands at Folsom Field in his hometown of Boulder and introduced himself to Walter Iooss, Jr. Iooss paid him $12 to carry his equipment around, and Reilly saw him shoot the game that wound up on the October 1, 1970, cover. He'd always been angry the week that the swimsuit issue arrived—fewer sports stories—until he turned 13 and saw the whole matter in a different light. As a teenager, he'd closely followed the media storm caused by Douglas S. Looney's critical piece in *SI* on Colorado coach Chuck Fairbanks. Later, Looney came to speak at Reilly's high school, and the young *SI* fan eagerly showed him around. Reilly asked him about the fallout from his Colorado story. "Well, yeah, I get a lot of letters," Looney said. "Most of them are in crayon because they don't give these people sharp things." That day, Rick Reilly knew he wasn't going to be an athlete, and because of his adenoidal voice, probably wasn't going to be an announcer. But he would be a sportswriter.

He went to work at the *Boulder Daily Camera* in college and at the *Denver Post* right out of school, and was a staff writer at the *Los Angeles Times* by the age of 24. In 1985, he got a call from *SI* staffer Jill Lieber, to say the magazine wanted to talk to him. *SI* flew him up from Vero Beach that March, where Reilly had been covering the Dodgers at spring training. Mulvoy took Reilly to lunch on the 47th floor, where the nervous writer managed to open his menu so clumsily that he knocked a glass of water onto Mulvoy. But he was hired and given a clear mission: he'd write college football and he'd cover the majors in golf. Mulvoy wanted him to be the next Jenkins. It was pretty close to what Rick Reilly had always wanted to be. At the *Times*, Reilly's puckish one-liners and irreverent style had drawn comparisons to Jim Murray. But raised on *SI*, he'd been influenced by a variety of Laguerre-era writers. In his work, there were clearly visible flashes of Deford's sentimentality, Kirkpatrick's ear for pop cultural references, and, as much as anything, Jenkins's sarcasm.

From the start, Mulvoy and Reilly had an affinity. The editor found a captive audience for the details of his golf exploits. And the writer found someone who knew he could be a star. When the hiring was made official, in the spring of 1985, Mulvoy sent Reilly a bottle of Dom Perignon.

Reilly would earn it. His breakthrough came with two stories in the April 21, 1986, issue, a feature on one of his sportswriting heroes and a news lead that evoked comparisons to another. The feature was "King of the Sports Page," a look at the turmoil-filled middle age of legendary *SI* alum Jim Murray, a former mentor of Reilly's at the *Los Angeles Times*. In the news story, writing about Jack Nicklaus's improbable victory at the Masters, Reilly's prose even had the rhythms of the Jenkins style: "Here had come Nicklaus, an American legend still under warranty, armed with a putter the size of a Hoover attachment, denting the back of Augusta's holes with 25-foot putts at an age when most guys are afraid to take their putter back."

At *SI*, there was jealousy about Reilly getting such choice assignments, as well as some resentment at his all-too-apparent attempts to emulate Jenkins. "You just wanted to pull him aside at one of those tournaments," said one fellow staffer, "and say, 'Hey, Rick, wherever did you get the idea to drink scotch and coffee at the same time?'"

• • •

By the mid-'80s, Jule Campbell had carved out her own little empire within the *Sports Illustrated* realm. The production of the swimsuit issue had become a year-round job, with planning, location scouts, fashion markets, and model interviews, culminating in several weeks of dawn-to-dusk shoots.

Campbell's fashion influence extended beyond mere swimsuits. A one-piece nylon ski suit that she'd asked a designer to make in 1967 became the blueprint for the next generation of ski fashion. And Marquette coach Al McGuire had been so impressed with her fashion sense that he'd asked her to design a set of uniforms for the Warriors. The sequined gold and powder blue pullover combination was worn by Marquette when it won the national championship in 1977.

More significantly, she had become one of the few people in the fashion industry who could literally make a career. Cheryl Tiegs was only the first of a series of *SI* cover girls who became household names. In 1974, Campbell discovered a 150-pound California teenager named Christie Brinkley, giving her the break that would effectively launch her career. In the early '80s, Campbell booked a young teenager from Czechoslovakia named Paulina Porizkova without meeting her (the first time she'd booked a model for a shoot without a face-to-face interview). Porizkova was destined to become a multimillionaire at any rate, but the *SI* spots would establish her as an American star.

In 1984, Campbell interviewed an athletic 17-year-old Australian novice named Elle Macpherson. When the teenager showed for her face-to-face interview at *SI* in leggings and an oversize sweater, she brought her skimpy beginner's portfolio without the requisite swimsuit photos, only head shots. Campbell was encouraged but noncommittal. "I can't really see what your body looks like," explained Campbell. "I'll have to talk to you again later, because you don't have any pictures."

At that, the determined Macpherson smiled and stood up, pulling her sweater over her head to reveal her toned, naked torso.

Campbell blinked and glanced out her window; her office had a nice view of the Equitable office building across the street, and the Equitable building, in turn, had a nice view of her office.

"Would you put it on again, please?" she said evenly. "I get the idea."

Macpherson got the booking.

Campbell developed friendships with several of *SI*'s models over the years. But she was vital in turning Macpherson from a preening schoolgirl into a supermodel. On their first shoot in the fall of 1984 on Shark Bay in Australia, she wanted Macpherson and Porizkova to work together, because they had become friends. Porizkova was as natural as a model gets, all fluid moves and languorous disposition.

"And when Elle would get in front of the camera," remembered Campbell, "because she was brand new, her chest would come out and her butt would come out. And I'd say, 'Elle, you don't have to do all that for us. Your body is beautiful in repose. That's not what I want—just be yourself.' And she would start crying, 'Can't I do anything to please you? Paulina is so perfect.' And I would say, 'No, you have your own look. Just project to the camera and be yourself.' At first it didn't come naturally to her, like some of the others, but she did learn."

In subsequent years, Macpherson would strike an assured, novel pose and Campbell would exclaim with surprise, "Elle! I never saw you do that before."

"I know," Macpherson would say proudly. "I practiced it just for you."

As Bob Miller and Mulvoy sat in a meeting in the fall of 1984, they agreed that the magazine hadn't really done enough to promote the swimsuit issue. Campbell concurred. She'd tried to pitch the idea of marketing a *Sports Illustrated* swimsuit calendar to Philip Howlett, the previous publisher, but he'd rejected it as impractical. Miller embraced the idea and Mulvoy, for his part, decided to expand the number of pages of swimsuits, from the 22 pages that Rogin had devoted in 1984 (itself an all-time high) to 30 in 1985. Because the swimsuit issue traditionally had a larger editorial page budget, due to the increased ad sales, efforts had been made in the past to load the issue up with minor sports, travel pieces, and other departures from the formula. "We've got to fill the pages anyway," reasoned Mulvoy, "so why not fill them with swimsuits rather than a story about a kayaker?" For his part, Miller decided that since advertisers were so eager to get into the swimsuit issue, *SI* should start charging more for it, updating the rate base by one million for that issue alone. With that in mind, he began to promote it more vigorously. The cover would be unveiled Tuesday morning, the day before newsstand sales, in *USA Today* (which traditionally gave it front-page play in its Life section). The swimsuit model who made the cover (in '85, it was Porizkova's second straight cover; in 1986, Macpherson's first) would then be trotted out to talk shows, sometimes along with Jule Campbell, sometimes not, to further drum up publicity.

The results were dramatic. The 1983 issue, with Tiegs on the cover, sold 300,000 copies on the newsstand. The 1984 issue, Rogin's last and Porizkova's first cover, sold a record 451,000 copies on the newsstand. But then the issue took off: in 1985, newsstand sales were 791,000; a year later they went to 1.18 million, and in 1987 they just missed 1.5 million. The commercial success only pushed the magazine further into ancillary marketing; by the late '80s, both the *Sports Illustrated* swimsuit wall calendar and desk calendar were hits; the "sunshine issue" had become big business.

• • •

The first year of Mulvoy's reign had been a kinetic success, but it had left some bruised egos in its wake. Some of his more daring commercial choices (like putting Hulk Hogan on the cover) were treated as heresy by the writers, but what they really resented was having their stories cut to make way for larger pictures. The December 17, 1985, issue of the *Village Voice* brought much of the new dissension into the open. Writing in the paper's Jockbeat column, David Herndon quoted anonymous sources saying that morale was low and that articles were being shortened by an average of 25 percent to make way for more and larger pictures. Mulvoy's responses only heightened the furor. Mulvoy, wrote Herndon, "denied there is a morale problem among the writers—'and anybody on the edit staff who says there is doesn't know what he is talking about.' He termed the observation that stories are running 25 percent shorter 'a patent lie,' explaining that stories formerly printed at 200 to 225 lines are now appearing at a length of 150 to 175 lines (okay, so math wasn't his favorite subject)."

Within months, John Underwood had seen enough, and was so alienated from Mulvoy that he sent his resignation to Ray Cave, who had gone from *Time*'s managing editor to the number two executive position as editorial director. Underwood's letter was a long, soulful lament, from one Laguerre disciple to another:

Professionally, I think the magazine is only a facsimile of the one I was originally drawn to and reflects little of the philosophy that fired it up and spun it into orbit years ago. As you know, I have always steered clear of that portion of the editorial process, and the office politics that go with it, but I am doubtful of a judgment that would make journalism out of a massive April Fools' joke and a Jim Brown "comeback" at age 48. It might just be the curmudgeon coming out in me, of course. But I wonder if a quality publication can live forever on impetus and that kind of thinking, or withstand the editing and writing it now suffers. I hold to the belief that *SI* must never be tempted into becoming a slick, weekly version of *Sport*, for its strength is in its universal appeal and not its ability to reek of the locker room, but I think that is exactly where it is heading. I hope I am wrong.

I am on firmer ground, of course, with my complaints as a writer. They can be summed up in a sentence: the editing at *SI* now is the worst I have ever encountered. The reason is not hard to ferret out. Editors, newly consecrated, who themselves never wrote a meaningful sentence for a meaningful publication, are making decisions on the worth of writers and their stories and handling their copy as superiors.

Few were suprised by Underwood's exit; many felt he had lost his love for the games long ago. In 1979, he wrote *The Death of an American Game*, a darkly ruminative look at the state of college football. The severity of his worldview was occasionally a source of mirth among his colleagues. "The National Football League draft is the most demeaning form of labor oppression I know," he said in one pub memo. And yet, Underwood's resignation would be the final exit of a decade-long exodus following Laguerre. With the exception of Deford and Kirkpatrick, who endured, many of the stars were gone: Jenkins, Underwood, Kram, Blount, Shrake. The heart of an extraordinary magazine had left, often bitterly. Some of the cases, in retrospect, couldn't be helped. But all of them together signaled a loss of responsiveness on the part of the people in power.

"The other writers of consequence bucked heads with Mulvoy and left," said Deford. "It's as simple as that. More and more authority was congregated with the editor. That's not to say that Laguerre and Terrell did not have authority, but they allowed writers more freedom. More and more it became an adversarial relationship."

Underwood's letter also complained about Mulvoy's reluctance to conduct investigative pieces in the wake of Ariel Sharon's libel trial against *Time*. Coming right on the heels was *SI*'s own day in court, with former South Carolina University women's basketball coach Pam Parsons, who sued *SI* for libel after a piece by Jerry Kirshenbaum and Jill Lieber that was published shortly after she resigned. The story, in the February 8, 1982, issue, quoted sources who charged that Parsons had a sexual relationship with one of her players, Tina Buck. *SI* won the case with a spectacular surprise witness, who had seen a report on the trial on the Cable News Network. The witness recalled seeing Buck and Parsons at a lesbian bar in Las Vegas, and called the Time Inc. customer service number, where an alert operator took her name and number. Parsons and Buck subsequently served four-month prison terms on perjury charges. But while the Parsons case ended in a rousing reaffirmation of *SI*'s reportorial practices and results, the long-term effect was less positive. One of the magazine's investigative reporters said that Kirshenbaum was shaken by the experience. "When Jerry came back, he was a completely different editor." Instead the magazine began running more "checkbook journalism," first-person stories written by athletes with *SI* writers, from Don Reese later in 1982, Gary McLain (who revealed his cocaine addiction while playing for national champion Villanova) in 1986, and South Carolina football player Frank Chaikan (who told of his steroid abuse) in 1988.

• • •

In 1986, Mulvoy was brought upstairs for a nine-month tour of duty on the 34th floor. The summons was unusual in that he'd only been editing the magazine for 18 months. To many staffers, it seemed further proof that while the executives respected the quality of leadership at *SI*, they didn't care much about the creative continuity of the magazine. Deford was upset, and wrote a letter to Grunwald complaining about the repeated intrusions. As Mulvoy left for 34, it was announced that assistant managing editors Ken Rudeen and Jerry Kirshenbaum would take turns editing the magazine.

But Mulvoy took the appointment with equanimity and decided it would be a perfect time to redesign the magazine. Gangel's award-winning design, conceived in 1960, was a clean, organized answer to the misguided jumble of the '50s *SI*. But his was a magazine designed to heighten the effect of black-and-white photography and occasional color. The attempts of his successors, Harvey Grut and Rick Warner, to update that format for the all-color *SI* had been ineffective at best and garish at worst.

The magazine in the '80s was plagued by numerous inset photographs, often inexplicably outlined in lime green or electric blue. To splash some more color, the departments were being introduced with loud, two-tone banners running across the page, a long way from the understated use of typography that Gangel had in mind.

Mulvoy had grand ideas of an updated *SI* for the next generation. He toyed with scrapping the full title in favor of running simply "SI" in large type on the cover, and he wanted to have the opportunity to feature a second photograph on the cover, a "teaser" picture similar to the upper-right-hand corner "flap" effect developed by Ray Cave and Walter Bernard in their 1977 redesign of *Time*.

The man hired to interpret Mulvoy's vision was a youthful, assured designer named Steven Hoffman, who had worked in the Time & Life Building through much of the summer of 1986, designing a prototype for a prospective women's fitness magazine called *You*. His work had attracted the attention of both Joe Marshall and Larry Keith, *SI* editors who had been detached for the project. Hoffman had attended the California Institute of the Arts, where he studied design and photography. But the *Esquire* covers of George Lois in the '60s beckoned him into magazine design and after five years as an associate art director at *New West* magazine, he moved to a similar job at *New York* magazine, before becoming a freelance design consultant for several magazines.

While Mulvoy worked on 34, Rudeen and Kirshenbaum were proceeding without incident. Kirshenbaum, who along with Larry Keith had been promoted to an AME position in 1985, had become a significant addition to the edit side, valued more for his comprehensive knowledge of the Olympics than for his line-editing skills (writers shared a mortal fear of having one of their stories "Kirshen-bombed"). But his affable demeanor and studied professionalism were a welcome antidote to Mulvoy's more combustible management style.

As the summer drew to a close, Mulvoy decided he wanted to give Deford a chance at the ME's chair. The offer surprised and pleased Deford and spoke to the odd relationship that the two men enjoyed. For curious reasons, Mulvoy and Deford managed to coexist, even though they grated on one another. Mulvoy, fresh off the smarting jolts of the loss of Jenkins and Underwood, wasn't about to alienate his last established star writer. And while they were certainly not suited for each other by disposition, they maintained a wary respect. Which didn't stop Deford from laughing with others about Mulvoy's obsession with money. And didn't stop Mulvoy from going into paroxysms of indignant bewilderment when he'd see one of Deford's two-minute television commentaries on NBC, which occasionally wandered off the topic of sports into more esoteric areas. Deford's television persona was that of a dashing, sartorially resplendent dandy; the patina of mildly affected southern courtliness had been accepted after a time by his colleagues, but Mulvoy found it pretentious.

But while he might have viewed Deford as a rival, he also recognized him as an asset. Deford accepted the offer to top-edit the magazine, and took over for a ten-week term that September. It was an extraordinary period; before taking over, Deford read through the files of stories that staffers had submitted but, for one reason or another, Mulvoy chose not to publish. Several were resurrected (one by Bill Nack, on jockey Laffit Pincay, won an Eclipse Award, as the year's best story on horse racing) and the writing staff, newly emboldened, relished the brief "Era of Good Feelings." Alex Wolff, a fellow Princeton graduate, remembered how the writers "were just pleased to be working with this legend." Another young staff writer, Austin Murphy, recalled "almost weeping with gratitude for Frank's touches." Few of those touches were placed on copy. In the let-Reagan-be-Reagan spirit of the times, Deford let his writers write, and elicited strong pieces throughout his brief term.

In Deford's second week as acting managing editor, he was working late one night when a young woman from the copy desk came in with a piece of text that needed Deford's initials to be sent out for typesetting. The woman handed Deford the paper, he initialed it, said, "Thank you," handed it to her, and went back to what he was doing. He realized, after a moment, that the woman was still standing there. "Is there anything else?" he asked.

"No, I just want you to know, I've been here five years now and that's the first time I've heard those words in this office."

Deford sat in his chair, dumbfounded.

"I'll tell you, I almost cried," he said, remembering the exchange a decade later. "I had to sort of catch my breath. And that was the way Gil and Mulvoy ran the show, in which it was this total, rude, arrogant display. I never got over that. I remember that moment at *SI*, sadly, more than I do any other. It was like learning something awful about your family."

In late October '86, as Deford's tenure was nearing completion, Mulvoy paid him a visit. Mulvoy's beloved Boston Red Sox seemed to be on a divine charge to the world championship, having come from a pitch away from elimination to vanquish the California Angels in the American League Championship Series. Mulvoy, working on the redesign, had stayed clear of Deford, but now, with Boston up three games to two on the Mets, Mulvoy was searching for the ideal cover blurb to celebrate the end of the Red Sox curse.

"We've got to come up with something *just* right," said Mulvoy.

"I've got it!" exclaimed Deford, grabbing a piece of scrap paper. He was pleased with himself.

Mulvoy came around behind his desk and looked over his shoulder as Deford sketched a dummy cover. In large letters, he sketched out his idea of the perfect cover headline. And it said: "BEAU SOX!"

Mulvoy's eyes widened, and his face contorted into a mask of repulsed indignation.

"What the *fuck* is that!?"

"Oh, come on," said Deford, still proud of his pun.

"What the fuck is that? *Beau Sox*!? No, Frank, I can't let you do that."

That evening at Shea Stadium, with Mulvoy in the crowd, Bill Buckner would muff a grounder in the bottom of the tenth. Two nights later, the Mets won game seven and the entire point would be moot.

The staff gave Deford a going-away present, a caricature signed by everyone. It was about this time that some staffers started referring to him as Mr. Roberts. "All I remember is when Mulvoy came back and took over for Deford again, he kept knocking Deford because the pictures weren't right," said Nack. "He was so jealous that people liked Frank and nobody liked him, nobody trusted him."

• • •

Down at *Discover*, the *SI* alumni were longing for the old days. Peter Carry had followed Rogin to the science magazine and, together, they engineered a remarkable turnaround in the magazine's editorial fortunes— it would go on to win a National Magazine Award for general excellence in 1986—but the bottom line was still problematic.

Back under his mentor, Carry worked well, although he hated the lack of urgency in a monthly magazine, and longed to go back to *SI*. On more than a couple of occasions, Mulvoy told him he'd be welcome back any time—he was finding that Keith, Kirshenbaum, and Bingham just couldn't handle the multitudinous details at which a trusted number two man like Carry had been so proficient.

Rogin missed his old job, and was made more miserable by the difficulty he was having with his girlfriend, Jacqueline Duvoisin. In the early '80s, the Human Dynamo had decided that, rather than continue a career as a social worker, what she really wanted to do was be a sports photographer. And while Rogin could be a fanatic on ethics issues, he'd developed another blind spot about her merits. He'd eased her into some *SI* assignments while he was managing editor, urging his staff to give her instruction. And when he moved to *Discover,* he made arrangements for her to continue getting assignments.

"When I got the job, Gil asked me to do one thing," remembered Mulvoy. "'Don't forget Jackie,' that's all he asked me. He had been a rabbi and everything else for me, and I don't think that's unreasonable. At the same time, she did about 10 percent of what he thought she should do. I mean, to him, she should have covered World Series, Super Bowls, every other goddamned thing."

Duvoisin was both insistent and abrasive; her lack of sports knowledge (one photographer insisted she stood on the infield before the Kentucky Derby and asked, "Which way do the horses run?") and her hyper persona (her tantrums and lack of decorum would get her thrown out of the British Open on more than one occasion) were proving a headache to much of the staff. "Jackie, being the person that she is, never made it important to get to a point where she could stand alone, on her own," said Myra Gelband. "She has always depended on Gil to fight her battles and to make headway. That has built resentment of her, not just at *SI* but outside the magazine."

Staffers crossed Duvoisin at their own risk. The week before the 1983 Super Bowl, veteran photographer Brian Lanker spent a day in the bathroom of his Beverly Hills Hotel room, explaining to Duvoisin the rudimentary concepts of lighting. Despite the help, she was furious at Lanker later in the week, when he left the lobby of the hotel to head to the game (she had been late to meet him in the lobby). Another day, Duvoisin was heard screaming at a man who was pouring coffee at the Time Inc. cafeteria, "My boyfriend's managing editor of *Sports Illustrated,* and you're not going to be here much longer!" It would go on for years, *SI*'s dark family secret and the single greatest blight on Rogin's brilliant but turbulent career.

When Time Inc. gave up and finally sold *Discover* in 1987, at a loss of more than $50 million, the move set in motion a chain of events that would affect *SI* well into the next decade. Before Rogin had left to go to *Discover,* Grunwald had promised him a job on 34. Having completed his mission, Rogin collected on his chit and was given the position of corporate editor. But by now, Jason McManus was the new editor-in-chief, and his dour, laissez faire attitude was a far cry from the Teutonic authoritarianism of Grunwald. McManus had been the surprise winner over Cave in the editor-in-chief succession struggle, and the move meant that Cave's days at the company were numbered.

On the 34th floor, there had existed a bias against executives directly overseeing a magazine that they had top-edited. Of course, the editor-in-chief was ultimately responsible for all the magazines, but his issue-by-issue critiques generally went to magazines he hadn't worked on. The same was true for the editorial director and all others who were working on the floor. Despite all this as precedent, Gilbert Rogin was assigned editorial oversight duties of *Sports Illustrated*.

McManus okayed the unusual arrangement for a variety of reasons. "I had never worked on *SI*," he said. "While I was a large baseball fan, I was not interested in other sports. And secondly, with Mulvoy, one of the frequent problems we had was the best writers would become the editors, the best editors would become the managing editors, and along the way, they sometimes had very little experience in actually developing managing skills, as opposed to writing and editing skills. Mark needed the tutelage in the early years, and obviously Rogin could provide that. The third most important reason was that Rogin was Mark's mentor and, even more than that, they were truly intimate colleagues. Normally the new managing editor would say, 'Give me anybody except the guy I just succeeded.' Whereas Mark wanted Rogin's help."

Also, Rogin insisted. And yet what resulted was a situation in which a Time Inc. executive (Rogin) was making calls and personal pleas on behalf of his girlfriend to the managing editor. Even Rogin's staunch defenders, like Myra Gelband, found the entire affair "imprudent." Peter Carry, who had stood by Rogin in the face of his own rejection to succeed him at *SI*, would eventually part with his mentor over the Duvoisin situation. And Mulvoy and Rogin, the old compatriots, were reduced to screaming matches. "He'd call, and I'd just say, 'Goddamnit, Gil, this is destroying me,'" remembered Mulvoy. "'I can't sleep because of this. I'm fed up with the whole goddamn thing.' Then he would back off for six months."

During Mulvoy's nine-month stay on the 34th floor, he had asked Neil Leifer (who had joined Cave at *Time* in the late '70s) to do a six-week study of the entire running of the photo department, where both production and morale were falling under Barbara Henckel. Leifer's stature had only increased since his days at *SI*, but he was still an *SI* shooter at heart. After interviews with dozens of people related to the photography department, Leifer submitted to Mulvoy a confidential 70-page memo that laid much of the problem at Henckel's managerial ineptitude, but also criticized Mulvoy's harsh managerial style.

The memo included a grave warning, though, that an even larger problem was looming. If Mulvoy didn't do something about "the Jackie situation," Leifer wrote, it could have terrible repercussions for the magazine. Leifer was not concerned that an underqualified girlfriend of an executive was working at the magazine. What did concern him, as well as others in the department, was that Rogin was deflating morale throughout the edit floor by intervening on her behalf.

"I said, 'Look, Gil Rogin is your boss. I understand that. If my boss called me in and said she's working for me, then she'd be working. I'm not going to lose my job over it. If I'm the picture editor of *SI* and I'm told that Jackie is one of my photographers, I may not like it but occasionally the boss does things like this. But I would not allow the idea of Gil coming down and complaining about the layout, and saying more of her pictures should be in there.' I know it happened. I investigated it pretty closely. That I wouldn't allow to happen. Not once. I will agree to have her work at the magazine; I will treat her as well as I can. I will keep in mind the fact that she sleeps with my boss. But not this."

But Mulvoy let the hectoring continue. And in time, it grew worse.

"It was a stick of dynamite already lit, standing there ready to go," said Peter Carry. When it finally blew, it would take a few careers with it.

CHAPTER 16

# LOVE AND INFAMY

## By 1987, even some of Mark

Mulvoy's harshest critics were grudgingly admitting that he had become a surprisingly effective managing editor. Mulvoy was placing his imprint on *SI*: the look of the magazine was bolder and more dramatic, *SI*'s enterprise stories were making news, the swimsuit issue had become a newsstand powerhouse, and Rick Reilly had grown into a star writer of the first magnitude. Internally, Peter Carry had returned from *Discover* to his executive editor position, and most of the problems in the photo department had been solved with the hiring of a new photo editor, veteran shooter Heinz Kluetmeier, who brought a persona of pleasant toughness to the job.

The most obvious change was the redesign, which allowed Mulvoy to drastically alter the internal look of the magazine and more reliably deliver on *SI*'s inherent promise to bring the reader the defining moments in sport. The new format premiered in the year-end double issue of 1986, with Sportsman of the Year Joe Paterno on the cover, but even then it was a work in progress. As it continued to evolve, Steve Hoffman showed a willingness to experiment further. The cover logotype was tweaked with the third issue, with Hoffman thickening the logo so that the letters of the title ran together in a bolder display. A few clearly misguided flourishes, such as the four-column format for the Scorecard, Inside Baseball, and Inside Football departments—were quickly scrapped. The redesign would continue to develop for years, but Hoffman had established a format in which Mulvoy's vision of larger, more vivid photographs could thrive. The one editorial innovation was Point After, Mulvoy's idea for a back-page column in which writers would have a forum for traditional sports commentary.

As design director—the designation was symbolic of title inflation common in the magazine business—Hoffman was a constant presence in the Mulvoy years, serving as something of an alter ego to the rough-hewn Mulvoy. He was less a loyal soldier on the edit side than a more clearly detached and self-contained design conduit. Not much of a sports fan, the sardonic but cheerful Hoffman was as able as the rest of the staff to laugh if he inadvertently referred to a team's practice as its "rehearsal."

Peter Carry returned from *Discover* in the summer of '87 and moved seamlessly back into the role that he'd had as heir apparent to Rogin, chief assistant to the managing editor, and liaison to the writers. Mulvoy and Carry weren't social friends, but grew closer over time. The two would play good cop–bad cop, with Mulvoy doling out annual raises to writers, and Carry giving them the often critical annual reviews. Carry maintained the master writers' list, a record of who was working on what and when it was due. And when it came to firing or demotions, Mulvoy often left the job up to Carry, who carried out his duties with stoic resolve. The reliability would make Carry a key factor in Mulvoy's editorship, and also branded Carry for the rest of his career as the heavy—Mulvoy's henchman. With Carry's return, Mulvoy moved out of the red-pencil business. For nearly three years, he'd performed the final line edit on every story that went in the magazine, but he gave Carry this job upon his return, freeing up Mulvoy to focus on his passion for picture selection and layout. With Carry back in place and the magazine's profitability continuing to grow, Mulvoy felt he was ready to take *SI* to a new level.

But first, he wanted to make a major change in the magazine's schedule. For more than 30 years, the edit staff had worked a Thursday–Monday workweek, the only Time Inc. magazine to regularly work on both weekend days. The schedule was good for office unity, nearly guaranteeing a number of incestuous relationships in the process, but bad for morale. Some editors complained that they never got to see their kids' little league games; staffers with spouses who worked a regular work week were in even more of a bind. With all that in mind, Mulvoy made a pitch to new editor-in-chief Jason McManus to allow *SI* to move to a four-day workweek, eliminating Saturday from the regular work schedule. Sundays and Mondays were often 12-hour days anyway, reasoned Mulvoy. And Saturdays had become slack days, in which staffers did little more than "sit around and watch football games."

"I didn't like it," McManus said of his first reaction to the plan. "He had to really talk me into it. He showed me the unusual and predictable work flow of a sports magazine. Unlike *Time*, there are no surprises. Unless someone dies, every event is planned two years in advance. Are you gonna cover it? What issue do you put it in? How much space do you give it? And because the events occur over the weekend, most of the work is done on [Sunday and Monday]. For all these reasons, plus the fact that people don't have their weekends, like the rest of the world, we felt that managerially it would work and the staff deserved it. But of course, I said, 'This is a test. If the quality begins to fall off or you're missing the deadlines, or production costs go up, we'll go right back.'"

When Terrell first brought up the idea of a four-day workweek in the early '70s, Ray Cave had dissented. And when Mulvoy pushed for the four-day week, Cave, as editorial director under McManus, argued against it again. "There is no question that a weekly can be turned out in four days, probably in three, and perhaps in two and a half," he said. "But that is not what this game is about. Be it *Time*, *SI*, or whatever, the fifth day matters. It allows time to talk about ideas, to slow the pace, which is frenzied as is, perhaps even, heaven forbid, to think a little. Layouts get done earlier in the week. Some stories get finished earlier. The entire pattern of the magazine takes shape earlier. If you have not done the early work, you do not have as much time or the people available late in the week when events force you to tear up part of an issue and start again. Few things discourage a staff more than having a magazine torn up in its closing day with insufficient time and staff to do it well. The first few times it is exciting; after that it is merely fatiguing."

Joe Marshall would compare the four-day workweek to a Chinese fire drill, but granted that "it was a tremendous blessing to get that Saturday off. I don't think it hopelessly compromised the magazine. We probably lost a little bit of creativity and closeness, but I think we probably lost more of that allowing writers to live out of town."

In a four-day workweek, there was also less time for meetings and discussions. Even more so than under Rogin, who trusted his senior editors to suggest story assignments, authority in a four-day workweek rested with the managing editor. With an autocratic, domineering leader like Mulvoy at the controls, magazine-making began to resemble a one-man show. Meetings were often perfunctory affairs that Mulvoy entered having already decided on a chosen course, from which he rarely wavered. "On the fly you couldn't do it," said John Papanek. "And you could never change Mark's mind in public."

But for all the squawking about Mulvoy's bullying leadership and often thoughtless indifference to subordinates, the fact remained that the magazine, a different sort of *Sports Illustrated*, more aggressive and less reflective, more judgmental but less sophisticated, thrived under his leadership. Mulvoy had spent enough time watching André Laguerre work to know that story mix was a crucial factor, and though his conception of the sports universe was much smaller and more literal than Laguerre's, he was mindful of the need to construct a week's issue from disparate elements. Though he loved hockey, he didn't overplay it. And he knew the value of getting a crucial off-season story, in any sport, into the issue, to break up the expected routine. He was also adept at anticipating events *before* they hit the general sports media. In the first issue of 1986, he placed a little-known teenage heavyweight named Mike Tyson on the cover, beginning the drumroll of hype for the next superstar of boxing. He could also seize the moment for one big issue, such as 1987's thematic cover and 63-page centerpiece "One Day in Baseball." For the 1988 Super Bowl lead story, Mulvoy opened with a 10-page portfolio showing the rapid-fire succession of events leading to Washington's second-quarter annihilation of the Broncos. It was an updating of the old principles of *Life* photojournalism, brought into full color by *SI*'s crack team of photographers. The spring of '88 included a timely Jack McCallum cover story on the decline of the center in pro basketball (with a vintage '60s-era cover shot of Bill Russell and Wilt Chamberlain) and Gary Smith's memorable account of Tyson's crumbling marriage to Robin Givens.

But the most riveting piece was Smith's cover story on Muhammad Ali's entourage. Smith didn't look or act anything like a sportswriter; he hadn't read *SI* before writing for it, and spent much of the mid-'80s living abroad with his wife in Bolivia, teaching English to teenagers at a local orphanage in the city of Cochabamba. Upon returning to the United States in 1987, he began working on a story on the coterie of followers who had been near Ali throughout his boxing career. The piece began with a vision of Ali dressed in black, months after voluntarily going off the medication for his worsening Parkinson's syndrome, sparring three rounds in the training room of his Michigan farm. It then ran through the mostly sad second acts of Ali's longtime aides de camp—Dr. Ferdie Pacheco, his cook Lana Shabazz, his bodyguard Howard (Pat) Patterson, and manager Herbert Muhammad—before closing with a visit that would amount to a eulogy for the Ali era. Smith traveled to a Los Angeles flophouse and found Drew "Bundini" Brown, Ali's perennial alter ego. For a generation, Brown's fascinating ramblings had been documented by *SI*'s fight writers, from Maule to Putnam, Plimpton to Kram. And now here was Ali's motivator, broke and alone, ranting to everyone and no one in particular, mulling the $9,000 he needed to get his possessions out of storage. It was a classic example of a writer getting out of the way to let a story tell itself. As with "One Day in Baseball," Mulvoy understood that Smith's story wasn't merely a good bonus piece, but was a stirring account of an icon that many of *SI*'s readers had grown up and grown old with. He turned it into a journalistic event. The cover story of the April 25, 1988, issue, "Ali

and His Entourage" featured Gregory Heisler's black-and-white photographs and ran throughout a 24-page section, on heavier-coated paper,
in the middle of the magazine.

The summer continued with a brilliant set of issues: Deford's updated
version of "Casey at the Bat," William Oscar Johnson's cover story on the
relationship of the beer industry to sports (which predictably angered
many of the magazine's advertisers), a special report on sports in China,
and a college football preview issue that highlighted the emergence of the
state of Florida as the top proving ground for college talent. (The timing
was perfect: for each of the next five seasons, at least two Florida teams
finished in the top four in the final Associated Press college football poll.)

In addition to a greater sense of vision, *SI* had gained speed under
Mulvoy, a willingness to roll with the events of the weekend and throw
out the carefully constructed story budgets with which the magazine had
begun the weekend. Laguerre used to refer to the occasional last-minute
shuffling of stories and placement as an "El Rippo"; under Mulvoy, they
became a common occurrence. When Ben Johnson blitzed Carl Lewis in
the 100-meter dash at the 1988 Summer Olympics in Seoul, Mulvoy
decided to put Johnson on that week's cover, which would hit the newsstands prior to the final weekend of competition. It was about five o'clock
New York time on a Monday, just about the time that the magazine's last
line of "late read" editors were changing a last typo or caption, that the
story broke from Seoul that Johnson had failed his drug test, coming up
positive for steroids, and Lewis had been declared the winner. *SI*, with
dozens of reporters in Seoul, had the talent and numbers to blanket the
breaking story. Mulvoy called Seoul (where it was 4 a.m. Tuesday) and
woke up Jerry Kirshenbaum with the news. Kirshenbaum called track
expert Anita Verschoth and the Seoul staff went to work. Verschoth
staked out the hotel where the International Olympic Committee was
meeting, writer-reporter Richard Demak was dispatched to the lab and
spoke to the technician who'd performed Johnson's drug test, writer Shel-
ley Smith left on the plane back to Canada with Johnson. All submitted
files and William Oscar Johnson filed a story within 12 hours. On
Wednesday morning, the cover story with plenty of investigative background—Verschoth had contacts who'd grumbled about Johnson for
months—hit the stands. Mulvoy kept the very same cover shot, but
changed the headline from "WOOOSH!" to "BUSTED!"

It was an example of the *SI* monolith at its best, and was one of the
main factors contributing to *SI*'s long overdue industry recognition, earning it the National Magazine Award for general excellence among publications with a circulation above one million. The results were positive on

the publishing side as well, where the magazine showed a stunning 23 percent increase in ad revenues, to $323 million dollars. Circulation, which had finally inched over the 3 million mark in 1987, rose again, to 3.22 million.

And as he vowed he would, Mulvoy was making a star out of Rick Reilly. Reilly had established himself as the most popular of *SI*'s new writers, and earned the sort of plum profile assignments, like a bonus piece on Pete Rose shortly before he broke Ty Cobb's career hits record, that earlier would only have gone to Deford. But even as he was succeeding, Reilly still looked, felt, and acted like the high school class cut-up, someone who was only as good as his last joke. The insecurity was eating him up inside. "I just kept waiting for the bottom to fall out," he said. "I kept thinking that at some point this magazine was going to realize that they made a terrible, terrible mistake and just come up with a giant truck and pull me away."

Like Jenkins two decades earlier, Reilly had arrived as a writer immediately comfortable with the larger stage. Covering the college football beat in 1986, he had plenty of material for his caustic, biting wit. In a piece on the University of Miami, Reilly led with the remark (oft repeated since then) that the Hurricanes were the only squad in the country to have their team picture taken from the front and from the side. In December 1986, *SI* reporter Austin Murphy traveled to Miami to collect some notes for Reilly to use in his Fiesta Bowl story. Murphy was listening to Jimmy Johnson's thoughts on how he would attack Penn State's defense when the young and still thin-skinned head coach veered from his point and blurted out, "Who is this *Rick Reilly*? Talkin' about how much mousse I have in my hair—I don't even *know* the man!"

When he started, Reilly had asked Doug Looney for his advice about being an *SI* writer. Looney emphasized that at *SI*, editors simply wouldn't accept a writer missing a deadline. "They don't care—there's no excuses," he told Reilly. "If you need to get to Bumfuck, Montana, and all the airports are closed in the middle of the winter, you've got to find some crazed Vietnam war vet to fly you there on acid, because *they don't care*." Reilly had taken this advice to heart. In 1987, Mulvoy moved him to the pro football beat, where his popularity, and the deadline pressure, only increased, often leaving him doubled-over with stomach pains brought on by nerves. On opening day of the regular season, Reilly covered a division showdown between the Seattle Seahawks and

Denver Broncos. After John Elway engineered another fourth-quarter comeback, Reilly drove to his suburban Denver home to write. He was up all night, eating Mexican food, drinking coffee, and polishing his one-liners, fighting through the debilitating pain in his stomach that grew so bad that, by the time he finally filed at 7 a.m., he was writing from a near-lotus position, bent at the waist over his laptop. Reilly wound up in the hospital that evening, with duodenitis. He continued torturing himself in the following months—"My stomach saw Sunday on the calendar and it just started freaking"—until, after a third episode in 1988, he vowed to take it easier.

Of course, among the people Reilly most desperately wanted to impress was Dan Jenkins. He'd first met Jenkins at St. Andrews at the 1984 British Open, which turned out to be Jenkins's last assignment for the magazine. He'd paid homage at countless press tents and barrooms after then, but couldn't get the approbation he craved. Jenkins had a few friends among the younger generation of sportswriters, but to Reilly he was cordial but standoffish, and far from relaxed. After reading Jenkins's deadline story on the 1986 British Open in *Golf Digest*, Reilly sent him a note congratulating him on his lead. Several weeks later, he saw Jenkins at the PGA Championships at Inverness.

"Hey, Dan," he said, "did you get my note?"

"I get a lot of notes," said Jenkins.

A year later, on a Sunday night just hours after Scott Simpson won the '87 U.S. Open at Olympic, Jenkins was sitting around the Washington Square Bar & Grill with Ron Fimrite, Pete Axthelm, skier Suzy Chaffee, and a few *SI* reporters when Reilly walked in. "Reilly came in and he was sort of a caricature of a drunk," said one witness. "Like he thought that was how a Runyonesque sportswriter should behave. It was affected and you could tell that it wasn't going over with Jenkins and Fimrite. I just remember the tension in that room being remarkable. Rick's fascinated with those old *SI* guys and I think he would die happy if he could just sort of overhear Jenkins saying, 'Shit, this kid is good.'"

• • •

Having become one of the company's largest moneymakers, *SI* was flush, looking for new horizons. They'd arrived at an idea hatched by publisher Don Barr and assistant managing editor Larry Keith for a monthly youth sports magazine. *Sports Illustrated for Kids* would be aimed at a coed audience of eight-to-thirteen-year-olds, with publication beginning in January 1989. The preteen market was burgeoning, increasingly lucrative, and fairly mad about sport. They were also the next generation of potential readers of the parent magazine. But the editorial product was a sticking point. The early plan had been to farm the editorial out to *Gray's Sports Journal* in Massachusetts. Mulvoy, who was overseeing the project by then, took one look at the first dummies and determined that the product would have to be done in-house. Late in July, he brought a signature of dummy pages to show senior editor John Papanek, who had a similar reaction.

Papanek spent a couple weeks going back through the issues of *SI* he'd read while growing up, pulling bound volumes from the early '60s out of the *SI* archives, and spending hours poring over the issues again. "I remembered pictures, layouts, covers, graphic elements, not so much stories, contents, and words. But I remembered the way things were laid out on a page. I found myself remembering almost exactly the order of the pictures as you turned the pages, with Frank Gifford coming before Y.A. Tittle, and then came Bobby Hull, and so I knew the pictures would have to be played crucially, and that tremendous care had to be taken in the way things looked. I said I thought it would be a mistake if they didn't employ first-rate photographers, first-rate designers, because the competition at that time was MTV and Nickelodeon on television."

Shortly after Papanek turned his suggestions in, Mulvoy met with McManus. They agreed not only that Papanek's suggestions were apt, but that he was the right man to put them into play. In mid-August, Mulvoy invited Papanek out to Westchester for a round of golf ("Mulvoy loved to take me to play golf, just so he could do a week's worth of jokes about how bad I was or how I wore the wrong shoes or had a sweater off the hook"), and proposed that Papanek could be the managing editor of the start-up.

Almost to a person, the staff was pleased to see the elevation of Papanek. He had been the very last edit hire of the Laguerre era, a Long Island–raised University of Michigan grad who was caught up with the times, marching against the war during the week, cheering for that noted reactionary Bo Schembechler on weekends. Papanek's story was similar to many of the bright, precocious reporters hired in the '60s and '70s. After graduating from Michigan, where he had been the sports editor of the school paper, he sent out résumés to five major newspapers and *SI*. After the magazine was the only publication to respond with more than a form letter, Papanek concocted an excuse to come to New York for an interview. Six weeks later, he was working at his mother's house when chief of research Merv Hyman called. "I was outside and I came running in, and he said, 'John, are you doing any work now?' I said, 'Yeah, I'm hanging storm windows on my parents' house.' He said, 'No, no, I meant did you have a job.' I said no, I didn't. He said, 'Well, a job's opening up at *Sports Illustrated*, and I would like to hire you.'"

Papanek started in December 1973 and quickly fell in with a bright, socially active crowd ("I felt like I was at a university just loaded with great teachers"), sitting at tables listening to Jenkins soliloquies, dating reporter Susan Adams for a while. He became an effective NBA writer later in the '70s, eliciting sensitive interviews from such notoriously diffi-cult personalities as Bill Walton, Kareem Abdul-Jabbar, and Julius Erving. After undergoing eye surgery for corneal transplants in 1981, Papanek spent much of his recovery time editing, rising through the decade into one of Mulvoy's most trusted senior editors.

After accepting the editorship of *SI for Kids*, Papanek brought over senior writer Craig Neff to help him, and spent the rest of the fall in intense preparations for the launch. The first issue, dated January 1989 with Michael Jordan on the cover, included a page of "SI for Kids" trading cards, echoing the foldout feature of Topps baseball cards in the first issue of *SI*. When the issue came out, Papanek encountered ad veteran John Marin in the halls. Marin congratulated him warmly for his institutional memory. But Papanek had never seen that first issue of *SI*. It was a coinci-dence, one in many cases of serendipity that made *SI for Kids* such a pleasant surprise. Starting with a target of a paid circulation of 250,000, the magazine had 400,000 paid subscriptions its first year, 500,000 in its second. Scheduled to break even in its fifth year, it was profitable by its third.

Mulvoy's last official act of 1988 was to announce the promotion of Julia Lamb to assistant managing editor. The first female AME in the mag-azine's history, Lamb was emblematic of the gains that women had made at *SI*, as well as the ways they were still marginalized. A reliable, attentive editor who had worked at the magazine since 1962 (she was hired as a copy clerk), Lamb, who had a degree from Vassar in medieval history, had taken the usual route to female success. She toiled as a newsmarker and researcher for 16 years, before requesting an editing tryout in 1978. By 1980, she was a senior editor, overseeing the soft beats that female editors so often received. "Women, animals, and foreigners" was how the female senior editors who'd had the job jokingly referred to their coverage responsibilities, which included the America's Cup races, the Winter Olympics, figure skating, and horse racing.

For all that, she had excelled as a coordinator of special issues, editing the 1984 and 1988 Winter Olympic previews. And with the appointment, Mulvoy announced that Lamb would edit the 1989 25th anniversary swimsuit issue.

The swimsuit special was envisioned, by both Mulvoy and Barr, as the Mother of All Special Issues. Since Miller had pumped up the marketing and Mulvoy had added the pages, the swimsuit issue had increased its profile through the late '80s. The hype helped, because the magazine had lost its ability to shock. The debate that accompanied the issue in its third decade had to do with context, not cleavage. The swimsuit issue had become America's premier annual cheesecake event, the most notorious special issue in American magazine publishing, reliably profitable but increasingly criticized for being a sexist anachronism.

Deford, asked by Mulvoy to write a piece about the history of the issue, mentioned Laguerre's influence, but also its cultural pervasiveness. For Deford, who had examined such purely American examples of kitsch as the Harlem Globetrotters, the Miss America pageant, and the Roller Derby, the swimsuit issue was a natural. The 284-page issue included profiles on the 19 women who had graced the 25 previous covers, and new pictorials of Cheryl Tiegs (in the Seychelles), Yvette and Yvonne Sylvander (Florida), Christie Brinkley (Kenya), Carol Alt (Kauai), Paulina Porizkova (St. Barthélemy), and Elle Macpherson (Australia). There were also 26 pages of new suits, including shots of 25th anniversary cover girl Kathy Ireland. It was a crowning achievement for Jule Campbell, who by 1989 had been at *SI* for 33 years. While others were more responsible for the magazine's journalistic success, a case could be made that Campbell had been directly responsible for more of *SI*'s profits than any other single person, even before the anniversary bonanza. Single copy sales for the 25th anniversary issue generated nearly $10 million, and sales of the *SI* 25th anniversary swimsuit issue video brought in another $5 million. *Business Week* estimated that the issue would gross nearly $30 million all told, in a year when *SI*'s profits were topping the $100 million mark and total ad sales were $375 million.

The coordinated multimedia sales effort was predictably viewed as crass overkill in many circles. The video, directed by Albert Maysles of *Gimme Shelter* fame, was reviewed in the *New York Observer* by media critic Ben Yagoda, who dubbed the issue as the paragon of a form of softcore porn called "mush-core," adding that the video was "a piece of pseudo cinema verité that severely compromises Mr. Maysles' reputation."

The principal presence in the film is Julie [*sic*] Campbell, the *SI* senior editor who's been in charge of the swimsuit issue since its inception. As captured by Mr. Maysles, she is a benevolent but strict madam, always making sure her "girls" are properly fetching. "Steffie, you can make the suit smaller right here," she tells Stephanie Seymour. "Open your shirt," she commands Christie Brinkley. The video even touches on kinkier areas, notably sadism. Cold water is dumped on one model's chest (remember those nipples), another is compelled to sit on hot rocks for a long period and a third is ordered not to squint even though she is staring into the sun. "She manages to look pretty even when she's in pain," Ms. Campbell says approvingly about one model. . . . *Sports Illustrated* is hardly the only mush-core purveyor in America today— merely the most canny in marketing it in a slick and "respectable" way.

But it wasn't just the deconstructionists. Supporters of women's athletics were becoming increasingly vocal in their criticism of the issue. Inside the magazine, the issue rekindled the larger question of the treatment of women. Ever since Pat Ryan left in 1978 (and subsequently rose to ME at *People* and, later, *Life*), it had been clear that there was a glass ceiling of sorts at *SI*. While the appointment of Lamb was designed to show that this was a new age at *SI*, many had their doubts.

They weren't assuaged by a pair of unrelated incidents in the late '80s. In 1987 in Calgary, where a group of *SI* staffers were convening to prepare for the following year's Winter Olympics, Mulvoy had made an innuendo-laden speech filled with wisecracks about the intelligence of *SI* marketing staffer Coco Vanderslice. She filed a sexual discrimination suit against Mulvoy and the company, eventually settling for $50,000. In November 1989, the young writer-reporter Julie Vader finished her tenure at *SI* with a tearful screaming match with Carry. At the end of a nine-month writing trial, which in Carry and Mulvoy's opinion she failed, she was called in for a conference with Carry. Vader wasn't surprised at the verdict (Carry's unenthusiastic attitude during her trial had been sign enough), but before she walked out she tried to explain why she thought it was more difficult for a woman writer to make it at *SI*. "This is a place where men slap you on the ass when you walk down the hall," she said. "I don't think you know what that does. People propositioning me, then not giving me assignments." The discussion deteriorated into a screaming match, and shortly thereafter Vader left the magazine.

• • •

In 1989, purely by accident, Mulvoy made the best hire of his tenure. After Alex Wolff wrote a piece in 1986 on the Gus Macker three-on-three basketball tournament in Michigan, he received a letter from a Marquette University freshman named Steve Rushin. Even then, the bespectacled, fair-skinned Rushin demonstrated a vaguely impertinent manner and a bone-dry wit. Rushin and Wolff exchanged letters, and Wolff eventually recruited the college student to help him as a research assistant on his book about sports nicknames. In '89, on Wolff's recommendation, Rushin was hired as a researcher.

It was almost literally a dream come true for Rushin, who looked like the bookish comic-strip character Funky Winkerbean. He'd grown up just outside the Twin Cities in Bloomington, working the concession stand at Minnesota Vikings and Minnesota Twins games at Metropolitan Stadium, in the days before the Met was razed and the Mall of America was built in its place. During his first days in the office, he betrayed a rather dazed aspect. "I don't know what I was expecting," he said later. "Maybe Frank Deford in a smoking jacket, standing by the Xerox machine."

Rushin took to the intense, collegial life of a beginning researcher, playing catch in the halls on the long Sunday nights when stories would trickle in, adhering to the rules of checking every word in the magazine, no matter how insignificant the piece of information or how ridiculous the imposition. It was 3 a.m. one Monday when Rushin and fellow researcher Albert Kim flipped a coin to decide who would get stuck calling Joe Paterno to check what color car he drove. Kim lost, and Rushin pulled up a chair and watched with a macabre smile. "If you didn't have to do it," he remembered, "you always wanted to look on and see the carnage."

Rushin rose quickly, and even in his early writing assignments showed a playfully sharp, though often overreaching, sense of humor. In the words of one of his colleagues, Rushin in his early years was "very clever and very funny and, partly because of those things, just a terrible writer." But more than anyone else in years who'd moved up through the reporter-researcher ranks, Rushin showed promise.

Nineteen eighty-nine was another banner editorial year, with Mulvoy showing a little more flexibility, taking more chances, especially with bonus pieces; Gary Smith delivered a piercing profile of Sugar Ray Leonard; Alexander Wolff, rapidly becoming a star on the college basketball beat, caught up with several former NCAA scoring leaders; Franz Lidz wrote about the game show *Jeopardy*; the polished Richard Hoffer (hired from the *Los Angeles Times*) wrote compelling portraits of Oakland Raiders svengali Al Davis and former heavyweight champ George Foreman, who had been out of the public eye for more than a decade. *SI* would win the National Magazine Award for general excellence for the second straight year, an unprecedented feat for a mass circulation magazine. But for all its accomplishments, the 25th anniversary swimsuit issue in February, the 35th anniversary issue in August, the year was a calamitous one for the magazine, and not just because of the March 4 announcement that Time Inc. was merging with Warner Communications to become Time Warner, the largest media and entertainment company in the world.

While the merger was troubling to many at the company, *Sports Illustrated* was facing a different set of financial headaches. Through the late '80s, the magazine's stunning growth in circulation was masterminded by mercurial, strong-willed circulation director Michael Loeb. With cable television in general and ESPN in particular giving *SI* a chance to advertise affordably on television, Loeb viewed the electronic market as the key to *SI*'s future. The commercials he ordered, greeted with anguished derision by virtually everyone on the editorial side, seemed to accentuate the magazine's sizzle at the expense of its content. Most of the television spots during the period were depressingly uniform, emphasizing a bonus gift for subscribing, and the swimsuit issue, with the magazine itself mentioned almost as an afterthought. Through different seasons and different promotions, the formula remained the same: an announcer would give a voiceover mentioning the appeal of a premium, such as a telephone in the shape of a sneaker. Then, while rock music blared loudly in the background, a group of astonished-looking white men would exclaim endlessly about how "cool" or "awesome" the item was. Then came the pitch: the sneakerphone is yours free with a one-year subscription to *Sports Illustrated*. In the next breath, if not in the same, the announcer would remind readers that this included the annual swimsuit issue.

The sort of readers the ads brought into the magazine were a departure from the typical profile of *SI*'s subscriber base. They were not, generally, the thoughtful upscale readers who were drawn to *SI*'s journalism but, rather, the sort of people who would be coerced to subscribe to a magazine because they'd get a free phone or a blooper video. While circulation went up, it was accompanied by myriad problems. Fulfillment, the process of getting the customer to pay for the subscription that was ordered, became more difficult. The churn, the constant turnover of nonrenewals and new subscriptions that needed to be kept equal for circulation to remain steady, became more active and more expensive. Subscribers were less likely to renew after their first year, choosing to wait, often for another premium, to re-up. And in an age when VCRs had penetrated much of the nation's households and Blockbuster video stores became as prevalent as movie theaters, the perceived value of a video (the most popular premium) was dropping rapidly.

Bob Miller, by now working as the head of Time Inc.'s magazine group, had been looking with growing skepticism at Loeb's projections, which he finally decided bore no resemblance to reality (at a time when renewals were growing increasingly difficult to acquire, Loeb's projections that were fed into the main business model showed renewals at an all-time high). Miller removed Loeb from his job, though he was reassigned to the circulation department of the new Time Inc. magazine *Entertainment Weekly*. The hangover from Loeb's approach, and the publishing side's unthinking, tacit support of it, would be felt well into the next decade. He was removed from his job with circulation at an all-time high of 3.44 million. It would drop to 3.22 million in 1990, when *SI* pulled back slightly on the aggressive marketing tactics, and it never again reached the heights of the Loeb era.

For all the calamity that it brought, there was little talk about Loeb that spring of 1989. Instead, everyone at *SI* seemed to be whispering about Frank Deford.

• • •

Writing in the August 1, 1988, issue about the tradition of the All-American Soap Box Derby in Akron, Ohio, Deford observed:

> Culturally vulgar institutions that endure are invariably blessed by serendipity. Anyone who sat around with his thinking cap on and tried to invent the Miss America Pageant or trick-or-treating or hog-calling contests or the All-American Soap Box Derby couldn't. . . .
>
> But a lot has happened. Some of the Midwest has gone to the Sun Belt and some to Japan. Chevrolet walked away from the All-American in 1972 and right after that, during the former vice president's Watergate troubles, the All-American champion was caught cheating, and his father said, Hey everybody does it. A lot of local tire factories have closed and now Akron doesn't want to be called the Rubber city anymore . . . but then Akron is like the rest of America. It isn't a place where things are made anymore.

Deford had become an institution at *SI*, the master of the bonus piece, the biggest name at the magazine, and one of the most emulated, respected, eagerly read writers in the country. "There were times, like when Deford wrote his piece on Billy Conn fighting Joe Louis, that I would get off my fat butt, walk up to the copy machine, and print forty copies and put them in everybody's mailbox, just to share the joy of reading this stuff," said *Washington Post* sports editor George Solomon. "When Deford wrote a piece, you just said, well, there's an hour that I'm really going to enjoy life."

For all his strengths, Deford's success had engendered some jealousy, as well as some skeptics. Some of the younger staff writers thought his bonus pieces had become shallow exercises in pop psychology, labeling him "Frank DeFreud." Senior editor David Bauer once remarked of a Deford piece that "this story wouldn't run in the magazine if Frank Deford hadn't written it." Significantly, though, no one accused Deford of phoning it in or resting on his laurels. In fact, if Deford was teased about anything within the halls of *SI*, it was his rectitude. "If I approved his expense account for seven years of writing," Mulvoy said, "I don't think he ever spent a dime on entertainment. Frank was not an entertainer. He'd go on the road, he'd fly coach; Frank never spent a dime." Deford was so honest, in fact, that he couldn't conceive how others were being dishonest. He never quite figured out how they were able to fix their expense accounts to make so much money. A friend once explained to him a couple tricks—fabricating a $24.99 expense, or taking a blank receipt and picking a figure—and Deford's eyes widened. "Yeah, but, well, now that's *fraud*!"

He was honest and he was conscientious and he was consistent. And he was burning out.

By 1989, it had happened a few times. Deford would sit in his study at his sprawling house in Greens Farms, Connecticut, starting to write another patented Frank Deford bonus piece, when it would occur to him: *I've said this before.*

After 27 years at the magazine and six consecutive National Sportswriter of the Year awards, he felt he needed to take a step back. He'd spent much of the past year trying to change the rhythm and pace and structure of his bonus pieces. He extensively researched *Casey at the Bat* and wrote an updated version; he did a profile of Arkansas coach Nolan Richardson, whose daughter died of leukemia, in stage play form. He was searching for a change of pace.

The plan, agreed to by Mulvoy, would have been for Deford, his wife Carol, and their adopted daughter Scarlet to go to England for a year. His son Chris had just started college, and Deford was ready to take a sabbatical from his weekly National Public Radio spots. He thought that a year in England, perhaps writing about soccer and cricket, going into London to cover Wimbledon, maybe coming back to the States once or twice to do a pressing *SI* story, would recharge his batteries. Deford would get a year away from the grind, and *SI* would have their star writer acting as de facto European correspondent and Bigfoot Abroad. While he was in England, he could write his big nonsports novel, the World War II–era romance, *Love and Infamy*. There was a spot picked out in Knightsbridge, and plans were being made for a late May flight. The Defords' house had even been put on the rental market.

But late one February evening, Deford got a call at home from his old Princeton friend Peter Price, a year behind him in school, who was business manager of the school newspaper and who, along with Deford, edited the Princeton humor magazine. Price, the former publisher of the *New York Post*, had a strange urgency in his voice.

"I want to see you," Price said.

"Yeah, sure," replied Deford. "Why don't we have lunch sometime."

"No. I'd really like to see you *right away*."

Deford was planning on driving into the city the next morning to interview baseball commissioner Bart Giamatti at noon. They agreed to meet at Deford's office at *SI* before the interview.

And it was there, on the morning of February 28, 1989, that Peter Price laid it all out: he'd been approached by Mexican media magnate Emilio Azcarraga, owner of the prominent Mexican-based international telecommunications company Televisa (whose American subsidiary was Univisa), who was interested in launching a national sports newspaper in the United States. Throughout Europe, many countries had more than one national sports newspaper. Why couldn't it be done in America? Price was interested in the idea, but knew that the enterprise would need a powerful figurehead, someone like Frank Deford.

Deford *was* intrigued, but still skeptical. After the short meeting, he went up to the Time Inc. archives and pulled the clip file on Azcarraga. Details were sketchy—Azcarraga was a somewhat mysterious figure in the States, and both respected and feared in Mexico—but there was nothing that dampened Deford's interest.

In late March, Price and Deford met again, this time in Azcarraga's New York office. They were still conceptualizing, trying to figure out what such a job would have to entail before Deford would consider it. Price's original projections for the staff, estimated at the size of the *New York Post* sports department, were far too low. And both men agreed that the way to get the industry's attention was to go out and grab three or four big names, like a Jim Murray or a Mike Lupica, to show that the fledgling enterprise meant business. Deford said that he'd need a three-year contract, guaranteed whether the enterprise failed or not; Price countered by insisting on a five-year deal, so that there could be no question he was in it for the long haul. Energized by the promise of a new challenge, Deford agreed in principle.

There was just one sticking point. Price wanted to move immediately. But Deford was just three months away from a handsome payoff at *SI*. At the Los Angeles Olympics in 1984, Rogin had given both Deford and Kenny Moore golden handcuff deals, deeds to 1,500 shares of Time Inc. stock that each writer could cash in only if he were still employed with the company five years later, on July 1, 1989. With takeover talk swirling around the company in the spring of '89, the value of Time Inc. stock kept going up. The value of 1,500 shares, after the Time Warner merger, would be over $200,000.

"Look," said Deford to Price. "I can do it, but I can't start until the middle of July. I ain't gonna walk away with two months to go. If this was two years to go, yeah, sure. But I'm not gonna walk away from this. It's a lot of money to me."

Price came back a few days later with a suggestion.

"Here's the deal," Price said. "Do you think they will give you the stock even though it's two months shy?"

"No, I don't think they will, because as I explained to you, the whole point of the thing is to keep me there. I just doubt very seriously whether they will."

"Will you ask?"

"Sure, I'll *ask*."

"If they'll give it to you, fine. If not, Emilio will give it to you."

But, said Price, there was just one thing. Because he was still arranging other elements of the deal, he had to insist that Deford couldn't tell anyone about the project.

It would put Frank Deford, notoriously honest, scrupulously honest, castigated-for-not-taking-part-in-the-expense-account-gold-rush honest, into a difficult situation. He would be asking for a $200,000 favor without telling his employers that he was about to take a very visible position as the point man for a nominally competing venture, a national sports newspaper. Years later, he would say that, had he to do it all over again, he would have told Price that he would go ask for the money, but only if he could tell Time Inc. exactly what he was doing. But he didn't do that.

Instead, the next day, he went to see Mulvoy, who was traveling. Not wanting to wait, he rang up Ann Callahan, who had moved with Gilbert Rogin to the 34th floor when Rogin became corporate editor. She told him to come right up. Deford had always been one of Rogin's favorites; it was Rogin who had worked out the terms of Deford's sweetheart deal that afforded him three months off a year in 1977; it was Rogin who'd given Deford the privilege of going over any edits made on his stories word by word; and it was Rogin, after all, who'd given Deford the stock bonus in 1984.

That afternoon, Deford told Rogin that he was going to work for Azcarraga at Televisa, but that he couldn't tell him right then what the project was. "And Gil was terrific about it," Deford remembered. "'Great—it sounds like a great opportunity. I'm so happy for you. He even said, 'I wish something like this had come along for me.' I remember this all very clearly, and I remember very distinctly what I said because it was so important for me to say exactly the right thing."

When Deford hesitatingly mentioned the stock bonus, Rogin suggested they go talk to Munro that instant. The chairman-of-the-board's office wasn't open to everyone, but as a former *SI* publisher, Munro knew both Rogin and Deford well. He wasn't in that day, but an appointment was set for a couple of days later.

Before seeing Munro, Deford reached Mulvoy by phone, and they had a curious conversation, which each man would remember differently.

"I said, 'Mark, I'm leaving,'" remembered Deford. "And he first thought, I remember this, that that meant I was going to London early! So we finally get that straightened out, and I said again, 'Mark, I can't tell you what I'm gonna do.' There's no questions from him on the phone, which you wouldn't have expected on the phone. And then he says, 'We're gonna give you the greatest party ever.'"

Mulvoy's memory of the conversation was almost diametrically opposed to Deford's: "I said, 'What do you mean you're leaving *Sports Illustrated*?' He said, 'I'm going to work for Emilio Azcarraga. Doing some television stuff.' And I said, 'You're not competing with *SI*?' He said, 'Oh, no.' So I said, 'Well, that's great.'" (Deford laughed ruefully at Mulvoy's account. "What he remembers didn't happen, because I wouldn't have said that.")

The day after talking to Mulvoy, Deford went into Munro's office. Munro had spoken to Rogin, been briefed on the situation, and already made arrangements. Deford could leave *SI* May 1, but would technically still be on the Time Inc. payroll through July (receiving regular payroll checks for literally no money—$0.00), so he could receive the bonus.

"What you've given this company over the past twenty years, this isn't a problem," said Munro cheerily.

"I'm really sorry I have to be so secretive, but you know what Peter's like," said Deford, "and he doesn't want me to say anything yet." Munro laughed. Then inexplicably, almost out of some visceral need to set Munro's mind, or perhaps his own, at ease, Deford said, "Dick, also, I just want you to know—*it's not another sports magazine.*" The two spent another 15 minutes talking and then Munro put his arm around Deford and walked him out of his office.

In talking to *SI* communications director Art Berke, who would compose the press release announcing Deford's exit, Deford agreed on a statement that said, "This is a once-in-a-lifetime opportunity to develop sports media projects, both national and international in scope. In this new venture I'll work closely with Univisa president Peter Price, an old friend from Princeton days. I can tell you that we have no intention of producing a sports magazine."

That this statement, like his statement to Munro, was technically true is without question. Equally clear is that those at the magazine were misled. "Frankie shaved it," is how Rogin would characterize it later. "As I recall, he said it wasn't going to be anything about sports. The impression was, and believe me, if Frankie was here, I'd tell him the same thing, the impression was that he wasn't going into a competing business. I think he's an honorable person generally speaking. And I think he was trying to have the best of both worlds. I know the impression was clear that he wasn't going to have anything to do with sports journalism."

"They obviously *knew* I was going into sport," protested Deford. "What did they think, somebody was going to hire me to write opera?"

And yet, it would have been quite plausible for Deford to move away from sport. He'd built a career on being slightly above the sporting fray, never one to sit around with other scribes like Jenkins, and uncomfortable being classified a sportswriter ("I'm a writer who happens to write about sports," he wrote in the introduction to his collection of essays). His other far-flung enterprises—the National Public Radio spots, the commentary on NBC, the Lite Beer commercial, the deal for a big and decidedly non-sports novel—could have easily led his colleagues to believe that he was going into a non-sports-related enterprise.

Deford left the office for the last time on May 1, as the magazine was going to press with his 100th bonus piece, on boxer Archie Moore. Five days later, the story of his involvement with the new enterprise, which would be called *The National*, broke in the *New York Post*. Mulvoy was furious, but far more upset about the implications—that Deford was considering going to *SI* to stock his writers for the new newspaper—than about the loss of his star writer.

But there was also a personal element to the split. From Mulvoy's perspective, the Deford debacle only ratified his long-held view of human nature: it *was* about money. Not knowing that Deford was going to get his $200,000 either way, Mulvoy assumed that he'd been "ultra-vague" as a way of tricking Time, Inc. into honoring the stock deal. Chagrined by what he viewed as a clear betrayal, Mulvoy spoke publicly about Deford's "dishonesty" to both the *New York Times* and *7 Days* magazine, turning the bitter private contentiousness into a very nasty public struggle. And as he heard that Deford was wooing prized writers like Bill Nack, Alexander Wolff, and Rick Telander, he grew increasingly angry.

In late May, Mulvoy called Deford and asked for a meeting at the University Club in midtown Manhattan, where Mulvoy spent his Sunday nights and got his weekly massages. In the genteel surroundings, the two had a heated discussion.

"I want you to stop raiding my staff," said Mulvoy.

Deford took quick umbrage, and asserted that he had the right to hire people from anywhere he wanted. "And so do you," he added. "You just took Peter King from *Newsday*."

"That's different," said Mulvoy, visibly angered. "We're *Sports Illustrated*!"

"Oh, Mark, come on!"

The meeting ended shortly thereafter.

In Mulvoy's view, Deford's inexcusable ethical breach was raiding the *SI* staff while still technically on the Time Inc. payroll. In Deford's view, he didn't start recruiting people until he left the building (although, in one conversation with articles editor Rob Fleder, he did mention that he wanted to talk to him "when I'm out of here").

Though Deford categorically denied that he'd ever agreed not to hire any *SI* staffers, Dick Munro would recall later that he "kinda told our people—didn't tell me—'I won't take any of your people.' But even if he didn't say that, to leave and be treated extraordinarily well, and then five minutes later start raiding the place that was so nice to you—to bite the proverbial hand that feeds you—is really out of order. It drove people at *SI* insane. And then, after he did that, Mark and his colleagues came to me and said that, 'You know, Dick, this guy that we all loved and treated so well has just put a knife in our backs, so we want you to rescind what you did,' and I had no problem in doing it. So we reneged on him. We took it back."

On Saturday, July 1, Deford received a letter from Mulvoy, which read: "It is with regret that I must conclude that in recent weeks you have engaged in conduct clearly detrimental to *Sports Illustrated*, in violation of the Company's conflict of interest policy and your express representations to me and others. Accordingly, I feel I have no choice but to remove you from the Company's payroll effective immediately." The letter simply meant that Deford wouldn't get the money from Time Inc., but instead from Azcarraga. But for weeks, the money had been far from Deford's mind. He was now fighting for his name, in the face of Mulvoy's accusations.

That weekend, Deford wrote a letter to Munro asking for "the opportunity to contest [Mulvoy's] rank allegations against me. . . . You are a decent man, and surely you will provide me the chance to answer these willful attacks upon my honor. I will meet you in private or in the company of any others you may choose to invite. I appreciate that these are hectic times for you, but I will call in a day or so, trusting that you remain fair and of good will."

Munro had read the letter, and described himself as "touched" by it. He sent a copy to Mulvoy and Rogin and waited for their reaction. "Now Frank can write a very nice letter, which he did. But I called and said, 'Guys, you've read the letter, I've read the letter, and do you still feel the way you feel?' Well, they would have removed his testicles." So Munro never responded.

Deford called Munro's office three times that week. But when he rang the third time, he could tell that Munro's secretary, whom Deford had known casually over the years, was under a terrific amount of stress. "He's not . . . available . . . right now," was all she could say. And in that moment, Frank Deford realized that it was time to let it go. "Don't worry," he said. "I'll never do this to you again. I'm sorry." With that, he stopped trying to explain himself to Time Inc. A twenty-seven-year relationship ended in bitterness and silence.

The root of the animosity revolved around several misunderstandings. It seems almost certain that Deford didn't directly lie to anyone at the building. He probably didn't tell Gil Rogin that the new project didn't "have anything to do with sports" (as Rogin would remember later); his answer to Jerry Kirshenbaum's question about what he was going to do next was probably not, "Jerry, I don't know" (as Kirshenbaum would remember); and he probably never told Mulvoy that the still-unnamed venture was a television enterprise (as Mulvoy would insist he did). Deford was hypersensitive to what he said, and when presented with the dearth of information, the people he spoke to at *SI* might well have drawn their own conclusions. Even the name of Azcarraga's company, Televisa, could have led to a misinterpretation of Deford's words.

At the same time, Deford clearly should have known that *SI* would view a national sports newspaper as a competing enterprise. It wasn't merely that the fledgling publication would later hire away articles editor Rob Fleder, and had already make offers to several writers (Rick Telander, Bill Nack, Steve Wulf, Alex Wolff, and Curry Kirkpatrick). *The National* would amount to nothing less than the most direct challenge to *Sports Illustrated*'s hegemony in the magazine's 35-year-history. By taking the concept of the *SI* bonus piece and putting it into a newspaper format (where it was renamed The Main Event) as well as installing Fleder to oversee it, *The National* attempted to beat *SI* on its own turf. A daily sports newspaper would inherently be more timely than *SI*, and if it also could match *SI* in depth of coverage, it would marginalize the magazine, leaving *SI* as little more than a loud picture book for teenagers, which some old-guard writers thought it was becoming anyway.

Deford's failure to woo any senior writers from *SI*, despite the money he was offering and the goodwill that he'd generated with his peers, was a sign of how much had changed in little more than a decade. When Laguerre left for *Classic,* nearly a half dozen staffers had followed him. But *SI* writers in the late '80s had become, relatively speaking, financially comfortable. *SI* was paying many of its writers in the neighborhood of $100,000, plus liberal benefits and expenses, plenty of vacation and personal freedom and, not incidentally, showcasing their work in one of the best-looking, best-selling magazines in the world. The writers might gripe to one another about how bad the editing was, or smirk about the Mulvoy tyranny, but when the time came, not a single one left.

Nack was tempted. He'd long had a stormy relationship with Mulvoy, and had worked his way into and out of Mulvoy's doghouse on several occasions. After the offer came, Nack called for a meeting with Mulvoy. His resentment over his handling, the editing, and the general running of the magazine had been building up for years, and he showed up at the meeting ready to vent his spleen.

"Well, what do you think you're going to do?" Mulvoy asked.

"I just might take it," Nack said, before launching into a litany of complaints, his voice rising with each sentence. "The morale around here is desperately low, and people are just miserable, and you're the reason behind it. You are a back-biter, and you are mean, and you are cruel, and you go behind people's backs, you're notorious . . . "

Nack looked over and noticed for the first time that Mulvoy's office door was still open. "You better close the door," he said. "I'm not done yet."

Mulvoy got up, floated over to the door, and shut it.

"Your problem, Mark, is that you came from a one-story walk-up in Dorchester, and you never got used to the fact that you rose to become a managing editor of *Sports Illustrated.* And in order to defend your turf, you're mean and difficult, and you get even with people like an alley fighter."

Mulvoy protested. "Morale's not low here."

"Stop making fucking excuses!" Nack yelled. "I know what the morale is like around here. Nobody is going to tell you because they're afraid of you, but I'm not afraid of you, 'cause I'm probably getting out of this fucking place, and you're the reason I'm leaving!"

Mulvoy's face was burning, but he didn't yell back. And as Nack opened the sliding wooden door to walk out of his office, confronting a few editors sheepishly waiting outside, he said, "I don't know what I'm going to do."

Mulvoy walked to the doorway and called after him, "Well, let me know what you decide."

Nack yelled back, "Yeah, I'll get back to you, but for now I'm fucking out of here."

But he stayed. He'd heard that other writers at *The National* were making more money than he had been offered, and he decided that he wasn't ready to return to the grind of daily journalism.

He called Mulvoy at home two weeks later to give him the news.

"Mark, Nack."

"Yeah, how are you?"

"Fine. I have decided to stay at the magazine."

"Oh, okay. All right. Good. I'm glad to hear that, Bill. Now, this isn't a raise, because we're not raising people because of this, but I'm giving you a bonus of $10,000 for staying."

"You don't have to do that," said Nack. "I certainly didn't expect anything. But I appreciate it."

"Now this isn't a raise—this is a one-shot thing."

"I understand that, Mark."

The two men talked for a few more moments and then said their good-byes. But before hanging up, Mulvoy said, "Oh, Bill?"

"Yes."

"It was a *two*-story walk-up."

# CHAPTER 17

# "PRAGUE SPRING"

In late September 1990, the top editors at each of Time Inc.'s core magazines—*Time, People, SI, Life, Fortune, Entertainment Weekly,* and *SI for Kids*—flew to Los Angeles, to "meet the cousins," Warner Bros. studio heads Bob Daly and Terry Semel. It was a get-acquainted session among corporate counterparts at the newly created Time Warner, as well as a tenuous first step toward corporate synergy, the dubious notion that the multimedia conglomerate, by working together, could be more than the sum of its parts.

The timing of the trip was perfect for *SI for Kids* managing editor John Papanek. The morning after the editors arrived, *SI for Kids* was featured in a laudatory story on the front page of the *New York Times* business section, delivered at dawn to each ME's room. At the breakfast that morning, Papanek received much good-natured kidding about his ability to plant a story.

After spending the day in meetings with Daly and Semel and touring the Warner lot, the editors returned by limousine to the Beverly Hills Hotel, where Mulvoy pulled Papanek aside and asked him to stop by his room later that evening.

When he got there, Mulvoy was practicing his golf swing.

"They want me to be publisher," Mulvoy said matter-of-factly, still working on his follow-through while Papanek sat and listened. "I had to think about it because, you know, I've often talked about maybe being publisher someday, but not yet. Not till I've done all I wanted to do at the magazine. But it's something I've often played around with, and they need something done now. And I had to think now, that if I say no, will I ever get another chance? It's something I think I could do. So, to make a long story short, I said I would do it. I want you to be the managing editor of *Sports Illustrated*."

"Oh, man."

"You know you can do it. We all know it. Gil's behind it, Jason's behind it. You've proved for two years that you can run a magazine. You've done a great job. The staff, everyone who works for you is happy."

Mulvoy was right; the appointment made sense. In many ways, it was the clearest succession choice since Laguerre had taken over for Sid James in 1960. Papanek had been at *SI* his entire adult life, had been an accomplished writer, a gifted editor and, in less than two years, taken a risky start-up project and turned it into a clear success. He would also be inheriting a magazine that was on a remarkable winning streak. In 1990, *SI* had already run Nack's award-winning story about the death of the great colt Secretariat; Ron Fimrite's historical bonus on the courageous Roy Campanella; E.M. Swift's probing profile of sports magnate Mark McCormack; even an excerpt of H.G. Bissinger's haunting Texas schoolboy football chronicle, *Friday Night Lights*. Earlier that September, Mulvoy had made his most eye-opening hire to date, bringing on the precocious Sally Jenkins, Dan's daughter, who had gone to the *San Francisco Chronicle* and, eventually, the *Washington Post*, after graduating from Stanford. The younger Jenkins was, like Rushin, a natural, and her hiring seemed to be proof that *SI*, enjoying record profits, was going to be able to bring even more writing talent to the magazine.

After talking with Mulvoy, Papanek returned to his room to call his wife. He was giddy with elation, his mind searching around in a strobe of fascinating questions about what the job entailed, what his colleagues would think, what the merger would mean to the job. Through the blur, though, a single nagging thought kept popping up: *Is Mark really ready to let go of this?*

Papanek had to keep quiet for a couple days, because Mulvoy was breaking a confidence (McManus having sworn him to secrecy). And he had to act surprised when McManus offered him the job Monday in New York. The first call Papanek made then was to Carry, whom he described as "distraught." But Carry continued as the trusted number two with Papanek's promise that he would take a more active role in Papanek's regime than he had in Mulvoy's.

When the news that Mulvoy was out and Papanek was in was announced in the office, the response on the staff was one of surprise and, in some corners, almost comic elation. Mulvoy's bullying bravado was usually good-natured, but it could be oppressive nonetheless, and many greeted his exit with a palpable sense of relief. Sarah Ballard compared the news to the fall of Juan Perón. Another editor, upon hearing the news, ran down the hallway singing, "Ding, dong, the witch is dead!" But some were still skeptical. At Mulvoy's going-away party, where Papanek and Mulvoy talked about a "new partnership" between the ad and edit sides, one writer whispered to another, "I'll believe he's gone when I see the stake through the heart."

Papanek was universally regarded as an excellent choice. After his eye troubles took him off the road in 1981, he went on the editing track and quickly established himself as a bright, responsive editor. He earned the respect of many of his fellow editors with his work at the 1984 Masters. When Ben Crenshaw won at Augusta, breaking a well-publicized, career-long drought of majors, Dan Jenkins wrote a story that seemed, to those who read it, to be underplayed. Researcher Jane "Bambi" Bachman Wulf was fretting, Mulvoy was nervous, and Rogin was furious, but Papanek saved the piece. "Papanek was the one who called Dan back and made him rewrite it, and explained to him that this was what they needed him to do," remembered Bachman Wulf. "He talked Dan into writing this terrific story. It was almost as if Dan was so close to Ben and so close to this that he couldn't capture the emotions at having watched Ben finally win the Masters. And the second story that Dan did was just a brilliant story. Papanek was a great editor."

He was also an increasingly rare item: an *SI* editor who had distinguished himself earlier through his writing. His sensibilities were far different and he was considerably younger than his two predecessors. He didn't have Rogin's hair-trigger temper or Mulvoy's bruising notion of diplomacy. Papanek was a classical music aficionado who was comfortable with new age gadgets (computers neither scared nor perplexed him) and new age thinking (he signed some of his memos "Much peace"). He and Kareem Abdul-Jabbar had discovered that they had nearly identical jazz collections during an interview for a bonus piece in 1980, and he was a talented musician who played both the clarinet and the saxophone, the latter in a bar band with *SI* senior writer Rick Telander.

But Papanek had also been a longtime sports fan with sufficient leadership skills to successfully oversee the tricky launch of *SI for Kids*. He had been well liked at the start-up, and returning now to the parent magazine, he had the support of both writers and editors, who welcomed him back with an uncommon enthusiasm. In many ways, he seemed the ideal person for the ideal job.

There was nothing to suggest that he was about to walk into what another Time Inc. ME would later describe as "the most disgraceful moment in the magazine's history."

• • •

Only in retrospect does Papanek's situation seem to have been untenable. He arrived at the precise moment that the company was imposing across-the-board cuts that required a 10 percent reduction in expenses from a magazine that had made more than $100 million in 1989. Especially odd was that the cutbacks came just one year after Time Inc. had spent millions on "retrofitting," modernizing the offices at *SI*, which moved to the 18th floor.

The week Papanek moved into the ME's office at *SI*, he received a memo about a company-wide hiring freeze. While his predecessors had possessed broad latitude to juggle personnel, Papanek was essentially stuck with Mulvoy's staff. He was also stuck with Mulvoy's problems, in particular a corporate editor, Rogin, who still wanted to top-edit his magazine and made frequent calls to the managing editor's office to find out how many of Duvoisin's pictures were going to be in the magazine.

And, finally, Papanek was stuck with Mulvoy. The new publisher hated his job almost instantly ("It was only a couple months before he started talking about it being a big mistake," said his brother Tom). Restless, disillusioned, and displeased with Papanek's changes, Mulvoy went back to his old routine, working the phones, kvetching daily to the AMEs and senior editors working below Papanek.

"It was clear right away that I was going to have two former managing editors very close to me, both of whom I knew well enough to know that they were incredibly possessive and protective of their particular perception of the franchise," said Papanek. "I knew from day one that I was going to have to live with these two guys. And you know, perhaps a bit naively, I thought that I could handle it. If only because, frankly, I had never had any trouble living with anybody that I had worked with in my previous 17 years at the magazine. The understanding, when the baton was handed over, was 'You're the managing editor, it's your magazine. I'm the publisher, I've got my job to do.' Mark was never able to abide by those rules. Not for a minute."

Meanwhile, Papanek was trying to get his new regime off on as positive a note as possible. He flew virtually all the staff writers in for a summit conference in December, at which he announced, "My entire life, I've wanted this job. It's what I've always dreamed of." One of the senior writers, E.M. Swift, recalled the moment: "I don't know why, but I thought, *That's too bad*. Somehow, he held it in too much reverence."

Papanek had conceived the conference as a cathartic session that would clear the acrimonious air between writers and editors. And the writers, newly emboldened by a chance to vent their grievances, complained that they often didn't get a chance to see the edits made to their stories before they went to press, and that many editors either disregarded or didn't understand rhythm and tone. Sally Jenkins said that in her first experiences of writing for the magazine, she felt that the pieces that ran were unnecessarily generic, that the editing was often "brutal." Rick Telander presented a laundry list of editing atrocities: "Perforce" had been put into one of his sentences, as well as "come a cropper" and "schneid." Not only wouldn't he use those words, he said, he didn't really know what they meant. And in his story about 300-pound college golfer Chris Patton, the burly Patton's quote while nursing a hangover, "A drunk motherfucker is a dangerous motherfucker," came out "A wounded animal is a dangerous animal." Telander wasn't arguing for the profanity, only for the expletive deleted dashes, so as to retain the flavor of the sentence. While Peter Carry fumed, Papanek set about trying to explain things from the editors' view. The one concrete thing that came out of the meeting was that editors would try to fax proof pages, the typeset stories, laid out for the page, to writers, so they could see what had been done to their stories.

Meanwhile, Papanek immediately altered the magazine's story mix, tapping into a wider, more disparate strain of subjects. December brought a Maryanne Vollers essay on endangered animals in Zambia, as well as a bonus piece from *SI* veteran Robert T. Jones on his golden retriever, Luke. A bonus piece by Franz Lidz about Don King's hair had been trashed by Mulvoy as insignificant and rambling. But when Papanek asked his senior editors for any stories they liked that had been killed, it was the first piece that article editor Chris Hunt volunteered. "From Hair to Eternity" ran in the December 10, 1990, issue.

Not all of his choices were so well received. With writing pronounced as the new priority, many staffers were surprised when Leigh Montville was installed as the regular Point After writer. The former *Boston Globe* columnist had written several solid feature stories for *SI*, but his bonuses were frequently self-conscious and overwritten, and he was disastrously miscast for the role of Point After. Barring that misstep, 1991 began well. A slight tweak in the magazine's design was overdue. Steve Hoffman had always viewed his design as evolutionary and under Papanek he set about working on a different headline typeface. More important, Papanek focused on the Scorecard section, which he felt needed a major overhaul. Papanek, Hoffman, and Steve Wulf, who would edit the section, set out to re-create it. They came up with a more colorful, relaxed look, and added a feature that looked back to an *SI* issue and small writing sample from past years. The retooled Scorecard, which opened to positive reviews in the 1991 swimsuit issue, was at once progressive while at the same time acutely aware (especially under Wulf) of its heritage, possessed of a rich institutional history. Mulvoy hated it. "Mark used that, I think, more than anything else to support his belief that somehow I was the devil incarnate," said Papanek.

While Papanek was hearing rumors about Mulvoy's complaints, the comments of his old mentor Rogin were more vituperative and more direct, coming in weekly critiques of his issues in red or blue ballpoint ink, correcting editing mistakes, mocking dull headlines, and grading each and every story from A to F. In light of Papanek's inexperience, having such an accomplished veteran to judge his work should have been a plus. He knew that Rogin could be a brutal critic, but in the first few weeks of critiques, he saw something else: a profoundly unhappy man who was still heartbroken over being pushed out of his dream job five years earlier.

"He's the most complex, strangest character I've ever encountered in my life," Papanek would say later of Rogin. "I consider him to be brilliant, and my greatest ally, and irrational, and my worst enemy at the same time. When I think over the twenty years I worked under him, I feel like I'm spinning in a centrifuge trying to figure him out. I saw him do things to copy that made my jaw drop in the way that listening to Mozart makes me feel sometimes. That's no exaggeration. And later on, when he was in a position to do whatever he wanted, I saw him do things that were just so incredibly wrong, that I couldn't believe he could do it."

Rogin's curious animosity toward talented writers was evident in his critiques, which veered toward the irrational. Gary Smith's award-winning bonus on basketball on an Indian reservation (judged by the American Society of Magazine Editors to be the best-written feature story in American magazines in 1991) earned a B-minus in Rogin's estimation. William Nack's equally accomplished story on Sonny Liston, "O Unlucky Man," merited only a B.

While he was prone to bizarre inconsistencies, much of Rogin's hammering criticisms in the weekly critiques had credence. Rogin's main substantive complaints centered on the look of the magazine. Much of the criticism was directed at photo editor Karen Mullarkey, who went outside SI's network of staff and contract photographers to commission more posed shots. The results were often embarrassingly cloying: a bonus piece on Billie Jean King included a four-column opening photograph of a smirking, tensed-up King, almost gruesomely mugging toward the camera, flanked by a placid, unsmiling Martina Navratilova and Tim Wilkinson, whose own smile had been frozen so long he'd gone cross-eyed. "What is this shit!!" scrawled Rogin on the critique copy of the issue, and others wondered the same thing.

While Scorecard was an aesthetic success, the design in the rest of the magazine seemed to surge out of control as Hoffman was given freer rein to assert his will, taking frequent and inexplicable departures from his previous stylistic blueprint. Double-truck bonus piece openings were often replaced by single-page shots facing off against postmodern typographic flourishes, usually followed in turn by thematically unrelated second spreads that only served to distract the reader from the story at hand. "An ME has to come down on his art director every once in a while, or else he'll take over the whole goddamn magazine," said one veteran editor. "John never did that, and so Steve Hoffman ran off with the thing." Hoffman was free to experiment more than he ever had before, and while a few of the daring presentations worked, many didn't, leading to design blights like the yellow, 5½-inch deep capital letter that opened a feature story on Dennis "Oil Can" Boyd. For the first time since the late '50s, longtime readers frequently couldn't tell where they were in the magazine or, occasionally, what magazine they were in.

It would become the central paradox of the Papanek regime: while much of the writing that appeared in the magazine was among the best of the post-Laguerre era, the packaging of that writing, including covers, layout, story mix, and design, was frequently less coherent than at any time since the '50s.

It was, for a mass-market weekly magazine, a fatal flaw. John Papanek, given time, patience and constructive criticism, might have grown out of it. But instead he was bombed by Rogin's critiques from above and Mulvoy's back-channel criticism from his flanks. Papanek could handle writers. He wasn't prepared for the rest of it.

Just as surely, Mark Mulvoy wasn't ready to be publisher, at least not under the difficult circumstances in which he took the job. Don Barr's publishing tenure had lasted five years and while the magazine had enjoyed astounding success over that time, it was now forced to contend with a hangover from Michael Loeb's circulation transgressions and a general downturn in the ad environment. Annual ad dollars, which had risen about $100 million, to $336 million annually during Barr's first four years on the job, stalled in 1990 at $335 million (and the added revenue was due solely to a rate increase; the magazine had lost more than 300 ad pages from the previous year). A retrenchment was occurring throughout the company. The new media monolith Time Warner was weighed down with $19 billion in accumulated debt, and the magazine division at Time

Inc. was one of the few assured profit centers. Inevitably, the magazines would be pushed to maximize their profit margins.

Bob Miller and his boss Reg Brack saw one possible solution. More companies were advertising in multiple editions of Time Inc.'s weeklies—*Time, SI, People,* and *Entertainment Weekly*—but to do so, they had to deal with four different ad staffs, none of which was authorized to cut them group deals. Rising business side star Don Elliman, the executive vice-president of marketing, suggested that the company pool its larger accounts and sell the Time Inc. weeklies as a package. While the move would take some authority out of the hands of publishers and ad directors at the individual magazines, it offered the possibility of securing more and larger contracts, a necessity in the deflated advertising environment. The new group, called Time Inc. Corporate Sales, was established just as Mulvoy was taking over, with Elliman playing a key role, as president of sales and marketing.

Mulvoy discovered very quickly that with the corporate ad sales strategy intact, much of the publisher's power was reduced. More important, the sensibilities required for the job were different. As ME, he had played golf and had drinks with publishing side execs and advertisers. He was always greeted as the conscientious leader, the busy but understanding editor who was taking time on a special occasion to see an advertiser. But as publisher, it was his job to see advertisers, his job to cater to their whims. Of Mulvoy's performance as a publisher, the consensus was that he was the wrong man for the position. "He wasn't paying attention," said one executive. "He didn't understand some of the things they were trying to do. I would view some of this with a grain of salt, because I think that Mark's experience as an editor made him more protective. But his fast-action approach to life was not suited to that job. Mark's attention span was very short, and on the business side they needed him to sit down and go through the numbers and make some very concrete decisions that had to be very carefully considered."

Instead, Mulvoy was watching what he viewed as his magazine being altered in ways he found unconscionable. It didn't bring out the best in him. In March 1991, on the day that the *New York Times* reviewed Franz Lidz's memoir *Unstrung Heroes*, Lidz was taking a congratulatory call from Rogin when Mulvoy stormed into his office and tore the handful of 50 photocopies of the review from his hands. "I turned to see Mulvoy, his face flushed a fire-engine red," Lidz recalled. "He screamed, 'Did you run these off on Time Inc. machines?' I shook my head. 'If you want to be a celebrity,' he snarled, 'you've got to pay the price.' As he stormed off, I thought, 'What a sad man.'"

For all his difficulties with Mulvoy and Rogin, Papanek seemed to have earned the staff's support until the spring of 1991 when he announced that *SI* was laying off senior writers Ron Fimrite and Pat Putnam. Presented with what the company euphemistically called an RIF (reduction in forces) directive, and an order to cut 10 percent off the magazine's overhead, Papanek decided to put Fimrite and Putnam (the two oldest writers on the staff) on contract. Fimrite had been home in San Francisco, eating lunch with his wife Linda, the day Papanek called. "He sounded embarrassed," remembered Fimrite. "He said, 'I hope you feel good about this—what we want to do is take you off the payroll and offer you this contract.'"

While the ensuing settlement prevented either side from discussing terms, it was well-known among the staff that Fimrite had been offered a contract for barely half of his annual salary, without receiving any of the benefits to which salaried employees were entitled.

"We still love you," Papanek assured the stunned Fimrite after mentioning the terms. "We just have all these young guys, and we need them to write the weekly stories. We know that you don't want to do that anyway, so we thought that this was the best way to do it."

"You're wrong," said Fimrite. "Not at those figures. That's absurd. Is this what I get after twenty years, this piddling sum?"

Across the country, Pat Putnam, the longtime boxing writer and devoutly conscientious journalist, the second oldest writer on the staff behind Fimrite, was called in and offered essentially the same deal. "That's when I discovered what a prick Peter Carry was," said Putnam. "Boy, he fooled me for years and years and years. He was assigned to tell me they were going to send me off with a contract. They were letting me go, more or less. He called it a minor bump in the road. Jesus Christ! Papanek didn't even have the guts to tell me."

Fimrite's case, after Papanek's weak explanation, became an open-and-shut age-discrimination case, and *SI* was so eager to settle it that they wound up offering Fimrite a contract for *exactly* what he had been making before. They also ran a glowing pub memo about his longtime contributions. Papanek talked Putnam out of filing a suit, convincing him to go on contract with the understanding that he wouldn't be limited to its terms and could write as much as he wanted.

Even though Papanek made several efforts at damage control, the moves undercut morale throughout the magazine. "They didn't even bother to ask Ron [if he was ready to go on contract]," said fellow staff writer John Garrity. "They assumed it. It was the last thing on his mind. It was absolutely devastating, and it was insulting and it was disruptive. My reaction to this was that if it could happen to him, it could happen to anybody."

• • •

*The National*, launched in January 1990 with Frank Deford as editor, was a journalistic money pit from the start. The biggest expense was coordinating the logistics of putting several pages of local coverage within editions in each of the three markets (New York, Chicago, Los Angeles) in which the paper launched. It was a misguided, quixotic effort; *The National's* greatest appeal was to hardcore sports fans who turned to it to provide coverage of teams that their local papers weren't covering. When the paper scrapped the localized notion and went to a single national edition, the handful of highly paid local columnists rotated on a single spread (it came to be known as "the million-dollar page" among *National* staffers).

An even graver problem occurred over deadlines. Readers paying 50 cents (eventually the single-issue price would go to 75 cents) for an all-sports newspaper, properly expected the paper to have all the West Coast results from the previous night. But *The National* was piggybacking onto existing presses throughout the country, meaning it was slotted into earlier deadlines. Its distribution deal with the *Wall Street Journal* meant that the paper had to go out at an earlier hour anyway. This alienated even the most avid fans. When the newspaper launched, Deford was one of 33 subscribers in the Westport, Connecticut, area. By the time he canceled his own home subscription, out of frustration with the shoddy delivery pattern, only two other people in the area were still subscribing.

*The National* was often a success journalistically, frequently beating or outperforming *SI* on news stories and long features, and bringing a level of sophistication to the presentation of statistical information that *USA Today* couldn't match. But very quickly, its real journalistic accomplishments were overshadowed by its money troubles. The newspaper used a discount phone service that required reporters to dial 31 digits to make an outside phone call. The handling of finances was so strained that Deford once had to step in to prevent a fistfight between two department heads. And in the fall of 1990, when business manager Dan Correa was fired, he left the office with his desk locked. When the bottom drawer was pried open, Televisa executives found over $2 million in unpaid invoices. "He did the same thing with bills for *The National* that we used to do with our phone bills in college," said one *National* staffer. "Hey—I don't see it, I don't gotta pay it!"

The paper was clearly in trouble early in 1991 when *SI* tried to hire away Mike Lupica, *The National's* star columnist, to become the sole writer of the back-page Point After column. Lupica, the tough-minded but sentimental writer who'd become the best-read sports columnist in New York, had broken out to a national audience in the newspaper (he was also making regular appearances on ESPN's *The Sports Reporters*). Papanek's long courtship of Lupica ended only after *SI* blanched at his price tag (reported to be $250,000), and Lupica bolted the sinking *National* to return to the *New York Daily News* in the spring of '91.

The newspaper folded just months later, on June 13, 1991. Azcarraga's enterprise was fraught with miscalculation and mismanagement, and beset by more than $100 million in losses. *SI* made no mention of the newspaper's demise; Deford's messy exit and the challenge for writers had left deep wounds, especially among the upper-level managers. When Papanek tried to hire Rob Fleder back as an assistant managing editor, Mulvoy went to McManus and protested. (He was eventually brought back, under the new title of features editor, making the identical salary he was making when he left. Mulvoy had come off his absolute ban on *National* employees, but he was determined that staffers shouldn't be rewarded for defecting.)

The day *The National* crashed, Papanek wrote a short note to Deford, remarking about the sense of loss that "all sports fans" felt about the paper's demise. "I remain a great admirer of yours, anxious to learn what you plan to do next," wrote Papanek. "Might it be possible, do you think, for Deford and *SI* to ever get together again?" The query would prompt a fascinating, foreboding correspondence. Deford wrote back five days later, thanking Papanek for his kind words:

> I remain, John, as affectionate as ever about the people and the institution that is *Sports Illustrated*. I have never wavered in my warm feelings for that good place. Alas, the man who runs *Sports Illustrated* is the only person I have known in my life who has chosen to defame me.
>
> Mark Mulvoy has publicly called me a cheat and a liar; he has made accusations against me which have no basis in truth whatsoever. Out of gratuitous malice, he strived to deny me a considerable sum of money promised me in good faith. In private conversations (at least the ones repeated to me) he has been even uglier with his slurs upon my character.

I'm sure Mark has his own reasons for being so spiteful. But obviously, so long as he is in the saddle, there is no way I can ever return to *Sports Illustrated.*

Deford's words unintentionally struck a nerve with Papanek. He responded quickly, hoping to make clear exactly who was in charge at the new magazine:

> Dear Frank,
> I can understand your bad feelings for Mulvoy, but surely you don't believe that the publisher "runs" *Sports Illustrated.*
> I can hear you chuckling at that one, Frank, but seriously, Mark does not run the magazine, I do. I have made it clear to Mark, Gil Rogin and Jason McManus that I would welcome your writing in *SI* if you were to indicate an interest.
> If it's Mark's association with *SI* that keeps you away, so be it, although that saddens me. But please—he's strictly business-side now, and hands-off with edit.

• • •

In the summer of 1991, the wheels came off. There was a void at the center of the magazine, a lack of clarity in story ideas and a lack of discipline in execution. In August, 23 years after Olsen's piece, *SI* would revisit the Black Athlete, in an unfocused series that was doomed from the outset. Senior editors Sandy Padwe and Roy Johnson conceived of the series, but there was little oversight in terms of cohesiveness, direction, or themes, only Padwe's baleful pub memo reflection, "Have things gotten better? I'm not so sure. Let the readers decide." When it premiered, *SI* didn't even tell readers how many weeks the series would run, only that it would be a "multipart series on the black athlete that begins with this issue." And while Olsen's '68 series had been a fount of bracing, unconventional wisdom, much of the new series was nothing but scattershot platitudes, as diffuse as the ten different voices in a "roundtable discussion" article that ran in the opening week of the series. (Padwe said he'd planned other stories for the series, but couldn't get them through the editing gauntlet.)

By splitting the writing among several writers, *SI* was guaranteeing a loss of focus. The series did have a reliable linchpin, in Kenny Moore's two-part series "A Courageous Stand" and "The Eye of the Storm" revisiting the events that led up to Tommie Smith and John Carlos's black-gloved salute, and the fallout from that protest. It included one of the most evocative design presentations in the magazine's history, opening with a crisp, eloquently shadowed black-and-white Brian Lanker collage of Smith's and Carlos's track pictures and memorabilia. But much of the rest of the series descended into flabby leftist cant, and earnest hand-wringing. One AME put it best: "Olsen's piece shocked people out of their complacency; all we did was sit around and express profound concern."

But the botching of a major series wasn't even the biggest problem. The storm that Neil Leifer had forecast five years earlier finally came to pass. Gil Rogin had been hammering Papanek regularly about the perceived misuse of his girlfriend Jacqueline Duvoisin, and as the golf season heated up, the complaints became almost manic in their intensity and irrationality.

Rogin's general critiques of the magazine were always fervent, but usually apt. However, about photography, especially when Duvoisin was even tangentially involved, he seemed to lose all judgment. Papanek recalled the tone: "It was like, 'Here's this week's issue, here are ten terrible pictures, but here's one brilliant picture.' And gee, isn't it funny that the brilliant picture was taken by Jackie? But the terrible pictures were taken by Ron Modra? And it was so blatantly obvious! If you take two pictures, the Jackie 'brilliant' picture and the 'terrible' Ron Modra picture, and put them in front of any twenty people, all twenty would say the good picture is the Ron Modra picture, that the bad picture is the Jackie picture. But he would see it as exactly the opposite. And then, without any qualms whatsoever, argue the point, beat it to death that Modra's picture was too posed, it shows no sophistication, it's this, it's that. Jackie's picture, on the other hand, is naively innocent, it's innocently wonderful, it's a 'great snap.'"

At the 1991 U.S. Open golf tournament at Hazeltine, where Payne Stewart beat Scott Simpson in a playoff, the entire crew of four photographers had come back with subpar work. When Rogin called to find out what the picture situation was, Papanek informed him that there were "slim pickings." Rogin didn't believe it, so Papanek invited him down to see for himself. And then, in the layout room, Papanek looked on in disbelief as Rogin, surveying the unchosen slides on a nearby light table, chose a pair of what Rogin described as "perfectly excellent" shots that were taken by Duvoisin, then publicly suggested, with photo technicians and subeditors and design people staring on dumbly, that the two Duvoisin pictures would be ideally suited to be the two pictures on the story's opening spread. Papanek gritted his teeth and said nothing, choosing to accede to Rogin's suggestion. Many who were there perceived his lack of action as tantamount to a surrender. It was the day he lost the troops. "He just let Gil completely castrate him in front of the picture people and the researchers and whoever was there," said one longtime staffer. "It was just brutal, and yet I say that's Papanek's fault if he let him get away with that. And, you know, Rogin has no shame. He hurts everybody."

While the Duvoisin situation was the flashpoint, Papanek and Rogin's relationship was deteriorating over a variety of issues. The Michigan grad's politics were conventionally liberal, and Rogin's were, at first glance, identical (Jerry Kirshenbaum, who wrote Scorecard during much of Rogin's ME tenure, said he felt the magazine strived for a "good liberal" slant). But Papanek was hearing some unconventional criticism in his meetings with Rogin, who excoriated him for devoting a bonus piece by Rick Reilly to filmmaker Spike Lee. "I get called on the carpet," remembered Papanek. "I get called up by Gil Rogin because he's not a mainstream sports figure, is another black and, 'Do you have a social agenda?' and 'By the way, that story on women sportscasters, you know, no one really cares about women sportscasters. You trying to change society? Are you trying to use the magazine as some weapon of cultural change? Do you have an agenda, a political agenda?' And then he would start counting the number of blacks on the cover." (Rogin would later deny doing so.) Rogin bemoaned Papanek's editorial slant, which he deemed to be "stories about suicides and drugs, and the travail of black people." From Papanek's side, it mattered not that Rogin called himself "the rabbi to the blacks," didn't even matter that Rogin's good friend Quincy Jones referred to Gil as Mack Daddy G. All Papanek knew was that he was trying to cover the world as he saw it, and Rogin was obstructing him.

It finally fell to Peter Carry to take a decisive stand against Rogin's meddling. Papanek was vacationing in the summer of 1991 and Carry was top-editing in his absence when Ian Baker-Finch won the British Open at Royal Birkdale. Rogin, making the usual calls, pressed his old protégé for assurances that Duvoisin's pictures would appear. But Carry, who'd spent nearly a year watching Papanek wither in the Rogin-Mulvoy vise, was in a fighting mood. Screaming at Rogin on the telephone, Carry could be heard throughout the floor. And with that episode, finally, the spat went public. Staffers leaked news of the flap to the news media, and both *Newsweek* and *New York* magazine published small items, reporting that McManus had finally intervened, and taken Rogin off oversight duties.

But even that wasn't quite true. McManus, who as editor-in-chief ran the company with all the decisiveness of a painfully shy freshman at his first college mixer, chose not to confront Rogin directly. Instead, he requested that Rogin send his critiques thereafter to McManus rather than Papanek.

Through it all, Rogin remained a staunch defender of Duvoisin (who would, by the mid-'90s, develop into a credible golf photographer). But he was blinded to the residual damage he was doing to the magazine. When confronted with the issue later, Rogin cited examples in the Time Inc. culture of editors doing far worse than he. "Managing editors have fucked people on top of their desks!—who were their employees!"

Of Rogin's meddling on behalf of Duvoisin, McManus would only say that "when I became aware of this, I took the necessary steps to look into it. Mulvoy never complained about it. You must go back to the fact that Rogin was his mentor and best friend, and he had no desire to upset Gil on that subject. Mulvoy's a fixer, and he didn't consider this a big problem."

But the idea that McManus was unaware of "the Jackie situation" found few takers and was rejected outright by those closest to the situation. "McManus is full of it," said Papanek. "He, along with everyone in the building, had known of Gil's meddling on behalf of his girlfriend for years and years, largely because Mulvoy would tell stories about it all the time, even at managing editor lunches! Only when it got into the outside press did it become public enough to embarrass McManus." On this point, Papanek and Mulvoy were in agreement. "He knew," said Mulvoy of McManus.

After pulling Rogin off direct oversight of *SI*, McManus made another miscalculation, choosing Mulvoy as Rogin's replacement. "I knew Mark well enough that he could keep this Chinese wall, these two jobs, in his head," said McManus later. "I never heard any criticism of Mark." Suddenly, 67 years after Henry Luce and Brit Hadden had firmly established the church/state separation between the editorial and business sides, one man was overseeing both. Not only did McManus suggest that Mulvoy critique the issues, he also invited him to come in and help Papanek with Sunday night closes. It wouldn't last long.

For a time, the odd arrangement seemed to be working. With Mulvoy's assistance, Papanek focused more on layout and design, and there was, initially, a marked improvement in the magazine's visual appearance. Jimmy Connors's adrenaline-pumping run through the U.S. Open had been the *only* story at that tournament, and Papanek put the semifinal loser on the cover as "The People's Choice."

A month later, Steve Rushin turned a corner, solidifying his stature as *SI*'s rising young star. On September 5, his mother had died of a sudden illness. He returned home to the Twin Cities, where he remained for several weeks. Upon his return to work, Papanek decided to give him lead writing duties for the World Series between the Twins and the Atlanta Braves. Atlanta led after five games, as the series headed back for game six at the Metrodome.

After a tense, 12-inning duel, Kirby Puckett pushed the series to a seventh game with his solo homer in the bottom of the 12th, sending the pressbox into hoots of disgust. A drained Rushin blinked and looked around quizzically, then finally figured it out: Puckett's homer meant a game seven, which meant all the newspaper writers who'd booked Sunday morning getaway flights would now have to stay a day longer. Sitting in their midst, not yet 25 years old but already at the top of his profession, Rushin quietly marveled at the collective cynicism of his colleagues, and promised himself never to turn into one of those writers who could cheer only for deadlines.

The next night, Tom Glavine and Jack Morris faced off in an epic pitchers' duel before the Twins finally prevailed. After spending three hours in the locker rooms, Rushin headed to his parents' home to write the most important story of his brief career.

"I set up down in the basement and it was just like a term paper," he said. "Now you've got to get the whole thing done in one night. It was the greatest sports event I'd ever attended. It was just—if you couldn't be fired up about that . . ."

He started writing at three, and sent the story less than five hours later. The kid who'd forged his birth certificate so he could sell beer at the old Metropolitan Stadium in Bloomington was now reporting on a dramatic World Series, and he didn't flinch. "The truth is inelastic when it comes to the 88th World Series. It is impossible to stretch. It isn't necessary to appraise the nine days just past from some distant horizon of historical perspective. Let us call this Series what it is, now, while its seven games still ring in our ears: the greatest that was ever played." André Laguerre would have changed it to "best," but he could have had few complaints about the rest of the story, in which Rushin artfully extracted the drama of the series in his bright prose, free of inordinate puns or self-referential humor. He did note that, in game six, Kirby Puckett had "leapt high against a Plexiglas panel in centerfield, hanging there momentarily like one of those suction-cup Garfield dolls in a car window, to rob Ron Gant of extra bases and Atlanta of an almost certain run."

Despite the improved appearance of the magazine, Papanek and Mulvoy weren't working well together. "Every Sunday, he would come in, sit in one of the offices, attend the Sunday picture shows," said Papanek. "Occasionally he'd take me aside and make some suggestions, which I was happy to receive. But far more frequently, he'd wander down the hall, walk into Jerry Kirshenbaum's office, and say, 'Why is he doing four pages instead of six? Why is he leading with the Bills instead of the Raiders?' He would do this constantly."

By the end of October, every day seemed to bring a new incident. The biggest was Papanek's decision to use men in the swimsuit issue. He felt that the best way to defuse the sniping about sexism would be to go coed with the portfolio of beautiful bodies. He'd start small, using a few tasteful shots of one beloved athlete. Through August and September, as Jule Campbell was lining up locations for the shoots that November, Papanek was holding quiet talks with Earvin "Magic" Johnson, who enthusiastically agreed to become *SI*'s first male supermodel.

Like virtually everything else in the Papanek era, this plan self-destructed.

Papanek was returning from lunch on Friday, November 1, when senior editor Roy Johnson met him outside his office to give him the news that Magic Johnson was announcing his retirement that afternoon because he had tested positive for HIV, likely the result of years of sexual promiscuity. In the blizzard of calls and planning that followed—*SI* scrambling to scrap their planned stories for that week's issue and giving assignments for a kaleidoscopic look at the Johnson situation—Papanek called Johnson's agent, Lon Rosen, to negotiate for an exclusive as-told-to story by Magic Johnson and Roy Johnson (the two were not related, but had collaborated on a book two years earlier).

Rosen called back later that day with an okay from Johnson to do the story. "One other thing," Rosen said, "Earvin specifically asked me to tell you that he still very much wants to be in the swimsuit issue photo shoot."

There was a moment of silence, as Papanek searched for the right words of response. "I just don't think it would be appropriate, Lon, for Magic to be in a bathing-suit issue with all these models."

Papanek spent the rest of the day making assignments: Jack McCallum wrote an overview of Johnson's career and E.M. Swift covered the culture of sexual licentiousness in professional sports. On Saturday, Papanek spoke with Roy Johnson from L.A. and talked further with photo editor Karen Mullarkey about getting pictures.

There was a big slide show on Sunday morning, where Papanek and Mulvoy clashed over the choice of pictures for the contents spread. Later that day, Papanek called a meeting with his senior editors. He didn't invite Mulvoy. When the publisher learned of it later, he walked out of the building, called McManus later, and asked to be taken off the oversight detail.

Four days later, McManus called Papanek into his office to say that the Mulvoy plan obviously wasn't working either. The new plan would have editorial director Richard Stolley, whose knowledge of sports made McManus look like Bob Costas by comparison, supervising and critiquing the issues.

But while Mulvoy wasn't dealing with Papanek on a daily basis, his presence was still felt throughout the floor. "It was as obvious as it could ever possibly be that he wanted the job back," said Papanek. "And he told me a hundred times, 'I don't want the job, I don't want the job back, I've had the job. I've done it. I've done everything I want to do.'"

Just before Christmas 1991, Neil Leifer stopped in at the barbershop in the Time & Life Building to get his hair cut. That morning, the year-end double-issue of *SI* had hit the stands. It was The Year in Pictures issue, with an overhead shot of a discus thrower on the cover. In walked Mulvoy, who gave him the customary greeting, "Hi, Leifer," and sat down for a shave.

Leifer remembered it as "like the first scene in *The Untouchables*, where Robert DeNiro's all stretched out flat and they've just put the hot towel over his face."

As they sat next to each other, Mulvoy spoke first.

"What do you think of that fucking cover today?"

"What?" said Leifer, a little taken aback.

"Was that a—*piece—of—shit* or what?"

"Well, you know, Mark, it is 'The Year in Pictures'; it's a very unusual picture."

"Bullshit! I've got to sell that magazine for two weeks with that crap on the cover."

There was a moment of silence, and then Mulvoy spoke again.

"And did you see that opening spread?"

Papanek by then had been inundated with reports of rampant Mulvoy criticism from back channels. "'Between you and me.' He'd say that a hundred times a day, and he could be standing on top of the Empire State Building shouting at the top of his lungs thinking that he's talking to one person, 'between you and me.'"

• • •

Despite a rocky 1991, Papanek went into 1992 hopeful and intent on improving his performance. He'd actively recruited two of *The National*'s best writers, the acerbic takeout writer Charles Pierce, and Norman Chad, the one surprise star from the brief life of the newspaper. Pierce was a contentious, irreverent Bostonian whom Papanek had tried to recruit in the mid-'80s, but his idiosyncratic submissions didn't fit into the Mulvoy mold. With his old boss Fleder back at *SI* as features editor and Papanek as ME, he wrote several features on a freelance basis for *SI*.

Chad had been the prototypical couch potato as a copy editor at the *Washington Post*. He'd written a TV column one day a week, but was hired away by *The National* because *Post* sports editor George Solomon wasn't convinced the paper needed a full-time sports TV critic. Rather than writing in the quick, elliptical style of *USA Today*'s Rudy Martzke, Chad wrote from the spleen, from the stance of the intelligent, long-suffering sports fan who, in the modern age, was subjected to all manner of electronic-media indignities just to watch his beloved games.

Papanek envisioned a regular spot for Chad, in the retooled, expanded Scorecard section. The idea was to give Chad his own column, of about 700 words a week, which would run boxed in Scorecard.

With a contract that began in January '92, Chad would attempt a signed column, something that had never really been done before in *SI*. William Taffe had written a TV/Radio column, but it had a strong reporting component, a far cry from the pointed irreverence of Chad. For all of the freedom that the magazine offered its writers, the magazine had never supported a regular opinion column; there was no analogue to the regular signed columns of John Lardner and, later, Pete Axthelm in *Newsweek*. Chad entered with high hopes, but he was soon discouraged by the ominous warnings he heard from his friends on the staff. *SI* alum and fellow *National* refugee Suzie Kamb told him, "Norman, I know you are very responsible, and you are a great deadline player, but do not turn the columns in any earlier than you need to."

Writing about his time at *SI* later, Chad was rueful about the entire experience. "I was hired by *Sports Illustrated* to write a weekly humor column on sports and TV. This was not a good idea for either party. I was writing for a group of editors, very Caucasian and very male, who were pretty well educated, pretty well insulated, pretty darn middle-aged and, to borrow a line from *Good Morning, Vietnam*, pretty much more in dire need of a blow job than any white men in history."

Chad soon learned that, with writers flung all over the country, communication was difficult. And while Rick Reilly and William Nack were routinely consulted about changes made to their copy, others were not. It became necessary for Chad to heed Sally Jenkins's advice to "follow the damn column from start to finish." And sometimes, receiving faxed copies of the edited column didn't help. "This really fooled me," he said. "I can't believe I fell for this for the first few weeks. It's on the page already, I'd call them and say, 'Yeah, okay, this is fine.' Then they'd change it. That wasn't the final edition. They saw me coming from a mile away. What bothered me then was the general deceit or misleading way that they would do it, because they didn't want to deal with writers."

Chad's problems would underscore a stasis that had been setting in at *SI* for a decade. As writers moved away and editors began to work shorter weeks, the time available for one-to-one consultation on stories began to shrink. Writers heard that there "just wasn't time" to fax an edited copy of their stories back to them. The lack of communication led to a flagging morale, not to mention egregious errors, as when an editor changed investigative reporter Lester Munson's story and referred to Don King as Mike Tyson's "manager." Writers, as long as there is paper to print their stories on and alcohol to drink after they've been written, will bitch about editing. But the institutional arrogance at *SI*, where out-of-sight writers were often out of mind as well, damaged both morale and the quality of the magazine. It was as Bob Creamer had long suspected: too much rough handling left writers defeated, uncaring.

Mike Tyson's rape trial provided a glimpse of the workings of the magazine. Much of the staff had already flown to Albertville, France, for the 1992 Winter Olympics. When the verdict came back, at 11 o'clock on a Monday night, *SI* was looking at a last-minute turnaround that would place Tyson on the cover under the headline "GUILTY!"

Bill Nack was covering the story from the Indiana courthouse and had 90 minutes to write about 125 lines. "I'm looking at the clock, and the clichés bombard you at first, 'cause they're the easiest. So I try to focus on the final, culminating moment of the trial, when they announced the verdict. All of a sudden, out of nowhere comes *The Second Coming*, by William Butler Yeats. I don't know why it came up, but it came up. The line was, 'And what rough beast, its hour come round at last / Slouches towards Bethlehem to be born?' And so I thought: 'The hour had come round at last,' and judge so-and-so had done this. So I started from there and finished in, like, an hour."

Nack filed the story and called senior editor Steve Robinson, who pronounced himself pleased with it. "Steve, I got one request," said Nack. "The opening line is from a poem by Yeats, called *The Second Coming*. All the Yeats scholars who read *SI*—both of them—will smile when they read the line. I would like it to stay intact, word for word: The hour had come round at last . . ."

"I like that," said Robinson.

Now Nack was excited. He called his friend Munson, who (along with fellow investigative reporter Sonja Steptoe) had done superb reporting throughout the Tyson–Desiree Washington case. "I think I got Yeats in the magazine!" Nack said.

The phone rang in Nack's room at nine the next morning. It was Robinson.

"Nack," he said, "I got one bad piece of news for you."

"The lead, right?"

"I couldn't help it. You know, Peter—he took out the word 'round.'"

Nack, by his own estimation, "went nuts" and began screaming at Robinson. "THEY TOOK OUT THE WORD 'ROUND'?! Now it's a CLICHÉ! 'The hour came at last'? 'Round' was the word that made the whole fucking sentence!"

"I know," said the apologetic Robinson. "I'm sorry. There's nothing I can do. I told Peter it was important to you, I told him it was a line out of Yeats."

"Well, what did he say?"

"He said it was excessive."

That sent Nack off on another tirade, which subsided into a slow burn that would continue for several weeks. When Papanek returned from Albertville, Nack stopped in the office and sat down with him, showing Papanek his original version and the edited one.

"Who did that?" asked Papanek.

"Peter."

Papanek shook his head. "He just doesn't get it, does he?"

• • •

As the strain on Papanek grew greater, he tightened up. His voice seemed taut and constricted, he seemed to lack clear judgment, and even letters that used to routinely bear the farewell salutation "Much peace" now ended with a perfunctory J.P. He snapped at his editors, dug his heels in on arguments with Hoffman or Mullarkey, and had taken to using a gloomy gallows humor in talking about his estranged dealings with Rogin, whom he often referred to as "Hannibal Lecter."

But the issue that likely sealed his fate came in the spring of 1992, during the weekend of the NCAA basketball tournament regional finals. That Saturday evening in Philadelphia, Christian Laettner took a full-court pass and hit a turnaround jumper at the top of the key as time ran out, to give Duke a 104–103 overtime win over Kentucky. Five years later, ESPN would run a special titled "The Greatest Game Ever?" But in covering the game for *SI*, Papanek stuck stubbornly to his plan, giving Duke-Kentucky about the same space as the other three regional finals.

The cover subject the next week was Kirby Puckett, part of the Baseball '92 Preview. The tease banner running above the logo announced "The Final Four: Why Michigan Will Win." The lead piece, "Boys to Men," was Curry Kirkpatrick's preview of the Final Four. On the third spread, came Alex Wolff's 110-line piece on the East Regional final. With little room to maneuver, he provided some cogent details of the final moments (Duke coach Mike Krzyzewski telling his team during the last time-out, "First of all, we're going to win, okay?"). There was a photo, by Damian Strohmeyer, of Laettner's game-winning shot, but nothing in the overall layout or presentation that would indicate that the contest was one of the great college basketball games of all time. And there was little space for Wolff to argue, as Jenkins had done after the '71 Oklahoma-Nebraska game, as Maule had done after the '58 N.F.L. title game, even as Rushin had done following the 1991 World Series, that the game would become an instant classic.

In covering the Duke-Kentucky game so casually, *SI* was abdicating its central mission: to produce compelling journalism about the most important dramatic events and characters in the world of sport. Instead, the general drift was toward hyping the upcoming event. Papanek wanted to predict the future, and so ignored the past. As the spring wore on, his handling of the Duke-Kentucky game was often cited to support the argument that he was unable or unwilling to roll with the changing events of a weekend in the way that Mulvoy had. Rogin hammered the point home in his weekly memos to McManus, stressing that it was by now clear to everyone that Papanek was overmatched in the job.

"John always looked a little stunned when I saw him there at the end," said Nack. "Like he was trying to keep up." The uncertainty cast a pall over the entire floor. Assistant managing editor Bill Colson and his wife, associate editor Victoria Boughton, had their third child early in 1991. In September '91, Boughton came back from her maternity leave to what she described as "the shittiest morale I have ever seen." Two other staffers described the mood on 18 as "funereal."

Sitting up on the 34th floor in a frowning, chain-smoking daze, growing increasingly horrified with the personnel problems, internecine squabbling, declining subscription and ad revenues, and overall downward arc of *SI*'s progress, McManus finally decided in May that a change had to be made. "It was no single issue that was terrible," he said. "It's Chinese water torture, the lack of improvement over time."

He decided to assign Papanek to head up Time Warner's New Media division forming in Arlington, Virginia. And when he called him in, he framed the move in the form of a promotion. He also told Papanek that he was confident that, given the time, he was sure Papanek would have proven himself as a managing editor. "But it's a little more complicated than that," said McManus later. "Because I don't believe that if he had a totally fair chance, he'd have been able to do the job."

That Thursday morning, the 30-odd staff members who gathered in the handsome, slightly claustrophobic *SI* conference room were greeted with an ashen Papanek. Speaking in a grim voice decidedly lacking in intonation, he announced that "I've been offered a position I'm profoundly interested in, which is to help shape the future direction of the company in the New Media division. So I will no longer be your managing editor."

One staffer who was there remembered that jaws literally dropped.

Steve Robinson blurted out, "Who's taking your place?"

"Mark is," said Papanek softly.

"Oh, my God!" said photo editor Karen Mullarkey.

And with that, Papanek said a few more words, got up, and walked out of the room. Later that day, Mark Mulvoy returned to the managing editor's desk, the corner office with the view, 1869.

Outside the building, reaction to the move was shock for a different reason. Mulvoy had been named managing editor again, but McManus decided to keep him on as publisher as well. "So much for the separation between church and state," said one writer when he heard the news. "Harry Luce is fucking spinning."

It was months before Papanek could talk to casual friends about the experience, and two years later, when reporters called to ask him about the magazine's 40th anniversary, he declined all interview requests. He received an invitation to the 40th anniversary dinner—with his name misspelled. The tenure that had begun with such promise had ended in ignominy. And even if Papanek had been given what he regarded as a plum job, he'd still been removed from the only place he'd ever worked.

For *SI*, the experience proved convincingly that the modern editorial formula articulated by Rogin and codified by Mulvoy—hard sports, big pictures, a narrower focus, an emphasis on reporting rather than writing, shorter, more reader-friendly stories—had become bigger than anyone in the managing editor's office. The job was not the ME's to mold anymore; all one could do was make minor adjustments.

After the fact, several of *SI*'s writers, from staffers to freelancers, began referring to Papanek's editorship as the Prague Spring. "With John playing the part of Dubček," noted Charles Pierce. "Then suddenly the empire strikes back, and Mulvoy returns. And now John's out working in a hydroelectric plant somewhere in the Carpathians."

Pierce's opinion was shared by some, but not all, of *SI*'s staffers. Even as many were bemoaning the unfair sacking of an managing editor they liked, they also admitted that they had missed Mulvoy's assured, decisive leadership.

"The thing about it is that, with that job, you have to eat, drink, and sleep sports seven days a week, and there are only so many people that can do that," said E.M. Swift. "I am not one of them and John Papanek was not one of them. John Papanek would take his day off and go to the opera. And that does not do you any good if Wayne Gretzky gets traded. Mulvoy moved on a story quicker than anybody. That was a flaw in Papanek's style: he wanted to work four days a week and take three days a week and be a 'normal' human being."

"When you're in a job where 60 or 70 people on a Sunday night are pulling you in a lot of different directions, you need to have somebody who can be a bad guy, who can make decisions that are going to really, really, piss people off," said pro football writer Peter King. "And you need to be able to do that almost without a conscience. That's the thing I liked about Mulvoy."

# CHAPTER 18

# WALSH'S REVENGE

**Mark Mulvoy had been out** of the managing editor's chair for only 18 months, but by the time he returned to the job in May 1992, the magazine's place in the sports media universe had fundamentally changed. The real story of the new decade for *Sports Illustrated* was that, for the first time since the late '50s, it had been eclipsed as the predominant media entity of American sporting culture. ESPN, the once-bumbling cable channel better known in the '80s for bowling tournaments and late-night college basketball reruns had become, almost overnight, a potent presence that altered the very rules by which *SI* operated.

The crucial moment had occurred in 1987, when ESPN president Steve Bornstein hired John Walsh—the brilliant, eccentric editor of the first incarnation of *Inside Sports*—to do some consulting for the network's floundering news shows. Walsh was the rare sports media professional who was equally comfortable in both television and print media. While ESPN had been throwing much of its money toward rights fees, to acquire programming of major sports like college football and, later, the NFL and major league baseball, Walsh understood that the key to the network's presence was its thrice-daily news show "SportsCenter." In January 1988, Bornstein hired Walsh to run the show full-time, purposefully changing the position's title from "executive producer" to "editor." ESPN's increased profile through major sports coverage would bring it new viewers, but it was the emergence of "SportsCenter" as, in Walsh's words, "the gathering place of the culture of sports," that kept them turning back to the network again and again.

And across the spectrum, other hints of the show's significance were evident. The station became a constant in pro sports locker rooms. In 1992, *The Sporting News* reported that "ESPN has raised the standard of sports television to the point where ABC, CBS and NBC are playing catch up." Renowned sports fan George Will wrote in his May 16, 1994, *Newsweek* column that "if someone surreptitiously took everything but ESPN from my cable television package, it might be months before I noticed." Jack Craig, writing in the *Boston Globe*, compared ESPN's hold on viewers during moments of crisis in sports as similar to CNN's in moments of international incidents. "Real fans know where to turn for breaking stories," he wrote. "Egos at ESPN are large, but not as large as at the networks, and its young staff provides a great deal of drive."

Less than a decade after Time Inc. had passed on a chance to acquire the sports network, ESPN's reach had dwarfed *SI*'s. It had become America's largest cable network, available in more than 60 million households. And, most ominously, it had become a journalistic presence. "John Walsh coming in and making 'SportsCenter' such an editorial powerhouse," said Mulvoy, "forced *Sports Illustrated* to rethink, or redefine, the way we had presented the news." By the end of '92, when people asked Mulvoy who the magazine's chief competitor was, he answered quickly: "'SportsCenter.'"

It also didn't help that the ads *Sports Illustrated* ran on ESPN had a desperate, breathless quality to them, while ESPN's print and television campaigns, produced by the same Portland firm of Weiden & Kennedy that produced Nike's iconographic spots, were cutting, confident, and clever. While the days of the sneaker-phone had passed, *SI*'s shrill ad efforts still demeaned its core product. Hubert Mizell, writing in the *St. Petersburg Times*, decried the magazine's televised pitches, "where viewers are offered *Football's Nastiest Hits* or *Shaq Attack* or some other wham-bam videotape, if they will only subscribe to the magazine. Wouldn't it be more fitting if *SI*'s ads on cable television told of the publication's wonderful writers, photographers, and features? It can sound as though you're being forced to accept the mag in order to get *Shaq Attack*."

No one was more aware of the fact than Rick Reilly. "I'll tell you, what pisses me off is our ads are boneheaded and targeted to the couch-potato fat guy," he said. "And ESPN's ads are so clever and it almost seems like we've got it reversed. I mean I think our readers are intelligent and smart and would love these clever ads and we could write them. And ESPN viewers are pretty much keeping couch springs down and they get these great ads. It's infuriating!" But true: a mid-'90s study of brand recognition by the firm Total Research showed that ESPN (at number 8) had passed *Sports Illustrated* (at number 25) in perceived quality among 139 leading media brands.

Because Mulvoy spent more time watching sports on television than anyone on the staff, he had sensed the danger of ESPN's emergence as journalistic rival long before anyone else at the magazine and, upon returning to the managing editor's chair, spent long nights wondering how to adapt.

But his rethinking led to little more than shorter stories and a narrower editorial focus, brought about by Mulvoy's greater reliance on reader surveys. "It got to the point where you could not get anything in the magazine," said Bill Nack, "unless it was about some famous asshole who weighed 300 pounds and who was nine feet tall. But the beauty of the magazine for years and years were these surprises."

Increasingly, the magazine was defined and dominated by action photography, but for a variety of reasons, the pictures lacked the snap and dazzle of *SI*'s best photography of the '60s and '70s. Part of the problem was the mass of signage everywhere. Gone were the days when Hy Peskin could use strobes and backlighting to create the ghostly, cinematic tableaux of the '50s. With advertising everywhere, on courts, rinks, scorer's tables, scoreboards and, increasingly, uniforms, athletic events seemed to be taking place at a strip mall, not a stadium. Equally problematic was the fact that the *quality* of pictures had grown sterile and blandly competent. Walter Iooss, Jr., once an innovator, had become an anachronism, virtually the only photographer around who still shot manually focused photographs. The pictorial savant Gil Rogin could tell the difference. "They're all fixed position stuff, you know?" he said. "The cameras are fixed to the backboards and they're all auto-focused. Yes, everything is in focus, but there's a certain artificiality about auto-focus pictures. It's difficult to describe, but it's there, and other people recognize it, too." With more photographers working the sidelines, there was less freedom, and simply fewer frontiers to conquer. "A camera has been put in just about every conceivable place you can think of," said veteran photographer John Zimmerman, "except for a place or two you'd like to shove one every once in a while."

As editor pro tem (a designation that McManus made to show that he didn't intend for the union of church and state to last indefinitely), Mulvoy quickly moved to change the magazine back to his original conception. The photo editor Karen Mullarkey was out of a job by sundown the day of the announcement, with Mulvoy bringing back Heinz Kluetmeier to the position. He scrapped the changes in Scorecard, which he despised, and returned to the grayer, more self-serious format that had existed before.

He virtually did away with departments, instituting in their place an occasional section called Sports People. The idea had come to him while planning for Barcelona. "It dawned on me that we were giving too much space to this judo player," Mulvoy said. "And I knew from my reading studies nobody was reading it anyway. This way you can still get those people in the book—it's a perfect way to handle some NCAA championships." It was also a way to narrow the magazine's focus even further, relegating any athlete or endeavor that strayed too far from the "core sports" to a single color picture and a text block.

"Mark became even more Mark when he came back," said Rob Fleder, who argued in vain against the Sports People idea. "His vision of the magazine became more narrow. Maybe that's what people wanted. Certainly if you listen to the business side guys and the circ guys: 'More and more NFL.' A lot of things—some of the quirkiness of the magazine and the unpredictability that it used to have, even in previous incarnations—tend to be lost."

The last writer to figure out that the old days were gone was Curry Kirkpatrick. He still might have looked like a twentyish cub reporter, but he was well into his forties by this time, and the enfant terrible act that had played so well in the loose, slangy atmosphere of the '70s had become dated. Mulvoy had long resisted Kirkpatrick's television work for CBS sports (he'd been a sideline reporter for college basketball games), insisting that he do it on his own time and that he not do any TV work at all while he was on assignment for *SI*. The final round of trouble began in the spring of '92, when Mulvoy discovered that Kirkpatrick had turned in expense accounts to both CBS *and SI* for a recent trip. "If that had been the only thing he'd ever done, he might have been okay," said one staffer. "But Curry'd been a problem for a long time. And then he just dug his grave in Barcelona."

Kirkpatrick had been a late addition to the *SI* team covering the Summer Olympic Games in 1992 in Barcelona. His assignment was to write a humorous piece about the hospitality ships that various companies were docking in the Barcelona harbor during the first week, and then write about the first Olympic tennis competition in the second. *SI* staffers said Kirkpatrick spent much of his first week in Barcelona avoiding Olympic editor Jerry Kirshenbaum, neglecting his ships story (he made it onto one ship, the *SI* hospitality ship the *Vistafjord*, for a publisher's party). Kirkpatrick spent most of his time badgering *SI* support staffers for tickets for him and his family to choice Olympic events. Word got back to Mulvoy after a Kirkpatrick tantrum left one staffer in tears. When Mulvoy discovered that Kirkpatrick hadn't done any reporting on the ships story, he revoked his *SI* credential and sent him back to the States. By the end of

August, Kirkpatrick was out of a job. A subsequent legal settlement prevented either side from talking about the details, but staffers said that Mulvoy had essentially forced Kirkpatrick out, threatening to turn evidence of the double-dipping on expenses over to the IRS if he didn't leave without a fight. It was a desultory end for another *SI* principal. "I did what they said," Kirkpatrick said in conceding his wrongdoing to another writer. "But I thought everyone knew it."

If Papanek's tenure had been a Prague Spring, then what followed thereafter were the Mulvoy purges. In addition to the sacking of Mullarkey and Kirkpatrick, Mulvoy did away with Norman Chad, Pat Putnam, and the gifted writer Tom Junod, who had started working for *SI* on contract, within months of his return. Chad's column was iced (Mulvoy killed eight of his columns within the space of four months), with Mulvoy objecting to his penchant for "Curry-isms," the cheap-shot one-liners that might anger advertisers. After Papanek was moved out, Putnam sent a letter to Mulvoy asking for assurances that his arrangement with Papanek was still good. After three weeks without a reply from Mulvoy, he hired a lawyer and filed his own age discrimination suit. Early in 1993, he was dropped from the masthead. "They had to pay me off until the end of the contract," Putnam said. "Which, as a stockholder, pissed me off."

Tom Junod was just finishing a dark, troubling piece about the life of Nebraska football player Scott Baldwin in the fall of 1992 when Mulvoy returned, found it too representative of Papanek's downbeat view of the sports world, and killed it. Several other Junod pieces were either killed or drastically cut and he left the magazine after his contract ended in 1993. Junod was quickly hired by *GQ*, where he would win back-to-back National Magazine Awards for feature writing.

More than ever before, the culture of *Sports Illustrated* was dominated by the editors. With the loss of Deford, there were still a few stars at the magazines, but no more legends, and certainly none walking around the halls—even New York writers rarely came into the office. Those who occasionally dropped by, like Sally Jenkins, often felt they weren't welcome. "Oh, no, you don't want to go onto the deathstar," said one senior writer about a visit to the city. "The editors would rather not see your face—they want to deal with you over the phone." Anyone might find their copy obliterated, and many of the best writers found it so unbearable that they simply stopped reading their stories in the magazine. The problem had been growing worse for years. George Plimpton, after writing a story about tossing horseshoes with George Bush in the 1988 holiday double issue, wrote a letter to Mulvoy protesting the "wholesale tin-eared butchery" performed on his story. "Sentences that showed any flair at all were made as dull as Associated Press leads," complained Plimpton in the letter. "Words I have never used (or will) crept into the text such as 'forsook' and 'far-flung locales.' . . . There were dozens of inconsequential changes, changing 'team' to 'squad,' that sort of thing. At times, it almost seemed as if the blue pencils were being wielded just for the sake of something to do." Plimpton never received a response from Mulvoy, never got another assignment during Mulvoy's time at the magazine, and was dropped from the masthead without notification less than a year later.

And for those with the institutional memory, who'd seen Andy Crichton coax a story on deadline out of Plimpton or watched Pat Ryan spend a month fencing with Mark Kram, all to elicit a gem of a bonus piece, the present rank of senior editors and AMEs seemed not only impersonal, but ineffectual and distressingly literal. "I just think the editors at *SI* have deteriorated hugely, not as human beings and not as personalities, but as professional editors, they are terrible," said one veteran senior writer, who'd been with the magazine since the Laguerre era. "They edit more now than they used to. You have trouble getting your stuff through, and you hit a brick wall with these guys. The arbitrariness of the editing is really just stupid. A lot of these editors are perfectly intelligent, nice guys, but a lot of them shouldn't be allowed to touch copy."

And so as *SI* became more efficient, it also became less compelling. From the sidelines, where those who cared about the magazine watched, the signals were not good. "*SI* in the last ten years has not been what anyone would describe as a writer's magazine," said Bill James, the influential baseball writer who had written a few pieces for the magazine in the '80s. "It is an editor's magazine. And it is so successful at what it does, that it's naturally not going to find a brilliant young writer and turn itself over to him. There's a question at some point of how long you can survive without a strong influence from writers. That to me is the essential question of how long it will stay on top of the world. It has a corporate face. It has a tendency to find editors who went to the best journalism schools and got the best grades, who are never going to be the best writers. So, do I fault it for hiring the best graduates from the best journalism schools? Absolutely not. Do I fault it for being an editor's magazine rather than a writer's magazine? Absolutely not. At some point, though, there's going to be a writer's magazine which will be strong enough that it will force *SI* to reexamine itself."

• • •

It wasn't as though Mark Mulvoy really wanted both jobs. He had never liked the publisher's job in the first place, and while performing double duty at Barcelona had been an exhilarating experience—editing the magazine by day, entertaining advertisers by night—the problems he'd had on the business side were waiting when he returned to the States. One point was resolved: the corporate ad sales strategy that had robbed publishers of much of their autonomy was mercifully killed. But even after winning that long war, Mulvoy wanted out. McManus gave him the choice of the two jobs and, not surprisingly, he chose to keep the managing editor's position.

Succeeding him as publisher was Don Elliman, one of the architects of the failed corporate ad sales plan and, with 25 years of experience, as much of a survivor on the business side as Mulvoy was on the edit side. A trustee at the New York Yacht Club, Elliman combined the sort of upper-crust background long valued at Time Inc. with a forward-looking, go-for-the-jugular aggressiveness honed in the market confusion of the '80s. The immediate problem, though, was that the new culture at Time Warner dictated a close relationship between the managing editor and the publisher, who would often be expected to work hand in hand—and Don Elliman and Mark Mulvoy couldn't stand each other.

Elliman was cordial verging on unctuous, possessed of a smoothness that remained static when dealing with all but his most trusted colleagues. Around Mulvoy, he adopted the same 200-watt smile and vapid, talk-show host tone that he took with prized advertisers. One found it hard to have an intimate or direct conversation with him, because he maintained a forced air of cordiality that never seemed to waver. Mulvoy, whose favorite phrase remained the conspiratorial, sotto voce "me to you," was the antithesis of that unruffled Time Inc. business approach. Mulvoy also bristled at any hint of condescension, and because Elliman had made it clear to his peers that many of *SI*'s problems were the fault of his predecessor, the two were almost doomed to an antagonistic relationship. Mulvoy exclaimed in wonderment to fellow staffers that the man who had "presided over this disaster" in corporate ad sales could receive a promotion for it. And when Elliman was named not only publisher but also president of *Sports Illustrated,* Mulvoy's response was predictable: "This is the biggest pile of crap!" he groused to one editor. Elliman's dual title was evidence of little more than nominative inflation on the business side of all magazines. At most titles, publishers were glorified ad directors. And because Elliman was going to be responsible for an expanding multimedia division that was bringing in revenues of more than a billion dollars a year, he was given the president's title as well.

The general recession that had hit the magazine industry at the beginning of the '90s was particularly painful at *SI*, because it hurt the magazine's ad revenues in its three largest categories: automobile, tobacco, and wine and spirits (the troika referred to by ad men as "drinking, driving, and smoking" or, after a few cocktails, "booze, buggies, and butts"). The record profits of 1990, of around $110 million, went into free fall, dropping to $88 million in '91 and $74 million in '92.

Though they hardly spoke, Elliman and Mulvoy made a better team than Mulvoy and Papanek had. Elliman moved aggressively to diversify *SI*'s "brand recognition," pushing into ancillary markets like television and special-edition publishing (with *SI* producing special minimagazines that would be used as premiums for other company's products, like Wheaties). Elliman's first move was to create SItv, an arm of the magazine that would specialize in producing television projects. The man Elliman wanted to hire was Ted Shaker, the former CBS Sports chief who had been a long-time rival of Mulvoy's, from the days when Curry Kirkpatrick was working for CBS (Mulvoy felt Shaker didn't live up to a verbal agreement to identify Kirkpatrick as an *SI* writer whenever he appeared on the network). The fleshy, garrulous Shaker had won several Emmys, primarily for his event coverage, and presided over CBS's lucrative contract to cover the NCAA basketball tournament. But he would agree to come to *SI* on one condition—that he wouldn't have to report to Mulvoy. Editor-in-chief Jason McManus and Time Inc. president Don Logan signed off on the arrangement. Less than a dozen weeks after presiding over *SI* as both editor and publisher, Mulvoy sensed that his powers were slipping away due to Elliman's maneuverings.

Shaker quickly cut a deal with ABC's "Wide World of Sports," in which SItv would produce a five- to seven-minute spot related to a story that had run that week. In trying to branch out to the new medium, the spots were unable to answer the central question: Why TV? A writer's piece would show up in the magazine on Thursday. If he or she then made an appearance on "Wide World" that Saturday, the writer could either rehash what was in the story (in which case, readers had no need to watch) or provide new information not appearing in the story (in which case, readers would properly feel shortchanged). The *SI* spots had no effect on "Wide World"'s flagging ratings; at the time, Mulvoy described it to editorial side colleagues as "seven minutes that nobody watches out of ninety minutes that nobody sees."

Early in 1993, Elliman appointed David Long as publisher. Long was a savvy magazine executive and a onetime friend of Mulvoy's, but the two had been at odds for years. "Mark had a personal animosity based on the breakup of Long's marriage," said one staffer. "He says he's a terrific ad salesman but he's a son of a bitch; he didn't want anything to do with Long." For his part, Long respected the editorial franchise, and showed a greater willingness than any of his predecessors to make deals with advertisers, at discount prices not listed on the magazine's rate card. "Going off the card" had been a practice strongly discouraged at Time Inc. in the past, but in the '90s, virtually every mass-circulation magazine in the country was doing it, and advertisers expected it.

While relations between Mulvoy and the Elliman-Long team were barely civil, the chilly crucible of edit and publishing did yield a pair of profitable innovations at the beginning of 1993. The first one occurred by accident. On Friday, January 1, Alabama pounded Miami 34–14, to win the Sugar Bowl and college football's mythical national championship. But Mulvoy didn't want to put an event that occurred on a Friday on the cover the following week. It was viewed as old news. Instead, he chose to devote the cover of the January 11 issue to a Gary Smith bonus piece on Jim Valvano. But old traditions die hard, as *SI* would discover over and over again in the '90s. For decades, one of the fringe benefits that local fans could look forward to upon winning a major sports championship or national title was a cover in *Sports Illustrated* the following week. After receiving hundreds of protests from readers and radio stations in Alabama, Mulvoy put out a special edition of the same issue, sent only to Alabama, that featured Alabama running back Derrick Lassic on the cover, and provided several extra pages of Sugar Bowl coverage inside.

With that as a precursor, Mulvoy planned ahead a few weeks later, and produced a separate newsstand-only commemorative issue devoted to the Dallas Cowboys' Super Bowl win. The issue featured reprints of articles written earlier in the season about the Cowboys, and retrospectives of their past Super Bowl wins, along with a reprint of Rick Telander's Super Bowl game story and extra pictures that hadn't made it into the regular magazine. That issue, distributed on newsstands in Texas, sold out all 188,000 copies, and a tradition was born. In April, *SI* did essentially the same thing, putting out a special issue to commemorate North Carolina's NCAA title. The advantages were obvious. By repackaging earlier articles and leftover pictures, *SI* could easily put together a souvenir of any championship team's season that, capitalizing on championship pride, would be a guaranteed newsstand winner with a remarkably high ratio of actual newsstand sales, all for a relatively minor editorial investment.

The series worked spectacularly through the next year, until the summer of 1994, when word leaked out, during the New York Knicks–Houston Rockets NBA championship series, that *SI* was planning a commemorative only if the Knicks won, but wouldn't do one in the event of a

Rockets win. The perceived slight renewed decades-old charges of an East Coast bias in *SI*'s coverage, and soon became a popular topic on Houston sports radio talk shows. Afterward, Mulvoy was quick to distance himself from the decision. "All these were driven by the ability of the wholesaler in the region to guarantee sales," he said. "And they had to guarantee a sale or we wouldn't do it. So in 1994, we did the Cowboys again, we did Arkansas [which won the NCAA basketball title], which was boffo. We did not do Florida State because the wholesaler said it wouldn't sell in Florida. So when Houston was involved, the New York wholesaler told us he'd sell 300,000 or 400,000. The Houston guy said he would maybe sell 40,000. So there's no business." When word got out, everyone from Time Inc. CEO Reg Brack to Houston mayor Bob Lanier was irate. Mulvoy's penchant for listening to surveys, for making decisions based on sales estimates, had gotten him in trouble. Because the flap occurred so late, *SI* didn't produce a separate special issue when the Rockets defeated the Knicks in game seven. Instead, newsstands in the Houston area received a special issue with Hakeem Olajuwon on the cover and extra pages of Rockets coverage inside.

For longtime *SI* readers, who'd grown up feeling that *SI* should stand as an authoritative surveyor of the sporting scene, the entire affair smacked of small-minded financial opportunism. And *SI*'s self-righteous scolding of major college football programs seemed hypocritical in the light of a commemorative celebrating Auburn's undefeated 1993 regular season, achieved while the school was on probation for numerous recruiting violations.

The week that North Carolina's commemorative hit the stands, *SI* embarked on a another ancillary publishing venture, one that was both more lucrative and less controversial. At an *SI* party at the '93 Masters, attended by the usual klatch of national and golf-related advertisers, media reps, and tournament officials, Mulvoy gave a speech announcing that the magazine would launch, in January 1994, a special editorial section sent to a targeted list of readers called Golf Plus. *SI* had sent questionnaires to all of its subscribers in 1993, identifying those who described themselves as frequent golfers (26 times a year or more) and, combining that list with their own demographic research of high-income subscribers, compiled a list of 400,000 readers who would receive the special section, bound into the center of the magazine. Early estimates predicted that the section would run from four to eight pages through the spring and summer, but advertisers jumped on it immediately. *SI* wound up with 350 ad pages during 1994, double its estimates.

The brunt of Golf Plus material was written by the solid Jaime Diaz—

wooed back to *SI* after four years at the *New York Times* and *Golf Digest*—and longtime *SI* writer John Garrity, whose more lyrical prose had appeared in *SI* for a decade. Garrity (whose sister Jane, under the pseudonym "J," had written the salacious '70s bestseller *The Sensuous Woman*), prided himself on his talents as a generalist, having written for a wide range of publications, including *Rolling Stone* and the *Village Voice*. Now, however, he would be doing most of his writing for a small fraction of *SI*'s audience.

Notwithstanding the substantial editorial talent, Golf Plus was never anything more than an ad-driven scheme to pick off some of the high-end golf equipment market from *Golf Digest, Golf World,* and *Golf* magazine. By targeting only 400,000 readers, *SI* could provide a single-page rate at a far cheaper price than a page in the general magazine would cost. And with 400,000 golfers on the Golf Plus list, advertisers could target much more specifically than they could by buying space in one of *SI*'s upper income select editions (sent out to the subscribers in the top one-third zip code demographics).

The exclusionary nature of the Golf Plus section served to anger many readers who were golf fans but hadn't responded to the original survey, or didn't golf the requisite 26 times a year. Suddenly, for reasons they couldn't fathom, they weren't getting the "full" *Sports Illustrated*. And while "select edit" was ostensibly conceived to give the reader a choice, the fact remained that most of the choices belonged to the business side. When *SI* inaugurated NFL Plus in 1994, with extra coverage of each of the six divisions, readers had to choose one—meaning that for the first time, its most avid readers were unable to get all of *SI*'s coverage on its number one sport. Football South, a similar section of coverage of SEC and ACC college games, was conceived as a lure to southern advertisers, and so was available only to subscribers in those states. The Alabama alumnus living in Seattle had no way of getting the extra coverage.

• • •

In the spring of 1993, Mulvoy announced that he would be taking three lengthy vacations in the coming months, during which three different men would get a shot at editing the magazine. The parallels to 1983, when Mulvoy had outperformed Peter Carry and Ken Rudeen, were both obvious and intended. Privately, Mulvoy was telling his closest friends that he planned to step down after the 1996 Olympics, perhaps to retire outright or maybe to serve as a supraeditor, presiding over all of *SI*'s multifarious enterprises.

None of the three candidates looked like an obvious heir apparent:

- Steve Wulf, the painfully soft-spoken *SI* writer and baseball editor, had been eyeing the job for years. Prematurely white-haired like Bob Creamer, Wulf was an heir to Creamer's throne as *SI*'s baseball expert. But while he was an indefatigable reporter, his stints on the editing side had been less successful. His communication skills were so poor that people literally couldn't hear what he was saying to them; Rick Reilly bought an amplifier for his phone so he could better decipher Wulf's slurred mumblings. While some found him a good line editor, Wulf's ambition and management style quickly annoyed many of his colleagues who liked him personally. The perpetually laconic senior editor Mike Bevans referred to him simply as "Mr. Baseball." It was not a compliment. Wulf's wife, Jane (Bambi) Bachman Wulf had been a longtime ally of Mulvoy's, although their relationship had cooled since Mulvoy's return in '92.
- Bill Colson had been an *SI* editor since the late '70s, working his way up from reporter. Seen by many as the "Mulvoy candidate," Colson was an intelligent and sensitive editor, less obviously ambitious than the other two candidates. Colson's wife, associate editor Vic Boughton, had worked editing advance text, the featurish essays that ran in the special editions of *SI* sent to the most attractive demographic markets. Colson was at the forefront of a trend that would mark *SI* in the '80s. Increasingly, the magazine's top-level editors were staffers who had advanced from lower-level editors rather than former writers who chose to come off the road, as had been the case with Terrell, Rogin, Mulvoy, and Papanek. Their dispositions and make-up were different. And, in the opinion of the writers, there was no question that the new breed's ability to line edit was inferior. "Bill's smart, but he's just so *literal*," complained one senior writer. "If he doesn't get something right away, you're dead."
- Finally there was the expatriate returnee Rob Fleder. He had remained as features editor since returning from *The National*, editing and assigning the bonus pieces. A graduate of Columbia Journalism School, Fleder served stints at *Esquire* and *Playboy* before coming to *SI* in '86. Bright, compact, and animated, he was the most experienced and extroverted of the three prospective successors but also, in Mulvoy's mind, the one whose loyalty to the *SI* formula was most in question.

For those involved and the staffers who were eagerly handicapping the process, it offered the opportunity to see who might fill the vacuum left when Mulvoy departed. "Mark has been great at what he's done," said one staffer. "But he had a real problem. He couldn't deal with people that he thought he had to compete against. And so he surrounded himself in this job by yes men. And Mark really did put out the magazine by himself. Everything under his reign was totally his. Everything was his idea. You can't be everything. You need help. You can't be the sole source of story ideas. And Mark would run these meetings where if you brought up this story idea, he'd make this silly comment and embarrass you. And it got to the point where meetings weren't about communication. They were a dictatorship. Mark just told you what he was going to do, and that was this and that was that and that was the end of the meeting."

There was also a growing generational gap and a simple difference of sensibilities between Mulvoy and his staff. Mulvoy's emerging friendship with Dan Quayle was cause for office consternation. The pair went on a Scottish golfing vacation shortly after Quayle and George Bush left office in 1993. Throughout the '90s, Mulvoy had vetted many of Quayle's most important speeches, including his infamous "Murphy Brown" broadside on values in media, which Mulvoy judged as "pretty all right." Mulvoy was a suburbanite, conservative, Catholic, and never much of a reader, all traits that were at variance with a majority of his staff. With the power he held, he was more than happy to play the role of the wisecracking, no-bullshit Mr. Big. When he looked out in the rain one Sunday morning, minutes before the start of the New York Marathon, he announced, "Good: all those dumb fucks are going to get wet."

His lieutenants, mostly liberal and instinctively suspicious of his Machiavellian tendencies, often had trouble understanding that humor. He might brag about "really getting to know" Stephanie Seymour on a swimsuit issue shoot, but for all his sexist jokes and bluster, Mulvoy was still a rather prudish Catholic boy at heart. He'd passed, with extreme prejudice, on an E. Jean Carroll piece about NBA groupies that Papanek had commissioned ("Love in the Time of Magic" wound up in *Esquire* instead), and he'd spiked a Rick Telander piece on Martina Navratilova's lifestyle before Telander could even start writing it.

Each of the three contenders spent four weeks top-editing and, afterward, much of the staff agreed that all three men comported themselves well during the trial. Colson seemed temperamentally unsuited for palace intrigues in the first place, and Fleder and Wulf were good friends, and longtime competitors in the original Rotisserie Baseball League.

Colson's trial was first, in the spring, and while the look of the issues was largely unchanged from Mulvoy's blueprint, he displayed a surprising dramatic flair, opening a lead story on the ascendance of Hakeem Olajuwon with an arresting shot of Olajuwon praying. He loosened up the magazine's opening weekend coverage of the NCAA basketball tournament, and created a format by which Alexander Wolff, *SI*'s superb basketball writer, could write a free-flowing yet readable rundown of the opening weekend's highlights.

Wulf's tour started in June, under a mood of recrimination. Mulvoy had pulled one of his planned bonus pieces and a Point After that he'd commissioned—Karl Malone responding to Charles Barkley's "I Am Not a Role Model" Nike ad— for the last issue prior to his editing run. Late in the four-week cycle, Wulf chose to put a Gary Smith story about the boating accident that had killed Cleveland Indians Steve Olin and Tim Crews on the cover, and ran Smith's bonus piece in the lead news hole, ahead of Sally Jenkins's account of Pete Sampras's July 4 Wimbledon final win over fellow American Jim Courier. (The unassuming Smith possessed a serene manner and deep empathy that made him perhaps the most natural interviewer in the magazine's history. Before he traveled to Cleveland to write the story, Indians manager Mike Hargrove had already decided exactly what he'd be willing to discuss with Smith and what emotions and feelings he would withhold. But as Hargrove would explain to a friend later, "And then, when we started talking, I told him everything.")

Mulvoy didn't like the issues, finding them too soft. "I knew immediately after my tryout that I had somehow blown it, because Mark had a meeting right after—the editorial meeting before my last issue," said Wulf. "And he went out of his way to praise Colson and never said a word about my issues. I knew after that I didn't have a future at *SI*." Within a year, he'd leave to write sports for *Time*.

Fleder's tour started on Labor Day weekend, with a skeleton crew. Mulvoy insisted that the magazine run a bonus piece on sports owners, the longest of the year, and then took virtually the entire edit staff on a field trip to Boston the Thursday and Friday before Fleder's first close. Because Monday was the Labor Day holiday, Fleder had one day during the week at full strength. He led with Joe Montana's regular season debut with the Kansas City Chiefs. The following week featured a cover on Pernell Whitaker and his disputed welterweight title fight draw with Julio Cesar Chavez. The night before work was to begin on the third issue, Mulvoy called Fleder at home, informing him that he was promoting senior editor David Bauer to AME. Fleder had been above Bauer on the masthead, and the curious timing of the promotion seemed to serve notice that Fleder had already flunked his trial. The final two weeks found Fleder in a listless, nearly sullen mood, going ahead with a cover story on New York Jet quarterback Boomer Esiason and his handicapped son that Mulvoy had criticized beforehand as "too local."

Well before Fleder's term was finished, the winner was clear. Mulvoy had been telling people for weeks that Wulf was only getting a shot as "a favor to Bambi," and now he was repeatedly dismissing Fleder's performance. While there were objective grounds to declare Colson the winner anyway, the preemptive manner in which it was done only exacerbated interoffice tension. As Mulvoy returned to his office, there was still no consensus in the staff's eyes about who should be the next managing editor, and significant doubt whether Colson had the vision to lead the magazine, the decisiveness to preside over a hectic weekend close, and the strength to distance himself from his boss's shadow.

"Who knows who it'll be?" said a veteran staffer who used to edit Mulvoy's choppy hockey copy. "Colson is being groomed, but I just don't see it. I can't see anybody else besides Mark doing it. He's such an overwhelming presence. Basically, *SI* is now whatever Mark Mulvoy wants it to be. And nobody in that position has ever known more about marketing, publishing, readership studies, demographics. He's the ultimate modern magazine editor."

• • •

Nineteen ninety-four was to be a year of celebration at *Sports Illustrated*. As it looked toward its 40th anniversary in August, the magazine's leading indicators—circulation, ad revenue, newsstand sales—had all recovered significantly since Mulvoy's return and Elliman's promotion. But the spirit of celebration was tempered long before the September anniversary dinner, and throughout the year, the magazine itself seemed less decisive, more conventional, often arbitrary at times.

The year began with *SI* still in retreat from a previous story gone wrong. New staff writer Ned Zeman's October 25, 1993, piece, "Southern Discomfort," about the incidents leading to high school basketball prospect Allen Iverson's conviction on manslaughter charges, was so badly botched that the magazine had to run two separate corrections, the last one in the February 21 issue. Zeman resigned, but the fallout served to further chill the environment for investigative features.

After Florida State edged Nebraska 18–16 in the 1994 Orange Bowl, Bobby Bowden and the Seminoles earned their first mythical national title, outpolling a Notre Dame team that had beaten them less than two months earlier. Rick Reilly's lead piece on the New Year's Day games cast serious doubt on whether FSU was a worthy choice for number one. After analyzing the merits of FSU, Notre Dame, Nebraska, and unbeaten Auburn, Reilly, in the tradition of Jenkins, rendered his verdict:

And so, ladies and gentlemen, here and now we present the undisputed champion of college football, the team that proved itself to be far and away the best in the land, a squad that truly deserves to be etched in history as the finest of 1993. . . .

Nobody.

It's no disgrace. Happens all the time. Some weeks nobody wins the lottery. Every now and then, no one is deemed worthy of a Pulitzer or a Nobel Prize. Lots of trials end in hung juries. Why shouldn't it be the same in college football?

Forcing the football world to pick a national champion this year is like asking a woman to choose her favorite Baldwin brother. They are all lovely to look at but far too alike to tell apart.

Presented with such a story, Laguerre would have taken his writer's opinion to its logical conclusion (as he had with Jenkins in the infamous "Furor Over No. 1" cover after the Notre Dame–Michigan State tie). But the cover of *SI* seemed to bear no relation whatsoever to Reilly's story. It was a conventional shot of FSU's Matt Frier celebrating with a cheerleader. The headline read: "No. 1 At Last."

In March, spring training camps were electric with excitement over Michael Jordan's unlikely bid to join the Chicago White Sox. In the mid-'80s, Jordan—*SI*'s all-time most popular cover subject—became the first individual athlete with whom *SI* ever did promotional tie-ins (offering a video of Jordan highlights with a subscription). In 1991, he received a reverential Sportsman of the Year treatment, with a hologram cover and three separate stories, by Jack McCallum, Curry Kirkpatrick, and David Halberstam. But by late 1993, Jordan had grown tired of *SI*'s coverage of his gambling habits, his retirement, and his father's death (which the magazine erroneously hinted was related to his gambling).

When the time came to cover Jordan's appearance in spring training, Mulvoy was determined to bring him down a notch. "Bag It, Michael!" read the headline accompanying the cover shot of Jordan taking a high and wild swing at a low pitch. The subhead said "Jordan and the White Sox Are Embarrassing Baseball." Jordan was so angered by the tone of the story that he vowed that week never to talk to the magazine again. "He was disgracing baseball," Mulvoy would say later, with a bit of defensiveness in his voice. Steve Wulf, who had written the story, attempted to distance himself from the flap, arguing that the cover and interior headline "Err Jordan" didn't reflect the tone of the piece. But Wulf's story called Jordan's effort a charade, and scolded the White Sox for taking part in it ("shame on them for feeding Michael's matchbook-cover delusion—

BECOME A MAJOR LEAGUER IN JUST SIX WEEKS!"). Other staffers wondered how Jordan could possibly "embarrass" a sport so rife with acrimony, fan alienation, and the sort of self-destructive tendencies that would lead to the cancellation of the World Series later that year.

Back in Chicago, senior writer Rick Telander instantly understood what the cover meant, and how Jordan would respond. "I'd been at the thing with Michael Jordan as Sportsman of the Year. He came in and it's about 50 of the highest rollers in advertising at *SI*. And Michael Jordan came through there, and he had silver pens, and they had these stacks of *SI*s there. And he worked the room as any movie star would. And the goodwill he brought to the magazine was astonishing."

But Mulvoy and the magazine had wanted it both ways. *SI* featured Jordan and his "Come Fly with Me" video prominently in its subscription promotions in the late '80s. Jordan had cooperated with numerous photographic and one-on-one interview sessions over the years, including a day-long session for the Sportsman of the Year hologram. Then the magazine chose to publicly ridicule Jordan. This might have been a justifiable journalistic decision in a different context. But the line between edit and business, publicity, and journalism had been so willfully blurred by the magazine in the preceding years that Jordan's anger was perfectly understandable.

"When we named him Sportsman of the Year," recalled Jack McCallum, "I could tell it really meant something to the guy. I've only talked to him once since we did that baseball cover, but obviously he's been really hurt by it. Somewhere, deep inside, I thought if we ever really had to get to him, would they send me out again to see if he would do it? And my suspicion is that he would just say, 'How you doing, Jack? Fuck you; I'm not talking to *Sports Illustrated*.'"

Mulvoy blithely ignored all criticism over the issue. After all, he reasoned, Jordan was retired from basketball and was never going to be a baseball player anyway. *SI* didn't need him.

For the 40th anniversary, Mulvoy had conceived of a series of reprints, over the course of the year, of 40 "classic" *SI* stories from the magazine's history, which in the words of the January 7 publisher's memo, "will allow us to revisit the work of some of *SI*'s own legends, such as Frank Deford, Dan Jenkins, and Mark Kram." The same pub memo promised a "double issue of *SI*'s greatest photographs" (later downsized to a special section in a regular issue), but it didn't mention the two special anniversary issues Mulvoy was planning.

The first, running in the nominal anniversary issue, dated August 16, 1994, was the sort of ambitious literary effort that made Mulvoy so hard to typecast. In November 1993, Mulvoy had summoned Steve Rushin to New York and assigned him to write a long piece on how sport had changed in *SI*'s time. Titled "How We Got Here," Rushin's 22,000-word opus viewed the past 40 years in sport through five different "pods." The first four pods examined the experience of four men: television executive Roone Arledge, the single most important figure in the history of sports television; Houston multimillionaire Judge Roy Hofheinz, who built the Astrodome and launched a trend toward bigger and more modern superstructures; maverick sports league architect Gary Davidson, who had a hand in launching the American Basketball Association, World Hockey Association, and World Football League, and the explosion of free agency that necessarily followed; and legendary running back Jim Brown, whose glory years presaged the ascendancy of the black athlete in American culture.

In the spring of '94, Mulvoy traveled to Minneapolis–St. Paul and visited Rushin, to get an update on the long article for the anniversary issue. "We were looking for a last pod," remembered Rushin, of his evening with Mulvoy at the sprawling new Mall of America. "Like a place to land. And we thought about doing some superstar like a young athlete in the NBA because that was the sport of the moment. Shaq or Chris Webber, who in '94 was just signing a gigantic contract, and just following this person around for a week or something. Mark had come to the Twin Cities for something, he was laying over here and we were having dinner at the Megamall—the Bruins were in the playoffs and he wanted to see them on TV."

As Mulvoy marveled at the monument to American commerce that had been built on the very site of the old Metropolitan Stadium, he started pondering the irony of a 16,000-car garage crowded with Japanese models, and the way that sports and society had changed since his childhood. And as they were passing yet another store with Shaquille O'Neal's Orlando Magic jersey displayed in the window, Mulvoy said, "Maybe this is where you end up." Rushin understood immediately, and decided to spend a few days just wandering around the mall. It would serve as the last of the five pods, and the coda to the longest single piece in the magazine's history, and one of the best.

A month later, on September 13, 1994, more than one thousand guests gathered at the Museum of Natural History in New York City for a dinner to celebrate the publication of the other anniversary issue, whose theme was "Forty for the Ages," a ranking of the forty most influential figures in the past four decades of sport. Muhammad Ali, number one on the list from the moment it was conceived by Mulvoy, ambulated slowly through the crowd at the beginning of the evening, smiling and waving with the heartbreaking fragility that seemed to mock his earlier triumphs. Peggy Fleming paused to shake hands with fellow honoree Wayne Gretzky. At another table, Joe Namath laughed about a Super Bowl story. Don King, the most controversial name on the list, entered to a mixture of cheers and low-level hissing. There was subdued, respectful applause for baseball labor leader Marvin Miller, coming on the eve of baseball's management group announcing the cancellation of the World Series.

The night's program began with Mulvoy standing behind a podium, looking nervous and uncomfortable. He traded snippets of a sterile speech with *SI*'s president Don Elliman, who stood behind another podium, sporting a similarly stiff grin.

Bob Costas, the nation's most respected sportscaster and the emcee for the rest of the evening, stood in the shadows and listened to Mulvoy and Elliman introduce corporate executives and swimsuit models. Costas, who made his home in St. Louis, had flown in to preside over the affair (he would also host a one-hour special, which would be nationally televised in prime time the next night on NBC). In the moments before arriving, he had mentally prepared a few remarks gently noting the absence of Mickey Mantle, Wilt Chamberlain, Willie Mays, and Red Auerbach from the "Forty for the Ages" roster. But as he looked out at the audience, another thought struck him. Searching the crowd in the moments before going on, Costas wondered to himself, *Where are all the writers?*

Others in attendance were wondering the same thing. After a year in which *SI* ran 40 classic stories, the 40th anniversary dinner seemed the ideal time to note the magazine's remarkable legacy and to reunite many of Laguerre's most distinguished protégés. But André Laguerre's name wasn't even mentioned during the evening's speeches. And as a new generation of *SI* staffers scanned the crowd for their predecessors and mentors, crucial figures in *SI*'s history like Dan Jenkins and Frank Deford, Jack Olsen and John Underwood, Mark Kram and Curry Kirkpatrick, Roy Blount, Jr., and Robert W. Creamer, photographers Neil Leifer and Walter Iooss, Jr., they were disappointed. None of those people were mentioned, and none of them attended. Because on the very night that *Sports Illustrated* was celebrating its history, none of those people had been invited.

The bruised feelings left in the wake of what should have been a celebratory evening simply served as a further reminder that in the '90s, *Sports Illustrated*, like so many other institutions in American sports, was about business first. Upon receiving his invitation, Roy Terrell had planned to make a rare trip to New York for the ceremony. Then he found out that his old friend Jerry Tax, the loyal company man who after 39 years was still coming to the office to help out with editing and late read-out, had not been included on the guest list. "When Tax told me that he had not been invited I couldn't believe it," said Terrell. "I still can't believe it. How could they conceivably . . . ? So I didn't go. By the time the 50th rolls around they probably won't even invite *me*."

•  •  •

Where *SI* had historically been out front in seeing the broad issues of sport in the '60s and '70s, one of the central failings of the magazine in Mulvoy's second tenure was its lack of vigilance in observing equally seismic changes in the '90s. It remained attuned to the pulse of the sports world, but often seemed blind to the big picture. In the last issue of 1986, Rick Reilly had written a Sportsman of the Year essay about Penn State football coach Joe Paterno.

A funny thing happens to a Penn State player after four years of Paterno's preaching "us" not "me," and "M.B.A." not "NFL." They get to sounding like Paterno. The team's famous boring uniforms? "I hated our uniforms at first," says safety Ray Isom. "Now I think they're beautiful." Before last season's Orange Bowl game, Paterno brought out the traditional patch (a tiny orange) for affixing to the team's jerseys. "Everybody was quiet while Joe held them up to the jerseys," remembers Isom. "Then everybody started saying, 'Nah, nah. Too flashy. Too gaudy.'" The offending, garish, end-of-civilization-as-we-know-it patches were vetoed.

Less than a decade later, on October 15, 1994, Penn State took the field for a key late-season game against Michigan. Nike had been supplying the team's uniform for more than a year by then, discreetly placing its distinctive swoosh logo near the bottom of the sleeve, just as other athletic apparel manufacturers had been doing with other team's uniforms for years. But as the undefeated Nittany Lions came out for their warm-ups at Michigan Stadium, it was very clear that something had changed. The swoosh had moved now to the *front* of the jersey, close to the collar on the left shoulder pad, perfectly visible for every nationally televised close-up shot of a Penn State player. The reasons were obvious: Nike offered the athletic program more money for the increased exposure. Joe Paterno not only agreed, but did so over the objections of his own players; unlike the case of the Orange Bowl patch, this time there was no vote.

As fans watching on television could quickly see, the Nike logo was showing up hundreds of times a game, a constant reminder of the sponsor and, sadly, the product. By the New Year's Day bowl games of 1996, several other manufacturers had followed suit, placing their logos on the front of the jerseys being supplied to the telegenic national powers.

The fact that Joe Paterno, one of the best men in sports, had taken a leading role in the rush toward a system in which commerce could co-opt an amateur sport was a development that demanded to be decried or defended, or at the very least, examined in greater detail.

And *Sports Illustrated* never covered it. Never noticed it, evidently.

Increasingly, the magazine didn't seem to stand for anything, or if it did, seemed to reach those decisions gratuitously. In the '60s and '70s, Jenkins often weighed in with his Heisman Trophy choice in mid- to late November. In '94, *SI* made its Heisman choice in September, putting Alcorn State quarterback Steve McNair on the cover with the billing "Hand Him the Heisman." While *SI* might piggyback onto a newspaper investigation about improprieties among major college football programs or a drug scandal in the pro ranks, the magazine rarely broke those stories anymore. And about the larger problems—commercialism, increasing violence, the disaffection between athletes and fans, the increased control of the games by television media—*SI* was often silent. Under the Mulvoy regime, the sense of imminent crisis in the world of sports didn't exist. Among its writers, only Steve Rushin seemed capable of consistently articulating a grasp of what was at stake.

But Robert Creamer, back home in Tuckahoe, knew what was going on: "Commercialism has now taken over and runs everything. At the Millrose Games last Friday night—sorry, the *Chemical Bank* Millrose Games—there was business-stuff everywhere. Even the finish-line tape is an ad; it no longer serves to determine the winner in a close race or the time of the winner; that's all done by photo-finish electronics; the tape, now an inch or two wide compared to the old slender string, survives only to carry an ad message (Chemical Bank, Chemical Bank, Chemical Bank). Commerce has triumphed and editorial independence is observed fitfully. So long, Norman Chad."

Twenty years after being known primarily for its first-rate journalism, *SI* embarked on its fifth decade as a wildly profitable mass-market magazine best known for its swimsuit issue. Wherever they went, whatever they did, *SI* staffers were hounded by the specter of the *SI* s.i. It seemed to inform the perceptions of most of *SI*'s readers, even though it appeared one week out of the year and though it was produced by a scant portion of the staff. "Of course, the magazine's readers see it as a whole," explained former *SI* writer Julie Vader in a 1993 column in *The Oregonian*. "So everyone on the staff gets those annoying wink-wink, drool-drool questions about the swimsuit issue, as if scantily clad models were hanging out by the Xerox machine and arguing the designated hitter rule in the cafeteria. This, naturally, is an affront to serious journalists who are busy trying to figure out another way to whine about fighting in the NHL or mispredict the Super Bowl."

The magazine might have deflected some of these complaints if it had done a better job covering women in sports. But it became a truism that the only time a woman was on the cover was when she was, in the words of one staffer, "a victim or a babe, or both." Monica Seles made the cover alone after she was stabbed in a tournament in Germany, but not after any of her eight Grand Slam singles titles. (She shared a cover with George Steinbrenner and Jack Nicklaus after winning the French Open in 1990.) Nancy Kerrigan graced the cover after being clubbed, but not after winning the U.S. figure skating championships.

Vader's column put the blame on the entrenched sexism she'd encountered in the building. "While working on an important, breaking story, I was slapped on the butt by an unattractive, married editor who told me to 'loosen up.' On an Olympic junket, a powerful editor invited me to engage in close, personal friendship activities, which might have been tempting if he were not also unattractive and married. And a particularly unattractive editor, who later became the top editor, sent me flowers and inappropriately affectionate notes, which stopped after I suggested he might want to develop a more close personal friendship with his actual wife."

Two days after the column ran, with the office still buzzing about it, Mulvoy opened the Thursday morning staff meeting by noting that, "I think we can start now—all the unattractive, married editors are present."

Gender wasn't the only hot-button issue. In January 1995, Roy Johnson, the magazine's only black senior editor, left after it became apparent that Mulvoy had no plans to promote him to AME. Johnson's exit only underscored the lack of racial sensitivity throughout the floor, which was almost as pronounced as the lack of diversity. Fleder voiced the majority opinion that, while Johnson clearly wanted a promotion to AME, "he hadn't earned it. He came to the magazine in the late '80s, he never edited a story, he didn't have an editor's skills. He knew stuff and he knew people, and he was very much a part of the community of journalists. But he's not a seasoned, experienced editor." But it was indicative of *SI*'s seemingly dubious diversity efforts that in a world of sports increasingly dominated by black culture, the magazine had a single black senior writer (gifted *National* alum Phil Taylor, who covered pro basketball) and a single black senior editor (Bobby Clay, also a former *National* staffer, who was hired shortly after Johnson left). Many wondered if *SI*'s minority outreach program consisted of anything other than Mulvoy occasionally asking Taylor if he "knew any good black writers."

Morale at the magazine did not improve in March 1995 when Mulvoy named *Time* senior editor Paul Witteman assistant managing editor, over a group of internal candidates. Witteman was a pleasant veteran of the *Time* news desk who seemed out of his element, if not his depth, in the new job. Mike Bevans, one of the senior editors passed over for the job, began referring to Witteman as "RuPaul, the magazine editor impersonator."

● ● ●

Just six months after the anniversary celebration, *SI* witnessed, from the outside looking in, a glimpse of the sports journalism environment in the 21st century.

On March 19, 1995, Michael Jordan unretired, returning to the Chicago Bulls for their Sunday afternoon, nationally televised game at Market Square Arena against the Indiana Pacers. It netted two more cover appearances for Jordan, both before and after his first comeback game.

Jordan's 7-for-28 shooting performance against the Pacers wasn't the story, as Phil Taylor pointed out in "Resurrection," *SI*'s lead piece the following Thursday ("A man cannot win when he confronts his own legend.") It was both the suddenness of Jordan's return and the media onslaught that greeted it. Both the *Chicago Tribune* and the *Chicago Sun-Times* produced special *sections* for both the Sunday return and the first home game, at the United Center Arena where Jordan once vowed never to play. What resulted was a classic case of media overkill.

The event provided a microcosm of *Sports Illustrated*'s problem in the '90s. In an age when every daily newspaper in the land had learned to package big stories, by sending multiple reporters to cover every possible angle of a major event, the blanket coverage affected sports events to an unnerving extent. Media covered the event and then covered the media's coverage of the event, in a self-referential, self-perpetuating echo chamber of superficial reportage.

For *SI*, the new pack mentality posed multiple problems. It wasn't merely that the eight reporters at the *Tribune* might rob *SI* of any interesting angles for covering the story, but that those eight, as well as the hundreds of other print, radio, and TV reporters assigned to the event, ensured that the valuable intimacy that *SI* had historically enjoyed had vanished. It was also the fact that *SI*'s cavalier, bitchy coverage of Jordan's baseball career had effectively killed any chance for special access for his basketball comeback. There'd be no more hanging around until the rest of the media had gone home, as Steve Wulf was accustomed to doing during his years on the baseball beat. There'd be no more driving Larry Bird back to the hotel, as Jack McCallum had done on numerous occasions when trying to get the inside story on the NBA beat.

Athletes didn't view the print media with such reverence in an age when ESPN provided around-the-clock coverage of the sports world. The central question, as Mulvoy had repeatedly noted, was how to respond to a world in which "there are at least 12 'SportsCenters' between the time an event occurs and when *SI* readers get the magazine." But it ran deeper than that: with big events, competing media coverage increased, making *SI*'s four-day time lag between deadline and street date even more noticeable. Between the time Taylor left Market Square Arena on Sunday evening, sports fans would be able to: hear Jordan's return being discussed on the postgame show, and the post-postgame sports talk radio call-in show after the game; see highlights on both the local news and ESPN's "SportsCenter" (which would devote special coverage to the return in its Breakdown segment); read several stories about it in both local newspapers and *USA Today* the next morning; read even more stories about it on a special America Online area that evening; see highlights of Jordan's return every half hour at 20 and 50 past for more than a day on CNN's "Headline News"; and read about it in the national edition of the *New York Times* and in both *Time* and *Newsweek*.

The collective function of the orgy of saturation coverage was to speed up the news cycle in which events played themselves out. By Tuesday or Wednesday, most knowledgeable sports fans knew more than they wanted or needed to know about Jordan's return. And it was in this environment that Taylor's story arrived two days later, on Thursday. It didn't matter that it was the best-written piece on Jordan's return or that it included pictures of such vivid clarity that no other news medium could match it. The central fact was that news of Jordan's return was perceived by much of America as over, done. Frank Deford, surveying the situation from afar, was somewhat empathetic with the magazine's plight. "It's harder now than it was 25 years ago, when I was doing it."

Mulvoy sensed that *SI* was hemming itself in, but he had no ready answers. To not cover the event would be to violate the magazine's central charter. The magazine's most loyal subscribers still hoped for, in fact, felt they deserved, an insightful, reasoned, funny, informative take on the event. In this case, that's what Taylor provided. But in too many other weeks, *SI*'s last word hadn't been definitive, only last.

It was against this backdrop that the war over the future of *SI* would be waged. Two combatants would take different sides in the most extended argument over the magazine's direction and purpose since André Laguerre had taken over. In medieval days, it would have been called a joust. In the old West, it was a duel. At Time Inc., where collegial euphemism concealed even the most dire of internecine battles, it would be called a bake-off.

# CHAPTER 19

# THE BAKE-OFF

On a late September afternoon in 1994, Norman Pearlstine stepped out of a cab at Fifth Avenue and 54th Street, in front of the staid University Club, for decades a popular gathering place for wealthy midtown Manhattan businessmen.

Two weeks earlier, Pearlstine had been named Time Inc.'s next editor-in-chief, becoming the first outsider in the company's history to hold the position. Now, befitting a man who regularly woke up at 4 a.m. and was in his office by six, he was getting a jump start on his new job, which didn't officially begin until January 1.

Pearlstine entered the University Club and walked into another era. From the overstuffed chairs in the U Club's lounge, fairly reeking with quiet, old-money privilege, it might well have been 1944, save for the copy of *USA Today* being scanned by Mark Mulvoy, the man Pearlstine was there to see. It was to be a get-acquainted meeting, part of Pearlstine's informal discussions with his new lieutenants, the managing editors of Time Inc.'s core magazines. But just moments after the Amstel Lights arrived, Mulvoy sprung a suprise on him, informing Pearlstine that he intended to retire as *Sports Illustrated*'s managing editor after the 1996 Summer Olympic Games in Atlanta. Furthermore, added Mulvoy, he'd already decided on a successor, assistant managing editor Bill Colson. With that, the tone of the meeting changed. As editor-in-chief, Pearlstine's most important duty was choosing managing editors and now, within minutes of their first meeting, he sensed that Mulvoy was trying to preemptively push on him a man he'd never met. Pearlstine's noncommittal response was clear to Mulvoy, who in turn sensed that after 30 years of serving the company, and a decade of shaping *Sports Illustrated*, he might have encountered a new boss with the temerity to ignore his final and most important recommendation.

It was not the beginning of a beautiful friendship. The two men were temperamentally ill-suited. Mulvoy's Boston-bred Irish Catholicism had its grounding in a kind of conspiratorial conversational style; he always said a bit *too* much, went a tad too far in giving details, providing criticism. Pearlstine, on the other hand, was as unreadable as an accountant on a poker vacation in Vegas. Staffers had taken to calling him "The Sphinx," and even his closest aides weren't always sure of his opinion in crucial personnel matters. When he did get down to it, Pearlstine could be as blunt as Mulvoy, but he was more calculating and more cerebral, and chose his words during the rest of the meeting with painstaking care.

Just two weeks after meeting Mulvoy, Pearlstine had a longer, more relaxed meeting with Daniel Okrent, the managing editor of *Life*. Pearlstine and Okrent had a history, having been casual social acquaintances and occasional lunchtime companions for decades. They met in 1971, when Okrent was an editor at Knopf and Pearlstine, then an energetic young reporter, came pitching a book idea about the oil industry. In the late '80s, Okrent wrote a music column in *Esquire*, describing the 1968 album *John Coltrane and Johnny Hartman* as the best recording ever. Pearlstine called him a few days later to say he agreed, and they went out to lunch. Throughout the '90s, they'd seen each other at magazine industry functions and social affairs. Most significant, in the culture of Time Inc., they were both outsiders. At their meeting, Pearlstine asked Okrent the same pro forma question that he asked all the managing editors: "What do you see as your future with the company?" Okrent allowed that he was perfectly happy where he was, but added that "if the job at *Sports Illustrated* ever came open, I'd sure love a shot at it." It was a plausible idea, but also an audacious one. Okrent had won two National Magazine Awards at the now-defunct *New England Monthly*, and had even added some snap to the irrelevant *Life*, but he'd never top-edited a weekly magazine before. And *SI* was weekly magazine-making at its most intense; AME Rob Fleder had once described sitting in the managing editor's chair at *SI* as "like driving a very fast sports car for the first time."

Pearlstine didn't tell Okrent that the job would be opening, but he filed it away as an element to consider in his future study of *SI*. But before that, he spent the first two months of his tenure shaking up *Fortune*. By mid-February, Walter Kiechel had been replaced by Pearlstine's longtime friend, executive editor John Huey, sending rumors of an outsider's purge running through the halls of every other magazine in the Time & Life Building. Immediately after promoting Huey, Pearlstine turned his focus to an analysis of *SI*. He spent hours going over old issues, assessing the magazine's competition, in both print and electronic media. He was aware that

Rupert Murdoch was considering launching a weekly sports magazine to directly compete with *SI*, and that the Hearst Corporation was linking up with ESPN to develop their own magazine, *Total Sports*, which might convert from special issues to a weekly publishing frequency somewhere down the road. The question of competition loomed large for Pearlstine, who tended to see competitors everywhere. Like Bill Gates at Microsoft, he operated with an assumption that his company's preeminence was constantly being assaulted.

On February 23, 1995, after an evening meeting of Time Inc. division heads held at the Tarrytown House just north of the city, Pearlstine shared a ride back to Manhattan with his deputy, editorial director Henry Muller. It was on that ride that the possibility of a contest was first broached, and that Muller and Pearlstine discussed the brutal history of "bake-offs" at Time Inc. In the original bake-off in 1977, *SI* alum Ray Cave had outdueled Jason McManus for the top job at *Time*. At *SI* in 1983, Mulvoy's daring had moved him past Peter Carry to the managing editor's job succeeding Rogin.

The rationale for a bake-off rather than a decision by fiat was compelling. While Pearlstine, after editing the *Wall Street Journal*, had been thoroughly conversant with *Fortune*'s publishing environment and its problems, he was on less certain terms with *SI*. He didn't particularly like the autocratic Mulvoy, and wasn't comfortable promoting Bill Colson on Mulvoy's word alone. By the time they reached the city, Pearlstine and Muller had arrived at the idea of a contest, between Colson, Okrent, and perhaps one other candidate.

Pearlstine assigned Muller, who had been overseeing *SI* (and critiquing the weekly issues) since early 1994, to set up the timing and terms of the contest. Both men would get three months to edit the magazine—May through July for Colson, August through September for Okrent—with the possibility of a third candidate to come later. (Later in the spring, Pearlstine offered a tryout to Carol Wallace, deputy managing editor at *People*, but she declined.)

Both candidates were decent, intelligent, well-liked men, with solid credentials. But they were shaped by vastly different backgrounds. Okrent was urbane, witty, assured in a crowd, a man who seemed comfortable in his own skin, both a confident leader and an adept corporate politician. About Colson there was an aura of goodness so genuine as to seem almost endearingly antiquated. He seemed literally guileless, and spectacularly ill-equipped for the sort of political in-fighting and strategic calculation that usually accompanied these ascension struggles.

Colson's father was the trial lawyer William Colson, a University of Miami law school grad who would go on to a distinguished career, arguing many civil rights cases throughout the South in the '60s and becoming the head of the American Trial Lawyers Association. He and his wife Martha raised their two sons and one daughter in the comfortable Miami suburb of Coral Gables, just a block away from Salvadore Park, whose leafy boundaries housed a complex of ten tennis courts. In the increasingly competitive Florida junior tennis scene, Salvadore Park became a magnet for talented juniors and Bill Colson, Jr., quickly became one of the best.

In a high school athletic career straight out of a Gil Thorp comic strip, the young Colson became perhaps the only schoolboy athlete ever to play on two mythical national championship–winning teams in the same school year, as Coral Gables High was voted national champ in both football and tennis in his senior year. In one of the most competitive tennis-playing regions in the country, Colson was undefeated in three years of varsity singles and doubles. He was named best all-around graduate by the students, athlete of the year by the coaches, and scholar-athlete of the year by Florida sportswriters. The June 14, 1967, *St. Petersburg Times* included this account of his performance in the state tennis finals: "With the temperature 90-plus in the clubhouse and close to 100 on the court, he looked cool, confident and comfortable, never seeming to work up a sweat. He remained calm even in the most crucial situations and played his same steady game, refusing to become rattled." In the national doubles high school championship, Colson and Alabama junior tennis standout Charles Owens beat future pro tour stars Brian Gottfried and Roscoe Tanner. Colson was the fourth-rated junior tennis player in the country when he graduated from high school in 1968, touring with the U.S. Junior Davis Cup team that summer.

He was recruited by over one hundred colleges across the country. Everyone wanted him for tennis, but Michigan and Stanford also expressed interest in him as a football prospect, while UCLA and North Carolina invited him to play both tennis and basketball. But William Colson, Sr., had always made it clear: sports was a means to an end, not an end in itself. There was a hint of noblesse oblige, both in Colson's manners, forthright and self-effacing, and in his college choice. He elected to forgo all the athletic scholarships and instead attended Princeton, where he wound up as captain of the tennis team.

After Princeton, he went to Indiana University for a Ph.D. in English, then came to New York in 1976 to take an assistant editor's position at

*Family Weekly* magazine. In the fall of 1978, he started as a researcher at *SI*, and worked his way up. He wrote a few pieces, but soon realized that his talents lay in editing, not writing. He moved quickly up the editing ladder, on the strength of his work ethic, native intelligence, and an otherworldly ability to concentrate, to screen out distractions. But he also exhibited a restless, pixilated intelligence, which could make him seem abrupt, even rudely indifferent at times. Many wondered if he had the people skills to be a leader. At the beginning of 1995, Colson went to the Center for Creative Leadership in North Carolina—"charm school," Mulvoy called it—where he would be steeped in management theory. No one knew whether it would take.

If Colson was the quintessential scholar-athlete, Okrent perfectly fit the description of the thoughtful fan.

His first words in *Sports Illustrated*, a freelance submission that ran as the April 28, 1980, bonus piece, were testament to his level of his zeal for baseball:

> On a warm night last June—the night I realized it was possible—I was sitting on one of the old Briggs Stadium seats bolted to my backyard patio. The voice of Ernie Harwell scratched in the night, traveling with the aid of 50,000 watts from Detroit, across Ontario and New York and into our western Massachusetts hills. My dog Willie, named for Mays, was curled at my feet. Spread before me were the American and National League schedules, anchored against the breeze by the weight of *The Baseball Encyclopedia* on one side and a genuine Seattle Pilots ashtray on the other. As usual, my wife took little notice of the Washington Senators cap I was wearing until I threw it into the air with a whoop of triumph.
>
> This is what was possible: I could, in 13 days, travel to 13 different ballparks, watch 13 games, see all 26 major league teams in action and see no team twice. I could, with the aid of a good travel agent, a light suitcase, and my wife's characteristic tolerance, enter baseball heaven. I could go looking, without distraction, for the game itself and for others who love it as I do.

Okrent and Colson had one thing in common: their fathers. Okrent's dad was a personal injury lawyer with similarly progressive political views. Harry Okrent was a charter subscriber to *SI*, and dutifully brought Dan to his first major league baseball game the summer that *SI* was launched, though he had disavowed the Tigers for their reluctance to integrate (only the Red Sox waited longer to sign a black player). Dan Okrent granted the point, but fell in love with the Tigers anyway. After drifting away from sports at the University of Michigan, he came East to work in the book publishing industry, began subscribing to *Sports Illustrated* again, and renewed his love for the game.

While the 1980 piece would introduce Okrent to *SI* readers, a story that he wrote earlier would eventually have a larger impact on the magazine and baseball. In 1979, he wrote a letter to Robert Creamer, his favorite *SI* writer, inviting him to write a chapter for Okrent's ambitious brainchild *The Ultimate Baseball Book*. Creamer accepted, and told Okrent to send some freelance ideas to *SI*. Okrent had been entranced by the mimeographed, self-published baseball newsletter of a night watchman in Lawrence, Kansas, named Bill James. After getting approval for the story, Okrent flew to Kansas to interview him. It was, improbably, a historic meeting of the two men who would most change the way baseball was discussed, reported, televised, and played in the modern era. James, of course, would soon bring sabermetrics ("the search for objective knowledge about baseball") to the masses and become the most influential thinker in the sport. Okrent, a year later, would invent Rotisserie Baseball.

*Sports Illustrated* killed the article.

Kathy Andria, then *SI*'s researcher on the baseball beat, disagreed with James's assertions. She was skeptical of some of James's more startling conclusions, and cited errors in his numbers. But the inaccuracies were minor and due entirely to the fact that major league baseball didn't even publish the sort of statistics that James was writing about. Okrent gladly granted that James might be a few percentage points off because he was working from newspaper box scores, but that his larger theories were correct. Only a year later, after Andria had left, did Creamer intervene on Okrent's behalf. "This is unfair to Okrent," he said to baseball editor Larry Keith. "And it's unfair to James."

The story, "He Does It By the Numbers," finally ran in the May 25, 1981, issue. The publicity that James got from the piece allowed him to clinch the book contract he'd been angling for, and quit his job as a security guard. Fifteen years later, after James had become the most quoted, influential writer in baseball, he still pointed to the *SI* piece as crucial in launching his career. "That article made me what I am," he said. "In one way or another, I've made a living off that article ever since then. That article didn't guarantee me a living, but it gave me the opportunity to get a book contract, and made me credible as a media personality. It gave me the opportunity to do what I do for a living."

To introduce the world to Bill James was a noteworthy feat. And yet as Okrent often ruefully noted, he could bring peace to the Middle East and develop a cure for cancer, but when he died, his obituary would still say "Okrent Dies, Invented Rotisserie Baseball." By the mid-'90s, the novel game that Okrent had conceived on a plane in 1980 had become the centerpiece of a thriving "fantasy" sports industry that had changed the nature of sports coverage in all media.

After editing the evocative coffee-table tome *The Ultimate Baseball Book*, Okrent wrote *Nine Innings*, a microscopic look at a single baseball game. In 1984, he started a magazine called *New England Monthly*, which won widespread media acclaim and two National Magazine Awards before folding in 1990. Okrent became a contributing editor at *Life*, late in 1989, before taking over as managing editor in 1992. In 1994, he was prominently featured as the lucid, ruminative "guy in the red sweater" on Ken Burns's exhaustive documentary *Baseball*. Secure in his accomplishments and his credentials, he viewed *SI* as the perfect job, as well as the perfect capstone to his career in magazine journalism.

• • •

What followed was the most public and potentially divisive succession battle in the history of Time Inc., carried out under all the more scrutiny for being seen as the first real opportunity for Norman Pearlstine to put his stamp on the company. There had been bake-offs before, of course, but never ones that were covered concurrently in the media, with *New York* magazine, the *Washington Post,* and the *New York Observer* (the gossipy weekly newspaper that was required reading for New York City's media industry types) all running stories on the battle while it was going on. "[Pearlstine's] closely reviewing issues, forming high-tech committees, bombing editors with E-mail, tweaking stories with suggestions such as a greater use of sidebars," wrote Richard Turner in *New York* during the early phases of the competition. "And in doing so, he's messing with the most independent island in the Time Inc. archipelago, long ruled like a Samoan princedom by the larger-than-life Mulvoy, who for a decade roamed the halls with a golf club and about as much subtlety as a Big Bertha driver."

The timing of the two trial periods assured that each man would be forced to address his perceived editing shortcoming. Colson, who had yet to establish himself independent of Mulvoy, or show that he had the reservoir of ideas to keep the magazine fresh and interesting during slow news periods, would preside over a summer season that promised to be more difficult than usual, since baseball's new three-division format would inevitably dilute the drama of the pennant races. Okrent would get his first taste of weekly magazine editing during the overstuffed fall sports glut, when football games and baseball playoffs meant several 11th-hour assignment decisions and a staff pushed to its maximum capacity. If an ME couldn't shift gears in moments following a big upset, he might underplay a big event, or miss it altogether.

In just the second week of his trial in early May, Colson made a series of decisions that would mark him as his own man. Throughout the basketball season, the staff had been hard-pressed to adequately document the calamitous effect that Dennis Rodman was having on the league. They'd covered Rodman in the past, with a Bruce Newman story on his background in 1988 and a Rick Telander profile in the 1993 pro basketball preview. But since then, Rodman had ascended to a whole new level of weirdness and rebounding superiority, and basketball editor Dick Friedman wanted to take another shot at him. With the magazine's NBA writer Phil Taylor already following the playoffs, Friedman and Colson agreed that new senior writer Michael Silver, only six months removed from being a beat writer at the *Santa Rosa* (California) *Press*, might be the right man to profile Rodman. At 29, Silver was a rising writing star with a background in rock 'n' roll and social dissent (he'd gone to Berkeley, his parents had marched against Vietnam). Perhaps, guessed Friedman, Silver was just loose enough to be able to hang with Rodman, to find some common ground where other writers had been perplexed or put off.

Silver got the assignment on a Wednesday, and though he was backed up with other stories, he was in no position to turn this one down. He flew from Oakland to Los Angeles, where on Friday night he walked into the San Antonio Spurs locker room before their playoff game at the Forum against the Lakers and introduced himself to Rodman. The two hit it off immediately, earning Silver a nickname (Si, "for your magazine") and an invitation to Sanctuary, a terminally hip L.A. after-hours club where he would get a full sense of the weird cultural crossroads—gay culture, rock 'n' roll rebellion, nihilism, sexuality, and celebrity—in which Rodman operated. After a trip to San Antonio, Silver followed Rodman for a night of gambling in Las Vegas, and then, the next morning, was getting ready to return to Oakland when Rodman urged him to come back with him to San Antonio and continue the interview on the plane.

That left Silver, hours after telling his wife Leslie that he'd be home shortly, calling her again to explain that he was now in San Antonio at Rodman's house. After a few soft "I love you's," Silver hung up the phone and found himself at the mercy of Rodman's taunting.

"Si—damn!" said the laughing Rodman. "Who wears *the pants*, man!? What the fuck is that?"

Silver took his teasing good-naturedly, and forged on through the night ahead in which he and Rodman visited a gay bar and talked further about Rodman's sexuality, his attitude toward basketball, and his relationship with Madonna ("She wanted to have my baby. She said, 'Be in a hotel room in Las Vegas on this specific day so you can get me pregnant'").

That Sunday, a dazed Silver banged out his story while Rodman posed for a variety of shots for photographer John McDonough. He offered to pose nude for the magazine, but settled on a series of cross-dressing sessions instead. The next morning, in the *SI* color room, Colson looked on in sincere wonder as the slides were shown. For the cover, he decided on the most arresting shot of Rodman, sitting defiantly in gold lamé hot pants, a black leather vest, and a studded dog collar, with a parrot on his shoulder.

The piece closed at about 4:40 p.m. on that Monday afternoon. Silver had just answered the last fact-checker's question and gone over the last edits with Colson when his phone rang again. It was Rodman, sounding significantly less carefree than he had over the weekend.

"Yo, man. You've *got* to do me a fucking favor, man. You've got to help me out."

"Dude, what do you want?" said Silver. "The story closed exactly five minutes ago."

"You've got to take that Madonna shit out of there. Man, she is so fucking pissed off at me."

Silver couldn't resist: "Dennis—*who wears the pants*, man?!"

Rodman did persuade Silver to fax an explanation to the singer confirming that Rodman had spoken highly of her. Two days later, the issue hit the stands to *SI*'s biggest media response of the year. It was the best-selling May cover in a decade. In only his second week, Colson had already exceeded expectations. But he didn't stop there.

The furor over Rodman had barely died down when Colson prompted an even bigger one. He'd grown up watching George Mira at the Orange Bowl when the University of Miami was the only game in town. But ever since the Hurricanes trash-talked their way through an unseemly 46–3 humiliation of Texas in the 1991 Cotton Bowl, the program had endured one damaging revelation after another. With numerous allegations surfacing about NCAA rules violations, Colson decided to use the magazine as a bully pulpit, assigning Alexander Wolff to write an open letter to Miami president Edward "Tad" Foote, urging him to shut down the football program. The starkest cover in years featured the school colors: the *SI* logo in orange on a dark green background with a large, white headline filling the page, which read, "Why the University of Miami Should Drop Football."

This was news everywhere, but it hit with particular force in the households of Colson's father, a former University of Miami trustee, and his brother Dean, a present trustee. The Colson family was inextricably bound up in the life of the university; in the '70s the Colsons had sold their Coral Gables house to the daughter of former Miami football coach and athletic director Jack Harding. "I don't agree with Billy, and I told him my reasons why," said Colson senior. "But I'm proud of him for standing up for what he believes." The pride was not shared by much of the Miami community. The most pointed retort came from Edwin Pope of the *Miami Herald*, whom Wolff described in his piece as a Miami rooter who had finally been pushed over the edge by the latest round of misbehavior. After criticizing *SI* for using "the *Herald*'s investigative reports as the source for almost all the magazine's own information," he took "total exception" to being characterized as a cheerleader, as well as with the sanctimonious tone of the piece. Even conscience-stricken purists like Underwood, who knew both Bill senior and Dean, were upset by the piece. "I think it was ridiculous," he said. "First of all, a lot of schools have done a lot of bad things, and I'm a great critic of the University of Miami. I think they've disgraced the university for the past ten years. But that doesn't mean you throw the baby out with the wash. I don't know where they got the idea that was something they should do, because a lot of schools made similar mistakes."

Others wondered about the odd juxtaposition of *SI* celebrating Rodman's scattershot deviance just weeks before getting on its moral high horse. But after a sluggish spring under Mulvoy, the magazine had become a hot topic again. In July, Colson ran a cover story asking "Should We Root for Mike Tyson?" Two weeks later, *SI* secured an exclusive interview with Monica Seles, on the verge of her own comeback. "A pattern very quickly developed," said Henry Muller. "Any editor could get lucky and do the Rodman thing. The story comes in, the pieces fall in place. But week after week after week the magazine is good and imaginative, and they were being talked about. They were doing what a magazine ought to do, which is to get attention beyond just the community inside the building. They were innovative, they were newsy, they were quick. That was pretty clear, I think."

There was grumbling that Colson had run too many "concept" covers, and not enough action covers, but virtually everyone at the magazine agreed he'd exceeded expectations. Some had questioned his story selection or his management style, but no one questioned that he had stepped out of Mark Mulvoy's shadow.

But Dan Okrent, outsider, award-winning editor, and longtime aquaintance of Norman Pearlstine, had the last shot.

• • •

On Thursday, August 3, as Colson's final issue was hitting newsstands, Okrent presided over his first editorial staff meeting.

He had spent the three months since learning of the bake-off planning his attack. For years, he'd sensed that *SI* was becoming too earnest about sport and society. Okrent, for all his literary aspirations and alliances, belonged to a tradition of sports fan that viewed sports less as a prism through which to interpret the rest of society than an oasis to escape from those very realities. He wanted to reinstill the magazine with that spirit, though he would try to do so with a staff that was inherently suspicious of any outsider.

As he sat with the 40 or so senior staffers and department heads that routinely attended the Thursday morning meetings that marked the beginning of *SI*'s workweek, Okrent tried to explain exactly what he had in mind.

"There's no point in doing things the way you do them," he said in preface. "I'm the outsider because I presumably would do things differently. So I'll experiment with things you're not going to like. I'll start something and I might throw it away two weeks later. I will change my mind. I will be going down one street one day and down a different street the next day, because I'm new to this and, as an outsider, I feel compelled to do things differently. I don't think Norm would have asked me to partake of this if he expected me to do the things you do."

Okrent also said that he wanted to "celebrate sports," a phrase that his critics would bring up often as a sign that he wanted to soften the magazine's coverage, to give it a wide-eyed credulousness that the magazine hadn't exhibited since the '50s. Word had already spread about Okrent's intent to bring back Steve Wulf from *Time* if he got the job, and with Fleder (another Rotisserian) already on the staff, the prospect of a cabal of like-minded, fortysomething baseball aficionados taking over the magazine seemed real enough. "It's going to be Revenge of the Roto-nerds," predicted one dubious staffer.

In July, Okrent called Bill James to discuss his first story idea: a profile of Atlanta Braves pitcher Greg Maddux that, rather than focusing on Maddux's understated, self-effacing personality, made a case for Maddux as the best pitcher of the modern era. He also hoped to show the advantages of print over television. ESPN could bring the details of Maddux's performances, even break down his pitching style, but there was something too ephemeral about trying to argue the case on television, where even the strongest statements—especially about sports—would be lost in the normal tide of hyperbole. "That's what makes *SI* special," said James. "Their way of conferring onto Greg Maddux the status of [historical] stardom. It's almost impossible for him to get it from 'SportsCenter' or anywhere else." James expressed reservations about the story idea ("I thought it was too soon; I was afraid Maddux would wind up 12–7 and we'd all look stupid"). Instead, Maddux went on to win his fourth straight Cy Young award, and Tom Verducci's cover story ran at an ideal time.

But that August 13 issue, the first of Okrent's trial, was perceived as a disaster among bake-off handicappers. The week leading up to it underscored the inherent difficulty of an interloper running the magazine. There was an air of self-conscious cordiality through the floor that was all the less convincing for the gravity of the stakes involved. Okrent, while he took a self-effacing tone in the first meeting, was determined to make his own statement and show he was in charge. He would quickly clash with design director Steve Hoffman, who had been telling colleagues, at least half-jokingly, that "I'm in a position to decide who wins this." After laying out the opening spread to Okrent's specifications—an unfocused, multiple-exposure photograph of Maddux filled up three-fourths of the opening spread, with the headline type and body copy reversed in white against a dark brown blob of background color—Hoffman realized that, whatever the intent, the spread looked terrible. On the Sunday morning of the first close, he showed up in Okrent's office with the dummy spread. "Just for what it's worth," he said, concentrating on not seeming confrontational, and coming off as just that, "this isn't up to the sort of quality that we'd normally run in the magazine." Okrent leaned back in his chair, clasped his hands behind his head, and grimaced, eventually forcing a smile. "I'm gonna run it," he said.

The opening spread of the first issue would only grow in infamy. Frank Deford, watching the bake-off from afar, called it "one of the worst things I ever saw in my life, just unbelievably bad." Internally, Okrent's machinations with a split-cover earned as much criticism. He wanted to put Alabama coach Gene Stallings on the cover in Alabama, where interest was high in the just-announced sanctions from the NCAA. But that meant Stallings was on the cover throughout the Southeast, including Atlanta, where Braves fans were denied the Greg Maddux cover.

A week later, Okrent called the senior editors in to discuss long-range story ideas, in a planning meeting that he would later describe as "the most depressing thing that I've ever been to." After opening the floor for story ideas, he sat in growing amazement as most of the magazine's senior editors shifted in their seats. Only Steve Fine and Heinz Kluetmeier, from the photo department, seemed to have a ready list of coherent ideas. Years of serving under Mulvoy seemed to have left the editors unable to think on their feet, and unwilling to risk public rejection. They sat in a reactive stance, often shooting down ideas that Okrent tossed out. No one was more outwardly resistant, both in the meeting and throughout Okrent's trial, than Steve Robinson, the tough, often humorless senior editor who had been unimpressed with Okrent's recent performance at *Life* (where Robinson himself had worked in the early '80s).

Okrent had wanted to get the mood inside an NFL locker room. His idea was to hand out disposable cameras to every member of, say, the San Francisco 49ers, and see what they would come up with. Robinson, who viewed the idea as a gimmicky soft feature that at best would yield an embarrassing collection of poorly lit, unpublishable photographs, dismissed the idea out of hand. And incidentally, he added, the 49ers would never give them permission.

"Turn it into a collaboration," Okrent suggested. "Tell them we'll go over all the pictures with them, and pick them together."

Robinson glared at Okrent, a Puritan witness to a spoken heresy. "Why . . . would we want to do that?" he asked incredulously.

There was a tense, combustible silence, before Peter Carry interjected some conciliatory words and suggested tabling the discussion until later. But after a couple of similar incidents, AMEs Jerry Kirshenbaum and Fleder both met privately with Robinson and asked him to be more cooperative. "He could be your boss one day," pleaded Fleder. Senior editor Michael Bevans, more laconic and less diplomatic, simply swung by Robinson's office after one meeting and asked, "Don't you like working here?" Later in August, veteran deputy photo editor Steve Fine went to Okrent and issued an apology, on behalf of the staff, for Robinson's behavior. "We're all worried about this," Fine told Okrent. "Steve is a valuable member of the staff, but we all can see that if you get this job, you're gonna fire him immediately because he's acting like such an asshole."

Some of Okrent's ideas *were* weird and, as often as not, misguided in both concept and execution. But beyond the miscalculations, there was a curious arrogance that informed much of the staff's reaction to his performance. "He's just *such* a fan," said one senior editor. After 12 years of Mulvoy, the staff had become locked into the notion that *SI* should be the "conscience of sport." But for many staffers, their fierce adherence to this line blinded them to both the larger questions (like the broad hot-button issues that the magazine used to tackle regularly under Laguerre) as well as the more surgical ones that Okrent was asking. They seemed all too quick to use the journalistic integrity club to beat on Okrent for asking simple, pointed, fans' questions, like "Why Is Deion Sanders Worth $35 Million?" In a *New York Observer* piece, one senior writer peevishly complained that the *real SI* would ask "*Is* Deion Sanders Worth $35 Million?" and that the formulation of Okrent's question amounted to "buying into the hype machine."

From the start, Okrent instituted changes in Scorecard. He agreed with Fleder that the section had become a "dinosaur," lacking any of the visual urgency of front-of-the-book sections in *Newsweek, Entertainment Weekly,* and other magazines. Okrent tried several things. One was The Scorecard Poll, similar in conception to a feature that Jack McCallum had brought to his Inside the NBA column in '93 and '94. Less well accepted was The Standings, a survey of the current buzz similar to *EW*'s The Hot List or *Newsweek*'s Conventional Wisdom Watch. Most thought the concept, which first listed items by winning percentage, and later by games behind, was ill-conceived. But it was nothing like the internal, and external, opposition that greeted the introduction of boldface within the Scorecard items. This conceit was derivative of the breathless communiqués in women's magazines like *Self* and *Cosmopolitan*. The practice debuted in the August 21 issue, and senior editor Sandy Bailey, who hated the idea in the first place, was further upset by what Okrent chose to run in boldface. A story on a golf course in Mâcon, France, mentioned that, "Apart from one phallus-shaped hole, **the course is an oversized relief of women's buttocks, breasts and thighs.**"

For all the internal conflict, Okrent eventually seemed to be getting close to what he wanted, a freer flowing amalgam of writers and ideas, a looser mixture of color and artwork. The September 11 issue, which opened with a magisterial illustration of Cal Ripken on the cover, was one of Okrent's best. The bonus piece was Richard Ben Cramer's elegiac meditation on the man and the city, Ripken and Baltimore. The lead Scorecard item made the key point (albeit one that had been made two weeks earlier by ESPN anchor Keith Olbermann), bolding up the simple fact that Gehrig's streak ended for one reason: **"The Iron Horse was suffering from a fatal disease."** The lead story, on a season-opening NFL game between New England and Cleveland, featured a gatefold opening spread of New England's Curtis Martin bursting over the goal line for a touchdown.

In early September, Scorecard editor Jack McCallum returned from his summer break. The gifted basketball writer had taken well to an office job. He was an amiable curmudgeon, a slouchy, assured writer-editor who would casually flip his wedding ring (as if conducting a pregame coin toss) during story conferences to let off nervous energy. One of the most unassuming staffers in the office, he was also one of the best-liked. On his first day back, McCallum walked into Okrent's office and confronted him with good-natured candor: "I like standings, I'm ambivalent about the polls, and I absolutely hate boldface." Office handicappers would later say that Okrent had realized the device was an abject failure and that he was looking for an excuse to kill it. But Okrent said he discontinued it solely out of respect for McCallum.

But Okrent was growing depressed by the resistance he was encountering at virtually every turn. Many in the staff hadn't warmed up to him, and he sensed that he'd been outflanked by Colson. With the inside man's strong performance raising eyebrows, and his younger, hipper issues serving as an antithesis to Mulvoy's ossified leadership, there was no logical place for Okrent to go. He could try to "out-Colson Colson," and might succeed, but the perception would have been that he was doing so out of desperation.

At the beginning of the bake-off, staffers assumed Okrent would edit the magazine like it was *New England Monthly,* or one long nostalgic baseball reverie. Instead he went against the grain, employing a Nixon-in-China strategy to put out what was often as much of a picture magazine as *Life* or *People.* In certain weeks, virtually every story began with a double-truck photo spread. While this was an understandable impulse in a feature monthly like *Life,* it was a distraction at a weekly newsmagazine, where the way a story was played subtly communicated to the reader a sense of significance. If everything was important, nothing was.

What was most curious about Okrent's tenure, though, were the stories that *didn't* run. Okrent prevailed on Steve Rushin (on hiatus, working on a book conceived as an American sports fan's travelogue) to write 200 lines to accompany a pictorial on the verities of the summer game. Then it was dropped to 90. And when Rushin finally turned it in, Okrent killed it and asked Wulf to write some simpler text blocks in its place. When word got out that Okrent had killed Rushin's piece to run Wulf instead, many staff members viewed it as a dire hint of things to come. "What Rushin wrote was hilarious and wonderful," Okrent remembered later. "But the pictures were elegiac. The prose was out of sync with the pictures. These pictures were sort of twilit, emotionally gauzy, and here's this very hip, rhythmic, wise-guy writing, which I happen to like, but it was just wrong for this."

He also wanted to apply a different, more contrarian spin to the Point After opinion page—to have it read less like a newspaper column and more like a genuine *essay*—and asked Bill James, Wilfrid Sheed, and Allan Barra to write pieces for it. "I wanted so much to change Point After to have more play and more fun, and not have imperious, tendentious, essay-writing by people who are not born to write essays," Okrent said. "So Bill and all the people that I asked to do it, that I went to because they don't write essays of that nature, all wrote essays of that nature."

But the theoretical reasoning was unfathomable to those who weren't in his inner circle. Instead, it looked like he was buying up material from every good writer he could find, then *not running it*. As the final evidence of what seemed a self-doubting, self-defeating editorial madness, his iron determination to NOT be the guy in the red sweater, he chose not to run the submission by James, precisely the sort of writer that Okrent wanted to bring into the magazine. James's piece was a provocative essay arguing that sportswriters were missing the essence of the game in the pressbox, divorced and separated from the pulsing roar of the crowd.

As the trial continued, things got worse rather than better. While Okrent had been reasonably circumspect, Steve Wulf was not. He walked up to *SI* hockey writer Gerry Callahan at the World Series and introduced himself by saying. "I'm Steve Wulf. If Dan Okrent becomes the new editor at *SI*, I'm going to be his AME. We want you to write more baseball." When word got out that the new regime was already being planned, the tenuous level of morale at *SI* took another precipitous drop. And by mid-October, Okrent was adopting a dazed, Papanekian expression. Walking out of the office with staffer Schuyler Bishop one night, he volunteered that "I never knew people disliked Steve so much."

The most severe criticism came from the October 30 issue, Okrent's next-to-last in his trial. Poor planning had left him in a situation in which several bonus pieces were being pushed later and later into the trial. While Okrent had always wanted a more feature-oriented magazine, he now faced an issue in the heart of *SI*'s busiest news period with nearly a half-dozen potential bonuses. Gary Cartwright's piece on the Southwest Conference could have run earlier, but hadn't. Additionally, there was a story by Darcy Frey on East St. Louis high school football coach Bob Shannon, an inspiration for hundreds of ghetto kids and suddenly out of a job. And Peter King, *SI*'s pro football writer, had spent a week with the

Green Bay Packers, emerging with an exclusive glimpse of NFL MVP-in-waiting Brett Favre, who spent the week racked in pain, and gobbling pain-killers, from hits he took in the previous Sunday's game. Virtually any of the stories would have been plausible cover choices.

But what Okrent chose to put on the cover was: Bo Jackson.

Richard Hoffer had done a feature on the iconic two-sport star in retirement. It was exactly the sort of "What Happened To . . . " story that would typically grace the cover of *SI* in the lean weeks of February or in the dead of summer. But here was Okrent, with an embarrassment of logical options, taking the least urgent and least newsworthy one of all, over the confidential but strenuous protest of his friend Fleder.

While Okrent would admit later that he'd gone with the Jackson cover to be different ("There's some things you do because it's a bake-off that you wouldn't normally do"), his decision pointed up one of the inherent flaws of the entire process. The premise of the bake-off was simple: give both men the magazine for three months and see how they run it. The problem was, because of the very high-stakes nature of the competition, they *didn't* put out the magazine the way they normally would. "I don't think Colson suggests that Miami drop their whole football program if this isn't a bake-off," said one staffer. "And you damn well know that the World Series would be on the cover if Okrent wasn't playing to Norm."

Lost in the controversy over the Jackson cover was what was inside the magazine: a sharp, readable mix of seven stories, identifiably hewing to an *SI* style, but still varied in tone and pace. The issue's pieces covered the week's news from innovative angles, but also included memorable features that even longtime *SI* readers couldn't have predicted. In design terms, Okrent had improved throughout the trial period; his grasp of photography was assured, and he was becoming comfortable with the flow of *SI*'s pages. But on the 18th floor, the whispered talk was all about what a bizarre choice he'd made with the cover.

Part of the reason Okrent had run the Jackson story then was that Mark Mulvoy made it clear that he wasn't interested in running such a story once he returned. Okrent and Mulvoy's relationship was frosty, partly because Robinson was a well-known Mulvoy loyalist and partly because Okrent was sure Mulvoy was running him down to the *SI* staff. "Mark had acted like an asshole," said one executive. "Everybody knows that. There were times when during the bake-off, especially during the Okrent part of it, he was clearly out of bounds with the opinions he was expressing. But it's also easy to sympathize with that. The guy spends eleven years running the magazine. And the notion that someone other than your handpicked successor would get the job becomes unbearable."

By the time Okrent's main trial ended (he would stick around to oversee the two basketball previews, just as Colson had edited the two football
previews), the staff was in a feeding frenzy of speculation. Colson fans
liked the Rodman cover and the Miami cover, and hated Okrent's Bo Jackson cover and the split-cover fiasco with Maddux and Alabama. Okrent
defenders felt that Colson had gotten too conceptual with covers on Tyson
and Seles, while defending Okrent's stark, text-free covers of Mickey Mantle and the Braves' World Series celebration. The last two led to some
resentment among *SI* traditionalists. "We've run like three nonheadline
covers in the magazine's history," said one veteran staffer. "And now
Okrent runs two more in thirteen weeks. What gives him the right?"

Fewer people mentioned the more compelling omissions, the ones
that vexed *SI*'s most loyal readers. Even longtime readers who enjoyed
the Rodman cover wondered why the same issue had no coverage of the
dramatic seven-game Western Conference semifinal between Phoenix and
Houston, ending with Mario Elie's clutch three-point shot that sent Houston toward its second straight championship, after being down three
games to one. Many were also perplexed when the magazine didn't cover
the women's World Cup of soccer over the summer, an event that
received premium coverage in many American newsapapers. Those who
decried Okrent's tenure rarely mentioned his glaring news judgment
omission, declining to cover the one-game American League West playoff
on Monday afternoon, October 2. "We would have had to go to press
late, and we would have had a day less newsstand sales," said Peter
Carry, but that was a businessman's lame defense. The ineluctable fact
remained that 97 percent of *SI*'s readership subscribed, and they still
expected the breaking news.

As the bake-off came to a merciful close, speculation grew rampant.
And the strain of not knowing, as well as the cumulative anxiety brought
about by constant rumors, was taking a toll on a staff that was growing
snippier by the day. "There was like a rumor du jour," said senior editor
Sandy Bailey. "It'll be announced at the end of December. It won't be
announced until June. It'll be announced next week. They've told Mark
not to come back. Mark's coming back and taking over for a year. Or
they've already told Okrent he has the job, and he's assembling his new
staff in the hallway. We had no idea what was going on and, worse, how
much longer it was going to go on. As much as people wanted desperately
for one person or the other to get the job, there was beginning to be a
sense of just wanting to get it over with."

No one was in a more agonizing situation than Rob Fleder. Close
friends with Okrent, he'd also developed a productive professional rela-

tionship with Colson. During the bake-off, many of the staffers who were afraid to confront Okrent instead vented their complaints to Fleder, who knew his buddy was taking a beating in the internal opinion polls, but didn't know what to do other than the best job possible for both men. By all accounts, that's what he did.

In late October, Muller called both Okrent and Colson to arrange for separate lunchtime meetings to talk about their performance and their vision for the future of *SI*. The two three-hour lunch meetings with Pearlstine and Muller were held on consecutive days at the Rihga Royal Hotel near the Time & Life Building.

Colson reiterated his belief that the magazine wasn't broke, and needed merely to be modified. He also said that he wanted to redesign Scorecard, but chose not to tinker with the look during the trial. He then unveiled some boards of a Scorecard redesign that he and Hoffman had cooked up in the fall. Okrent was less specific, speaking further about his vision that *SI* needed to be "more sportsy" and more feature-oriented, less attuned to straight reportage on breaking news events.

Pearlstine asked both men if they could work for the other; both said no. It was an answer that he had expected, but it served to crystallize his alternatives, on the eve of the magazine's most important and most profitable year to date. In the Olympic year ahead, *SI* would be publishing a daily magazine during th summer games in Atlanta, in addition to its regular coverage. While Mulvoy's behavior during the whole affair had made Pearlstine furious, he also knew that a split with Mulvoy would be ugly. Mulvoy was privately telling friends, "me to you," that if Colson was named the new ME, he would gracefully step aside at the first of the year, but that if Okrent was named, Mulvoy would dig in his heels and run the magazine until the torch was out in Atlanta. There was no way that Pearlstine would allow such a protracted and agonizing interregnum, so the reality was that choosing Okrent, whatever else it meant, would necessitate the probable loss of Colson and an inevitably nasty and public split with Mulvoy.

On Friday the 10th, Okrent and Pearlstine met for a rambling, philosophical breakfast at Sara Beth's on Amsterdam and 80th. At the end of the meal, Okrent said, "The one thing I haven't done for you is really walked you through the issues and tell you what I did and didn't like." Pearlstine told him to stop by his office the following Wednesday afternoon. What Pearlstine knew that Okrent didn't was that Wednesday evening was a Time Warner board of directors meeting, in which Pearlstine intended to announce his decision to the board. A decision was imminent.

But first came the handicapping.

On November 13, Warren St. John's front-page piece in the *New York Observer* put a spotlight on the frayed nerves at the magazine. "Two Editors Strut for Pearlstine In Odd *Sports Illustrated* Pageant" read the headline, and the story went on to note that "Time Inc. oddsmakers put the safe money on Mr. Okrent" and that some *SI* staffers had termed the contest a charade because "Mr. Okrent was a shoo-in."

That weekend, Colson's wife Vic Boughton received a call at home from Franz Lidz. The eccentric senior writer lived far from the office, on a rural Pennsylvania farm. But as if to prove that he was a consummate reporter, not just a writer of quirky essays, Lidz stayed on top of the interoffice gossip. "Franz was pretty sure it was bad news for Colson," said Boughton. "He felt he had a source, very close to Pearlstine. And he sounded like it was pretty much a definite that it was going to be Okrent. You never ask Franz about his sources. I said, 'Well, I haven't heard anything one way or the other.' But between the Franz conversation and a few other things, I thought things were looking a little bleak. Then I was pissed off. I thought if this is true, then this is such a cynical exercise."

The rumors left Boughton depressed, and as they coursed through the rest of the magazine, they outraged Robinson and Mulvoy, both of whom placed angry calls to Lidz in the coming days. And they further perplexed Okrent. He knew he wasn't getting good reviews from the staff and he hadn't gotten any positive signals from his breakfast with Pearlstine. At the same time, many were saying it was a done deal, and Okrent was sure that at one point he'd heard Pearlstine tell him that "*when* you take the job, Mulvoy will have to go." As he went into Pearlstine's office the afternoon of Wednesday, November 16, he just didn't know.

The meeting was oddly uncomfortable, Pearlstine stoically listening along, less engaged than Okrent had ever seen him. After talking for about an hour, Pearlstine said he had to take a call, and asked Okrent to come back at 5:30 to talk further. When Okrent returned this time, his boss gave him the news instantly: "I've decided to go with Colson." There were reasons given in the agonizing minutes that followed, but Okrent comprehended little of it.

Okrent left in a fog and returned to his office, in a kind of muted shock. He called his close friend Jim Gaines, the managing editor at *Time*, and they agreed to meet for a drink at La Cité, the French bistro on the ground floor of the Time & Life Building. *Entertainment Weekly* managing editor Jim Seymore and AME Peter Bonventre met them down at La Cité, where Okrent passed on his news (and Gaines trumped this with his own news: he'd been bumped upstairs to corporate editor). The four talked awhile about the Pearlstine tornado (in his first 11 months as editor-in-chief, he'd replaced managing editors at *Fortune, SI,* and *Time*). What they didn't talk about, because Okrent was still stunned by it, was the bizarre, almost cruel way in which he was notified. Pearlstine feared a leak; there had been some already, and he knew that Colson wasn't talking to the media. He'd given Gaines the news about the coming transition at *Time* a week earlier, but he was compelled to hold out on Okrent. With the board meeting that evening, Pearlstine felt he simply couldn't afford to tell Okrent any sooner, lest word leak to one of the directors before the 6 p.m. meeting. Concealing the news from Okrent had bothered Pearlstine. "Is there any other way to do this?" he asked Muller a day earlier. They couldn't think of anything.

Back at La Cité, a few drinks were ordered. Okrent had a tight grin on his face. Eerily serene through it all, he left after an hour. "I've gotta go home," he said blankly, "and tell my wife." On the cab ride back to his Upper West Side co-op, Okrent was calm and crushed. He gave the news to his wife evenly, as though reporting on someone else's job. It was only after he told his children that he wasn't going to get to be managing editor of *Sports Illustrated*, and they went to him, hugged him, and told him they loved him anyway, that he began to weep.

Just then, at Michael's restaurant in midtown Manhattan, Norman Pearlstine was sitting down to dinner with Bill Colson. Pearlstine seemed uncomfortable at first, while they waited for their drink orders. But when the alcohol arrived, he raised his glass and said, "Here's to the new managing editor of *Sports Illustrated*."

It was about 10 o'clock that night when Vic Boughton stopped trying to keep herself busy. The kids had gone to bed, she couldn't sit through any more television, she was unable to read, so she just waited. And then her husband came in the door, a wry look on his face, but saying nothing.

"Well?" she said expectantly.

And with the same bashful, almost embarrassed smile that he'd had since high school, he said, "I got it."

*Bill Colson: still undefeated in varsity singles.*

No one was happier with the news than Mulvoy, who, for the first time, seemed to be at peace with his impending retirement. Before Colson could even ask, Mulvoy vowed to stay away from the office for the first several weeks of his tenure. There would be no Papanek replays. In the weeks following, when people asked him if he was *really* going to retire after the Olympics, he was unequivocal: "The torch goes out, and I go out."

The long process would help Colson, establishing him more clearly in the mind of his staff as their new leader than a simple stamp of approval from Mulvoy would have. "You want to do well for Bill," explained Bill Nack one day, "because he's just so nice. You want to reward goodness."

Afterward, Pearlstine was sanguine about the process. He understood that it had been traumatic for the staff, but he was satisfied that it had accomplished its purpose.

"There were a lot of people at *Sports Illustrated* who didn't know me and were sufficiently paranoid about the whole process as to assume that this was some sadistic charade for wanting to move Okrent in," he said. "And all I can tell you is that if I wanted Okrent clearly and unambiguously for the job, I just would have given it to him."

There was talk that the decision was an 11th-hour turnaround on Pearlstine's part, a move to provide some stability. *MIN*, the insiderish *Media Industry Newsletter*, reported the next week that the decision was "a clutch move . . . that shows Pearlstine really learned the lay of the land. He was leaning the other way, but that could have created very harmful factions at a very profitable property. The move he didn't want to make may turn out to be his best."

In fact, there was far less intrigue or suspense than the *SI* staff could have imagined. The sources leaking that Pearlstine was leaning toward Okrent were misreading him badly. But those in Pearlstine's inner circle had sensed his preference for months. John Huey, the *Fortune* ME who was close friends with both Pearlstine and Okrent, sensed early on that Pearlstine was impressed with Colson's performance. Late in Okrent's tenure, he asked for an hour of Pearlstine's time to make the case for Okrent, and midway through his presentation, realized he wasn't getting across.

Muller and Pearlstine had spoken regularly during the Colson trial but, as if by implicit agreement, stopped talking early on in the Okrent regime. Both men recognized that conversation on the topic would necessitate jumping to a conclusion. But both men were thinking the same way. Near the end of Okrent's trial, Pearlstine finally mentioned to Muller where he was leaning. "Well, if I had to make a decision today, it would probably be Colson," he said.

"Yeah, I think I agree with you," allowed Muller.

After the orals, they sat down together for an hour and Pearlstine made his final decision.

By trying to please his boss, Okrent had sealed his own fate. "What you want is an editor who's going to put out his magazine, not somebody trying to put out what they think I want," Pearlstine said. "Because that's a sure way to fail. I asked Colson the question: 'What would you have done differently?' And he said, 'Nothing.' And I believe him."

The morning of the public announcement, Okrent bravely asked to speak at the Thursday morning editorial meeting in which the news was given to the *SI* staff. He thanked everyone for their help and said he'd enjoyed himself through it all. Before he left the 18th floor that day, he stopped by Robinson's office and made peace with his main antagonist. And shortly thereafter, Dan Okrent walked out of the Time & Life Building, mulling an extremely uncertain future.

Along with Colson's appointment, effective with the January 15, 1996, issue, it was announced that Mark Mulvoy had been promoted to "editor." It was a ceremonial designation, by which Mulvoy would remain on the payroll in an advisory capacity through the 1996 Summer Olympics. But his tenure as ME would effectively end with the closing of the January 8, 1996, issue. Unannounced, but already agreed to, was that Mulvoy would retire in September 1996. He'd gotten everything he wanted.

But despite the highly public nature of the bake-off, the response to its resolution was oddly muted. Even this, the most visible transition of power in *SI*'s history, was hardly reported the next day in the press. Time Inc.'s announcement was made at the same time that Time Warner chairman Gerard Levin ousted longtime ally Michael Fuchs. That move led the *Wall Street Journal*'s coverage, which included just a single sentence devoted to *SI*. In their pieces on the Time Warner moves, neither *USA Today* or the *Chicago Tribune* even mentioned the *SI* change.

It wasn't until the *New York Observer* article that ran a week later that Bill Colson finally got a sense of how institutionalized and unchanging the media's fix on *SI* was. "Thursday, Bloody Thursday at Time Warner" read the headline, over two stories, one on the Levin-Fuchs contretemps, one on the Time Inc. moves. Above the headline was a whimsical Robert Grossman cartoon, superimposing the key players on a *Time* cover. Front and center was Levin, rolling Fuchs's head like a bowling ball off the cover, and Pearlstine, his arm around new *Time* ME Walter Isaacson, kicking Gaines up a flight of stairs. In the lower lefthand corner, Okrent stood frowning, chained to a ball that read "Life sentence."

And behind the *Time* logo, very small, was an illustration, barely larger than a line drawing, of Bill Colson. Walking toward a swimsuit model.

# CHAPTER 20

# "EXTENDING THE BRAND"

## Mark Mulvoy collected his

coat, and with a heavy sigh, shut out the light for the last time in the managing editor's office. It was four in the morning on January 3, 1996, and as he reached Rob Fleder's office, he ducked his head in the door. "Fuck Yogi," Mulvoy said. "It's over." Fleder got up and shook his hand, and with that, Mulvoy headed for the elevators. He had just closed his final issue of *Sports Illustrated*.

When he got out to the front of the Time & Life Building, a heavy snow was already falling, the early onslaught of what would become New York City's worst blizzard in years. Mulvoy looked at his watch and considered his options. He usually stayed in the city after a late close like this. But with snow expected to continue through the night, he knew that if he waited until the morning, it might be days before he got to his home in Westchester County. So he told the limo driver to take him to his house in Rye. "No hurry," he said. "Just drive slow."

And sitting in the backseat of the car, looking out of the tinted glass at the snow enveloping Manhattan, he thought about the 30 years that had brought him from a two-decker in Dorchester to the managing editorship of *Sports Illustrated*. He recalled the time as a teenager when he'd told his brother that all he ever wanted out of life was to write for the *Boston Globe* and belong to the Wollaston Golf Club. He thought about how large his world had grown since then, of cavorting with supermodels on beaches, dining with dignitaries at the White House. And he thought about his father. Mark Mulvoy felt proud and sentimental, exhilarated and relieved. But most of all, he felt empty.

Mulvoy's last night as managing editor had exemplified both the best and the worst of the modern *Sports Illustrated*. Against a deadline that required intensely complex planning similar to the old Laguerre days, Mulvoy presided over a 16-page section on Nebraska's 62–24 win over Florida in Tuesday night's Fiesta Bowl, the national championship game that had dwarfed in significance all the New Year's Day bowl games played Monday. The Cornhuskers' rout was the sort of one-sided affair that left college football writer Tim Layden very little room for game analysis. But true to *SI*'s mission, Layden found the larger truths in the blowout. His game story, "Runaway!!" served as something more than just an account of Nebraska's dominating victory. It was an incisive, reasoned consideration of the Cornhuskers' tumultuous 1995 campaign. Layden revisited the stormy season, and focused on its defining moment, a closed-door, players-only meeting in September not previously reported in the national media. The team captains who called the meeting were all fifth-year seniors, recruited by Osborne in 1991 when he was being dismissed as a milquetoast coach who wasn't smart enough, charismatic enough, or committed enough to win the big one. Layden's story attributed credit, assigned blame, and left the reader both enlightened and informed. It was just the sort of tour de force that *SI* always strived for in big-game reporting, and after the tortuous year of bake-off politics and questions about the magazine's future, it was exactly the sort of article that would argue for *SI*'s continued relevance. It was the best of *Sports Illustrated*.

And here was the worst: no one outside of Florida or Nebraska got to read it.

Rather than spending the extra money necessary to execute the first full-run Tuesday night close in the magazine's history, *SI* closed the January 8 issue the night *before* the Fiesta Bowl for 48 out of 50 states, sending that issue to more than 99 percent of its subscriber base. That issue had Atlanta Olympic Games organizer Bill Payne on the cover, and no mention of the Fiesta Bowl inside. Only subscribers living in Florida and Nebraska got the "Fiesta Bowl Special"—essentially the same January 8 issue, with the Fiesta Bowl cover and a 16-page section bound into the center spread. But subscribers were never the real priority. There were 140,000 *SI* subscribers in Florida, and 30,000 in Nebraska. The press run for the Fiesta Bowl special was more than 500,000, with the extra 350,000 copies distributed for newsstand sale in Nebraska, a lucrative decision that netted *SI* close to an extra million dollars in revenue. But it also left nearly three million subscribers without an *SI* story on the biggest college football game of the season.

In addition, it left Bill Colson in a lurch for his first issue as managing editor the following week. Since part of *SI*'s subscriber base had received the special edition, he couldn't repeat the game story, or even the sort of featurish wrap-up that *SI* usually provided when champions were crowned in the middle of the previous week. But he had to do something. What all of *SI*'s subscribers received a week later, in the January 15 issue, was a piece by Layden looking ahead to the next season, outlining how difficult it would be for any other teams to dominate in the '90s, and handicapping the national title race for '96. Readers wrote in angrily—they hadn't seen Layden's story, or his reference to Nebraska's extraordinary quarterback Tommie Frazier as "college football's Joe Montana." Most assumed that the magazine had simply ignored the game. "How could you make college politics a bigger story than the game?" asked a Kansas City reader. "Nebraska did something that no Division I football team has done in nearly 40 years," wrote a reader in Chicago, "and what *SI* writes about is that the Huskers recruit unworthy players, won't be able to repeat next year and are headed for a fall." The volume of letters only underscored the flaw in Mulvoy's thinking: the notion that only people in Florida or Nebraska cared about the national championship game was ludicrous on its face.

After the fact, even an embarrassed Don Elliman admitted that it had been a mistake. "We should have held the entire goddamn magazine, no matter what it cost, and run the issue with Nebraska and Florida," he said. "The production people at one point said, 'You cannot do this.' If we pushed harder, we could have done it. Somebody might have gotten their magazine late. Some people might have gotten it post-weekend, but we still should have held it." On the edit side, Time Inc. editorial director Henry Muller agreed: "It could have been done. Anything can be done; it just costs more money, that's all."

But when the time came to spend the money, the people who could have done so, Mulvoy and Elliman, had chosen to pull back. It wouldn't be the only time that the pressure to attain maximum profitability would clash with the principles of magazine-making.

• • •

"Extending the brand" became the hot phrase for the magazine division at Time Warner in the '90s, but it was merely a euphemism that camouflaged the harsher corporate realities at work. Ever since the 1989 merger that left Time Inc. part of a bloated megacompany weighed down with debt, Time Warner's executives had been applying pressure on every one of its divisions to streamline operations and expand profit margins. In the magazine division, the standard was 12 percent. That was the annual increase in *profits* within the division expected by Time Inc. president Don Logan. At a time when the universe of magazine advertising was shrinking, the extra money wouldn't come through an increase in national ad pages or rates, so it had to come elsewhere. Thus came the directive to each magazine—"extend the brand," move into other media, think of more special issues, one-shots, marketing tie-ins, ways to bring other advertisers into the magazine through special sections.

Since Elliman's arrival, *SI* had moved aggressively in these fields: Golf Plus had been a niche-marketing success, and the newly created division of *SI* Presents, the adjunct arm created at the beginning of 1995 that specialized in "custom publishing"—championship commemoratives, special one-shots, and preseason annuals—was instantly profitable as well. With the May 6, 1996, issue, the single-copy newsstand price went up nearly 20 percent, from $2.95 to $3.50, netting an extra $3 million in annual revenue.

But taken together, it wasn't enough to meet the 12 percent profit increase goal. More revenue streams were needed, and in 1996, *SI*'s business department ranged far and wide to find them. Suddenly, the *SI* "brand" was all over the place. The *SI* logo could be seen on the cover of David Wallechinsky's quadrennially published Olympic record book as well as on the new version of the computer game MicroLeague Baseball, even though *SI* had no direct involvement with either product. In June 1996, *SI* unveiled its promotion with Moosehead Beer. "Beauty and the Moose!" the ad exclaimed, announcing a sweepstakes to win a "100% Canadian Experience Hosted by *Sports Illustrated* Supermodel Stacey Williams!" The same issue included a full-page ad for a *Sports Illustrated* beach towel, with the purchase of "the 2.5 oz. Cool Water Eau de Toilette Spray, $42.50."

*SI* would meet its 12 percent goal in 1996, but as one former Time Inc. executive pointed out, "this year isn't the problem. You can do things this year or next year to grow the magazine. But when you've done them, then what do you do? At some point you have to start hurting your core product. Somewhere there has to be a limit."

While the brand was being extended, the magazine itself was shrinking. Another quarter-inch had come off the top of *SI* with the July 4, 1994, issue. This saved money two ways—on paper during printing and in weight during postage. After frequent trims, *SI* was nearly 13 percent smaller (starting at 8¾₆ by 11½ inches, it was now 8 by 10⅞₆ inches) and almost 30 percent lighter (from paper with a 45-pound basis weight at its inception, down to 32-pound basis weight in 1996) than when it began.

And while the caretakers of *SI* could talk blandly about not doing anything to compromise the magazine, they'd already passed the threshold; the flimsy 32-pound paper lost a significant measure of opacity. "I don't think we can go much lower than that," said production manager George Baldassare, stating the obvious.

The production department also had usurped an unsightly 1¼ by 3⅜-inch space near the bottom of the front cover, known as the "inkjet window," on copies sent to subscribers. Allowing the company to further streamline the delivery process by printing subscribers' addresses directly on the cover, it was hailed for its efficiency (all Time Inc.'s weekly magazines eventually adopted the format). But because it was part of the cover, the inkjet window, unlike the adhesive subscriber address label that had preceded it, couldn't be removed. Readers who treasured *SI* covers as framable keepsakes complained, but this was a minor aesthetic point at best. And in a corporate culture in which magazines were unironically referred to as "brands," minor aesthetic points were invariably lost.

Even the magazine's history seemed to be undergoing a downsizing, with the publication, in the fall of 1996, of an updated version of *The Best of Sports Illustrated*, the coffee-table book originally printed in 1990. The new book, priced at $29.95, as the original had been, was actually a cheap knock-off, a reprinted version that was 80 pages shorter, printed on thinner paper, lacking the cloth cover and patterned endsheets of the original, and, in keeping with the *SI* of the '90s, cut to smaller dimensions.

It was within this culture of churning commerce, blurred priorities, and bottom-line obsession that Bill Colson would be expected to chart *Sports Illustrated*'s future course.

• • •

He's a lousy writer, but he's a real good line editor. And he gives power to his AMEs. We've had 16 years of trickle-down management here. We grew, but the staff morale sucked. It's been 16 years since editorial fascism has been introduced at *Sports Illustrated*, and I think maybe Colson can bring that to an end.
—A longtime staffer, on Bill Colson

When Colson sat down on Thursday, January 4, to lead his first staff meeting as managing editor, the sense of generational change in the *SI* conference room was palpable. In suspenders and bow tie, Peter Carry sat at the far end of the long conference table, seeming very much like the longtime apparatchik now fading from power. Colson sat in the center of the long oval table, flanked by Rob Fleder, who had been given Colson's old office, at the head of the senior editors' hall, closest to the managing editor's corner office. (By September, Fleder would be promoted to executive editor, sharing the title with Carry.) Sitting to Colson's other side was his shadow, design director Steve Hoffman, by now a ten-year veteran. Colson and Hoffman had little in common besides the Swiss Army watches that both wore, but they had developed a collegial, complementary professional relationship.

The contrast between Mulvoy and Colson was pronounced. In the classic '80s corporate raider style, Mulvoy wore his clothes as a sort of flamboyant armor: French cuffs, monograms, double-breasted suits, and tie pins. Colson, from an upper-middle-class background, displayed the casually slangy dressing style of the comfortably well-off. He'd come in on off days in khakis and an old button-down shirt, looking like a close-out sale in a J. Crew catalog. And while Mulvoy had grown tired and distracted in the mid-'90s, as likely to want to talk about his round at Winged Foot as a personnel problem, Colson was both absorbed and energetic, walking the halls to solicit opinions on cover blurbs and headlines, imploring staffers to bring their ideas to the table. "There's just a general openness to the place that wasn't there before," said one editor during 1996. "The managing editor has an actual interest in what other people have to say."

Colson's first year on the job was one long siege of inexhaustible energy. He was in the office nearly every day, making the 40-block walk to work in the mornings from his Upper East Side condo, even walking to work when the city was paralyzed by snow. Sitting next to an empty chair in a meeting, he might idly spin it while he was talking. Even lounging back in contemplation, he'd repeatedly place a pencil between his lips and, with a burst of breath, blow it up in the air and catch it in his hands. Still without an ounce of fat at 45, he seemed to subsist on caffeine-free Diet Cokes the way André Laguerre had subsisted on scotch and water. And once he arrived at the office, he was usually in for the the balance of the day. One Sunday night in February, as secretary Joan Rosinsky was bringing him a cup of soup, editorial coordinator Trish Chesler shouted in mock surprise, "Colson's gonna eat?!"

"Only if you remind him," Rosinsky said.

Colson usually came in on two, if not three, of the staff's off days each week. On Saturday afternoons, he'd bring his three kids up to the mostly empty offices, giving them change to go to the candy machine while he made phone calls and worked on planning. Even Boughton marveled at this. "With his concentration, he's able to actually get something done." Colson's tunnel vision, an impervious concentration honed through decades of competitive tennis, was already renowned.

His likes were genteel. Colson was drawn to the courtly, urbane hallmarks of modern life. He loved the civilized give-and-take of *Frasier*, but the hectic melodramatics of most television shows left him frazzled. "He sat through a little of *ER* with me and just about had a heart attack," said Boughton. "'Shit, come on! Spare me! Get this shit off! I'm going to the kitchen.' He just couldn't take it."

Greeting a visitor in his new office one day, he was riffling through his still disheveled mementos when he stumbled across a framed picture of the Duchess of Kent. "Look at her," he said, beaming with admiration. "Isn't she classy? This is real class. Lady Di *wishes* she were this classy." The contrast couldn't have been more stark. Every managing editor had his feminine dream. Gil Rogin was obsessed with Mary Decker. Mark Mulvoy had a jones for Stephanie Seymour. And Bill Colson had a crush on the Duchess of Kent.

Just weeks after Mulvoy left the managing editor's office, Jule Campbell announced her own retirement, effective with the 1996 swimsuit issue, her 32nd. Tyra Banks—sharing the cover with Valeria Mazza—became the first African American on the cover of a swimsuit issue, although *SI*'s self-congratulatory diversity celebration was muted when Banks showed up in a bikini on the cover of *GQ* just days before *SI* hit the stands.

What should have been a more pleasant exit for Campbell ended with a hint of bitterness. Mulvoy had approached her in the early '90s with a plan for her to write a book about her experiences with the swimsuit issue, to be ghostwritten by E.M. Swift. But Campbell demurred, saying that the book was rightfully her own, and would come after her career at *SI* was done. "Well, you won't get a goddamn picture from us," said a rankled Mulvoy.

In 1995, *SI* published a glossy, oversize, full-color paperback book called *The Best of the Swimsuit Supermodels*. A collection of the most revealing photos accumulated from the sessions of Ireland, Brinkley, Kim Alexis, Tiegs, Porizkova, Macpherson, Seymour, Rachel Hunter, and Vendela, the book didn't even mention Campbell's name. "Mark informed me it was going to be a T and A book," she said. "And that's not what I'm trying to accomplish. I've always put one sexy picture, or tried to, in the story; I call that stirring the pot. It makes it controversial and wakes people up, you know? But you put 25 of those together, and it takes on a different color."

By 1996, opposition to the swimsuit issue over its perceived sexism wasn't limited to feminists anymore. Even some advertisers, most notably Nike, were pulling out, declining to advertise in *that one issue*. Increasingly, the swimsuit issue was seen in much the same way as a middle-aged man showing up at a dinner party with an 18-year-old beauty on his arm: less scandalous, in this era, than pathetic. Many inside the magazine viewed Campbell's exit as somewhat overdue. "It's tired," said Mulvoy, to more than one colleague, but when the time came for ways to update Campbell's formula, few had the first idea what to do differently.

Contemplating the future of the swimsuit issue a few weeks before taking over, Colson was almost fatalistic. "We've gone as far as we're going to go in the skin area," he said. "They're not going to take their bathing suits *off*. So what do we do? It's always cited as sort of the prototypical demeaning way women are portrayed in media. That's unsettling to me, a father with two daughters who don't quite understand the whole thing."

But he also realized that killing it was not an option—it simply made too much money. Other staffers had taken pains to come up with alternatives, in an attempt to distance the issue from the regular magazine. Alex Wolff wanted to make it a newsstand-only magazine, not sent to subscribers. Sally Jenkins had long wished that the issue focused on athletes rather than models. Other staffers had spent long hours trying to conceive of a different sort of special issue that would be as profitable. But even these discussions ended with a reality check. "If we could think of another issue that would make just as much money as the swimsuit issue," said one editor, "then they wouldn't replace it at all. They would just *add* it to the swimsuit issue, to make even more money. So it's hopeless."

After the astounding success of the 25th-anniversary swimsuit issue, which sold 2.7 million copies on the newsstand, the issue hit a slump in the '90s. While the swimsuit issue and its ancillary products (videos and calendars) still accounted for more than a tenth of the magazine's annual profits, its newsstand numbers steadily declined. After selling 1.7 million copies in '92 and 1.5 million in '93 and '94, sales dropped to 1.4 million in '95 and to 1.2 million in '96.

*SI*'s reader surveys, which increasingly guided thinking on both the business and edit sides, were particularly detailed for the swimsuit issue. For years, the *SI* publicity department had dealt with protests about the issue's sexist slant by pointing out that it had the highest percentage female readership of any issue of the year. But this was a canard, a result of statistical manipulation of pass-along readership. Of *SI*'s subscribers in 1996, 88 percent were male. Of those that bought the swimsuit issue at the newsstands, 87 percent were male.

In the surveys, readers were frank about what they wanted: more familiar models, in more provocative and revealing poses, for more pages. They cared little about exotic locales or imperatives of fashion or sunsets or travel pieces. In short, if the balance of the regular reader studies showed that the average reader wanted one thing—more NFL—the swimsuit issue survey results could be codified into a similarly simple desire: more skin. Page-by-page response numbers showed that pictures of black models scored consistently lower than those of white models. (Kathy Ireland remained the overwhelming favorite—over 60 percent of readers said they wanted to see more of her.) "They want the girl next door with an expression that says she wants to fuck them," was how Hoffman summarized the numbers.

In May 1996, Colson hired *Glamour* fashion editor Elaine Farley to replace Campbell. And he devised a compromise that, for the short term at least, would satisfy some of the issue's critics. Beginning with the 1997 edition, the swimsuit issue became a special issue unto itself, devoted entirely to swimsuits. Though it would still be sent to subscribers (who would get that, plus the regular *SI* during a week in February), it would no longer have to contend with the dubious juxtapositions or questions of context. Farley's tenure began with a bang, and an evocative cover shot of Tyra Banks, in February 1997. And Colson had given the readers what they wanted, which was more cheesecake.

• • •

At the 1996 Summer Olympic Games, as elsewhere during Colson's first year, *SI*'s journalistic performance was nearly overshadowed by the magazine's business concerns.

*SI* was one of ten worldwide sponsors paying an average of $40 million in cash, merchandise, and services for the privilege of full Olympic partnership. In addition to publishing a daily magazine that would have exclusive distribution within the Olympic village, *SI*'s business-side publishing arm was producing the official Olympic program and a business-side events staff of 140 entertained some 3,500 advertisers and their guests over the 17-day competition.

The editorial operation, which sent 130 people to Atlanta, was distinctly separate. But the effect of having the business side of the magazine promoting an event that the editorial side was covering was profound and distracting. *SI*'s coverage of the Atlanta Games had a self-consciousness to it, and the staffers had become overly sensitive about answering conflict-of-interest criticism. "The problem isn't that we can't slam the Olympics," explained Colson. "We can. The problem is that whenever we write something positive, it looks like we're sucking up." The SItv-produced special, *Prelude to the Olympics*, which aired on NBC the Wednesday night prior to the opening ceremonies, only exacerbated the perceptions that *SI*'s coverage was soft. *Prelude* was a featureish personality program, with many *SI* writers doing video equivalents to their Olympic preview issue pieces (Gary Smith profiled Michael Johnson, Alex Wolff revisited his piece on the break-up of Yugoslavia's national basketball team, with the help of *Hoop Dreams* director Steve James). But the special making news in the week leading up to the opening ceremonies was HBO's *Real Sports*, in which Frank Deford, exhibiting the interviewing skills that had launched one hundred bonus pieces, elicited a headline-making, self-incriminating exclusive out of International Olympic Committee president Juan Antonio Samaranch, who told Deford that the Olympics were "more important than the Catholic religion."

*SI* was more comfortable on its own turf. The 44-page *SI Daily* was a technological triumph. Printed in full four-color (on higher-quality paper stock, in fact, than the regular *SI*), the magazine went to press every night at a QuadGraphics printing plant in The Rock, Georgia, about 70 miles southwest of Atlanta, with recently promoted AME Mike Bevans serving as editor, assisted by senior editors (and fellow *National* alums) Mark Godich and Bobby Clay. Most nights, the *Daily* had to transmit the last page at 1 a.m. Eastern time, although when a bomb went off in Centennial Park, Bevans stopped the press run to get a short story in that day's issue. *SI Daily* was also embroiled in controversy, running a highly critical two-part E.M. Swift profile of world track kingpin Primo Nebiolo that earned the wrath of the International Olympic Committee, which had viewed the magazine as a quasi-official publication (with some justification, since the *Daily* had exclusive distribution at Olympic venues, where Olympic draw sheets for each day's competition were included with the issue).

Within the main magazine, the coverage of the games was the best in *SI*'s history, with Colson recruiting Roy Blount, Jr., for an essay on Atlanta in the preview issue and a series of scene pieces during the games. After the first weekend, Colson chose to lead with "It's Greek to U.S.," Gary Smith's withering critique of Atlanta as host city: "When you select, for cash and convenience, a landlocked city with little vestige of its past, one whose identity is tied to the mega-corporations it has enticed, in a country full of enterprising scrappers—over, say, Athens, which just happens to be the birthplace of the Olympics, not to mention of Western civilization, and the locale where one might look to plant the Centennial Games if ideals were what was at stake—well, then, don't you deserve all the plywood and tent poles you can get?" Three issues filled with event coverage culminated with Kenny Moore's examination of Michael Johnson's blazing 200-meter world record run. The story was published six days after Johnson's run, after it had received extensive coverage in dailies, on television, and in newsweeklies. Yet it still provided new information that hadn't been published before, as well as a stirring account of the events surrounding the run. Even in the media glut of Atlanta, *SI* could still deliver.

• • •

"After Atlanta," Mulvoy had vowed, "you're going to see the greatest disappearing act in history." After Mulvoy served for nine months in the largely ceremonial task of editor, his retirement was officially announced on September 2, 1996. While not exactly sanguine, he was acutely aware that his time was up. And so Mulvoy had one more surprise for everyone: a graceful exit. After Colson had emerged the bake-off winner, Mulvoy's legacy stood secure and he could finally rest. In December of 1995, he stopped chewing his fingernails, a habit he'd had since age three. During Colson's first months on the job, Mulvoy kept a respectful distance. He seemed more willing to let things go, with the understanding that the torch had been passed. When he came in the office, which was rarely, he stayed out of Colson's way, even stayed away from editorial meetings. While the magazine went on around him, Mulvoy sat in his new, humble, cramped office and spoke on the phone to old friends, inevitably about golf.

"I'm getting nickel—I don't like berillium . . ."

"I hit it past him twice, speaking of Tom Kite . . .'

"Shot my best score ever in competition—a 68. And let me tell you about the course. . . ."

And in the end, many of the staffers who had spent years grousing about Mulvoy's overbearing tactics felt a tinge of something resembling sadness. "Mark's like Lou Holtz," said Sally Jenkins. "You don't agree with everything he does. There's a lot of people that are going to criticize him but once the guy's gone, I think his work will stand on its own. I would have liked to have seen some different things in the magazine, some different issues attacked. But he put out a damned good magazine, too, so the bottom line on Mark is, he was a hell of an editor who in the long run I think was a little late coming to some issues."

Mulvoy's farewell column in the September 9 issue, a Point After in which he went through a box of sports mementoes that he'd accumulated over the years, struck many as fatuous. Even Colson confided in friends that he thought Mulvoy had missed an opportunity. "He could have said so much."

"There's a part of me that really likes him personally," said one long-time staffer. "I mean, he's a flaming asshole sometimes. He's overbearing, he's crude, he can be so gauche, you just say, 'I can't believe you said that in public.' But he's so insecure, he's so concerned. He really wants everybody's best wishes and kind regards and yet there's something very sweet about him. It's just like he sort of missed life's charm school lessons. He's been unspeakably cruel to certain people. But he's got four of the nicest kids you'll ever meet. Trish is great, but she can't do that singlehandedly. If you want to take the measure of somebody, you look at their kids."

Though he kept his vow not to bother Colson, Mulvoy wasn't quite finished. When Colson gave Curry Kirkpatrick a freelance assignment early in 1997, Mulvoy heard about it and placed a call to Henry Muller, arguing that in light of Kirkpatrick's firing, it was hypocritical for *SI* to hire him for any more stories. Muller conferred with Pearlstine and it was agreed; they instructed Colson to kill the story. Mark Mulvoy had shot his last bullet.

Still estranged from him, still vowing not to even consider a return to the magazine until he was gone, Frank Deford wasn't without some genuine affection for his old adversary. Deford could always read people, and Mulvoy was easier than most, though the irony of his antagonist's vulnerability often left him dumbfounded.

"I sometimes shake my head and I say, 'Hey, Mark—*you won*," said Deford. "You beat everybody. I don't know how you did it, but you won. When the chips are cashed in, you got more than anybody else over there."

• • •

It was left to Bill Colson to try to solve the conundrum that had faced *SI* for much of the '90s: how to gain editorial relevance, and retain spectacular profitability, in a media-saturated environment in which the competition wasn't merely ESPN but the entire sprawling cacophony of sports reportage that was flooding every medium imaginable, from talk radio and Internet websites to specialized niche publications like *Baseball America* and *Pro Football Weekly*, all vying for the attention of American sports fans. In the short term, at least, *SI* continued to be driven by the same centripetal forces at work throughout sports media and, in fact, all of contemporary journalism. More of the magazine's resources—in terms of writers, pages, photographs—were being pulled inward toward a few major sports, and more of the coverage of those major sports focused on a few players and teams. During the 1995–96 NBA season, the magazine ran 5 covers and 22 stories about the Chicago Bulls. From the beginning of the 1995 season through the end of June 1996, *SI* ran 5 covers and 30 stories on the Dallas Cowboys.

The concentration left sizable gaps in *SI*'s coverage of secondary sports. Without departments in which to play minor stories, without the For the Record page to note weekly results, with a narrowed story focus in the news section and feature well, *SI* was all but abandoning its implicit role as the magazine of record for boxing, tennis, track and field, soccer, and horse racing. "I'll be the first to admit," said Colson, "that I'm contributing to the narrowing of interest of the American sports fan."

But in his first year, he also proved that his bake-off performance hadn't been a fluke. The February 12, 1996, issue, with both Reilly and Gary Smith weighing in on Magic Johnson's comeback, was the first of several instances in which *SI*'s coverage of the news was itself newsworthy. Nack's evocative profile of Kentucky basketball coach Rick Pitino caused a firestorm in February, and in May, Reilly wrote the most human, and most damaging, portrait of Cincinnati Reds owner Marge Schott, accompanied by a classic Bill Frakes cover shot.

With Steven Hoffman given more freedom, covers were more impressionistic and less predictable (over a dozen in '96 were devoted to bonus-piece subjects). Scorecard finally underwent a redesign, and though the change was more cosmetic than editorial—the section ran an extra page but the average word count was the same—it did bring a long-absent zest to the front of the book. Colson gave the writers freer rein to express opinions that diverged with his own (Rushin even got a dig in at his own magazine for all but ignoring major league soccer in a story about the MLS inaugural season) and even showed a willingness, by the end of his first year, to try to bring some more outside writers into the magazine. Conversely, Colson's shortcomings were predictable. Though accessible around the office, he remained remote from his far-flung writers. He often delayed his desicions until the last minute, meaning that closings were frequently difficult.

What was still missing from the new *SI* was a sense of repose and meditation, a place for a reader to stretch out. Too many news stories were plagued by overlarge pictures that substituted for the sort of careful, insightful game analysis at which *SI* had specialized in the past. Even bonus pieces had a rushed, truncated feel, and many stories and Scorecard items were simply too short to be explored in the sort of depth that had been *SI*'s habit. On the same week that *Time* employed Pulitzer Prize–winning columnist Charles Krauthammer to write an extended essay on the implications of Garry Kasparov's chess series with a computer, *SI* ran a rimshot-laden Point After by Reilly and ignored the straight news angle altogether.

Reilly, the most popular writer on the staff, continued to be a brilliant schizophrenic, displaying his best skills (a deft comedic sense, genuine empathy) and his worst traits (an inability to tell his good one-liners from his bad ones) within the same stories. "I can't get through it," said one veteran writer. "I can't really watch a stand-up comedian without feeling bad for him. And that is what this guy is doing in print. He can't let a gag go by." But Reilly was simply too good too often to be dismissed as a mere gag writer. He could write news stories and bonuses with equal skill, and could switch easily from earnest Defordian seriousness to cranky Jenkins-esque irreverence.

He was also the most prominent of a group of bright writers of approximately similar tenor—Rushin, Wolff, Silver, Gerry Callahan, and Austin Murphy—all of whom were talented, thoughtful, sardonic, and overly prone to use words like "malodorous" and "odoriferous." Most of these writers had grown up devouring *SI*'s distinctive literary style, and they made a strong core group. But there was little journalistic counter-point, not enough feature writers of the caliber of Smith and Nack, and precious few other writers possessing real gravity. The magazine had long ago junked the eclectic story mix of the Laguerre era, and after 12 nearly uninterrupted years of Mulvoy, the range of voices writing in the magazine had narrowed as well.

Still, some insisted that the magazine was more consistent than ever. "Anybody who thinks the staff was better then than it is now doesn't understand the English language," said Rick Telander, just months after leaving *SI* to write a column for the *Chicago Sun-Times*. But most of *SI*'s new era of writers, from Steve Rushin to Michael Silver, Alex Wolff to Tim Layden, gladly recognized a debt to their predecessors. Though they might drink less and work harder than their antecedents, they were unde-niably influenced by the writers of *SI*'s glory years, by Deford's bonuses and Curry Kirkpatrick's one-liners and, most of all, by the body of Dan Jenkins's work.

"Dan started a tradition of snappy stuff," said Jerry Tax. "And an awful lot of kids dearly longed to be like that. And I tell you there isn't a damn one that's come along that can do it as good as Dan did. He was a master of lightening up every piece, so that if you didn't give a shit about golf, it didn't make a bit of difference."

More than anyone on the staff, Reilly was plagued by comparisons to Jenkins. The comparisons grew thicker after the 1996 publication of *Missing Links*, his golf novel and fiction debut. "Rick's truly funny," said one staffer, "but if you took out all the Jenkins influences from the novel, you'd have nothing left but pronouns and puns." After nearly 15 years at the magazine, Reilly realized that the specter of Jenkins, like jokes about the swimsuit issue or friends asking for tickets, had become part of the job. "Whenever I told anyone I was writing a golf novel, the first thing they'd ask was 'Is it going to be as funny as *Dead Solid Perfect*?' What can you do? Should nobody else write a golf novel ever again?"

At the Masters in 1996, Reilly received an award from the Golf Writers Association of America. Larry Dorman of the *New York Times* gave Reilly an introductory speech, in which he referred to his friend as "a writer who's been doing a pretty good Dan Jenkins impersonation for the past 20 years."

As he stepped to the podium to accept his award, Reilly's first words were, "I'd like to thank my wife June, my daughter Sally . . ."

Even Jenkins laughed.

Just weeks later, Reilly and Jenkins were both in Salisbury, North Carolina, for the annual dinner of the National Sportscasters and Sportswriters Hall of Fame, where Reilly would win his fourth Sportswriter of the Year award and Jenkins would, at long last, be inducted into the Hall. At the end of the night, when Jenkins took the stage to accept his award, he mentioned that he was delighted to be in the same place with the other honorees, including "Rick Reilly, who has his own voice and his own talent and doesn't need me to tell him a damn thing."

Later that night, Jenkins stopped by Reilly's table and sat down with him—it had always been the other way in the past—and the two men spoke for a long time. After the dinner, they went out for dessert. Jenkins, who'd recently given up smoking, seemed mellower, more ruminative. In time, he began grousing to Reilly about all the things he couldn't eat, drink, or smoke anymore.

"You know what it is, don't you?" Jenkins asked.

"No, what?" said Reilly.

"Dues—for all the good times I had."

It was the first time that Reilly ever felt Jenkins had accepted him as a colleague. "He can be kind of a hard sonofabitch sometimes," he'd say later. "But that night, he was really gracious. And I think he knew what he was doing. He'll always be the king, but now I've finally gotten more comfortable around him, gotten to the point where I've stopped sitting in pressrooms staring at Dan Jenkins. It doesn't feel like I'm having a cup of coffee with God anymore. "

• • •

"People talk about how *SI* changed," said Steve Rushin. "But we're in an age where a player not only rejects, but *angrily* rejects a ten-year, $70 million offer. Twenty-five years ago, the player wasn't making 200 times the salary of the average fan. A little bit of publicity wasn't necessarily a bad thing. But every year it becomes more of an impostion." *SI*'s ability to gain exclusive access had been an integral part of its success: Bud Shrake picked Muhammad Ali up at the airport and drove him to his hotel before his military registration appointment; Dan Jenkins and Darrell Royal drove around Fayetteville on the eve of 1969's Game of the Century. But in the '90s, *SI* couldn't get a one-on-one with Mike Tyson, and Michael Jordan wasn't even talking to the magazine. And many of those who did cooperate were less giving with their time, more guarded.

"It's a different generation of athlete today," says Jack McCallum. "Would they rather talk to Jack McCallum, who's going to somewhere along there ask 'em a question they're gonna get pissed off at, or would they rather go hang with Ahmad? Or with Willow? And the answer's clear. They'd rather go hang out with Willow Bay. The saturation of sports has really changed things, and made it more difficult for us, I think."

Additionally, the watered-down regular seasons throughout the sports calendar made many *SI* beats inherently less dramatic, presenting a far-reaching editorial problem. The San Diego Padres and Los Angeles Dodgers faced off on the final day of the 1996 regular season with the National League Western Division title hanging in the balance, but both teams had already clinched a spot in the expanded playoffs, so *SI* didn't even cover the game. A generation earlier in college basketball, regular-season intersectional showdowns and end-of-season conference tournaments had real meaning. But in the '90s, when 64 teams advanced to the NCAA tournament, the regular season had become analogous, in both purpose and significance, to the Indianapolis 500 time trials. When it came time for the games that did matter, playoffs, major tournaments, bowl games, *SI* was just one of an ever-growing throng of media, clamoring for time with athletes who were increasingly distant, uncooperative, or openly hostile to all print media.

During Mulvoy's later years, the magazine too frequently chased after individual stories while losing sight of the larger picture. With Colson, *SI* began to venture out, digging deeper to report not just the facts but also the broader implications. Stories like Rushin's essay on the political infighting over the Indianapolis 500, Richard Hoffer's pointed dispatch from Michael Irvin's drug possession trial, or Gerry Callahan's acerbic report on Jerry Reinsdorf's signing of free agent Albert Belle all showed a sense of a longer view, an ability to discern universal truths from specific situations.

The best example in 1996 was Gary Smith's June 24 cover story on troubled teenage basketball star Richie Parker, whose sexual assault conviction had cost him a shot at a major-college scholarship. Through a complex set of vignettes, Smith elegantly set out the chain of events that turned the Parker case into a divisive issue. Smith was uniquely aware of the resonance of the case, and the gravity of the stakes: "Sports, having somehow become the medium through which Americans derive their strongest sense of community, has become the stage where all the great moral issues have to be played out, often rough and ugly, right alongside the games." The story earned Smith and *SI* a National Magazine Award for excellence in feature writing.

On one of the biggest stories of the '90s, *SI* was out in front rather than behind. The magazine had been chronicling the ascension of golf prodigy Eldrick "Tiger" Woods since his earliest days as a child phenom. Perhaps because it covered golf so thoroughly in its Golf Plus supplement (with *SI* reporters covering every PGA tournament), the magazine recognized Woods's significance and spoke with a special authority about his impact on the sport. "Golf, as we know it, is over," wrote new staff writer Gary Van Sickle, after Woods won his first tour tournament in the fall of 1996. Some dismissed that as mere hype, and many sports columnists and commentators were critical of Colson's choice of Woods as Sportsman of the Year for 1996. But events in the ensuing months would bear out *SI*'s judgment, as well as the magnitude of Woods's talent. When the 21-year-old scorched the Masters with a record-breaking performance in April 1997, Colson placed "The New Master" on the cover and opened the 15-page news lead "Strokes of Genius" with a wide-angle gatefold shot of Woods sinking the record-setting final putt on Sunday afternoon. By that time, of course, Woods had quickly become America's newest sports superstar and everyone was on the bandwagon. But *SI*'s regular readers were prepared: they'd been reading about Woods for seven years.

• • •

There were more challenges looming on the horizon: in the summer of 1996, Condé Nast announced that it would launch a new magazine,

*Condé Nast Sports for Women,* in the fall of 1997, and hired Sally Jenkins away from *SI* to be one of its staff writers. *SI* had been toying with the idea of a select-edit section for women but had been dragging its feet in its coverage of women's sports for years. Colson had intended to provide more coverage of women's sports, but beyond the numerous stories of women's events in the Olympics, he didn't do so. *SI* didn't cover the regional finals of the women's NCAA basketball tournament, nor the championship series in the inaugural season of the American Basketball League. But once Condé Nast moved into the breach, *SI* responded aggressively, announcing that it would test a separate magazine, titled *Sports Illustrated Women/Sport,* with two issues in the spring and fall of 1997 (with plans to switch to a monthly frequency in 1998). The premiere issue—top-edited by Sandy Bailey, who had been promoted to Olympics editor after Jerry Kirshenbaum's retirement in 1997—was a journalistic success and another successful brand extension, though it again skimmed some of the magazine's best talent away from the main magazine.

In a time of brand extensions, the biggest one of all would be televised. Debuting December 12, 1996, the 24-hour sports news cable network CNN/SI was a joint venture between the magazine and Turner Broadcasting (also part of the Time Warner empire). The new network was clearly a belated attempt to try to gain some ground against ESPN, whose tagline "the world leader in sports" was starting to sound more like a fact than a boast.

"I believe ESPN needs to be gotten after by somebody, or they are just going to outbusiness everybody," said publisher David Long. It was unclear, though, how CNN, whose news program "Sports Tonight" had long ago been outstripped in both ratings and relevance by John Walsh and ESPN's "SportsCenter," could help *SI* slay the ESPN monolith on its own turf.

The channel was announced in the spring of 1996, and an internal memo explaining the launch went out to the staff, which was initially wary. "We got a memo that said what this was about, and we'll be expected to come on but nobody will *have* to appear against their will, which is good," said Steve Rushin. "Otherwise, it would be like those hostage videos in the Middle East. I didn't get in this to be a big TV personality. God knows, there's no great cry for me to be a TV personality. I've done a few of these things, and it seems to me it's easier than print journalism. But print journalism is what I got into, what I wanted to do, and what I'm doing."

Throughout the preparation phases of the project, both Colson and senior editor Steve Robinson (who moved to Atlanta to direct *SI*'s portion of the operation) took pains to say that the network would not scoop the magazine. But as Colson quickly realized, scoops weren't the problem. The best *SI* game stories combined insight and eloquence with an accumulation of details. The *SI* writers who went on the station were expected to withhold the sort of details they used in their story. "These people want Peter King," said Colson before the launch. "But I tried to explain that sooner or later, they're going to have to make their own Peter King." At any rate, it was difficult to see how doing spots for CNN/SI—and the network planned to interview writers during halftimes of games they were covering—would make *Sports Illustrated* a better magazine. Others wondered whether Robinson, who'd had a reputation as a literal-minded line editor, had the vision to lead the magazine in a new medium. (One of Robinson's duties was running CNN/SI's online entity. Ironically, one of the people he worked under in that capacity was Dan Okrent, who left *Life* to become the head of Time Inc.'s New Media division in 1996.)

ESPN responded quickly, announcing the launch of ESPNews, a similar channel promising 24 hours of news coverage and, for good measure, launching it November 1, more than a month before CNN/SI's kickoff. *SI* was attempting to break out of its print realm and battle ESPN for supremacy in electronic media. But the cable network would enter the fray with some built-in advantages: ESPN itself was in 60 million homes and ESPN2 was in 40 million; there was also a network of more than a hundred affiliates on ESPN's radio network; its website, ESPNet, was among the most popular on the Internet, while *SI*'s, like other Time Inc. magazines mired in the company's misbegotten, money-hemorrhaging Pathfinder online project, was a user-hostile triviality, little more than a repository to reprint stories in the magazine.

Against this multimedia giant, CNN/SI was launching in only a few million homes. Several staffers sensed a hint of desperation in the entire process. To many on the editorial side, the CNN/SI launch was marked by equal parts hubris and desperation, a belated and delusional bid by Time Warner to muscle in on ESPN's lucrative market.

"It's ridiculous," said one of the magazine's senior writers. "What could they possibly be thinking? We're a great magazine. And they get caught up in this TV stuff. Why do we even want to compete on it? What's the most in-depth thing they do on ESPN? "Between the Lines" with Bob Ley or something? We do that every issue. It's just frustrating that they bring in some previously employed clowns from TV or something and—what do they keep calling it?—*leveraging* the brand name? Extending the brand? The brand should be the magazine, and we should concentrate on ways to make it the best magazine possible."

Very shortly, they would be forced to do just that. In the fall of 1996, a 12-person committee, including John Walsh, Steve Bornstein, and Walt Disney Co./Hyperion publishing division chief John Skipper, held several meetings to consider a direct challenge to *Sports Illustrated*. By the spring of 1997, the word was leaking out: Walsh would oversee the launch of *ESPN*, an oversize biweekly sports magazine that would begin publishing in the spring of 1998. Rather than the haphazard design of Hearst's *Total Sports* annuals published under the ESPN name, the new magazine would boast a more sophisticated look, conceived by respected magazine designers Walter Bernard and Milton Glaser. Editorially, it would aspire toward a more forward-looking stance, with plenty of the regular departments that *SI* had long ago abandoned. Bornstein made it clear that Walsh would be directly responsible for the magazine, and because of that simple fact, the new publication would have to be taken much more seriously than any other challenge to *SI* in its history.

Colson welcomed the challenge. For decades the magazine had been competing mostly against its own self-image. Now there would be an identifiable outside source pressing *SI*, an external publication to judge and be judged against. Moving to preempt the ESPN challenge, Colson brought the select edit—the departments like NFL Extra and NBA Extra that were previously sent only to selected subscribers—into the regular magazine, to bolster coverage of the main sports. And the production department redoubled its efforts to implement a revolutionary new binding process that would allow *SI* to do away with the traditional staple and saddle-stitching technology. Just as *Inside Sports* had pushed *SI* to move more quickly to an all-color format in the early '80s, the ESPN challenge promised to keep it on the forefront of mass magazine technology.

The irony was that after years of relentless brand extensions, *Sports Illustrated* would now need to engage in a brand retrenchment. When *The National* folded in 1991, conventional wisdom within the magazine industry was that *SI* was invulnerable, but five years later, the perception had changed. It was 1980 all over again, and this time Walsh's side would have deep pockets. The war for supremacy in the world of sports media would now be fought on more than one front and, for the first time, on *SI*'s home turf.

• • •

When André Laguerre was editing *Sports Illustrated*, the American sports fan was just becoming aware of the excitement that existed in the packed gymnasiums and stadiums far from the country's media centers.

Well into the postwar era, there were vast spaces that were populated but still effectively empty and uncharted, at least in their relation to the national media. A holiday tournament in Alaska; a late Western Athletic Conference shootout in the Mountain time zone; another football factory springing up in the heartland. *SI* thrived in the '60s and '70s by reporting from those empty spaces, often with spectacular color photography, surveying the national sports landscape with unprecedented authority.

But TV, and especially cable TV, would break the equilibrium, fill up the spaces, shatter the intimacy, and eclipse much of the entree that *SI* enjoyed with athletes. It distracted the stars of the game as well as the fans, turning elusive, ineffable moments of magic into just another clip on the highlight loop. There was a moment, maybe in 1970 when "Monday Night Football" started, when television stood as the perfect complement to *SI*'s editorial mission, providing plenty of events, but only scant, stingy dollops of actual coverage. But TV wouldn't settle. Roone Arledge pushed toward more personality, John Walsh pushed toward more journalism. Television gobbled up the landscape and spit out *SI*'s beloved strobes.

By the mid-'90s, sports had become pervasive and the mystery and romance of the faraway, unseen game had vanished. There would be no more mornings in which a sports fan dropped the toast on the paper, bleary-eyed and disbelieving, at the just-published score from the night before last: Chaminade 77, (top-ranked) Virginia 72. Now television was reporting instantaneously from those far-flung locales, and by doing so robbing them of much of their charm and mystery. And suddenly, a write-up in *Sports Illustrated* meant less than a postgame chat with Dick Vitale or a touchdown pass in the highlight package on "SportsCenter." Television could not do what *Sports Illustrated* could do, but it incontrovertibly changed the environment, filled those empty spaces, altered *SI*'s universe.

"I do think that what they have lost is a sense of primacy that was there once upon a time," said Frank Deford. "That *Sports Illustrated* was it, and now that's not so true anymore. It just has lost that cachet. It's because of television. It's because of a lot of things, but it's because of television. It just doesn't mean as much as it once did."

It was also true that the *Sports Illustrated* of the Laguerre era could not exist in the '90s, partly because the sporting universe had changed so radically, but also because the company that published it had changed radically as well. In the Time Inc. of the modern world, the Laguerre-era *SI* would be considered too diffuse, lacking the sort of narrow hard-sports focus that would ensure maximum efficiency and profitability.

"No, it wouldn't be successful," said former art director Dick Gangel one summer afternoon, a look of sadness crossing his hardy, weathered face. "As a matter of fact, we are in an age of vulgarity. This is a vulgar, vulgar society, and any illusions about improving the breed through journalism are silly, absolutely silly. You see people lying and cheating and stealing, fighting and killing right in front of your face, you start to think about the messages you were taught when you were a kid. It's a very hard time. I know it's changed my attitude about art and about life itself. And I feel sorry in a certain way that kids coming up today didn't have the Winnie-the-Pooh ideal life that I had."

In his Connecticut farmhouse, Gangel was surrounded by the works of Andres Francois and Marc Simont, Arnold Roth, and Bernard Fuchs, reminders of the magazine's glory days, when *SI* achieved that rare confluence of pop cultural success: being commercially successful, critically praised, and culturally significant. It was the last of the truly sophisticated mass magazines, and the only sophisticated one to rise in the age of television.

"As an editor, Laguerre seemed to have had enough of war, politics, hard news, and what the prime minister might or might not say tomorrow," said Ray Cave. "He plainly decided that journalism in these areas was actually more limiting than sport. Of course, Laguerre's definition of sport, of leisure, was virtually limitless. So, for that matter, was Luce's. Laguerre infected his staff with a sense of the consequence of sport—to the society, and to each of us. He felt sport was a true mirror of the human condition, a meaningful mirror. It was a sophisticated view of sport, and he insisted that the magazine reflect that sophistication. In hindsight, and certainly in net profit terms, he was probably wrong. Maybe sport is, and was, no more consequential than the Bulls versus the Sonics. Laguerre believed otherwise. But there is no arguing about one thing: you make more money with a hard-sports magazine."

Shortly after Frank Deford returned from covering the Olympics in Atlanta for *Newsweek* and HBO, his old colleague and former *SI* staffer Bill Leggett died. Not a great writer, Leggett nevertheless served the magazine faithfully for decades, often taking frequent breaks for refreshment at the side of Laguerre. After the funeral service, in an August drizzle in New York City, Deford stood in the rain with Ann Callahan and Gilbert Rogin, and unashamedly reminisced about the old times. A few days later, the pressbox at Belmont Park was renamed in Leggett's honor. But *SI* made no mention of his death because, in one staffer's words, "No one really knew who he was. Also, you're going to have a lot of these people dying soon—and we can't run Pub Memos on all of them."

Back home in Connecticut after Leggett's memorial service, Deford sat for a while and considered his mixed feelings about his old magazine, of the nostalgia and resentment, longing and anger, that had washed over him steadily since Atlanta.

"It suddenly occurred to me," he explained later, "that the reason so many people are harsh about the current *SI* is that they grew up with the magazine. They started as kids. In that sense, *SI* is like their music or their clothes, or their first kisses. It is part of their growing up, and they have so idealized it (as we do so much of childhood) that the current version can't possibly measure up."

And yet for the staff members, he realized, it was something different: "*Sports Illustrated* could only be young itself once—and it just so happens that Laguerre was the father and we were all impressionable children and we were underdogs and it was all so new and exciting. And it can't ever be that way again, because now it is just a product."

# A FACE IN THE CROWD

## On a Wednesday in May 1996

at Whitney Tower's handsome two-story town house on the Upper East Side, a group of *SI* alumni have gathered for their annual reunion luncheon, an informal affair started two years earlier by Sarah Ballard. The numbers grow each year. This year, Ron Fimrite flies in from San Francisco, still recovering from hip-replacement surgery. Ballard and William Oscar Johnson are in from the Cape. Ray Cave and Pat Ryan stop by, Andy Crichton and Robert Creamer take the train down from Westchester County, Jule Campbell shows up, as do Susan Adams, Ann Callahan, Roy Blount, Jr., and Nancy Williamson. Stephanie Salter can't make it back from San Francisco, but she'll call later in the afternoon. Walter Bingham has just returned from Europe and sends his severely jet-lagged regrets.

Kisses are exchanged and stories are told. Andy Crichton has received doctor's orders not to drink, but he's drinking anyway. Ron Fimrite, gleam in his eye, shakes the ice in his glass absent-mindedly and someone comes by to fill it up. Roy Blount, Jr., bashfully updates old friends on the progress of his screenwriting career. They sit down for lunch, at two tables for eight, and after a while, Cave and Crichton are passionately discussing what's wrong, and what's right, with the current magazine. Soon enough, they'll be arguing over Laguerre again. What did he think of America? How did he hold all that alcohol? And what was that white stick made of anyway?

Then, from the other table, Whitney Tower taps a spoon on his water glass and stands up. "I'd like to thank you all for coming today," he says, and explains the absence of Bingham and Salter. Dan Jenkins is absent as well, he notes, attending the funeral of his old friend Bob Drum, but he's sent along a note, which Tower hands to Sarah Ballard to read out loud:

Dear One and All:

Sorry I can't be with you again. As you know, I missed last year's reunion because I was busy redoing my expense account for Terrell—the one from Beverly Hills that he threw across the room at me.

I hate not being present for Bingham's report on what everybody's salary was from 1967 through 1972.

I'm sure Cave can finish rewriting Maule in time to be on hand. As I understand it, he's turning the second paragraph into the sixth, the eighth into the third, the fourth into the 13th, changing the Packers to the Rams throughout, and polishing up the lead as he simultaneously reworks the Pub Letter and the last Scorecard item.

Of course, I'm as excited as everyone else about Olsen's proposal for a five-part series on white athletes in dreadlocks who want to be almost black.

I hope Creamer's bonus piece works out, the one on the third inning of the Yankee–White Sox game of Aug. 23, 1926.

No matter where I am, or what I'm doing, I promise I will be with you for the celebration when we hear that Rogin and Mulvoy died in a mid-air collision of corporate jets.

My excuse for being absent this time will not come as a surprise to some of you. The fact is, I'm trapped behind the radiator in Crichton's office, looking for my Texas-Oklahoma game story.

A mighty hug on all of you.

Love, laughs, and memories,<br>Dan

There's much to be learned from the laughter that still washes over the place, the urgent electricity still in the air minutes after Jenkins's sign-off. What's clear above all is that these people still care about this magazine, not just what it was but what it has become. Most of them still read it regularly, even as they claim not to. They had all participated in the consecration, had all traveled to midtown Manhattan for decades, pouring their talent, their time, their imagination, and often their own wrecked marriages, into André Laguerre's journalistic crucible. In 1975, Bob Oates of the *Los Angeles Times* wrote a lengthy story about *SI*, the longest, most in-depth portrait of the magazine to that date. It contained the only known media interview with Laguerre, who was, typically, concise. He'd just left the company and was bitter, but he knew what his magazine had accomplished. "We treated sports seriously," Laguerre told Oates. "We gave sports a new respectability." End of interview.

On the same afternoon that the enclave of *SI*'s past convenes, its present is nearby, just out of orbit, living in another world and still, somehow, the same one. It is perhaps appropriate that, as the group of *SI* alumni sits down to eat, a figure of some interest passes not far from Whitney Tower's front door, moving south down Park Avenue, bound for midtown Manhattan. In the hazy May heat, the man is dressed like a sloppy preppy in khakis and a loose-fitting jacket. He cuts an erect figure, hands in his pockets, eyes straight forward, lost in thought, deftly weaving left and right around oncoming pedestrians, marching against the grain of traffic and history and time. It is Bill Colson, bound for work on his day off, trying to come up with just a few more story ideas.

Susan Adams, Susan Alexander, Maury Allen, Bruce Anderson, Roger Angell, Gerald Astor, Bernard Auer, Sandra Bailey, George Baldassare, Sarah Ballard, Don Barr, Allan Barra, David Bauer, Walter Bernard, Michael Bevans, Betty Bredin Bingham, Walter Bingham, Tom Black, George Bloodgood, Roy Blount, Jr., Peter Bonventre, John G. Booth, Victoria Boughton, Robert H. Boyle, Christine Brennan, Bob Brown, Fran Brown, Dave Brumbaugh, Don Bryant, Art Buchwald, Ann Callahan, Gerry Callahan, Tom Callahan, Dita Camacho, Jule Campbell, Peter Carry, Gary Cartwright, Ray Cave, Norman Chad, Trish Chesler, Bobby Clay, Richard Clurman, Neil Cohen, Bill Colson, Dean Colson, William Colson, Jerry Cooke, Bob Costas, Robert Cowin, Robert W. Creamer, Andrew Crichton, Sheldon Czapnik, Lucy Danziger, Martin Dardis, Frank Deford, Richard DeFuccio, Mike Del Nagro, John Dewan, John Dominis, Martha Duffy, Karen Dunn, Don Elliman, Chris Evert, Clay Felker, Paul Fichtenbaum, Ron Fimrite, Steven Fine, Robert Fisler, Honor Fitzpatrick Scott, Rob Fleder, Dick Friedman, Jim Gaines, Ann Gallagher, Bill Gallagher, Jr., Dick Gangel, John Garrity, Myra Gelband, Herman Gollob, Ralph Graves, Tom Griffith, Henry Grunwald, Harvey Grut, David Halberstam, Richard Haskell, Andrew Heiskell, Margo Huber Heckler, Tom Hickey, Steven Hoffman, Johnette Howard, Philip Howlett, Chris Hunt, Walter Iooss, Jr., Bill James, Sidney James, Dan Jenkins, June Jenkins, Sally Jenkins, Dana Johnston, Elisa Johnston, Laurie Johnston, Roger Kahn, Suzie Kamb, Larry Keith, Greg Kelly, William Kelly, Jr., Jim Kensil, Armen Keteyian, Peter King, Curry Kirkpatrick, Jerry Kirshenbaum, Heinz Kluetmeier, Jim Knight, Pamela Knight, Tony Kornheiser, Mark Kram, Mark Kram, Jr., Dick Labich, Barbara La Fontaine, Claudine Laguerre, Leon Laguerre, Michele Laguerre, Nathalie Laguerre, Odette Laguerre, Julia Lamb, Tim Layden, William Leggett, Neil Leifer, Jack Leonard, Franz Lidz, Alan

Light, Don Logan, David Long, Douglas S. Looney, Henry Luce III, Melissa Ludtke, Mike Lupica, John Marin, Joe Marshall, Donald Matheson, Dorothy Maule, Jack McCallum, James McCluskey, David McCoubrey, John "Max" McGowan, Jason McManus, Jack Meyers, James Michener, Bob Miller, Vance Minter, Kenny Moore, Henry Muller, Mark Mulvoy, Thomas Mulvoy, Dick Munro, Lester Munson, Austin Murphy, Jim Murray, Skip Myslenski, William Nack, Helen Nathan, Marty Nathan, Richard Neale, Craig Neff, Merrell Noden, Michael Novak, Bob O'Connell, Daniel Okrent, Jack Olsen, Milt Orshofsky, Sandy Padwe, John Papanek, Joe Paterno, Norman Pearlstine, Paula Phelps, Charles Pierce, Nicholas Pileggi, Bernerd Platt, George Plimpton, Shirley Povich, Curtis Prendergast, Pat Putnam, John Rawlings, Rick Reilly, Steve Robinson, Jonathan Rogers, Gilbert Rogin, Gary Ronberg, Pete Rozelle, Steve Rushin, Pat Ryan, Stephanie Salter, Alvaro Saralegui, Vic Sauerhoff, Dick Schaap, Herbert Scheftel, William Scherman, Tex Schramm, Budd Schulberg, Ted Shaker, Morton Sharnik, Art Shay, Blackie Sherrod, Edwin "Bud" Shrake, Michael Silver, Fred Smith, Gary Smith, Liz Smith, James Snedecor, George Solomon, John Squires, Claude Stanush, Patricia Stenborg, Richard Stolley, Robert Sullivan, Kelso Sutton, E.M. Swift, Barry Switzer, Jeremiah Tax, Phil Taylor, Rick Telander, Roy Terrell, Lee Eitengon Thompson, Cheryl Tiegs, Whitney Tower, Sandy Treadwell, George Trescher, Tony Triolo, Joan Braun Truscio, Gene Ulrich, John Underwood, Julie Vader, Pauline Varangot, Garry Valk, Anita Verschoth, Kurt Vonnegut, John Walsh, Frank White, Michael Wilbon, Nancy Williamson, Paul Witteman, Robin Wolaner, Alexander Wolff, Connie Wood, Les Woodcock, Jane Bachman Wulf, Steve Wulf, John Zimmerman, Paul Zimmerman.

**ACKNOWLEDGMENTS**

I decided I wanted to write this book in 1991, after reading *Rolling Stone Magazine: An Uncensored History*, written by my friend Robert Draper. In his acknowledgments, Draper mentioned that he had grown up relying on *Rolling Stone* as his window to the world, an interpreter of events that he looked to for guidance in much the same way that his parents had looked to *Time* magazine or the nightly news. It occurred to me that, for better or worse, I'd grown up looking to *Sports Illustrated* in much the same way.

It was the first weekly magazine, and for years the only one, that I read regularly. My mother bought me a subscription as a Christmas gift when I was six and nearly thirty years later, its arrival in the mail still seems to announce the unofficial beginning of the weekend. But like so many of *SI*'s most loyal readers, I knew nothing of the drama behind the magazine. One January night in 1988, while I was interviewing Dan Jenkins, he mentioned the name André Laguerre with a tone of reverence that he does not frequently use. It's fair to say that if it wasn't for the generosity shown by Jenkins and Bud Shrake, in sharing their memories of the magazine and Laguerre, I might never have known that *SI* had a story worth telling.

I was hardly the first one to think of writing a history of *Sports Illustrated*. Others had toyed with the idea, either outsiders fascinated with the magazine's pull on American sports fans, or staffers who knew that their own memoirs would be inextricably bound up in the history of the magazine.

Many of the most crucial figures were reluctant to talk about their experiences at *SI*, but in the end, virtually everyone did. From the first managing editor Sid James, who spent a weekend with me at his home in Laguna Hills, California, to present managing editor Bill Colson, who endured my incessant phone calls and frequent visits throughout his first year on the job, the men who occupied the position were both crucial to my understanding of the magazine's history and unfailingly helpful. Mark Mulvoy made a special trip to Chicago to sit for a two-day grilling; Gilbert Rogin spoke candidly with me on several occasions; John Papanek spoke extensively and on the record about one of the most painful experiences of his life; and Roy Terrell, who had gladly left it all behind in 1979, reluctantly agreed to dredge it all up again for my benefit over a weekend at his home in Islamorada, Florida.

I'm also particularly indebted to Jenkins and Shrake, as well as Nathalie Laguerre, Andy Crichton, Frank Deford, Robert W. Creamer, Mark Kram, Bill Nack, Jule Campbell, Alexander Wolff, Roy Blount, Jr., Whitney Tower, Neil Leifer, Ron Fimrite, Daniel Okrent, Rob Fleder, Ray Cave, and Pat Ryan, all of whom were subjected to several rounds of phone calls. "Michael," said Okrent near the end of the process. "I've learned not to believe you when you say you have just one more question."

A small cadre of people helped transcribe the more than 500 hours of interviews I recorded for the book. I'm especially indebted to the precise, prolific Sharon Maslow—the "Hyper Typer" of Minnetonka, Minnesota. I also received extensive help from many others, including Donna Robinson, Brien Hindman, Dan Shumski, Patricia Tom, Lauren Mutter, Kari Bowser, and Catherine Tsai.

During my 18 months of travel and research, I imposed on many friends for both shelter and sustenance, and am particulary grateful to Dr. Reggie Givens, Rob Minter, Andy Bagnato, Patrick Taggart, Brad Garrett, Greg Emas, Terry McDevitt, Dana Colley, Barbara Morgan, Jenifer Miller, Laura Pfeifauf, Michael Oh, Jim Barrios, Jane Girson, Anne Smith, Susan Reckers, and my brother-in-law, David Frost, for their help and hospitality. I also received long-distance research assistance from Russell Smith, Chris Brown, Mark Leiser, Kristin Scudder, Jeff Zivan, Tim Shanley, and Kevin Lyttle (who in addition to his extensive research for the book, also agreed to act as interim commissioner of my geek baseball league, a thankless job if ever there was one).

I spent a lot of time at libraries, much of it at the Library of Congress, whose courteous staff guided me through the complicated process of finding the earlier incarnations of *Sports Illustrated*, from the mid-'30s and late '40s. The help of both James Baughman at the University of Wisconsin and Bryant Sapp at the University of South Carolina saved me from further journeys to libraries. My best library, however, was at home, thanks to the generosity of Sid James and Whitney Tower, each of whom loaned me more than a decade's worth of bound volumes from their personal collections, saving me countless trips to countless other libraries.

The *Sports Illustrated* publicity department was unfailingly courteous and cooperative, and I owe Art Berke and his assistants, Christine Cortez and Dave Mingey, as well as former *SI* staffer Roger Jackson, many thanks. I also received much needed help from Time Inc. director of communications Peter Costiglio and former Time Inc. archivist Kenneth Schlesinger.

In 1963, Malcolm X visited the *SI* offices, accompanying photographer Gordon Parks, who was stopping by to pick up a friend for a lunch date. This fascinating but ultimately inconsequential fact, and dozens of others just like it that distracted from the already careening narrative, were parsed from the original manuscript with the help of Patrick Porter and David Zivan, who read the work in the early stages, saved me from many of my redundancies and lapses in logic, and guided me toward completion. Porter also helped with literally every phase of the book, doing library research, transcribing tapes, reviewing back issues, proofreading, and supplying his own encyclopedic knowledge of *SI*.

I'm indebted to the support of Northwestern University professors Abe Peck and Donna Leff, two mentors who are also friends. Additionally, I would be remiss if I didn't thank Dr. Keith O. Garner for his help and guidance along the way, as well as Ken Bertken, Joanne Stouwie, James and Nicole Stubbe, John and Lois Stob, and, of course, Robert Draper, who has been down this road before.

I am quite sure that the standard writer-agent contract doesn't include room and board, but Sloan Harris of ICM showed an unstinting devotion to the project, as well as an undending tolerance (shared by his wife Jenny) for my frequent visits and extended stays at his home in Wilton, Connecticut. I am grateful to him, and grateful to Austin entertainment lawyer Rick Pappas for introducing me to him. Brian DeFiore at Hyperion Books gave me the time and the means to write the book, then helped usher it to its ultimate completion, along with his assistant Mollie Doyle, the superb line editor Leslie Wells, and all-seeing copy editor Henry Price.

Finally, my deepest thanks are due my wife, Danica Frost, who paid the bills, fed the cats, tended the yard, and pursued her own career while I was sitting in my office poring over past and present issues of *Sports Illustrated*. I am certain there were times when she must have wondered whether I was hard at work or just enjoying myself. As it turns out, both.

# Index